Essays on Church
Ordinary Christianity for the World

by

Phillip A. Ross

PILGRIM
platform books

Marietta, Ohio

ISBN: 978-1-7337267-1-9

Edition: 9.16.2020

Published by

Pilgrim Platform
149 E. Spring St.
Marietta, Ohio, 45750
www.pilgrim-platform.org

Printed in the United States of America

For The Church
Gathered and Scattered

Books by Phillip A. Ross

The Work At Zion—A Reckoning, Two-volume set, 772 pages, 1996.

Practically Christian—Applying James Today, 135 pages, 2006.

The Wisdom of Jesus Christ in the Book of Proverbs, 414 pages, 2006.

Marking God's Word—Understanding Jesus, 324 pages, 2006.

Acts of Faith—Kingdom Advancement, 326 pages, 2007.

Informal Christianity—Refining Christ's Church, 136 pages, 2007.

Engagement—Establishing Relationship in Christ, 104 pages, 1996, 2008.

It's About Time! — The Time Is Now, 40 pages. 2008.

The Big Ten—A Study of the Ten Commandments, 105 pages, 2001, 2008.

Arsy Varsy—Reclaiming The Gospel in First Corinthians, 406 pages, 2008.

Varsy Arsy—Proclaiming The Gospel in Second Corinthians, 356 pages, 2009.

Colossians—Christos Singularis, 278 pages, 2010.

Rock Mountain Creed—The Sermon on the Mount, 310 pages, 2011.

The True Mystery of the Mystical Presence, 355 pages, 2011.

Peter's Vision of Christ's Purpose in First Peter, 340 pages, 2011.

Peter's Vision of The End in Second Peter, 184 pages, 2012.

The Religious History of Nineteenth Century Marietta, Thomas Jefferson Summers, 124 pages, 1903, 2012 (editor).

Conflict of Ages—The Great Debate of the Moral Relations of God and Man, Edward Beecher, 489 pages, 1853, 2012 (editor).

Concord Of Ages—The Individual And Organic Harmony Of God And Man, Edward Beecher, D. D., 524 pages, 1860, 2013 (editor).

Ephesians—Recovering the Vision of a Sustainable Church in Christ, 417 pages, 2013.

Galatians: Backstory/Christory, 315 pages, 2015.

Poet Tree—Root, Branch & Sap, 72 pages, 2013.

Inside Out Woman—Collected Poetry, Doris M. Ross, 195 pages, 2014 (editor).

God's Great Plan for the World—The Biblical Story of Creation and Redemption, 305 pages, 2019.

John's Miracles—Seeing Beyond Our Expectations, 210 pages, 2019.

Essays on Church—Ordinary Christianity for the World, 385 pages, 2020.

TABLE OF CONTENTS

INTRODUCTION

This book contains most of the articles that have been on my website (www.Pilgrim-Platform.org) over many years. They are included here to provide hard copy and to preserve them. They provide my thoughts and experiences of the Christian church as a pastor with more than forty years of ministry behind me. Here you will find a series of essays that are intended to be helpful to churches now and in the future. Many church members today will wonder what my problem is. The main problem is that too many church members today don't see the problem. They are content with the church as it is.

They likely think that the church has always been like it is today, and faithfulness means keeping it the way it is. But this is not true. The church is quite different than it used to be. Many fundamentally leaning Christians believe that we need to return to the way the Early Church was, which is amazing when you read Paul's letters. Paul was always chastising the church for its faithlessness and problems. History doesn't flow backward. God's intentions for His church have always been future directed. God is working on the future, and to this effort these essays are directed.

The first article is a response to the market crash of 2008. At the time, Stephanie and I were financing our three children's college costs. We lost about forty percent of our assets, and had to shift that burden to college loans, which still haunt us—and them. You might wonder what the market crash had to do with the church. The point of the essay is to suggest that credit and credibility are moral concerns, and therefore church concerns.

Find a comfortable place to sit and enjoy the read.

CRISIS OF ...

What? The American economy? The Stock Market? Eight years of conservative policies? How about a hundred years of liberal indoctrination!

If we can't see the right problem or see the problem rightly, we cannot find the right solution. If we don't understand the disease, we cannot prescribe the right medication. Apart from a proper diagnosis, doing something may be worse than doing nothing. We are all in serious denial of our real situation, so seeing the problem, putting the problem in the correct context is everything.

WHAT CAN WE DO?

The first thing to do is to see the problem in its proper context, its historical context, its cultural context. That is what these essays are about, helping people see the problem. But unrepentant sinners do not want us to see what the Bible is trying to show us because the perspective of the Bible threatens them—and rightly so. For the past hundred years or so unrepentant sinners have had increasing control of American public education, media, and religious institutions. We have been steeped in godlessness for so long that we no longer even realize it. That's why these essays may seem to be so out of step with American culture and contemporary Evangelicalism.

We are today (2009) in the midst of a financial crisis, to be sure. But it is more than that! It is also a crisis of failed social and educational policies and curriculum—public and religious. It is also a crisis of moral failure. But more important than these, it is a crisis of faith—not faith in some generalized sense of personal confidence, but faith in Jesus Christ as the actual Lord of history.

The deeper, more important problem with our economy is that too many Christian churches and those who claim to be followers of Christianity today are not faithful to God's economy.[1] Is this news? Unlikely. Is it true? It's been true for decades, perhaps a century. It is a persisting condition that is now the accepted norm in too many families, churches, denominations, and seminaries.

---

1   *Oikonomia*, the Greek word for economy, is composed of two Greek words: *oikos*, meaning house, and *nomos*, meaning law. Hence, an *oikonomia* is a "house law," a family administration. Some versions of the Bible translate *oikonomia* as "administration," and others as "arrangement" or "plan." God's economy is His plan, His administration, His arrangement for household life, which includes marriage, family and work (employment). *Oikonomia* is God's plan for our lives.

THE REAL CHANGE WE CAN BELIEVE IN

These essays serve to call Christians to repentance, revival, and reformation—back to their historic roots, and to provide an alternative view on church growth and personal sanctification, an alternative to our contemporary understandings. Christianity today is not what it used to be, nor can it be. Yet it must be faithful to it's roots.

Who might be interested in these concerns? Christians, church members, and pastors who have an interest in theology, or who are concerned about the deteriorating condition of the churches. Anyone interested in Christianity today, whether contemporary or historic, will find much grist for the mill.

The concern here is the role of orthodox doctrine, which is the basis upon which unity and peace are founded. The concern here is how best to be the church in the midst of a crisis of faith that is bleeding the churches to death. The recent development and failure of the Church Growth Movement has added greatly to these problems. Honest self-analysis is the first step to the recovery of the distinctively Christian mission in the world. But we must be cautious because a prescription without a proper diagnosis can be harmful.

INCREASED SANCTIFICATION

Because the word *sanctification* means separated unto God or separated for the purposes and use of God, and because biblical wisdom opposes worldly wisdom[2] increased sanctification requires less entanglement with worldly ways and means. This, however, does not mean creating a Christian commune in the country or a Christian ghetto in the city. Rather, we need to stop responding like cattle to the influences of advertising and marketing, and begin responding to God's Word.

Our minds are filled with the sludge of those who are trying to affect us one way or another, who are vying for our attention. That sludge has captivated our attention by pushing our emotional buttons—and for what? Notice that the more "plugged in" to the world we are (social media, cell phones, Internet, TV, etc.) the less attention we pay to those people who are physically and geographically nearest to us at any point in our day. We are neglecting our neighbors in order to keep up with the world.

---

2   See Ross, Phillip A. *Arsy Varsy—Reclaiming the Gospel in First Corinthians*, Pilgrim Platform, 2006.

SEEING AND SPEAKING

The first thing to do is to see the problem. We know that people don't want to look at problems. They want to see answers. But failing to see the problems correctly leads only to the wrong answers.

The second thing we need to do is to talk about what we see. We must begin a real and serious dialog about the problem—not just our leaders, but we the people must help give them direction. Denial leads to death. I don't have all the answers, but I do have some important questions. And I trust that God has the answers. You can help.

KNOWING GOD

It takes one to know one. I can identify another regenerate person because I know what God's Holy Spirit has done to me. I know how He has changed me, so I can recognize similar changes in other people. But if a person has not been regenerated by the Holy Spirit, he will not know or recognize or value regeneration in others. Because the marks of regeneration are personal and subjective, and because regenerate people are intimately aware of how God has changed them, because they know that the changes in their own lives are real, they can trust that similar marks in other people are equally real. The reality of the Holy Spirit in their own lives provides a guarantee of the reality of the Holy Spirit in the lives of others who are similarly marked. The guarantee of God's reality and of the power and presence of the Holy Spirit is found in the heart of the believer. My own changed life is the proof and guarantee of God's reality. Your own changed life is the proof and guarantee of God's reality.

We are the proof of the existence of God. It is not found in an argument. It is not found in the Bible. It is not found in history. It is found in one's own regeneration, in your own regeneration. And if a person is not regenerated, it is not found at all apart from God's judgment.

The whole world stands under the judgment of God as a result of Adam's sin and is exacerbated by our own sins. When God's judgment is manifest, all doubt about God's reality is quelled because God's judgment has a drastic effect upon this world and the world to come, in eternity. By God's grace alone God moves to rescue people from this context of damnation in this fallen world. God's plan takes many generations to unfold in its full glory, and when it is complete all evil will be destroyed and all extant people will live in the context of God's salvation. In the meantime the process of salvation will be progressive in that evil will be diminished over time as increasing numbers of people find themselves regenerated by the grace of God.

WHAT IN THE WORLD IS ROSS DOING?

In 1983 I had an experience that culminated in 1985 in what is called regeneration. Ordained at First Congregational Church, Berkeley, California, after earning a Master of Divinity degree at Pacific School of Religion, I was confronted by the reality of the Bible as I taught the Bethel Series Bible Study Program at a church I was serving in St. Louis, Missouri. I had read and studied the Bible for many years, but the Bethel Series opened it up to me in a new way. It became real, and that changed me.

I began preaching and teaching differently from that time forward, as if the Bible was real history about real people. My preaching and teaching disturbed some of the people in various liberal churches that I served. Others in those same churches came to new life in Christ, much as I had. I began writing to preserve my preaching for later reflection and evaluation, keeping and reworking my sermons for more general consumption. Not everyone liked my preaching. The main complaint that I got was that I was too deep and expected too much from people. I thought I was just doing my job.

During that same period, wondering whether I was the problem, I decided to check my own theology against the historic, Christian testimony. Looking for a major, historical theological figure who was squarely in the historic, Protestant tradition, I turned to John Calvin by reading *Calvin's Commentaries* in twenty volumes. It proved to be an interesting read, not because I learned a lot, which I did, but rather because I discovered that I had become a Calvinist by reading the Bible prior to reading Calvin. My preaching effort during those years turned into a two-volume book, *The Work at Zion—A Reckoning* (1996)[3], which provides a kind of record of my growing theological perspective.

At the same time, the simple-minded, pie-in-the-sky, otherworldly, wishful-thinking of some of my new conservative friends disturbed me. It seemed to me that people from both ends of the political and theological spectrums had misunderstood the Bible, albeit in different ways. So, I set out to see if the kind of biblical misunderstanding that I observed among various people I knew was new. Were the contempo-

---

3   Books were written in the years preceding the publishing date, of course.

rary churches involved in something new? I discovered that they were not. There is a long history of misunderstanding the Bible.

Next, I turned to the book of James which had provided a corrective to the early church. Already in the first century the church had veered from the truth of the gospel. James saw it and spoke to it. I brought James' corrective to light in *Practically Christian—Applying James Today* (2006).

Looking for the original source of the problem of biblical misunderstanding, I began studying the story of Jesus' ministry. If the doctrines of grace were true, then Jesus would have preached them. He did. And interestingly, almost everyone had misunderstood Jesus during his earthly ministry. So I detailed this story about Jesus and His friends in *Marking God's Word—Understanding Jesus* (2006).

I then picked up the continuing story of the gospel in the book of Acts, only to find that people had misunderstood Paul in the same ways that they had misunderstood Jesus—until the dispensation of the Holy Spirit. Paul took up the gospel of Jesus Christ, teaching and preaching as Jesus did, and all hell was rallied against him. That story is found in *Acts of Faith—Kingdom Advancement* (2007).

Seeking some practical advice about the right way to live as a Christian, I then turned to a study of the book of Proverbs. The difficulty for many Christians is that Proverbs predates the ministry of Jesus. But it does not predate the reality of Christ. Historic theology teaches that the Christian faith is founded on the eternal consistency of God. God does not change, nor does God's wisdom. So I began looking for Christ in Proverbs and found Him on every page. That study became *The Wisdom of Jesus Christ in the Book of Proverbs* (2006).

Arsy Varsy—Reclaiming the Gospel in First Corinthians (2008) was begun at Covenant PCA in Vienna, WV, in order to provide a deeper understanding of the American church situation and its then current similarity with the ancient church at Corinth, and the reality of contemporary backwardness. Covenant was a Presbyterian Church in America new church start, and was struggling with how to be a successful church. Paul spoke to these same concerns in the large, influential, and successful church at Corinth.

Varsy Arsy—Proclaiming the Gospel in Second Corinthians (2009) followed as Covenant PCA in Vienna, WV, dissolved and/or morphed into the Mid-Ohio Valley Reformed Fellowship under my leadership. The issues that Paul spoke to in Second Corinthians have proven to be as applicable as those in First Corinthians. Many of the Corinthians had difficulty understanding Paul. Will we never learn?!

In 2004 I founded Pilgrim Platform Books as a publishing company, to provide my ongoing publishing needs. I could not find a publisher willing to take me on. My first project was to complete a small book on the first couple of chapters of Colossians that I had previously put together to test the quality of Wipf & Stock, a small publish-on-demand printer that was recommended to me by Douglas Vickers.[4] Applying the central insight that I call presuppositional trinitarianism to Colossians I coined a replacement motto for one of the Reformation's *solas—Solas Christos* or Christ Alone. The replacement is *Christos Singularis* or the singularity of Christ. Thus, was born *Colossians—Christos Singularis* (2010) as an antidote for misunderstanding the five solas of the Reformation.

Wanting to provide both theology and practice, I turned to an examination of Jesus' Sermon on the Mount, where Jesus calls for and defines a new humanity. Paul's take on this concern was that Christians are to put off the Old Man and put on the New Man—Jesus Christ. It is imperative to engage the definitions and practices that Jesus has given. This consideration is found in *Rock Mountain Creed—Jesus' Sermon on the Mount* (2011).

I had been watching an Intrenet dust-up among the small, conservative Presbyterian churches (PCA, OPC, etc.) for a decade (the Federal Vision controversy) when I decided to read John Williamson Nevin, the nineteenth century American President of the only seminary that the German Reformed Church in America ever had in Mercersburg, Pennsylvania. Somewhere along the line, I learned that Nevin's Mercersburg Theology provided source documents for what became known as the Federal Vision, a moniker that was attached to the developing theological movement around Douglass Wilson, James B. Jordan, Peter Leithart, etc.

I downloaded the Google Books electronic copy of Nevin's book, *The Mystical Presence* (1846). Two things bothered me about this book. First, Google's optical character reader (OCR) was atrocious, which meant that the book was full of typological errors. But that wasn't all. It also seemed to me that Nevin's editor(s) did not understand him, and provided little to no editorial help. Admittedly, Nevin is tough reading

---

4   Douglas Vickers, was a British, Christian economist whom I had met through the Reformed Congregational Fellowship. http://www.amazon.com/ Douglas-Vickers/e/ B000AQ3TBQ.

for both his terseness and breadth of consideration. I began correcting the typos for my own reading, but soon found myself providing significant editing and clarification of Nevin's ideas. I began adding footnotes, making corrections and extending Nevin's arguments because I found that he was saying what I had been trying to say. In some ways, his efforts far exceeded my own, but in other ways, I thought I was able to bring additional clarity and explanation to his arguments. I simply could not stop that project and worked on it day and night for about four months. The end process was published as *The True Mystery of The Mystical Presence* (2011), and I listed it as being co-authored with John Nevin because by the time I was finished, my comments were simply intertwined with his, and to separate them out would add a level of complexity that would not serve its readability.

Some time earlier a friend, David Gundlach, asked me about my interpretation of 2 Peter 3:12: "waiting for and hastening the coming of the day of God, because of which the heavens will be set on fire and dissolved, and the heavenly bodies will melt as they burn!" Are we to take it literally? And if not, why not? Isn't the plain reading the right reading most of the time? I had been thinking a lot about these concerns and decided to address them. Earlier, David introduced me to the work of R.J. Rushdoony and Cornelius Van Til.

I determined that much misunderstanding about such end-times concerns issued from a misreading of the Greek word *telos* that is usually translated as *end*. The word does mean *end*, but not as in the final *destruction* of the world, but as in the final *purpose* for the world. The world will end as the establishment of God's purpose is fulfilled in the world, given to and through Jesus Christ. But I couldn't just discuss Second Peter, I had to begin that discussion with First Peter. Those books were published as *Peter's Vision of Christ's Purpose in First Peter* (2011) and *Peter's Vision of The End in Second Peter* (2012).

In 2013 I discovered the work of Edward Beecher, son of Lyman Beecher and brother of Harriet Beecher Stowe. Edward Beecher received the first honorary doctorate from Marietta College. I studied two of his major books to learn more about the early theological position of Marietta College. His books were long out of print, so I edited and reissued them, adding a slew of footnotes to provide background information about the authors and theologians he cited. These books retained his original titles: *Conflict of Ages—The Great Debate of the Moral Re-*

lations of God, 1853, and *Concord Of Ages—The Individual And Organic Harmony Of God And Man*, 1860.

In 2012 I completed a study of Ephesians intended to show how the biblical understanding of the church has been warped over time. My hope was to provide a vision of the church for the twenty-first century, titled: *Ephesians—Recovering the Vision of a Sustainable Church in Christ* (2013).

I then discovered a book reflecting on the history of Marietta, Ohio, in the nineteenth century written in 1904 by a local Congregational minister. Established in 1789 by an Act of Congress, Marietta's history is long and involved, and in many ways is typical for Christianity in America. Marietta was founded by Congregationalists who intended to facilitate Christian unity in this "Western" frontier at the time. The story of that failure might serve as a model for rekindling that original vision of Christian unity. Time will tell. That book is titled *The Religious History Of Nineteenth Century Marietta—Reflections* (2012), which I edited and expanded with relevant footnotes and an appendix.

An Internet discussion in 2012 with an avowed agnostic about my understanding of Christianity turned into a small book titled *Buttal & Rebuttal—A Collision Between Belief and Unbelief* (2015). In that discussion it became clear that there was much biblical misunderstanding, even among the educated—*especially* among the educated. I published a companion volume intended to address the root of that misunderstanding, *Galatians—Backstory/Christory*, 2015. There I tried to show how Paul's understanding of law and gospel was rooted in the Old Testament.

In 2019 I published two more books. *John's Miracles—Seeing Beyond Our Expectations* is a study of John's treatment of Jesus' miracles that began in 1994, but not finished until 2019. It employs the idea of Jesus humanity and divinity to His miracles to produce some very interesting and surprising analysis of some very familiar stories. *God's Great Plan for the World—The Biblical Story of Creation and Redemption* (2019) came about in response to John Saggio, whom I have never met, but who sent me a copy of his gargantuan, self-published book, *The Destiny of Israel and the Twilight of Christianity*, subtitled: "In Quest of the Meaning and Significance of the Hebrew and Greek Scriptures" (www.TwilightofReligion.com). Saggio taught philosophy at Mesa Community College. It seemed to me that Saggio, who was highly educated, had misunderstood the central them of the Bible. So, I tried to lay out a clear, relatively simple presentation of the overarching theme of the Bible in a way that even highly educated people could understand.

PLEA

These books and others yet unpublished need support and marketing resources. This growing body of literature needs more public exposure, which will require money, talent, and connections. My marketing skills proved to pretty much match my marketing budget, practically nothing. So, my focus has been content development, not marketing.

I have labored to teach people how to read Scripture with the eyes of faith, to see the richness and depth of the biblical perspective. And it often involves disabusing people of some wrong (unbiblical) assumptions and expectations about the Bible, about ministry, about the church, about the world, etc. I'm convinced that those wrong assumptions and expectations are the very things that have gutted the churches, bled the larger society of its Christian heritage, and continue wreaking havoc in American culture. Thus, I believe that the condition of the Christian church is at the center of our the world's problems.

The solution to this problem is not to bring more lost people into the church's pews. As needed as that is, it won't help until the churches get faithfulness right. People are to be saved into the churches, but the culture of the contemporary churches is little different than the culture of the world. Few churches have any idea of what a biblically faithful Christian life would actually look like. Most churches just slap Bible study and prayer onto their existing worldly lifestyles and call it Christian. Consequently, the need of the hour is not evangelism, but sanctification.

The churches are, in part, institutions of religious education. But they are failing to adequately educate people. So, given this failure, they don't need more students to learn their failing methods. They need to make their education efforts more effective. We need to get the story right before we get it out. More students in a bad school only make things worse.

I am simply convinced that the truth will set us free, and that the loss of American freedom is directly related to the suppression of the truth of our own religious history.

What Can You Do?

If you appreciate what this ministry is about, you can help. If you "see" the concern, if you "get it," you not only *can* help but you *must*. This sin-soaked world needs you to help.

The first thing to do is to grow stronger yourself. If you understand what I'm talking about, please buy and read my books. Get some people together and read them as a study group. Give them to pastors, churches, and public libraries. Talk about the issues, you won't be disappointed. There is much grist for the mill in my work. Even if (when) people disagree—and they will!—it will only make the conversation more interesting and valuable.

Link

The perspective that is reflected in this ministry, which is really nothing other than the historic, Protestant, Reformed, born again perspective, needs to be more widely promoted. It has been and is being eclipsed by the dominant marketing perspective that has captured Western Christianity. Promotion takes resources—time, talent, and treasure. So, share this ministry as a way to promote it. Share these essays. That will help this ministry.

Partner

If you have skills that might be of help, please contact me. My website and books are not currently making any money, they cost me to produce them. This is a labor of love on my part.

This could change, if you have the business skills and/or resources to help make it happen. Producing these materials is more than a full-time job for me. I need help. However, it is very important that the purpose of this ministry not become the making of money. That cannot be the guiding principle, but on the other hand, without some support and resources nothing will come of it. Our guiding principle must always be the promotion of Jesus Christ. If you understand this and can help, please contact me.

DEFINITIONS

What do we do when the meaning of something is disputed? "...if the foundations are destroyed, what can the righteous do?" (Psalm 11:3).

Our world is currently in the midst of revolution, a drastic and far-reaching change in ways of thinking and behaving. The news is filled with stories about how different things are being redefined, retooled, and reinvented. It is as if we are in a race to scrap the past as quickly and thoroughly as possible.

What is driving this passion? In a word—*democracy*. The world seems to be deep in the process of the democratization of all things. We can see the process at work at Wikipedia, which claims to be "the free encyclopedia that anyone can edit."

What is Wikipedia? "Wikipedia is an encyclopedia collaboratively written by many of its readers. It is a special type of website, called a wiki, that makes collaboration easy. Many people are constantly improving Wikipedia, making thousands of changes an hour, all of which are recorded on article histories and recent changes. Inappropriate changes are usually removed quickly, and repeat offenders can be blocked from editing. Since its creation in 2001, Wikipedia has rapidly grown into the largest reference website on the Internet" (from Wikipedia/About Us).

The guiding principles of Wikipedia, the principles of democratization, direct that all "Wikipedia articles and other encyclopedic content must be written from a neutral point of view, representing views fairly, proportionately and without bias." Editors are directed to not state any opinions, but to stick to the facts. The guidelines state that there is a difference between fact and opinion. It's no more nor any less than what people learn in college. It is a helpful process, but it has a serious flaw. It is impossible to do because opinions are simply expressions from particular perspectives, and everyone has a particular perspective. Every expression of fact comes from a particular perspective.

The flaw becomes obvious when we explore the difference between fact and opinion? From the dictionary we learn that an opinion is a belief or judgment that is not founded on proof or certainty. Opinions are value judgments that issue from one's beliefs and/or presuppositions. A fact, on the other hand, is a statement or assertion of verified information about something that exists or has happened. Facts are existential, they don't appear to be dependent upon beliefs or presuppositions. They just are. And what is more, facts appear to be obviously true, self-evident, axiomatic (evident without proof or argument). In other words, facts seem to be true and are verifiable. A verifiable fact has an identified source, and the source is cited or assumed to be an authority on the matter.

Authorities are people who have studied and often written extensively on a subject. Authorities are the paragons of studied opinion. They have studied the opinions of many authorities and come to their own opinion, which they posit to be true and authoritative.

Do you see the circularity of the process? Opinions are not allowed, but facts are actually nothing more than well-established opinions. Philosophical and/or theological differences involve the interpretation of facts. All sides have their authorities.

Most serious disputes are not disagreements about facts, but disagreements about the interpretation of the facts, about what the facts mean. Wikipedia solves this problem by insisting that every viewpoint is equal. Wikipedia aims not to evaluate any viewpoint positively or negatively, but to simply present the "neutral" "facts." And while this sounds very good and fair and intellectual, there are no actual neutral facts. Nonetheless, Wikipedia claims to maintain a neutral perspective by claiming to state only neutral facts. Wikipedia is engaged in the democratization of opinion, by building a democracy of so-called facts. But, as we have seen, facts are nothing more than footnoted opinions.

Yet Wikipedia says that it is not a democracy. True, it is not setting up a government. However, it is setting up an authoritative social resource where every voice is equal. And while a voice is not a vote, voices (where participants have "voice" but not "vote") are intended to have an effect on votes, to sway votes.

Embedded in Wikipedia is the philosophy of Ayn Rand. "Jimmy Wales, founder of Wikipedia, has been a passionate adherent of Ayn Rand's Objectivism. From 1992 to 1996, he ran the electronic mailing list 'Moderated Discussion of Objectivist Philosophy'" (from Wikipedia). Such passions are not objective or neutral and they do not just go away. Rather, they form the foundation of one's worldview.

Here we need to challenge Wikipedia's assumptions about the neutrality of the democratization process. Wikipedia editors are carefully instructed to write from a very particular perspective in order to convey the impression of neutrality. This is a foundational philosophical concern. Political freedom, a pillar of the U.S. Constitution, guarantees the right to express political opinion in the public square, which is forbidden on Wikipedia on the grounds that it (Wikipedia) is not a "public entity." Yet, it could and has been argued that the Internet itself is public in nature.

The concern is not really about Wikipedia but about the broader issue of democratization. Wikipedia is simply an example of the process at work. The process is related to mass hallucination.

> "In most cases, mass hallucination refers to a combination of suggestion and projection, wherein one person will see, or pretend to see, something unusual, and point it out to other people. Having been told what to look for, those other people will consciously or unconsciously convince themselves to recognize the apparition, and will in turn point it out to others."

The idea that "Wikipedia has a neutral point of view" is a pareidolia,[1] a suggestion, not a fact. Suggestion and redirection are the very successful tools of prestidigitation—and of politics.

My intent is not to single out Wikipedia, but only to use it as an example. It is as much a fruit as it is a root. Wikipedia is successful because it represents what many people believe—that they can be neutral with regard to the deeper religious and philosophical concerns. The point to be made here—a point made in the Bible—is that no one can be neutral with respect to God. Belief in God requires that all facts be interpreted in the light of God. And unbelief in God means that facts are not inter-

---

1   A psychological phenomenon involving a vague and random stimulus (often an image or sound) being perceived as significant. Common examples include seeing images of animals or faces in clouds, the man in the moon, and hearing hidden messages on records played in reverse.

preted in the light of God. The two positions are mutually exclusive, impact the world of "factuality," and both cannot be correct.

I believe, on the basis of the Bible from a Christian perspective informed by the presuppositionalism of Cornelius Van Til (and many others), that such a belief in neutral factuality is an illusion, and a dangerous one at that. Consequently, we need to make every effort to define our terms on the basis of Scripture, as Daniel Webster did when he wrote his first *English dictionary*. You are hereby warned about this concern because our world and its Modern dictionaries have engaged in a systematic process of purging biblical definitions from the English language, and have made great strides over the past fifty or so years.

As a result, you may find much of the information in these essays to be unfamiliar to your contemporary sensitivities. But rest assured that these ideas have deep roots in Christian history.

CALVIN'S METHOD

From what has been previously said, it becomes apparent that Calvin's theology required a "Copernican revolution" of the traditional method recommending Christianity to non-believers. The traditional method of apologetics, developed best by Thomas Aquinas, constructed its view of man in relation to God and did so from the bottom up. Aquinas did not think that the philosophers mixed up heaven and earth simply because they did not know about the fall of mankind in Adam. He believed that Aristotle's philosophy must not be rejected, but supplemented by the Christian story. According to Aquinas, the Christian story needs the theism of the philosophers as its foundation. How otherwise, argues Aquinas, can believers show unbelievers that the story is reasonable.

Aquinas sought to show the unbeliever that the Christian story is in accord with logic and in accord with fact. Calvin sought to show that "logic" and "fact" have meaning only in terms of the "story." The unbeliever appeals to a "logic" that is above the Creator-creature distinction, to thought in general, human and divine, as identical with being itself. Aquinas thought he could satisfy the demands of the unbeliever with respect to the requirements of logic and reason as such. Calvin required the "philosopher" to give its proper place to the fall of man and recognize that the creature must submit his logical efforts to the Creator-Redeemer of man.

Aquinas thought he could satisfy the demands of the unbeliever with respect to the idea of facts, as such. Calvin required the "scientist" to give its proper place to the fall of man and recognize that facts are, and cannot be anything but, expressive of the all-controlling plan of God.

Aquinas offers Christianity to the natural man as an hypothesis that, in his open-minded search for truth, he will find to be better than any other. Calvin challenges the natural man to relinquish his claim to be the rightful judge as to whether the claims of Christ to be the way, the truth, and the life are true or false. And, with true repentance for following the god of this world, everyone needs to prostrate themselves before the Triune God of Scripture.

Man cannot know himself, except as he knows himself as a sinner saved by grace. When by the gift of the Holy Spirit he has become a Christian, he has therewith at the same time become a genuine theist. When he has thus become a Christian theist, he looks back to the pit from which he has been dug. "Hath not God made foolish the wisdom of this world, for after that the world by its wisdom knew not God, it pleased God through the foolishness of preaching to save them that believe."[2]

Following Calvin rather than Aquinas, we may today point out that in all the history of thought, except that which is based upon the Christian story, man cannot identify himself. He would have to do so in relation to a world of pure contingent factuality made correlative to an abstract, timeless principle of rationality which, in the nature of the case, cancel each other out. If modern scientists, modern philosophers, and modern theologians would escape their inability even intelligently to ask any question, let alone find any answer, they can do so only by accepting the answer the Triune God has given man in Scripture. Without submitting to this God, he is a prophet without a mantle, a priest without a sacrifice, and a king without a crown. (from www. vantil.info).

WHAT IS A CHRISTIAN?

What makes a person Christian? It sounds like a simple question, but it has been complicated by sin and history.

Jesus' first sermon set the standard: "Repent, for the kingdom of heaven is at hand" (Matthew 4:17). Clearly, Christians are repentant people. Repentance is the primary response to the gospel and includes the renunciation of sin that all Christians make. It was enough for the thief on the cross (Luke 23:42-43) who was about to die, but it was not

---

2   http://www.ligonier.org/learn/articles/calvin-as-a-controversialist.

enough for most other people. Why not? Because most people are not about to die. Most people are able to continue to live in faithfulness through repentance to obedience. So the Lord expects these things to happen.

We see this in Peter's first sermon. "Repent and be baptized every one of you" (Acts 2:38). Peter repeated the message of Jesus in Matthew 4:17. Peter's message on the Day of Pentecost concluded with a ringing call to repentance (Acts 2:38). Paul's message to the Greeks in Athens sounded the same note: God "commands all people everywhere to repent" (Acts 17:30). When Paul gives an accounting of his ministry, he says, "I have declared to both Jews and Greeks that they must turn to God in repentance and have faith in our Lord Jesus" (Acts 20:21). Notice how Paul calls his hearers not simply to faith, but to faith *and repentance*. In the last book of the Bible, the letters to the seven churches of Asia Minor all demand repentance (Rev. 2-3).

Obedience to the gospel means being baptized, among other things. There are exceptions that suggest that baptism is not a strict requirement (i.e., the thief on the cross), but it is still the general rule. Unless something prohibits baptism, baptism should be the first act of faithfulness on the part of a new believer. And with baptism comes worship, service, fellowship with other believers, and participation in the Lord's Supper. These things, of course, do not cause a person to become a Christian, but are marks of faithfulness.

HISTORICAL INHERITANCE

The Early Church was driven underground because Christians were persecuted by the Roman state. But when Constantine corrected this error by legalizing Christianity in 325 A.D. the church took its place as a public institution. Baptism was celebrated as a public statement, not just a church sacrament.

Apart from times of Christian persecution baptism and worship have always been matters of public expression—and rightly so. Christianity is a public religion, not simply a private affair. The effort to privatize Christianity is an effort to return Christianity to an ineffective and/or persecuted status in the public domain.

Suffice it to say that while baptism does not and cannot cause a person to be a Christian, Christians should be baptized as a public proclamation and recognition of their Christian identity. Baptism as a public ceremony is an announcement of covenantal identity. The individual, or his or her parents in the case of infant baptism, are publicly claiming to be members of Christ's covenant.

And yet, we find that not all baptized people can be characterized as faithful Christians. So, we must recognize two categories of Christian: 1) faithful and 2) unfaithful.

A person can be an unfaithful Christian. In fact, the very definition of unfaithfulness requires a prior commitment (beliefs, values, lifestyle, etc.) that one is *not* keeping. People cannot be unfaithful unless they first acknowledge a standard of faithfulness. Christ is the standard, and baptism is the acknowledgment.

CHRISTIAN IDENTITY

Recognizing, then, that baptism identifies a person as a Christian, we need to mention some of the things that do not make a person a faithful Christian. A person may be actively involved in one and/or all of the following and still not be a faithful Christian:

- attend or be a member of a church.
- financially support a church, or tithe.
- hold church office, i.e. Deacon, Elder, or Pastor.
- read or study the Bible.
- respond to an altar call.
- pray the sinners prayer.

These things may (and may not) accompany faithfulness, but none of them make people faithful Christians, though these things in themselves are not contrary to faithfulness. A person can do any or all of these things and still not be faithful. Why not? Because people lie, and self-deceit is rampant.

GOD CHANGES HEARTS!

Christians are people whose hearts (minds, beliefs, wills) have been changed into the increasing likeness of Christ by the power and grace of God. Becoming a Christian is an active response to God's call (Mark 7:14, John 3:3, etc.).

Unfaithful Christians are actually in a worse position than those who have never heard the truth of the gospel of Jesus Christ. Unfaithfulness is not a matter of ignorance. Whereas pagans and atheists may not know the truth, unfaithful Christians have actually turned their backs on the truth that they do know, which shows that becoming a faithful

Christian is more than being exposed to God's truth. Faithfulness is a matter of regeneration and responsibility, whereas unfaithfulness issues out of degeneration and irresponsibility (Matthew 13:3-9).

What About You?

Perhaps your knowledge of Christ is insufficient (who's isn't?). Yet, ignorance of the law will not keep you from being indicted. Or perhaps you have never really heard God's truth (Matthew 11:15, etc.), and you are open to hear it now.

If so, you need to know that Christians share many things in common as they encounter God's amazing grace. For instance:

- Recognition of your own personal failure and sin as shown by God's Word, the Holy Bible. There are two things to be recognized here—your sin and God's truth.
- Sin and failure are personally shown and acknowledged as sin and failure in the lives of believers by God's Holy Spirit. It is not just that sin is recognized in a general way, but that Christians recognize and agree with God's (the biblical) assessment (judgment) of our sin (Matthew 13:41-41; John 8:34, 16:8; Romans 5-8).
- Christians see their own personal helplessness in the face of their own sin and failure, and ask God for help. If you understand that you cannot change your situation, that you are caught in a web that you cannot escape without outside help, then pray. Are you actively seeking that help?
- This matter of asking for God's help is very important. There are no formulas or set responses to follow. In fact, following a formula or a predetermined response suggests a lack of seriousness and integrity on the part of the person asking the Lord for help. Use your own words. Don't be forced into a childish and immature response. This is serious stuff, and requires your serious attention. Go home and pray about it!
- The Bible says that Jesus Christ already paid the full price for the sin of all who submit to His authority.
- Through the Holy Spirit's leading, Christian's see that Christ's payment covers their own personal sin.
- In gratitude for their own changed hearts, they continue to trust and obey God's Word (starting with water baptism).

- Because of the mercy they have received from the Lord, they are merciful to others in return.
- Christians are humbled because of their personal conviction of failure and sin and the recognition of their own helplessness to fix it.
- Therefore, a Christian is a person who has rejected the way of sin and death by responding to Christ in obedience to Scripture.

APPLICATION

On the one hand, it is an error to suggest that becoming a Christian requires the advice, help, or blessing of anyone other than God. Salvation is an intensely personal affair between particular individuals and God Himself through Jesus Christ.

On the other hand, salvation is not a private affair, it is a public confession. Being restored to Christ means being restored to Christ's community, the Church, with other Christians. No one can be a Christian alone, apart from other restored Christians.

But also be aware that not every professing Christian is a faithful preacher or teacher of the truths of Christianity. Faithful preaching and teaching require spiritual maturity, a commodity in too short supply in our sin-soaked, youth-worshiping world.

It is very helpful to discuss these matters with other born-again believers who are experienced in the faith. It should be that faithful Christians can be found in every church, but things are not as they should be. We live in difficult times, unfaithful times. So, finding other faithful, born-again believers may be more difficult than it should be. But don't fret. There are many, many faithful Christians in every walk of life. Connecting with them is another matter, one that faithful Christians want to help with.

WHAT IS A CHRISTIAN? PART II

Again, it sounds like a simple question, but it has been complicated by sin and history.

The first and most inclusive definition of a Christian is a person who has confessed Jesus Christ as Lord and Savior (John 11:25-27—*Do not neglect reading and studying the verses cited. Don't just skim over them thinking that you already understand them. Take the time to actually study them*). And while such a confession is necessary, it is not sufficient. We know this because Jesus failed to recognize the faithfulness of some people who had confessed Jesus as Lord (Matthew 7:21-ff). Consequently, there are two aspects of being a Christian that must be addressed—that which is necessary, and that which is sufficient. And both must be understood in the context of God's grace.

TWO SETS

These things—that which is necessary and that which is sufficient—are not mutually exclusive. Rather, one (sufficiency) is contained within the other (necessity). It will help to see a picture of this relationship in terms of sets. (See Illustration 1 below.)

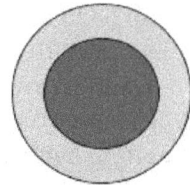

The outer circle or larger set represents that which is necessary, and the inner circle or smaller set represents that which is sufficient. Sufficiency always includes necessity, but necessity does not always include sufficiency.

Illustration 1:

Thus, we can see what Jesus meant when He said, "Not everyone who says to me, 'Lord, Lord,' will enter the kingdom of heaven" (Matthew 7:21). The implication is that some people are lying and/or self-deceived when they confess Jesus as Lord. This issue has caused much confusion. The liars and the self-deceived (who are lying to themselves) will not enter the kingdom of heaven because they are not Christians according to Jesus' own words, in spite of the fact that they think they are. People can be wrong, self-deluded. In fact, self-delusion is common inasmuch as sin is common. Sin is always a function of self-delusion.

While many people will find this idea objectionable and divisive, it must be noted because it is a foundational concept of Scripture and of Christianity. It is not my idea, or the idea of a particular denomination. Rather, it is biblical and pertains to the difference between the lost and the saved, the sheep and the goats, covenant keepers and covenant breakers.

COMPLICATIONS OF SIN

Sin has complicated our understanding of Christianity because sin has effected our ability to understand reality (truth). The crux of the confusion comes in thinking that we can understand reality (truth) apart from God. We cannot. And thinking that we can is the first fruit of sin. The first fruit of sin is self-deception, believing something about ourselves that is not true, or thinking that we are something that we are not. It is a misunderstanding of personal identity and personal ability. Consequently, the first sign of sin is disagreeing with God (Scripture), as Eve did in the Garden (Genesis 3:6). The bottom line is that being a Christian is more than simply saying you are a Christian. Yet, saying that you are is absolutely necessary (Romans 10:9).

The "more" that is involved is God's actual grace. But it is not something additional that is added on to one's confession of faith. Rather, it is something that necessarily precedes one's confession. It is the foundation that makes confession real. People can be confused about what that grace is, and the lost can deceive themselves about whether they have actually received it. This confusion has caused the definition of Christianity to have been understood in several different ways throughout Christian history. The various understandings or definitions of Christianity can be grouped into two categories: judicial and mystical. Christianity can be defined judicially and it can be defined mystically. Both definitions are important, and they must be distinguished if we are to avoid confusion.

To define Christianity judicially means that being a Christian is being susceptible to judgment. In other words, there are elements of being a Christian that can be evaluated by other people. For instance, I can testify that you have made a profession of faith in Christ if I have witnessed your profession. Such a testimony on my part contributes to an objective or public evaluation of your identity as a Christian. I can testify that you understand yourself to be a Christian. Such a testimony is clear, firm, discernible, and communicable. It is not merely subjective.

In contrast, that which is mystical or personal is not as easily discerned, and much of it is simply not discernible at all by others. The mystical or personal aspects of Christianity have to do with the inward reality (or subjective experience) of the fruits of the Spirit (Galatians 5:22-23). Christians are fruitful people. There is no such thing as an unfruitful Christian (Matthew 3:10, John 15:16). If there were such a thing as a fruitless Christian, it would defeat the power of God to make His people fruitful.

The problem with discerning the fruits of the spirit is that people are impatient and want instant results, whereas God is very patient (2 Peter 3:9). Impatience and Christian maturity are opposites. God's mercy and patience often cause people to doubt God's power and effectiveness to produce fruit in the lives of His people and in the life of His church—and this is where Christians often get into trouble.

GROWTH IN GRACE

Who is to say if you or I have love, joy, peace, long-suffering, kindness, goodness, faith, meekness, and self-control (Galatians 5:22-23)? Who can see the growth of the seed before it becomes a discernible plant? Who can say that you or I are not growing in our faithfulness, even though we evidence little outward fruit? And yet the unseen seed is no less a particular kind of plant than the full grown plant. Knowing the hidden things about a person requires subjective knowledge and experience of others that human beings simply do not and cannot have regarding one another (Luke 15:16). As such, Jesus counseled believers to refrain from making such judgments about others (Luke 6:37). Why? Because that which is mystical is subjective. It's an inner experience. It's private, not public.

There are two aspects of being a Christian:

1. A confession of faith in Christ that is open to public inspection. Others can hear it, testify about it, and witness the life you lead.
2. A personal spiritual relationship with Jesus Christ that results in spiritual growth, which is a subjective matter that is a personal matter between God and an individual.

When someone makes a confession of faith in Christ, we are obliged to believe it even when there is little or no evidence. Often the confession of a recently converted sinner comes without the evidence of fruitfulness because the converted sinner has not had time to provide evidence of his or her change of heart, and manifest a changed life. Nonetheless, the fact of the matter is that God changes hearts, and so we should expect to see evidence of sin in a Christian's life and evidence of some ongoing spiritual growth. Both elements coexist in the lives of believers (Romans 7:15). All Christians are sinners, and it is unrealistic to expect a person to ever be completely free of sin in this life. There should, however, be a renouncement of sin, some spiritual growth, some improvement over time, some increase in genuine righteousness.

Of course, sin is completely forgiven in the lives of Christians through the power of Christ, though it lingers in our lives. Even though it lingers, there should be less of it in a Christian's life over time. Christians do not celebrate sin, though they find themselves caught in it. Rather, Christians are convicted and abhorred by sin. They renounce it, and make every attempt to extricate themselves from it. Christian growth is a matter of becoming more aware of the sin that besets us, and better able through the power and presence of the Holy Spirit to become less susceptible to the power and temptation of sin, and more responsive and obedient to the power of God.

Discerning such growth requires judgment. But who's judgment? Of course, every Christian must be willing and able to make such a judgment, first and foremost about him- or herself, and then and only then about others who are under their jurisdiction and who claim to be Christian. The focus of such judgment needs to be on submitting ourselves to the judgment of others who are more mature than we are, and not on making unrequested judgments about other people. Christians are to live in submission to other Christians, to the judgment of other Christians through the authority of the church (Hebrews 13:17).

Christians are called to judge one another in order to help one another grow and mature in faithfulness (Luke 12:57, John 7:24). However, such judgments must not be made in private because Christianity is not simply a private affair. Rather, judgment (evaluation) must be done through the structures of the church. Christian confession is a public statement, made before witnesses, because it makes a claim about one's identity and one's social and public loyalties. Christian confession is social (public) because it effects one's public and social relationships.

It is not that Christians are not to judge one another, but that we are to judge one another righteously—correctly, fairly, honestly, biblically, with love and compassion, not in order to condemn one another, but in order to hold each other accountable, and to assist one another in spiritual growth and maturity (John 7:24). Christianity is a team sport, and all Christian success is team success. To suspend judgment of one another is to abandon the God of righteousness and the obligation to nurture one another in faithfulness. Judgment (evaluation) is the engine of spiritual growth.

COMPLICATIONS OF HISTORY

Becoming a Christian is similar to becoming a citizen of a nation. There were two ways to become an Old Testament Jew: birth and baptism. One could be born into Judaism, or one could convert. The same is true about national identity. And yet, many Israelites were unfaithful. In fact, the essential story of the Old Testament is the story of Israel's unfaithfulness, her innate inability to do and be what God had called her to do and be.

The nation of Israel was a temporary measure in the history of redemption. The advent of Jesus Christ put an end to the nation of Israel and gave birth to the church of Jesus Christ, the true Israel (people) of God. The Old Testament nation of Israel was never intended to be perpetual. Rather, it was the seed that gave rise to the Kingdom of God—the Church or Body of Christ. The form of the seed was not the form of the vine (John 15:5). The seed is destroyed as it becomes the plant. The nation of Israel was destroyed in A.D. 70 as Jesus changed many Old Testament practices though the establishment of the church.

The most important thing that Jesus changed was the idea of being born into a state of salvation or into God's Kingdom or favor. Rather, Jesus said, "You must be born again" (John 3:7). Birth was necessary—you had to be alive! But it was not sufficient. Regeneration was necessary.

Mere birth was no longer a consideration because God was taking the gospel to the nations. He was opening membership in the Kingdom of God to people of other nationalities. In Christ one's particular nationality or physical birth (ethnicity, race, and color) was a non-issue. It didn't matter (Romans 1:16, 2:9-10, 10:12; Galatians 3:28; Colossians 3:11). Christianity was not a function of one's blood, of being born into the right nation or the right family, tribe, or clan. It has nothing to do with the circumstances of one's birth. Jesus crossed the circumstances of human birth off the list.

The concern of physical birth shifted to spiritual rebirth in Christ. This was always the primary concern, but during the infancy of the church the Lord used the nation of Israel to symbolize and concretize the reality of regeneration in human history as a means of helping us understand how God's kingdom works.

Consequently, Christian identity is not innate to the human race. It is not natural. It is alien, not of this earth. Christ was—is—calling His people to acknowledge the preeminence of their alien citizenship, the fact that the Kingdom of God is not of this world (John 18:36) and that the jurisdiction of the Kingdom of God does not belong to this world, though the consequences of God's jurisdiction do effect this world, as well as eternity.

BAPTISM

Christian baptism is a ceremony that symbolizes the reality of regeneration. Baptism does not make a person Christian, it represents the way that God makes sinners into Christians. The ceremony of baptism is not a means of regeneration, it is a symbolic representation of regeneration in Christ. The symbol has real power associated with it because it re-presents the gospel of grace through faith. But it must be understood that the power lies in the gospel not in the ceremony.

Faithful Christians are baptized Christians, unless there is some compelling circumstance that prevents baptism. The ceremony of baptism is neither sufficient nor necessary, but it is a mandated act of faithfulness.

The efficacy of baptism does not rest on the faithfulness of those who receive baptism, though personal faithfulness is expected to increase over time. Rather, the efficacy of baptism rests upon God's faithfulness to accomplish His promises to His people as given in Scripture (Acts 2:39).

CHRISTIAN IDENTITY

So, how do we know who is a Christian and who isn't? The answer is at the same time both easy and difficult.

The easy part has to do with the judicial aspects of Christianity. A Christian first identifies him- or herself as a Christian by making the confession that Christ is Lord. And while it is true that such a confession includes the testimony that Christ is the Lord of his- or her own personal life (a necessary element of one's confession), such a confession is not sufficient because Christianity is not merely a private or personal matter, but it is necessarily a public and social matter precisely because Christians are called to love. And love cannot be private, but is always public and social because love has to do with others. Thus, one's confession must be that Christ is Lord, period! Christ is Lord of this world and everything in it. This is the missing element in too many Christian confessions.

The thing to realize is that Christianity is not about "me." It's about Jesus Christ. Of course, it most certainly impacts "me," but that is not its main feature or its main concern. While Christianity is about heaven, it is not so much about getting "me" into heaven, but about bringing heaven to earth. Jesus taught Christians to pray "Thy kingdom come, Thy will be done on earth as it is in heaven" (Mark 6:10).

Thus, the judicial elements of Christianity are the social elements, not the personal elements. This, of course, does not dismiss or demote the importance of the personal elements of faithfulness, for the social elements require the prior existence of the reality of the personal elements. Every Christian "shall love the Lord your God with all your heart, and with all your soul, and with all your mind, and with all your strength" (Mark 12:30). This First Commandment is intensely personal and must be in place first. This is the first priority of every Christian. But this cannot be easily discerned by other people because it is subjective, personal. This element of Christianity is between God and the individual. It is mystical in that it cannot be fully known. We are privy to our own personal relationship with God through Christ Jesus, but we are not privy to another person's relationship with God. We must not judge anyone else in this regard, apart from the formal structures of our own local church. This element of Christianity is absolutely essential, but it is not sufficient.

The Second Commandment is built upon the first, "You shall love your neighbor as yourself" (Mark 12:31). Here is the fruit of the root. I can know if you love me, just as you can know if I love you because unexpressed love is not really love. Love must be expressed, and it must be expressed socially, outwardly, publicly. Expressions of love must be available for public inspection because love is the glue that holds societies together—love, not law, love, not government, love, not economics. Love lives in the public realm because it is social (it necessarily involves others) and is subject to public observation and discernment. It shows when people love one another.

Yet, we must be careful here because we are not called to judge the quality or quantity (the passion) of one person's love for others. The best that we can do is to testify to our own love of others and someone else's confession or intention to love others. This is what marriage is about. It is a public confession of love and the intention to love one another. We are not qualified to evaluate the quality of the love between husband and wife, but we are qualified to witness marriage vows or pledges to love one another—the promises and intentions.

The same thing is true about the church. The church is a covenant institution. That is to say that membership is dependent upon a public confession of faith in Jesus Christ as Lord and Savior. We are in no position to evaluate how well or how poorly another person loves the Lord. But we can and must acknowledge and value their promise to do so.

Unfaithful

Can Christians be unfaithful? Of course. In fact, *only* Christians can actually be unfaithful because unfaithfulness means failing to honor one's pledge of faithfulness. Without such a pledge there can be no unfaithfulness. This means that all unfaithfulness is Christian unfaithfulness. A person cannot be unfaithful to Buddha, or to Brahman. There is no Zen equivalent to unfaithfulness because there is no Zen pledge. Jews can, of course, be unfaithful—the Old Testament is full of Jewish unfaithfulness. However, inasmuch as Christ is the fulfillment of the Old Testament Judaism, anyone who is still a Jew apart from Christ is necessarily unfaithful to the God of the Old Testament. And, of course, Muslims can be unfaithful to Mohamed, but inasmuch as their god is an impersonal force they can only be faithful to an impersonal force. Thus, the fruit of their faithfulness is both impersonal and employs the exercise of force against what is personal. Thus, Islamic faithfulness is necessarily Christian unfaithfulness, inasmuch as both root their faith in the Old Testament.

And of course, Christians can be unfaithful. That bears repeating—Christians can be unfaithful to the pledges of faithfulness that they have made personally and to those that have been made on their behalf. Church leaders make pledges on behalf of their congregations (i.e., a pledge to pay a mortgage, pledges that the members faithfully believe various biblical tenets or principles, etc.). And parents make pledges on behalf of their children (which means that they take fiscal responsibility for them, and promise to raise them in the love and admonition of the Lord (Ephesians 6:4).

And yet, it must be stated and understood that an unfaithful Christian is still a Christian, even though he or she is unfaithful. If there is unfaithfulness, then there is Christian unfaithfulness. Only the unfaithful can renounce God or turn away from Him. Furthermore, it must be noted that an unfaithful Christian is in a worse position than an outright atheist or pagan because an atheist or pagan has not broken a promise to the Lord. Rather, such a person has not yet made any such promise.

So, What is a Christian?

This brings us back to the original question, what is a Christian? The first answer to this question that the earliest Christians gave was that a Christian is a person who confesses that Jesus Christ is Lord. Such a confession is a necessary and social element in that it is public, objective, and judicial and defines a person as Christian. A confession of Christ takes place in time and is to be a matter of public record. That is to say that there are other people who testify to the factuality of the confession. Whether the person will be faithful to his/her confession is between him/her and God. But the fact of the confession itself is a matter of public record.

However, such a confession is not sufficient. More is required. The person making such a confession must actually believe (prior to the confession) and endeavor to live on the basis of that confession (after having made it). Christians must actually intend to live as if they believe that Jesus is Lord of the universe. This is the subjective element of Christian faithfulness. In order to be correctly defined as a Christian, this subjective (or informal) element of one's profession of faith must be real. The Christian's heart, mind, and soul must be changed by the grace of God. But it is not the place of other Christians to judge the reality or effectiveness of that change. That is the function of the Holy Spirit and the appropriate jurisdictional representatives of the Holy Spirit through one's local church.

There are, however, other Christians who can provide help and guidance on the way. Those who have been in the faith longer are able to help those who are newer. Help them do what? Help them grow in grace and godliness. Such help cannot be foisted upon anyone, but it can be graciously sought and received.

Grace Alone Through Faith Alone

Christians are saved by grace through faith, but not by faith in general. Too many people seem to think that "faith alone" means that faith in anything will do. As long as a person "believes" in something s/he will be okay. Of course people are saved by grace through faith. Faith is the instrument of salvation. And our personal faith is important, but it is Christ's faith that has saved us. Christ's faith led Him to the cross and to the propitiation of God. His faith provided the means of reconciliation with God—the cross. His sacrifice provided for our forgiveness and reconciliation. Our own personal faith in Jesus Christ and in the effectiveness of His sacrifice and atonement is necessary, but it is not sufficient (Matthew 7:21-ff). If it were, we wouldn't need Christ. Rather, Christ alone is sufficient! This does not mean that *our* faithfulness is not important. Rather, it means that we are saved first and foremost by *His* faith, and secondarily by our own personal trust (or faith) in the effectiveness of His faith.

Christianity is not about "me" or "you," or about "my" faith or "your" faith. Rather, it is about Jesus Christ and His faithfulness to Scripture. We are saved, first and foremost by Christ's faithfulness which has provided God's propitiation. Jesus Christ has atoned for the sin of the world. We are saved first and foremost by God's acceptance of the sacrifice of Jesus Christ for the propitiation of sin, and only then by our own acceptance of Jesus Christ as Lord and Savior. Both the order and the emphasis of this process of salvation are important—even critical.

To get this wrong is to take the emphasis off the work of Jesus Christ on the cross and to put the emphasis upon "me," upon *my* faithfulness, *my* efforts. To get this wrong is to turn from grace to works-righteousness, and to rely upon "myself," or "my" faithfulness rather than the faithfulness of Jesus Christ.

Christians are saved by Jesus Christ, not by their own faithfulness—though personal faithfulness plays a necessary role in the lives of believers. It is Christ who has grasped the hearts and minds and hands of His people in salvation. Sure we can hold tight to Christ's hand—and we should! But it is not our strength that holds us fast. It is Christ's strength. It is Christ's grip on us that brings us to salvation and holds us in salvation, not our grip on Christ. Our grip on Christ is necessary, but Christ's grip on us is alone sufficient.

OTHER VOICES

Lewis Sperry Chafer said, "In his attempt to state what a Christian is, the author falls, as many do, into the error of substituting a manner of life for the possession of life" (Lewis Sperry Chafer, Dallas Theological Seminary. 1935; 2002. *Bibliotheca Sacra,* Volume 92. Dallas Theological Seminary).

Habermas says, "A Christian is justified in making the assertion that the Holy Spirit provides a witness that they are, God's children" (Gary R. Habermas, Michigan Theological Seminary. 1997;2002. *Journal of Christian Apologetics* Volume 1. Michigan Theological Seminary, p. 64).

Turner says, "To be a Christian is to be indwelt by the Spirit" (M. M. B. Turner, *The Significance Of Receiving The Spirit In Luke-Acts: A Survey Of Modern Scholarship*, Trinity Evangelical Divinity School. 1981; 2002. *Trinity Journal* Volume 2 . Trinity Evangelical Divinity School, p. 145).

Albert Martin, a baptist pastor says, "According to the Bible, a Christian is a person who has faced realistically the problem of his own personal sin.... A biblical Christian is one who has seriously considered the divine remedy for sin.... A biblical Christian is one who has whole-heartedly complied with the terms for obtaining God's provision for sin... A biblical Christian is a person who manifests in his life that his claims to repentance and faith are real" (Albert Martin, *What is a Biblical Christian?* www.apuritansmind.com/ChristianWalk/AreYou ATrueChristian.htm).

Gordon Fee said, "A Christian is a person who walks in the Spirit, who knows Christ" (Gordon Fee, *Christian History: Paul and His Times.* 1995; Published in electronic form by Logos Research Systems, 1996 (electronic ed.). *Christianity Today:* Carol Stream, IL.).

Spurgeon said, "What is a Christian? If you compare him with a king, he adds priestly sanctity to royal dignity. The king's royalty often lieth only in his crown, but with a Christian it is infused into his inmost nature" (Charles Spurgeon, *Morning and Evening*, Ages Software, p. 252).

Augustine says, "Let the very fountain of grace, therefore, appear in our head, whence, according to the measure of each, it is diffused through all his members. Every man, from the commencement of his faith, becomes a Christian, by the same grace by which that man from his formation became Christ" (Augustine, *De Praedest. Sanct.* Lib. i. c. xv.; *De Bono Perseverantia,* cap. ult. See supra, chapter xiv. sec. 7).

Marshall says, "What cause for assurance can the Christian possibly have? Can it have anything to do with his works proceeding from his natural inclinations?" No, insists Walter Marshall, assurance rests on the work of God, originally as His will is expressed in the work of Christ, and derivatively as the merit of Christ is worked out in the Christian: "We must have some assurance of our salvation in the direct act of faith...before we can, upon any good ground, assure ourselves, that we are already in a state of grace, by that which we call the reflex act" (R. M. Hawkes, *The Logic of Assurance in English Puritan Theology,*

Westminster Theological Seminary. 1990;2002. Westminster Theological Journal Volume 52. Westminster Theological Seminary, p. 257).

Vos says, "To be a Christian is to live one's life not merely in obedience to God, nor merely in dependence on God, nor even merely for the sake of God; it is to stand in conscious, reciprocal fellowship with God, to be identified with Him in thought and purpose and work, to receive from Him and give back to Him in the ceaseless interplay of spiritual forces…. According to this the covenant means that God gives Himself to man and man gives himself to God for that full measure of mutual acquaintance and enjoyment of which each side to the relation is capable" (Geerhardus Vos, "Hebrews, the Epistle of the Diatheke," in *Redemptive History and Biblical Interpretation* (ed. R. B. Gaffin, Jr.; Phillipsburg: Presbyterian & Reformed, 1980, page 186).

Robert Haldane said, "A Christian is free from all things, above all things, faith giving him richly all things" (Haldane, R. 1996. *An Exposition of Romans* (electronic ed.). Christian Classics Foundation: Simpsonville, SC).

Matthew Henry said, "The life of a Christian is in heaven, where his Head and his home are, and where he hopes to be shortly; he sets his affections upon things above; and where his heart is, there will his conversation be" (Henry, M. E. *Matthew Henry's Concise Commentary*, electronic ed.).

Martin Luther said: "A Christian is at the same time a sinner and a saint; he is at once bad and good. For in our own person we are in sin, and in our own name we are sinners. But Christ brings us another name in which there is forgiveness of sin, so that for His sake our sin is forgiven and done away. Both then are true. There are sins…and yet there are no sins…thou standest there for God not in thy name but in Christ's name; thou dost adorn thyself with grace and righteousness although in thine own eyes and in thine own person, thou art a miserable sinner" (Martin Luther, *Werke*, Erlangen ed., 2.197; cited by Warfield, *Perfectionism* , 1:116).

Calvin said, "I speak in Christ, that is, as a Christian; to be in Christ and to be a Christian is the same" (John Calvin, *Commentary on Romans*, Ages Software, p. 578). Calvin also says, "That Christians are under the law of grace, means not that they are to wander unrestrained without law, but that they are engrafted into Christ, by whose grace they are freed from the curse of the Law, and by whose Spirit they have the Law written in their hearts" (John Calvin, *Institutes of the Christian Religion*, 2:8:57).

Again Calvin said, "But because believers stand invincible in the strength of their King, and his spiritual riches abound towards them, they are not improperly called Christians" (Ibid, 2:15:5). Calvin makes known that those who hold to the title "Christian" and do not believe do not really hold the title at all. He says, "For although the name 'Christian' now flits about among us, yet it is only an abuse if the name of God is not called upon by us. And we shall not be able to call upon Him (as says St. Paul) unless we have believed in Him" (John Calvin, *Sermons on the Deity of Christ*, Sermon 18, Ages Software, p. 236).

John Owen is quite blatant on what a Christian is to be and what his mind is set upon, "The glory, life, and power of Christian religion, as Christian religion, and as seated in the souls of men, with all the acts and duties which properly belong thereunto, and are, therefore, peculiarly Christian, and all the benefits and privileges we receive by it, or by virtue of it, with the whole of the honor and glory that arise unto God thereby, have all of them their formal nature and reason from their respect and relation unto the person of Christ; nor is he a Christian who is otherwise minded" (John Owen, *Works*, Volume 1, Ages Software, p. 145).

Charles Hodge says, "It is only faith in Christ, not faith as such, which makes a man a Christian. 'If ye believe not that I am he,' saith our Lord, 'ye shall die in your sins'" (Charles Hodge, *Commentary on Romans*, Ages Software, p. 139).

William Twisse, moderator for the Westminster Confession of Faith, says this, "Question: What is the hunger and thirst of a Christian as a Christian? Answer: An appetite after that which conserves the life of a Christian. Question: What is that? Answer: The favor of God to the pardoning of our sins, and to the saving of our souls" (William Twisse, *A Brief Catechetical Exposition of Christian Doctrine*, London, Old Bailey, 1645. p, 8).

William Bridge says, "Christ is in all believers" (William Bridge, *Works*, Volume 1, *Soli Deo Gloria*, p. 362). He makes this comment based on 2 Corinthians 13:5 where Paul says, "Know ye not how that Christ is in ye, unless ye be reprobates?" Paul does not say, "unless ye be Christians who do not believe." Rather, Bridge rightly asserts that believers have Christ and reprobates do not. Christians have Christ, and non-Christians do not. What then is the fundamental constitution of a

Christian according to the Westminster Confession of Faith and those who wrote it?

Thomas Goodwin says, "That our being in Christ, and united to him, is the fundamental constitution of a Christian" (Thomas Goodwin, *The Works of Thomas Goodwin*, Volume 5, Tanski Publications, 1996, p. 351). Goodwin uses Romans 16:7 as his text and meaning, "who also were in Christ before me," (i.e. converted before me.) Goodwin then says that being in Christ is meant individual "justification" (Ibid.).

Thomas Manton says the same. The Christian is one who "takes the law of God for your rule...takes the Spirit of God for your guide," and the "promises for your encouragement." This "closer walk," Manton says, are of those Christians who are "freed from wrath...taken in favor with respect to God...under special care and conduct of God's providence...hath a sure covenant-right to everlasting glory...hath a sweet experience of God's goodness towards him here in this world," and "hath a great deal of peace" (Thomas Manton, *Manton's Complete Works*, Volume 6, Maranatha Publication, Worthington. pgs 13-15).

Jeremiah Burroughs likewise distinguishes the Christian by conversion, "Christians who profess the gospel must have a great care for their conversation (behavior)...you think or hope, at least, that through the gospel there has been conversion, He expects that you will be careful of your conversations before men...if you would manifest that god has wrought any thru saving knowledge, any wisdom in you to save your souls, then know that god requires that you should show your good conversation (behavior), and that with meekness and wisdom" (Jeremiah Burroughs, *Gospel Conversation*, Soli Deo Gloria Publications, Morgan, PA: 1995. p. 8).

INFORMAL CHRISTIANITY[3]
What It Isn't...

- It is not a local church, but is the personal, internal, subjective faith that identifies church members as belonging to Jesus Christ.
- It is not formless, but conforms to the biblical reality described in Scripture.
- Its discipline is not strict and legalistic, but is free and gracious.

---

3 *Informal Christianity—Refining Christ's Church*, Phillip A. Ross, Pilgrim Platform, Marietta, Ohio, 2006.

- Its principles are absolute in their biblical conception, but gracious and merciful in their practical application.
- It is not concerned about titles or positions, but with genuine Kingdom membership.
- It is not a particular group or social organization. It is concerned about Kingdom membership more than particular church membership. Yet it does not ignore particular church membership.
- It is not concerned about organizational leadership, but with growing God's people.
- It is not concerned about voting, budgets, or committee reports, but with biblical integrity in the lives of individuals. Yet, does not ignore these things.
- It is not about denominations or associations, but with furthering the cause of Christ in the community.
- It is not a man-made corporation, but a God-given fellowship.
- It is not a non-profit organization. It offers no tax incentives for giving, but relies upon Christian charity.
- It is not about organizational names or constitutions.
- It is not about property ownership.
- It is not a legal entity, but a spiritual organism.
- It is not an institutional program, but a biblical family pattern.
- It is not about budgets or bank accounts, but is about friends helping friends informally.
- It is not a social, recreational or service club.
- It is not concerned about social status. It does not cater to the rich and famous, nor does it favor or pamper the poor and downtrodden.
- It does not exist for the sake of its own members, but for the gospel of Jesus Christ.
- It is not based upon worldly friendships, but upon spiritual fellowship. Favors are never owed nor collected.

This is not to say that Christians should not gather in churches or own property or have meetings, budgets, vote, etc. Rather, it is to say that these things are not to take precedence in the lives of Christians. It simply acknowledges that all to often such things pervert the primary purpose and structure of Christian fellowship.

What Informal Christianity Is...

- It is simple faith alone in Christ alone that makes Christianity an easy burden.
- It is lived in a casual, ordinary, and common way.
- Its application to life is unofficious, relaxed, suited for everyday use. It is a part of ordinary living, not apart from ordinary living.
- It is a sincere, unfeigned, genuine, personal love of the Lord Jesus Christ.
- It is willing obedience or conformity to Scripture and real cooperation among God's people, which means that it doesn't conform to the world.
- It is personal pleasure and delight in God's Word and God's Way.
- It is the application of the Bible to the structure and function of the church.
- It is the liberty to enjoy life to its fullest measure in Christ.

This is not to say that formal structure is not important, it is. But formal structure apart from the informal realities here mentioned robs the form of its original meaning, purpose and effectiveness.

Agape

The Greek word *agape* is usually translated as *love* in the new translations of the Bible, but the old King James version, as well as the Modern King James Version, translates it as *charity*.

Three-fourths of the time that the word *love* is used in the Bible, it is the Greek *agape* (or the verb, *agapao*). Three-fourths of the time! Agape is quite different from what we usually think of as love. *Agape* does not involve romantic attachments or sexual fulfillment. It is none of that! It is free from that kind of entanglement.

Agape is first and foremost an attitude, but it also results in action. That is why the King James Version translated it as *charity*. It is the kind of love that expresses itself in concern for others—but not mere concern. It is love-in-action. It is the kind of love expressed through generosity.

God's people are generous people. Whether they are rich or poor makes no difference. Christians do not give to others in order to relieve their conscience, as some people do. Rather, Christians share their bounty, be it great or small, because God shares His bounty.

Charity has gotten a bad reputation in our day. It's time we restore charity to its rightful place in Scripture and in the lives of Christians.

ORTHODOXY

Below is a graphic depiction of how various models of church leadership are related and how they can err.

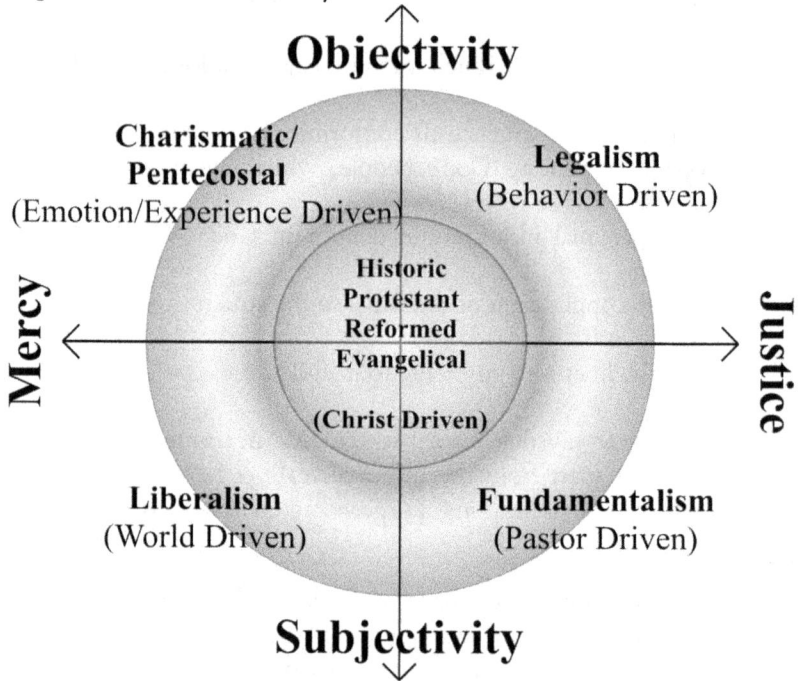

Objectivity

Charismatic/
Pentecostal
(Emotion/Experience Driven)

Legalism
(Behavior Driven)

Mercy ← → Justice

Historic
Protestant
Reformed
Evangelical

(Christ Driven)

Liberalism
(World Driven)

Fundamentalism
(Pastor Driven)

Subjectivity

LIVING BY FAITH

What does it mean to *live by faith?* The phrase is one of the most important in all of Scripture. It first occurs in Habakkuk 2:4. The Lord instructed Habakkuk to write a vision about a time when "the just shall live by his faith."

Later, in writing to the Romans (1:17), Paul said that such a time had come in Christ. Describing his own conversion, Paul affirmed the righteousness of faith when he said that he no longer lived, but Christ lived in him, and that he "lived by faith toward the Son of God" (Galatians 2:20), who loved him.

"Now, 'the Just shall live by faith. But if he draws back, My soul shall have no pleasure in him.' But we are not of withdrawal to destruction, but of those who believe to the saving of the soul" (Hebrews 10:38-39).

Martin Luther discovered that God's free grace is the key to the Scriptures. His discovery was made by reading Romans 1:17, "For in it the righteousness of God is revealed from faith to faith; as it is written, 'The just shall live by faith.'" The whole of the Protestant Reformation hangs on God's free grace.

Christian faithfulness means walking by faith, living by faith. Living by faith means trusting that the Lord will provide.

Endeavoring to practice this precept, ministry should not pay salaries or hire anyone to do ministry. This does not mean that ministers are not compensated, but that they are not "paid" to do ministry. Rather, we rely on Christian love—charity. Ours is to be a ministry of Christian love, of personal service to the Lord among friends of the Lord. You might say that this ministry is of the Lord, by the Lord, and for the Lord.

Walking by faith does not mean ignoring the material aspects of life. Walking by faith is not neglect of material responsibility. Walking by faith means trusting that the Lord will provide what is needed. Walking by faith is walking, not sitting. It is working, not loafing. It is working in order to share in the joy of giving. God is generous and God wants His people to be generous as well. That's *agape*.

CALVINISM & ARMINIANISM

Calvinism and Arminianism have offered rival biblical and theological interpretations for a long time. Some people think that both cannot be faithful to Scripture because they are mutually exclusive. It is our understanding that Calvinism ultimately trumps Arminianism in every measure as the more faithful interpretation of Scripture. Yet, this is not a denial of the role of Arminianism in the life of the believers. The following chart sets out the fundamental differences.

Calvinism	Arminianism
Inability or Total Depravity	**Free-Will or Human Ability**
Because of the fall, man is unable of himself to savingly believe the gospel. The sinner is dead, blind, and deaf to the things of God; his heart is deceitful and desperately	Although human nature was seriously affected by the fall, man has not been left in a state of total spiritual helplessness. God graciously enables every sinner to repent and be-

corrupt. His will is not free, it is in bondage to his evil nature, therefore, he will not—indeed he cannot—choose good over evil in the spiritual realm. Consequently, it takes much more than the Spirit's assistance to bring a sinner to Christ—it takes regeneration by which the Spirit makes the sinner alive and gives him a new nature. Faith is not something man contributes to salvation but is itself a part of God's gift of salvation—it is God's gift to the sinner, not the sinner's gift to God

lieve, but He does not interfere with man's freedom. Each sinner posses a free will, and his eternal destiny depends on how he uses it. Man's freedom consists of his ability to choose good over evil in spiritual matters; his will is not enslaved to his sinful nature. The sinner has the power to either cooperate with God's Spirit and be regenerated or resist God's grace and perish. The lost sinner needs the Spirit's assistance, but he does not have to be regenerated by the Spirit before he can believe, for faith is man's act and precedes the new birth. Faith is the sinner's gift to God; it is man's contribution to salvation.

Unconditional Election

God's choice of certain individuals unto salvation before the foundation of the world rested solely in His own sovereign will. His choice of particular sinners was not based on any foreseen response of obedience on their part, such as faith, repentance, etc. On the contrary, God gives faith and repentance to each individual whom He selected. These acts are the result, not the cause of God's choice. Election therefore was not determined by or conditioned upon any virtuous quality or act foreseen in man. Those whom God sovereignly elected He brings through the power of the Spirit to a willing acceptance of Christ. Thus God's choice of the sinner, not the sinner's choice of Christ, is the ultimate cause of salvation.

Conditional Election

God's choice of certain individuals unto salvation before the foundation of the world was based upon His foreseeing that they would respond to His call. He selected only those whom He knew would of themselves freely believe the gospel. Election therefore was determined by or conditioned upon what man would do. The faith which God foresaw and upon which He based His choice was not given to the sinner by God (it was not created by the regenerating power of the Holy Spirit) but resulted solely from man's will. It was left entirely up to man as to who would believe and therefore as to who would be elected unto salvation. God chose those whom He knew would, of their own free will, choose Christ.

	Thus the sinner's choice of Christ, not God's choice of the sinner, is the ultimate cause of salvation.
Particular Redemption or Limited Atonement Christ's redeeming work was intended to save the elect only and actually secured salvation for them. His death was substitutionary endurance of the penalty of sin in the place of certain specified sinners. In addition to putting away the sins of His people, Christ's redemption secured everything necessary for their salvation, including faith which unites them to Him. The gift of faith is infallibly applied by the Spirit to all for whom Christ died, therefore guaranteeing their salvation.	**Universal Redemption or General Atonement** The Spirit calls inwardly all those who are called outwardly by the gospel invitation; He does all that He can to bring every sinner to salvation. But inasmuch as man is free, he can successfully resist the Spirit's call. The Spirit cannot regenerate the sinner until he believes; faith (which is man's contribution) proceeds and makes possible the new birth. Thus, man's free will limits the Spirit in the application of Christ's saving work. The Holy Spirit can only draw to Christ those who allow Him to have His way with them. Until the sinner responds, the Spirit cannot give life. God's grace, therefore, is not invincible; it can be, and often is, resisted and thwarted by man.
The Efficacious Call of the Spirit or Irresistible Grace In addition to the outward general call to salvation which is made to everyone who hears the gospel, the Holy Spirit extends to the elect a special inward call that inevitably brings them to salvation. The internal call (which is made only to the elect) cannot be rejected; it always results in conversion. By means of this special call the Spirit irresistibly draws sinners to Christ. He is not	**The Holy Spirit Can Be Effectually Resisted** The Spirit calls inwardly all those who are called outwardly by the gospel invitation; He does all that He can to bring every sinner to salvation. But inasmuch as man is free, he can successfully resist the Spirit's call. The Spirit cannot regenerate the sinner until he believes; faith (which is man's contribution) proceeds and makes possible the new birth. Thus, man's free will

limited in His work of applying salvation by man's will, nor is He dependent upon man's cooperation for success. The Spirit graciously causes the elect sinner to cooperate, to believe, to repent, to come freely and willingly to Christ. God's grace, therefore, is invincible; it never fails to result in the salvation of those to whom it is extended.	limits the Spirit in the application of Christ's saving work. The Holy Spirit can only draw to Christ those who allow Him to have His way with them. Until the sinner responds, the Spirit cannot give life. God's grace, therefore, is not invincible; it can be, and often is, resisted and thwarted by man.
Perseverance of the Saints All who are chosen by God, redeemed by Christ, and given faith by the Spirit are eternally saved. They are kept in faith by the power of Almighty God and thus persevere to the end.	**Falling from Grace** Those who believe and are truly saved can lose their salvation by failing to keep up their faith, etc. All Arminians have not been agreed on this point; some have held that believers are eternally secure in Christ—that once a sinner is regenerated, he can never be lost.

And so it is that Calvinism and Arminianism are mutually exclusive at every point. There have been many attempts to combine or integrate these two systems of theology, but none can succeed without making a mess of logic and logical consistency. Thus, we thank God that salvation is not a function of our own human understanding, but by grace alone through faith alone in Christ alone according to Scripture alone to the glory of God alone. Being saved does not require an understanding of how we are saved, nor does mere salvation produce such knowledge.

And yet, we understand that the Bible does in fact teach that personal responsibility and right human behavior are necessary gospel ingredients. My attempt to explain this conundrum is found in my Statement of Faith, p. 34.

SALVATION

Soteriology: n. The theological doctrine of salvation as effected by Jesus.

Salvation is accomplished by the almighty power of the Triune God. The Father chose a people, the Son died for them, the Holy Spirit

makes Christ's death effective by bringing people to faith and repentance, thereby causing them to willingly obey the Gospel. The entire
process (election, redemption, and regeneration) is the work of God and
is by grace alone through faith alone in Christ alone according to Scripture alone to the glory of God alone. Thus God, not man, determines
who will be the recipients of the gift of salvation. However, God's determination is not merely about people as individuals, but is about the
imitation of the character of His Son, Jesus Christ. Thus, God's preference is not about individuals, for God is no respecter of persons. Rather,
God's preference is about the character qualities of Jesus Christ, the fruits
of the Spirit.

> "Christian! the only thing that makes you differ from the vilest
> being that pollutes the earth, or from the darkest fiend that gnaws
> his chains in hell, is the free grace of God!"
>   – Octavious Winslow

ESSAYS

NONCONFORMITY

The restoration of the English King, Charles II, in 1660 brought back into power all those spiritual influences which the Puritans had stood against prior to the English Civil War. Episcopacy (rule of the church by the clergy), compulsory liturgy, and uniformity in worship practices were again to be the state religion.

A meeting at the Savoy Castle in 1661 between Episcopalians and Presbyterians indicated the futility of any hope of accommodation, and rather than comply with the terms of the Act of Conformity, which was imposed upon all churches the following year, some two-thousand Puritans gave up their churches and livings by becoming nonconformists. This Great Ejection of 1662 was one of the most decisive events in the history of English Protestantism. The Great Ejection, the birth of nonconformity, was the beginning of Congregationalism (and of Presbyterianism).

However, I am not a Christian nonconformist for merely historical reasons. There is today another similar push to impose a kind of uniformity upon churches. It is not a formal writ or decree, but it is a movement that makes popular values and beliefs the mainstay in many churches. It is a kind of populism that is generated by mass media and advertising. The media industry is interested in generating sales, so it caters to the lowest common denominator in order to guarantee as much commerce as possible. Thus the media tends to both generate and to deliver this lowest common denominator mindset far and wide. For many years the churches have flirted with it, but of late they have practically surrendered to it.

I do not choose to conform to the standards of such popular media, which are so prevalent in today's churches. Yet, Christian nonconformity is not simply a matter of being different for the sake of being different. Nor is it a contrarianism that stands against everything that anyone else says. Rather, nonconformity celebrates the tradition of the historic, classic, Protestant Reformed churches by not conforming to the world or to neo-worldliness that is dressed in Christian garb.

Rather, all Christians should conform to the things of God, to the image of God in Christ, to Christ's character qualities, the fruits of the Spirit.

STATEMENT OF FAITH

By grace Through Faith In Christ

It all begins with grace…

Grace is the unmerited privilege of receiving God's favor or bless-ing. Grace is given by God to produce faith. Faith produces obedience. Obedience produces understanding. Understanding produces growth in faith.

And issues from God's sovereignty…

God, in His sovereignty, has determined the eternal destination of every person before time itself. But such knowledge is beyond human understanding. Because of the limitations of human beings, the gospel is couched in such a way as to appeal to the perception of free will in sin-ners. Because God predestines people to salvation, believers seek to un-derstand God's Word.

It's beyond our ability…

All people are completely unable to save themselves. Sinners strug-gle against God, but cannot bring about salvation.

But not God's…

God bestows His grace upon whomever He chooses. People cannot cause God to give grace. God's grace has already been given to His peo-ple from eternity. However, God's grace causes the faithful to desire to satisfy Him with their obedience. The Holy Spirit inspires the faithful to desire to fulfill the conditions of God's covenant. Obeying God involves proclaiming salvation in Jesus Christ to all people.

Christ already accomplished it…

The death of Christ on the cross provides atonement for all true be-lievers. God is perfect and makes no errors. Many sinners do not receive God's grace and salvation. Therefore, the atonement is effective only for those who are actually saved. Faith means trusting God personally for one's own salvation, and that Christ's atonement (sacrifice) applies to "me" personally. Christ's atonement works for "whoever believes."

God doesn't make mistakes…

Those whom God truly calls are elected and saved in fact, because God is perfect and makes no errors. But because sinners doubt God, they think that their own power is greater than God's, and that they are able to resist God's Holy Spirit.

Hanging in there…

Those whom God truly calls are elect and, in fact, persevere in sal-vation because God is perfect and makes no errors. Because sinners doubt God, they believe that the world of circumstances is more power-ful than God, and can doubt their salvation. But because God saves, and God is all-powerful, His saving is final. Obedience to God's Word (Bible) provides assurance of salvation.

Repentance

"Surely after that I was turned, I repented; and after that I was instructed, I smote upon my thigh: I was ashamed, yea, even confounded, because I did bear the reproach of my youth" (Jeremiah 31:19).

"We hence learn how blind the Papists are, who, speaking of repentance, hold that man, through his own free-will, returns to God; and on this point is our greatest contest with them at this day. But the Prophet briefly determines the whole question; for, as he had said before, that men cannot turn except God turns them, he now adds, that he had found this to be really the fact, that people had never become conscious of their sins though God had grievously punished them until they were turned, not by their own free-will, but by the hidden working and influence of the Holy Spirit; 'after thou has turned me, I repented.' The meaning is, that men never entertain a real hatred towards sin, unless God illuminates their minds and changes their hearts; for what is the turning or conversion of which the Prophet speaks? It is the renewal of the mind and heart. For let its definition be fetched, as they say, from what is contrary to it; what is turning away? It is the alienation of the mind and heart from God. It then follows that when we turn we are converted, we are renewed in knowledge, and then in heart, or in our affections; both of which the Prophet ascribes to the grace of God, for he says that the people repented not of their sins until they were turned or converted, that is, until they were renewed both in mind and heart."
—John Calvin on repentance, Jeremiah 31:19 *Commentary on the Prophet Jeremiah & The Lamentations* (Vol. IV, Baker Book House, Grand Rapids, MI, p. 102.)

1. Repentance is taking full responsibility for the sin
2. Repentance is turning from the idol we serve to the true God
     What do we mean by idols? How does that tie into sin? Sin is not just a transgression of a law of God. It involves a turning from God in unbelief and turning to something else as a "god." When I sin I am saying to God, "I do not trust you. I do not believe your way is good and best. I do not believe you are wise." In place of the true God I worship pleasure, a lover, a lie, my money, a career advancement, my reputation etc. We cannot worship God and sin. we cannot sin without worshiping idols. Deep in the heart of man there is a powerful pull of idolatry. We

want to worship this other god because of the pleasure it brings us. That love for sin and out false lover can actually keep us from repentance. (Mark Lauterbach, *The Transforming Community*, pgs. 142-144).

Baptism

Christian Baptism Is Trinitarian.

Christian baptism (Covenant baptism) is "one" in the same sense that the "Lord" and the "faith" are one—that is the Trinitarian sense of oneness. The unity of the Lord is not something that is built by human hands, or human understanding. It is not something that is decreed by human institutions, nor a function of human institutions. The unity of "one Lord, one faith, and one baptism" is given by God, not built or established by man. The unity of such oneness is established by God in eternity. But what kind of unity does this biblical, Trinitarian understanding of God describe?

Clearly, God's unity lies in the unity of the Father, Son, and Holy Spirit—three, yet one; one, yet three. Christian unity is a unique unity that is founded in the character of God and is reflected in God's creation. And because Christian baptism touches the leading edge of God's character in the reflected character of humanity, who was created in God's image, the unity of baptism follows the pattern of God's unity, which is trinitarian (small t).

The unity of baptism is found in the wholeness of its three constituent parts: 1) initiation, 2) spiritual reality, and 3) covenant responsibility. As God is one, yet three, so baptism into His church is similarly one, yet three—one in essence, three in manifestation. The elements of baptism are unified in Jesus Christ, who brings salvation, judgment, and the incarnation of the Holy Spirit.

Three Baptisms

"I indeed baptize you with water unto repentance: but he that cometh after me is mightier than I, whose shoes I am not worthy

38

to bear: he shall baptize you with the Holy Ghost, and with fire
(Matthew 3:11).

The three baptisms of Christ are analogous to the Trinity—Father,
Son, and Holy Spirit—three, yet one. These three baptisms are listed in
Matthew 3:11. They are 1) John's water baptism of repentance, 2) Jesus'
baptism of fire, and 3) the baptism of the Holy Spirit. Like the Trinity,
they are one, yet three.

1) **Water Baptism**

An interesting thing has happened over the long course of history,
baptism has almost always been associated with water. But that's not the
whole story. I want to show you that only one of these three baptisms
has anything to do with water.

Scripture speaks often of water baptism. The illustrations are too
numerous to list. But take Jesus' own baptism as an example.

> "And Jesus, when he was baptized, went up straightway out of
> the water: and, lo, the heavens were opened unto him, and he
> saw the spirit of God descending like a dove, and lighting upon
> him" (Matthew 3:16).

The first thing to notice is that when Jesus was baptized by John He
was in water—the Jordan River, where John baptized many.

People assume that this means that He had been immersed. But the
record doesn't say that. It only says that He "went up straightway out of
the water." Granted it could mean that He came up from having been
immersed, but it could just as well mean that He came up to the shore
after standing in the river in ankle deep water to be baptized by sprinkling or pouring.

John's baptism employs water. The traditional baptismal ceremony
reproduces John's baptism, however much water you understand to have
been used. It is a ceremonial baptism performed by men in the presence
of witnesses. This baptism is like a wedding ceremony. The ceremony is
not the love, nor the marriage. It's only a symbol.

2) **Fire Baptism**

The baptism least like water baptism is fire baptism. Fire baptism
and water baptism are mutually exclusive. Fire and water cannot coexist.
Unlike John's water baptism which is for believers, Jesus' baptism with
fire is for unbelievers. In water baptism believers confess Jesus to be the

Christ. In fire baptism unbelievers deny Jesus to be the Christ. The core of water baptism is the confession of the believer. The core of fire baptism is the rejection of the unbeliever.

Fire baptism is not only distinguished from water baptism, but is also distinguished from the baptism of the Holy Spirit. When John said that Jesus would baptize "with the Holy Spirit and fire," he didn't mean that baptism with fire was another way to describe the baptism of the Holy Spirit. Rather, the Bible teaches that there is a different baptism for unbelievers. The saved and the damned do not undergo the same change of character that is signified by baptism.

Michael Horton opened up this understanding of fire baptism for me. Horton writes, "God himself appears as a fire throughout biblical revelation, and is even self-described as 'a consuming fire' (Hebrews 12:29). But we automatically assume that this is a good thing—this business about being consumed by heavenly fire, set aflame by divine conflagration within the spirit. Some even want to be 'baptized' with the Holy Spirit and fire, not realizing the context."

The context, of course, is Matthew 3:10-12,

> And now also the ax is laid unto the root of the trees: therefore every tree which bringeth not forth good fruit is hewn down, and cast into the fire. I indeed baptize you with water unto repentance: but he that cometh after me is mightier than I, whose shoes I am not worthy to bear: he shall baptize you with the Holy Ghost, and with fire: Whose fan is in his hand, and he will thoroughly purge his floor, and gather his wheat into the garner; but he will burn up the chaff with unquenchable fire.

This baptism by fire is a baptism into destruction, into death and damnation, and is reserved for those who refuse Christ's salvation. Where water baptism is a baptism into Christ's Church, fire baptism is a baptism apart from Christ's Church. The symbolism of water baptism evokes regeneration by the Holy Spirit, but fire baptism is an unceremonious degeneration into eternal damnation apart from the Holy Spirit.

This insight is based upon two beliefs. First, when Jesus returns He will separate mankind into two groups, the saved "to the resurrection of life," and the damned "to the resurrection of condemnation" (John 5:28-29). Believers will be separated from those who don't believe.

The second belief upon which this insight is based involves the nature of baptism itself. What is baptism? What does the word actually mean? When we read the word *baptism* in our Bibles we are not reading an English translation of a Greek word. Sure, the Greek word is *baptizo*. However, the English rendering is not a translation, but a transliteration. That means that the word was simply incorporated into the English language without translation.

Early on, people associated baptism with a water ceremony. But to understand the three baptisms of Christ we must not limit our understanding of baptism to human ceremonies. Rather, we must discover the richer meaning and reality of baptism. It is a spiritual reality, as well as a sign that points to a spiritual reality.

The spiritual meaning of *baptism* is associated with the baptism of the Holy Spirit. Again, our understanding of the baptism of the Holy Spirit has been colored by the modern argument that it means speaking in tongues. There are modern denominations that base church membership upon this understanding and its manifestation. But this modern phenomenon is an aberration, a departure from the ancient understanding of the baptism of the Holy Spirit.

3) Spirit Baptism

The involvement of the Holy Spirit in baptism can be traced to Acts 2:38, where Peter preached "Repent, and be baptized everyone of you in the name of Jesus Christ for the remission of sins, and ye shall receive the gift of the Holy Ghost." The gift is not speaking in tongues, but is the Holy Spirit Himself, who then produces the fruit of the Spirit and the various gifts of the spirit in His people. The baptism of the Holy Spirit means receiving the Holy Spirit.[1]

This broader understanding of baptism is shown in 1 Corinthians 10:2, where Paul, describing some events of the Old Testament, said that the ancient Jews "were baptized into Moses." But what does it mean to be "baptized into Moses"?

Dip or Dye

The Greek *baptizo* literally means to dip or dye, as in the dyeing or bleaching of cloth. But the passion to defend immersion as a the only legitimate baptismal practice has shifted the attention of well-meaning scholars from the purpose—dyeing, to the process—dipping. People have latched onto the process of *baptizo*—to dip, and ignored the purpose—to dye.

---

1   For more on this see Ross, Phillip A. *Arsy Varsy—Reclaiming the Gospel in First Corinthians*, Pilgrim Platform, Marietta, Ohio, 2006 .

The process may involve dipping, but the purpose of dyeing material is to permanently change the color or character of the cloth. The process is important, but there are many possible dyeing processes. However, the purpose of dyeing is essential to the process. Purpose is always a primary concern of God. Therefore, because the ceremony of baptism does not cause the requisite change of character, we know that God is not limited to dipping (or pouring or sprinkling). God's greater concern is the end product, His purpose for changing people in the first place.

The question about being baptized into Moses must be divided into questions about the process and the purpose of such baptism. The purpose determines the process, so to rightly understand the process we must first understand the purpose. What was the purpose or result of being baptized into Moses?

The result was that Israel followed the covenant administration given to Moses. The people followed him out of Egypt. Moses, of course, lead according to the covenant that God had given him. The people of God were being changed into the likeness—not of Moses, but of the covenanting God who himself led Moses.

God has always been out to change the character of His people, to dye them, if you will, in various stages (covenant administrations) or baptisms, to bring them ultimately "to the measure of the stature of the fullness of Christ" (Ephesians 4:13). Yet, God is working to produce only one change, one baptism. Consequently, all this history, all these covenant administrations serve the same purpose, God's one true baptism, a change of heart that will affect a change in history.

The fact that God's eternal covenant—Adam's covenant, Noah's covenant, Abraham's covenant, Moses' covenant, David's covenant—has come to Christians through Jesus Christ is shown in Galatians 3:14, "That the blessing of Abraham might come on the Gentiles through Jesus Christ; that we might receive the promise of the Spirit through faith." God's covenant of grace, given to Adam, Noah, Abraham, Moses and David (and others) has, through Jesus Christ, been given to the Gentiles.

How has it been given? Always by the power of the Holy Spirit. How has it been received? Always by faith in Christ, the Messiah. The Holy Spirit falls upon His people, brings them to faith through a change of heart, thus fulfilling God's covenant of grace, so that they may fulfill God's covenant by faith in Christ.

The real issue of baptism is not sprinkling, pouring, or immersion—but being permanently changed (dyed) by the power of the Holy Spirit. Surely, God is more concerned about purpose than process. And even when the process plays a role, we know that God's power is not mediated by the ceremony of baptism, however we do it! The power is not in the ceremony, but in God's Word. Nor is the result of some outer affect, but a changed heart.

Surely, God can bring about the requisite change of heart, whether people are sprinkled, poured, immersed or none of the above. The real concern of baptism is the dyeing, the bleaching, the purification, the changing of one's character, the rebirth, the regeneration, the new life.

God is always after this one thing!

Christ's Trinitarian nature has produced three baptisms—the baptism of repentance by water, and the baptism of regeneration by the Holy Spirit, or the baptism of degeneration by fire. But these three baptisms, while different, are one in purpose. That purpose is the changing of human character to the glory of God. The one overriding purpose of baptism is the changing of human character into the likeness of Christ—and that involves more than getting wet.

Initiation

> "When ye come to appear before me, who hath required this at your hand, to tread my courts? Bring no more vain oblations; incense is an abomination unto me; the new moons and Sabbaths, the calling of assemblies, I cannot away with; it is iniquity, even the solemn meeting. Your new moons and your appointed feasts my soul hateth: they are a trouble unto me; I am weary to bear them. And when ye spread forth your hands, I will hide mine eyes from you: yea, when ye make many prayers, I will not hear: your hands are full of blood. Wash you, make you clean; put away the evil of your doings from before mine eyes; cease to do evil; Learn to do well; seek judgment, relieve the oppressed, judge the fatherless, plead for the widow. Come now, and let us reason together, saith the LORD: though your sins be as scarlet, they shall be as white as snow; though they be red like crimson, they shall be as wool. If ye be willing and obedient, ye shall eat the good of the land: But if ye refuse and rebel, ye shall be devoured with the sword: for the mouth of the LORD hath spoken it." (Isaiah 1:12-20).

Covenant baptism is required in order to draw near to the Lord, because He is Holy. God cannot tolerate the impurity of sin in His presence. And because we are not able to make ourselves pure and holy, He washes His people in the waters of baptism. The reality of Christian baptism that is pointed to in the symbolic ceremony of baptism is the fact that baptism is God's doing. He initiates it. He accomplishes it.

Consequently, the initiating aspect of covenant baptism pertains to God the Father in heaven. It corresponds to God as Father in the Trinitarian conception of the Godhead, and can be symbolized by sprinkling. Sprinkling was used in the Old Testament as a kind of purification (see Exodus 29:21, etc.). The word and ceremony of sprinkling in the Bible suggests both an initiation and a purification rite. God does much with little, like the parable of the Mustard Seed teaches (Matthew 13:31-32).

Spiritual Reality

The spiritual reality of covenant baptism is best demonstrated by the reality of the Holy Spirit, which was made most perfectly manifest in and through Jesus Christ. The birth of Christ in human history is the perfect manifestation of the reality of God and His Spirit. God was shown to be real because Christ was born a man. Christ took on the reality of human flesh.

> John 17:3: And this is life eternal, that they might know thee the only true God, and Jesus Christ, whom thou hast sent.

> John 20:31: But these are written, that ye might believe that Jesus is the Christ, the Son of God; and that believing ye might have life through his name.

> Romans 6:4: Therefore we are buried with him by baptism into death: that like as Christ was raised up from the dead by the glory of the Father, even so we also should walk in newness of life.

Christian baptism is both a literal and a symbolic pouring out of God's holy Spirit.

> Isaiah 44:3: …I will pour my spirit upon thy seed, and my blessing upon thine offspring.

> Joel 2:28: And it shall come to pass afterward, that I will pour out my spirit upon all flesh; and your sons and your daughters shall

prophesy, your old men shall dream dreams, your young men shall see visions.

Acts 10:45: And they of the circumcision which believed were astonished, as many as came with Peter, because that on the gentiles also was poured out the gift of the Holy Ghost.

Covenantal Responsibility

In Christian baptism we find God's giving and our receiving of His covenant responsibilities. In baptism God's people are engrafted into the body of Christ—not by the symbolism of the ceremony, but by the reality of the Holy Spirit. Participation in the body of Christ, then, necessarily entails covenant responsibilities. There is some common understanding of this aspect of baptism among the various traditions when it is applied to confessing adults. But a great deal of misunderstanding has arisen regarding its application to the children of believers. How can a child, much less an infant, assume any covenant responsibilities?

Clearly, children and infants are not able to do so to a significant degree. But that does not exclude them from the promises of God. As clearly as children are not able to assume covenant responsibilities, the Bible clearly teaches that the children of believers are recipients of God's promises, covenant, and blessings.

Deuteronomy 12:28: Observe and hear all these words which I Command thee, that it may go well with thee, and with thy children after thee for ever, when thou doest that which is good and right in the sight of the LORD thy God.

Acts 16:31: And they said, Believe on the Lord Jesus Christ, and thou shalt be saved, and thy house.

These and many other Scriptures confirm that the children of believers are recipients of God's covenant from birth.

Yet, they are not able assume their covenant responsibilities. Therefore, the covenant responsibilities that will belong to them in their faithful adulthood, must be assumed by those who have authority over them in their childhood—their parents, and in particular, their fathers. Fathers and parents are responsible for their children. The responsibilities that the children will take as adults are assumed by the parents for their children. The parents are the temporary custodians of their children's adult responsibilities. The same is true with regard to their covenant responsibilities.

God's covenant is a covenant of grace and obedience. God established the covenant, and has laid out its responsibilities. In Deuteronomy 28 we learn that if people obey God's covenant they will be blessed, and if they don't, they will be cursed. Thus, God's covenant brings necessary consequences for faithfulness and for unfaithfulness.

Regarding the baptism of children, God's covenant responsibilities do not change, but are applied to whoever assumes authority for the baptized child. If the baptized child assumes God's covenant responsibilities for himself as he grows, and makes an appropriate confession of Christ, and faithfully participates in the fellowship of the redeemed, then he and his parents receive and enjoy the promised blessings.

But if the child does not assume God's covenant responsibilities for himself, and does not make a confession of Christ, then he and his parents are liable to God's promised curses. However, because the parents of the child assumed the child's covenant responsibilities and the child rejected them, then the child must be formally disciplined by the church at an appropriate time. Because the child has not fulfilled his covenant responsibilities that were given by grace and taken on his behalf, those in authority over the child, those who took upon themselves the covenant responsibilities for the child, must bring formal charges against the irresponsible child that will result in church discipline, which would include formal censure from communion. The child must be formally disciplined because he was formally baptized to the Lord.

From infant or household baptism necessarily flows either the child's affirmation of the covenant made on his behalf, or his rejection of it, and the church's consequent discipline. Thus, there is an awesome parental responsibility attached to infant baptism.

The reason that this awesome responsibility is placed upon the parents of the baptized or dedicated child is to insure that the parents will take their responsibility for the Christian education of the child seriously. Baptism of children carries with it the potential joy of confirming them into the faith, or the potential sorrow of formally disciplining them.

> Matthew 20:23: And he saith unto them, Ye shall drink indeed of my cup, and be baptized with the baptism that I am baptized with: but to sit on my right hand, and on my left, is not mine to give, but it shall be given to them for whom it is prepared of my father.

Matthew 21:25: The baptism of John, whence was it? from heaven, or of men?

Romans 6:4: Therefore we are buried with him by baptism into death: that like as Christ was raised up from the dead by the glory of the Father, even so we also should walk in newness of life.

1 Peter 3:21: The like figure whereunto even baptism doth also now save us (not the putting away of the filth of the flesh, but the answer of a good conscience toward God,) by the resurrection of Jesus Christ.

Baptize Who?

And Jesus came and spake unto them, saying, All power is given unto me in heaven and in earth. Go ye therefore, and teach all nations, baptizing them in the name of the Father, and of the son, and of the Holy Ghost: Teaching them to observe all things whatsoever I have commanded you: and, lo, I am with you alway, even unto the end of the world. Amen (Matthew 28:18-20).

We have briefly discussed the three baptisms of Christ. The most important being the baptism of the Holy Spirit, which is a movement of God in the soul of believers. Water baptism is a ceremonial initiation into the fellowship of the church, and fire baptism, a hardening of the heart that rejects Christ. We learned that Scripture alludes to the heart or purpose of *baptize*, which is to dye, to cause a permanent change of heart or character. Of the three, only the ceremony of water baptism is under human control. The others are movements of God's Spirit.

Let's now look at who should be ceremonially baptized by the church. This concern is generally known in history as the controversy between infant baptism (*paedo* baptism) and believers baptism (*credo* baptism). We will discuss the importance of the dynamic and creative relationship between infant and believer's baptism, and their mutual dependence upon one another, both symbolically and for genuine, spiritual growth in grace. These differing baptismal ceremonies symbolize equally legitimate but different symbolic understandings of Christian faith.

Adults

There has never been any dispute about baptizing adult believers. Those who confess the faith before God's people are to be water baptized. The ceremony of baptism symbolizes reception into Christ's eternal Church. The traditional understanding is that baptism follows a legitimate confession of faith. Believer's baptism symbolizes the human response or decision for Christ.

> For God so loved the world, that he gave his only begotten Son, that whosoever believeth in him should not perish, but have everlasting life. For God sent not his Son into the world to condemn the world; but that the world through him might be saved (John 3:16-17).

Salvation always involves a response to or decision for Christ. Believer's baptism highlights the believer's necessary response to Christ, which is confession of faith and personal repentance.

Infants

The issue of infant baptism gets stuck on this particular point. Infants are unable to repent or confess their faith. So, how can the church baptize someone who has not yet responded to Christ's salvation?

Those who practice infant baptism have an entirely different concern. Infant baptism does not emphasize or symbolize the human response, but emphasizes and symbolizes God's unmerited gift of grace. Paul writes that "God commendeth his love toward us, in that, *while we were yet sinners*, Christ died for *us* (Romans 5:8, italics added). *Before any response or decision is made*, Christ has already acted for those who will someday confess their faith in repentance. God's gift was given before time itself. Paul reminds us in Ephesians 1:4-6 that God "hath chosen us in him *before the foundation of the world*, that we should be holy and without blame before him in love: Having predestinated us unto the adoption of children by Jesus Christ to himself, according to the good pleasure of his will, To the praise of the glory of his grace, wherein he hath made us accepted in the beloved" (Ephesians 1:4-6, italics added).

Infant baptism looks *forward* to the fulfillment of God's promise in Christ in the life of an individual—called from time eternal. And believer's baptism looks *back* upon the fulfillment of God's promise in the life of an individual—God's movement in a particular soul. One celebrates God's ability to fulfill His promises. The other celebrates the awareness of the beginning of the fulfillment of God's promises, God's presence in the life of an individual. On the one hand, Christians anticipate the accomplishment of God's promise, proclaiming the future fulfillment of promises not yet complete. And on the other, Christians celebrate God's past action, proclaiming the power of God's already accomplished promise in the cross and in the lives of believers.

The difficulty with this controversy as it has been historically discussed is that it forces people to choose between the promise of God's future hope and the fulfillment of God's past promises. It promotes a false dilemma and a false choice. Rather, faithful Christians must proclaim in worship and its symbolism both God's promise and His fulfillment—not wavering between them as if unable make up their minds, but boldly claiming and proclaiming both for the integrity of the faith. Christianity is a two-handed faith, proclaiming both God's past action and God's future hope.

Infant baptism reminds God's people that, as important as our human response or decision for Christ is, it is not *our* decision that saves us. We are saved only by the unmerited grace of God—not by anything that we have done or can do, but only by what Christ has done on the cross and will do in the lives of believers. That is the symbolism conveyed by infant baptism. The infant is completely passive in the face of the promise and power of God, just as we all are. But s/he is not to remain passive!

Clearly, it doesn't mean that every baptized infant will make the necessary decision or response to Christ. Rather, infant baptism celebrates the tremendous influence and responsibility that Christian parents and churches have for their children. Christian children have an extraordinary advantage over children whose parents are not Christian. Christian parents have the God-given responsibility to provide a biblical and moral education for their children, whether or not those children ever personally decide or respond to Christ. Christian parents who baptize their children are trusting in the fullness of God's promise.

> Then Peter said unto them, "Repent, and be baptized every one
> of you in the name of Jesus Christ for the remission of sins, and
> ye shall receive the gift of the Holy Ghost. For the promise is
> unto you, and to your children, and to all that are afar off, even as
> many as the Lord our God shall call" (Acts 2:38-39).

Just as Christians trust the Lord for their own salvation, Christian parents trust the Lord for the salvation of their children. Infant baptism requires that Christians clearly understand that the ceremony of baptism *does not save* anyone, nor does it empower the parents to save their children by right teaching. We are not saved by proper education, but by grace. And yet, this does not annul the value of an orthodox Christian education. It only allows parents to teach each child that God has already called him or her, and further, that the failure of the child to respond or receive Christ will result in Christ's fire baptism of destruction and damnation.

The child is to be presented with a choice—salvation or damnation —by the parents. That is their (the parents') baptismal responsibility. When the parents do this the child can see that his parents sincerely believe that God has already acted in his behalf by baptizing him or her. The parents teach the child that God's grace has already been extended to him or her. And indeed it is given to all who believe through the ordinary means of grace. Such a teaching is for the encouragement of the child to decide for Christ and make his own confession of faith at an appropriate time.

The faith of the child must still be confirmed by the child's own confession of faith. If a child was sprinkled as an infant, there is no problem with immersion after his confession, or to have no additional ceremony. Should an additional ceremony be chosen, it is not the advocation two different baptisms or re-baptism, but rather is to be considered to be a baptismal renewal. Just as married couples may renew their wedding vows after ten, twenty-five, or fifty years, so a person may renew his/her baptismal vows at appropriate times. Such a ceremony is not another baptism, but merely a renewal of baptism.

In addition, just as the ceremony is not a guarantee of salvation for infant baptism, it is not a guarantee for salvation for believer's baptism either. God's grace is not mediated by the ceremony, but by God's Word. Consequently, there is no harm in repeating the ceremony under the right circumstances.

The biblical warrant for such a service of renewal is 2 Timothy 1:6, "Wherefore I put thee in remembrance that thou stir up the gift of God, which is in thee by the putting on of my hands." Paul had already laid hands on Timothy, we assume in a service or ceremony. While the stirring up of Timothy's gift does not necessarily refer to a renewal ceremony, it may well have given rise to a commissioning service of some kind. Be that as it may (or may not) be, Paul goes on to say, "Quench not the Spirit" (1 Thessalonians 5:19). If such a renewal service would provide additional meaning in a Christian's life, it ought not be forbidden. Renewal is a significant theme of Scripture and must be allowed for liturgically.

Again, the significance of baptism is not the ceremony, nor the amount of water used, but the presence of the Holy Spirit in the life of the believer. Furthermore, the Holy Spirit is not limited to the moment of the baptismal ceremony. In reality, the Holy Spirit seeks, saves, and preserves the believer all his/her life. Baptism is the miraculous process of character change, initiated in an instant but lasting a lifetime.

The presence of the Holy Spirit always precedes the individual decision or response to Christ. If we do not clearly understand that God acts upon His people before they decide or respond to His call, we may be tempted to believe that people are saved by their own decision or response—that people save themselves by "deciding for Christ." But if we are saved by our own decision, we are not saved by God's grace.

Anabaptists—those who forbid infant baptism—claim that nowhere in Scripture does God specifically call for infant baptism. That's true. Scripture never specifically mentions any case of infant baptism, though it applies it to "you and your children" (Acts 2:39). And neither does Scripture specifically forbid it. We find allusions to baptizing entire households, and we know that God's covenant promise was given to the faithful and to their children, and that the sign of the covenant in the Old Testament—circumcision—was given to infants and adults alike. We find every indication that the New Testament sign follows the same guidelines as the Old.

"But," the *credo* (believers baptism) Baptist's say to the *paedo* baptists, "you follow the teaching and traditions of men and not of Scripture." To which the *paedo* (infant baptism) Baptist's respond, "Not at all. Infant baptism, while not being specified in Scripture, is inferred, just as the doctrine of the Trinity is not specified, but inferred." It is the logical conclusion of biblical fidelity and the wholeness of Christian doctrine.

Is baptism a sign, foreshadowing God's movement? Or a seal, confirming God's movement? It is both. So, who should be baptized? Believers should be baptized after they have made a legitimate confession of faith—and their children if they so choose to do so. That is, believing parent(s) may have their children ceremonially baptized after they have reaffirmed their own faith on behalf of the baptized child, to the glory of God.

The real reason there is so much difficulty and resistance regarding the baptism of infants is that Christian parents have not taken seriously their responsibility to raise their children in a Christian home. Nor have churches fulfilled their responsibility to baptize only believers and the

children of believing parents. Parents must provide a Christian education for their children—and that means more than bringing them to
Sunday School for an hour a week.

There is no higher calling than Christian parenting—no more difficult task, no greater responsibility, nor any greater joy. Christian Trinitarian baptism provides a structure for parental hope in Christ.

Baptismal Renewal

What has been traditionally and liturgically known as Confirmation
is a kind of ceremonial baptismal renewal. The service of Confirmation
developed out of the Jewish practice of *bar mitzvah*. *Bar mitzvah* involves a period of study and a celebration of the personal reception of
covenantal responsibilities by young men who were circumcised in infancy. So, Confirmation was developed as a period of study and a celebration of one's Christian covenant responsibilities by those baptized or
dedicated in infancy or childhood.

As part of that celebration, there is no compelling reason to forbid
the reapplication of water in the service of baptismal renewal. A baptismal renewal does not amount to another baptism, just as a marriage
renewal ceremony is not another marriage. Nonetheless, such renewal
celebrations may be beneficial to those involved for a variety of reasons.
However, this does not change the fact that such a renewal ceremony is
not necessary, not required. And may be more a sign of immaturity in
the faith, thinking that it is necessary. But neither are we to eschew or
chastise the immature. Rather, we are to trust that "he who began a
good work in you will bring it to completion at the day of Jesus Christ"
(Philippians 1:6) with or without such a ceremony.

Far be it for God's churches to forbid the working of God's holy
Spirit in the lives of His people. Rightly administered, however, baptism
is an ordinary means of grace provided through the ministry of the
church.

Baptismal Symbolism

The historic baptismal disagreement divides over the symbolism of
baptism. And the division is understandable because Scripture does not
specify the symbolism of baptism. Rather, baptism's symbolism is, like
the doctrine of the Trinity, a product of inductive reason. We can see
this by asking the question of both paedo and credo baptists, what does
baptism symbolize?

Credo baptists say that baptism symbolizes the reality of the Holy Spirit and represents the regeneration of the sinner. His commitment to Christ. For credo baptists baptism is about individual regeneration. And credo baptists forbid paedo baptism because infants cannot testify to their own regeneration, nor can they make any commitments. Credo baptism is about individual sinners coming to Christ as individuals and its symbolism is defined or bounded by philosophical individualism. Being careful to deny all suspicion of baptismal regeneration, credo baptists tend to understand baptism as being symbolic, like communion. It is not that it actually does anything, but that it symbolizes an inner reality.

Paedo baptists, however, do not understand the symbolism of baptism to be either that of personal regeneration or commitment to Christ. Rather, paedo baptists understand baptism to be an act of faithful obedience to Scripture. Paedo baptists say that baptism symbolizes the obedience of Christ and represents the obedience of believers. For paedo baptists baptism is about community obedience, not personal regeneration. Paedo baptists don't need to deny baptismal regeneration because that is not what baptism is about. Because baptism is not about personal regeneration but community obedience, paedo baptists have no stock in baptismal regeneration. Yet, they do and must claim that baptism actually does something. It doesn't regenerate individuals, rather it reinforces the role of God's covenant in the church(es) by acknowledging that the baptizand is believed to be under Christ's covenant. Paedo baptists do baptism as a public ceremony of covenant acknowledgment. The baptism is an acknowledgment that the baptizand is under Christ's New Covenant.

There have been many attempts to explain the doctrine of the biblical covenant, and much confusion. Consequently, a clearer taxonomy of biblical conventionalism is needed. The truth is that nowhere does the Bible say that baptism represents either regeneration or obedience, yet both are involved in the various baptism stories.

God's Eternal Covenant
By grace alone God created man (humanity) and established them in His covenant (Genesis 1:28). This is sometimes called the Covenant of Works and thought to apply prior to the Fall. However, such an understanding is incomplete because it addresses only half of the covenant —God's promise (and/or fulfillment) of blessing for obedience. A covenant by definition has two aspects or stipulations. It sets out an obli-

gation, which can be either honored or not honored. The first stipulation is the provision of some reward for honoring the obligation, and the second stipulation is the provision of some punishment for not honoring the obligation. Thus, biblical covenants are issued by the suzerain, who then either provides reward or punishment.

In the case of Adam, the context in which man was placed (the garden) contained the two elements of God's covenant: blessing, represented by the tree of life, and cursing, represented by the tree of knowledge or the self-determination of good and evil (Genesis 2:9). This two-sided covenant included all humanity and is eternal (Genesis 2:16-17).

God's covenant has gone through various iterations, most of which emphasized God's original intention to bless humanity—Noah (Genesis 9:17), Abraham (Genesis 17:9), Moses (Exodus 34:27), David (2 Samuel 7:8-16), etc. The essential structure of the covenant has been delineated in Deuteronomy 28. The understanding that God's eternal covenant includes both blessing for obedience and cursing for disobedience untangles much of the historic confusion. It underlines the unity and consistency of God's unfolding covenant, and the fact that God's covenant always applies eternally to all people.

As a consequence of Adam's sin, all of Adam's people are on the train to hell. Because Adam disobeyed God, the punishment element of the covenant has been in effect since that disobedience. It is God's covenantal jurisdiction that sends people to hell. People go to hell because of the stipulations of God's covenant (cursing for disobedience), just as people go to heaven because of the stipulations of God's covenant (blessing for obedience).

But Adam's sin rendered (or demonstrated) that man alone could not live in obedience to God's law. That is the central teaching of the Old Testament. So, God sent Jesus to replace Adam's covenantal headship and live in perfect obedience, which satisfied God's requirement for obedience. Christ died on the cross for Adam's (humanity's) sin, which satisfied God's demand for justice. And Christ released the Holy Spirit to inhabit God's people through regeneration, which did two things: 1) it satisfied God's expression of grace/mercy, and 2) it guaranteed that those who were inhabited by the Holy Spirit would eventually (in glory) acquire Christ's righteousness—which would release the fullness of God's blessings. Those who are in Christ will complete their sanctification because that is Christ's intention and He is God—and God accomplishes His own will.

So, Christ's New Covenant is both a renewed covenant (God's eternal covenant is still in effect because it is eternal), and a New Covenant because Christ is the New Covenant Head. Those who are caught up (reborn) in Christ's New Covenant are guaranteed God's ultimate blessings, not because of their own obedience or faithfulness, but because of Christ's obedience and faithfulness. However, God's blessings are not merely for individuals, but are for the corporate body of Christ (love requires others to be involved). Thus, there is not a one-to-one correspondence between individual faithfulness and blessings. But as the body of Christ continues to grow the blessings will also increase "across the board."

Understanding God's Covenant this way helps us understand why unbelievers go to hell, why Christ's birth and death on the cross were necessary, and the basis upon which people are saved—by grace alone through faith alone in Christ alone according to Scripture alone.

Paedo baptists understand baptism as covenantal obedience to God's covenant description found in various places in the Bible (Deuteronomy 1:39, 4:9, 30:1-2; 2 Chronicles 30:9; Psalm 115:14; Matthew 28:19; Acts 16:31). Whether we understand Christ's covenant as being a renewal of the Old Covenant or a New Covenant, it has the same character and structure of the Old Covenant. The central difference is Christ's fulfillment of God's Covenant, and the release of God's blessings through Christ.

One of the difficulties related to simply bringing the symbolism of Old Testament baptism into the New Testament is that the Old Covenant was mistakenly understood to apply only to genetic Israel. So, as a blood covenant it would come through progeny. Whereas a grace covenant would come through regeneration. Nonetheless, the Old Covenant was to be a model for the New, and both would find their greatest fulfillment in families. The New Covenant is no less family related than the Old.

Once a man was baptized he was expected to fulfill his covenantal responsibilities—to be obedient to Scripture. If he did, he could expect God's blessing—salvation. And if he didn't he could expect God's curse—damnation. Being baptized provides no guarantee of faithfulness, whether one is baptized as an infant or an adult. Baptism simply makes the human context clear. Those who are not baptized tend toward confusion about God and His expectations. Baptism, not simply the ceremony of baptism, but living in the light of God's covenant following baptism, removes the confusion about man's obligations to God. And the removal of confusion is helpful. That's what baptism accomplishes, not baptismal regeneration, but the clarification of God's expectations regarding one's self, a fruit of regeneration.

Thus, where credo baptists only baptize those who freely confess their sins and pledge themselves to Jesus Christ in repentance, paedo baptists do the same thing regarding adults. But once a person has been baptized, he is then responsible for his wife and family. And as an expression of obedience to Christ he gives his children the advantage of clarifying their responsibilities to God as members of the human race by baptizing his children as infants. The baptized head of household has his infant children baptized, not as a symbol of their regeneration, but in his obedience to God's command, God's covenant, God's promise to bless him and his children. He baptizes his children as a testimony of Christ's obedience and God's promise to bless future generations. Thus, infant baptism does not represent individual regeneration. It represents the covenant fidelity of the believing community to the commands of God.

Once the child has been baptized, he is taught that God's hand is upon him to either bless or curse him. The parents are then obligated to teach the child that God is who He says He is, that He is trustworthy, loving, just, and omnipotent—and that the child is already obligated to God by way of Christ's covenant.

BAPTISMAL PARALLELS

Compare and contrast believer's baptism and infant baptism. Note that they have much in common.

Infant Baptism Track	Believers' Baptism Track
Symbolizes God's initiating action in salvation.	*Symbolizes believer's response to God's salvation.*
Infant Baptism Ceremony (*a symbol of God's grace*) To be baptized as a symbol of God's Covenant is to be brought under God's eternal covenant with all its attendant promises and threat-	**Infant Dedication Ceremony** (*a symbol of God's grace*) To be dedicated as a symbol of God's Covenant is to be brought under God's eternal covenant with all its attendant promises and threat-

enings (Deuteronomy 28, 2 Samuel 7, Jeremiah 31:31-40, Matthew 26:26-30, Acts 3:12-26) by the blood of Christ and the power of the Holy Spirit in the hope of salvation, symbolized by the washing of water by sprinkling or pouring, and the parents' commitment to God's covenant.	enings (Deuteronomy 28, 2 Samuel 7, Jeremiah 31:31-40, Matthew 26:26-30, Acts 3:12-26) by the blood of Christ and the power of the Holy Spirit in the hope of salvation, symbolized by the laying on of hands upon the infant and the parents' commitment to God's covenant.
Dedication ceremony (*taking the vows of faithfulness*). Confirmation or dedication is a symbol of personal regeneration that involves the laying on of hands as an outward sign of an inward and spiritual receiving or the acceptance and forgiveness of Jesus Christ as personal Lord and Savior (Acts 9:17).	**Baptism ceremony** (*taking the vows of faithfulness*). To be baptized as a symbol of personal regeneration involves sprinkling, pouring or immersion with water of an individual as an outward sign of an inward spiritual grace, or the acceptance and forgiveness of Jesus Christ as personal Lord and Savior (Romans 6).
Church Membership Requires baptism and profession. Public assent to God's personal calling to unity in the Body of Christ through the common commitment of believers in a local church. Requires public assent to the local church constitution, by-laws, and Statement of Faith.	**Church Membership** Requires profession and baptism. Public assent to God's personal calling to unity in the Body of Christ through the common commitment of believers in a local church. Requires public assent to the local church constitution, by-laws, and Statement of Faith.

Paedobaptism & Paedocommunion

What follows was a discussion on the Reformed Congregationalist Discussion List (on Yahoo!) about padeobaptism (infant baptism) and credobaptism (believers' baptism), which brought up paedocommunion during the month of October, 2003. The following is a reconstruction of that conversation with corrections of spelling, etc.

It began with the moderator's description of a man whom he invited to join the list.

From: Darrell Todd Maurina

Date: Tue, 07 Oct 2003 20:49:49 –0000

Subject: [Reformed_Congregationalists] Re: The half-way covenant

Reply-To: Reformed_Congregationalists@yahoogroups.com

To clarify...the man is definitely Reformed, and would probably be one of the most pronounced Calvinists here. His views on church government are a bit unclear to me; he seems to advocate very strong elders in the local church but as a member of an independent church, he is a *de facto* Congregationalist, though he would advocate fairly close voluntary connections between churches.

The main issue for us is going to be his views on admission of young children to the Lord's Supper and his argument that it is un-Reformed to require a personal profession of faith before admitting people to church membership.

Regards,

Darrell Todd Maurina

From: Phil Ross

Over the years I have tried to respond to some of the issues of baptism. (See the preceding discussion.)

In addition, let me suggest that the missing ingredient in baptism and communion pertains to the jurisdiction of the family in relationship to the church. Headship plays a significant and widely ignored role in both of these sacraments. I suspect that this role has been in eclipse since long before the Reformation, and thus is not found in the literature of the Reformation (as far as I know).

In baptism, the head of the household testifies on behalf of the infant because of the jurisdiction of the head of the household. Infant baptism provides the foundational model for representational and covenantal government. The head of the household represents his family in the courts of the church.

That representation, then, extends to Holy Communion in that it is (or should be) the head of the household who first catechizes and judges the readiness of his family members to receive Communion. The church defers to his judgment as a way of supporting and honoring the jurisdiction of biblical headship, the most intimate form of representational, covenantal government.

It is, then, not the job of the church to set an "age of accountability," or whatever. The Deacons simply pass the elements to the head of the household, who then serves his family members according to his own judgment. His family is under his jurisdiction.

The job of the church, then, is to disciple the head of the household, who in turn, disciples his own family with the help of the church. Family discipleship by the head of the household is foundational to the biblical model of home and church, and their separate jurisdictions. Thus, the wife and children are directed to quietness in the church meeting, and should ask her husband/father should they have any questions. ("And if they will learn any thing, let them ask their husbands at home: for it is a shame for women to speak in the church," 1 Corinthians 14:35.) This reinforces family headship and representational, covenantal government in the lives and minds of impressionable children, which strengthens the authority of the church and of the state, and provides stability to the social fabric.

This will not be a popular idea, but I believe that it is the biblical model. The problem today (and for the last ____ number of years, fill in the blank) is that just as the state usurps the jurisdiction of the church, the church usurps the jurisdiction of the family.

Phil Ross

From: Kirk v d Swaagh
In a message dated 10/9/03 4:11:41 PM, prta@lubrizol.com writes:

"I am sorry if I am opening a can of worms or preempting the discussion this gentleman is being invited to participate in. But these are questions I have not found good answers to that are consistent with the reformed position on Baptism."

I must confess that I have been asking those same questions. If baptism is a covenant sign and we apply it to our children as such, should not the other covenant sign given to us by our Lord also be applied to all the members of the covenant community?

I have grown increasingly uncomfortable with the message that our children receive when we allow the signs of the covenant to be passed before them without letting them partake. Are we not saying that you are not really part of us?

This does not preclude the necessity for teaching and admonishment of our children as to what these signs mean and the privilege of receiving them. But setting the usual hurdle seems to me an arbitrary undertaking.

It would appear that the only passage which can be cited which would prevent our inclusion of our covenant children to the Table to receive this covenant sign is the 1 Corinthians admonition to self-examination. I believe it is possible to interpret that passage primarily as a corrective to the abuses in the Corinthian church. There is of course a wider application, but at its core it is a call for reverent and sober behavior at the Lord's Table. I do not see why this cannot be expected of our children. Even if we should insist on self-examination, could we not encourage our children in this regard? They might only be confessing that they were mean to the cat but confessing they are. In the process they are learning what it means to live a life of humility before a holy God.

Just some thoughts.

Grace and peace,

Kirk v d Swaagh

From: Phil Tabor

While I agree that the reformed churches have by and large not practiced Paedocommunion, the church as a whole did so prior to the middle ages and as early as at least 250 A.D. The change to this accompanied a number of other changes (such as withholding the cup from the laity).

In regards to the OT rites, you state, "It is quite likely that none but males participated in the Jewish feasts, including the Passover (Ex. 34:23). I am not even certain that Jewish boys partook of the supper until passing a rite into manhood." Does the fact that men are commanded to go up for the feasts exclude them from bringing their families? Or rather is this the typical biblical language that addresses men directly and includes their families implicitly?

Scripture does not speak of excluding children from the Passover or any of the feasts. We know from example that when Samuel's father went up to Jerusalem for the feasts, he took his family to participate. We also know Joseph took Jesus when he was twelve (before his rights of manhood). We know the children (both sons and daughters) partook of the sacrificial feasts.

Deuteronomy 12:7, 12 "There, in the presence of the LORD your God, you and your families shall eat and shall rejoice in everything you have put your hand to, because the LORD your God has blessed you... And there rejoice before the LORD your God, you, your sons and daughters, your menservants and maidservants, and the Levites from your towns, who have no allotment or inheritance of their own."

In regards to the Feast of Weeks, Scripture is explicit in the inclusion of children.

> Deuteronomy 16:9, "Count off seven weeks from the time you begin to put the sickle to the standing grain. Then celebrate the Feast of Weeks to the LORD your God by giving a freewill offering in proportion to the blessings the LORD your God has given you. And rejoice before the LORD your God at the place he will choose as a dwelling for his Name-you, your sons and daughters, your menservants and maidservants, the Levites in your towns, and the aliens, the fatherless and the widows living among you. Remember that you were slaves in Egypt, and follow carefully these decrees."

And again in regards to the feat of tabernacles.

> Deuteronomy 16:13-17 "Celebrate the Feast of Tabernacles for seven days after you have gathered the produce of your threshing floor and your winepress. Be joyful at your Feast—you, your sons and daughters, your menservants and maidservants, and the Levites, the aliens, the fatherless and the widows who live in your towns. For seven days celebrate the Feast to the LORD your God at the place the LORD will choose. For the LORD God will bless you in all your harvest and in all the work of your hands, and your joy will be complete. Three times a year all your men must appear before the LORD your God at the place he will choose: at the Feast of Unleavened Bread, the Feast of Weeks and the Feast of Tabernacles. No man should appear before the LORD empty-handed: Each of you must bring a gift in proportion to the way the LORD your God has blessed you."

Notice verse 16 contains the command to the men to appear, but from the previous text it is clear this includes the whole family.

Does the example of Old Testament sacrificial practice have a bearing on participation in the Lord's Supper? Let us consider Paul's thoughts.

> 1 Cor 10:14-22: "Therefore, my dear friends, flee from idolatry. I speak to sensible people; judge for yourselves what I say. Is not the cup of thanksgiving for which we give thanks a participation in the blood of Christ? And is not the bread that we break a participation in the body of Christ? Because there is one loaf, we, who are many, are one body, for we all partake of the one loaf. Consider the people of Israel: Do not those who eat the sacrifices participate in the altar? Do I mean then that a sacrifice offered to an idol is anything, or that an idol is anything? No, but the sacrifices of pagans are offered to demons, not to God, and I do not want you to be participants with demons. You cannot drink the cup of the Lord and the cup of demons too; you cannot have a part in both the Lord's table and the table of demons. Are we trying to arouse the Lord's jealousy? Are we stronger than he?"

Notice the direct comparison between those who participate in the Lord's supper and those in Israel who ate the sacrifices. Is this conclusive? Probably not. Is it significant? I think so.

For those of you interested in reading some excellent articles in support of paedo communion and to find out who is practicing it in the reformed community today, check out the site www.paedocommunion.-com.

God Bless,
Phil Tabor

From: Phil Tabor
Michael,

There was one more statement I meant to address in your post:

> But if we mean 'Christian' in the exact same way for adults with credible professions as we do for infants who cannot so much as exercise faith, much less profess (though they may be regenerate), then we must fall into a trap.

Infants cannot exercise faith? Is this a Reformed position we are to hold to? Is it supported by scripture? Certainly not.

Psalm 8:1-2: "O LORD, our Lord, how majestic is your name in all the earth! You have set your glory above the heavens. From the lips of children and infants you have ordained praise because of your enemies, to silence the foe and the avenger."

> Psalm 22:9-10: "Yet you brought me out of the womb; you made me trust in you even at my mother's breast. From birth I was cast upon you; from my mother's womb you have been my God."

> Psalm 71:5: For you have been my hope, O Sovereign LORD , my confidence since my youth. 6 From birth I have relied on you; you brought me forth from my mother's womb. I will ever praise you. ... 17 Since my youth, O God, you have taught me, and to this day I declare your marvelous deeds."

> Mark 10:13-16: "People were bringing little children to Jesus to have him touch them, but the disciples rebuked them. When Jesus saw this, he was indignant. He said to them, 'Let the little children come to me, and do not hinder them, for the kingdom of God belongs to such as these. I tell you the truth, anyone who will not receive the kingdom of God like a little child will never enter it.' And he took the children in his arms, put his hands on them and blessed them." (We need to exercise our faith like the little children, not they like us.)

> 1 Cor 7:14: "For the unbelieving husband has been sanctified through his wife, and the unbelieving wife has been sanctified through her believing husband. Otherwise your children would be unclean, but as it is, they are holy."

Do these passages give us a picture of infants and children being unable to exercise faith? No, the Reformed faith has long claimed that infants can exercise faith and that is why we baptize them. When we then turn and say that we withhold communion from them because they can't, then we are speaking out of both sides of our mouths.

Phil Tabor

From: Michael

Phil Tabor,

Thanks for your response. I frequently value your input.

Your quotes from the Old Testament were helpful. I would concede that families certainly did come down to Jerusalem for the Feasts. It did appear to be a family occasion. Maybe I need to refine my position. Certainly, the families partook of common meals at these festivals. But the "presentation of the males," the absence of any specific reference to wives and children actually partaking of the Passover Supper proper, and

Exodus 12:4, "every man [Heb, *ish*] according to his eating shall make your count for the lamb" make me uncertain. Then the final New Testament Passover seems to exclude all but adult Jewish males.

> Matthew 26:18-20: "And he said, Go into the city to such a man, and say unto him, The Master saith, My time is at hand; I will keep the passover at thy house with my disciples. And the disciples did as Jesus had appointed them; and they made ready the passover. Now when the even was come, he sat down with the twelve."

> Mark 14:15-17: "And he will shew you a large upper room furnished and prepared: there make ready for us. And his disciples went forth, and came into the city, and found as he had said unto them: and they made ready the passover. And in the evening he cometh with the twelve."

> Luke 22: 11-14: "And ye shall say unto the goodman of the house, The Master saith unto thee, Where is the guestchamber, where I shall eat the passover with my disciples? And he shall shew you a large upper room furnished: there make ready. And they went, and found as he had said unto them: and they made ready the passover. And when the hour was come, he sat down, and the twelve apostles with him."

We know that Peter had a wife from other passages in the Gospels. It was likely that she was there in Jerusalem for the whole Feast of Unleavened Bread. But there is a conspicuous absence of other family members.

Now, I admit there is always the possibility. But I am hesitant to embrace paedo communion on these arguments by themselves. It just doesn't seem conclusive.

I really think that when the rubber meets the road, the clincher seems to be the command that one must examine himself prior to partaking of the Lord's Supper.

> 1 Corinthians 11:28: "But let a man examine himself, and so let him eat of that bread, and drink of that cup."

> 2 Corinthians 13:5: "Examine yourselves, whether ye be in the faith; prove your own selves. Know ye not your own selves, how that Jesus Christ is in you, except ye be reprobates?"

Covenant children may have regeneration, or as some have said, the "seed of faith." I'll grant you that. But the Reformed churches (and if there has ever been a notable exception, I'd be open to hearing it) have withheld this ordinance unto infants until they come of age to make a credible profession of personal faith. Personal, profession of faith has always been an integral element of Reformed Christianity on both sides of the Atlantic.

> 1 Timothy 6:12: "Fight the good fight of faith, lay hold on eternal life, whereunto thou art also called, and hast professed a good profession before many witnesses."

The Reformed tied this to the ordinance of the Lord's Supper, precisely because self-examination of true and saving faith was a prerequisite for coming to the Supper.

I am leery of laying aside some four hundred years of Reformed ecclesiastical practice, especially when it was the Reformed faith that "rediscovered" and elaborated upon the idea of covenant. That some men in the last twenty years say they found a major blind spot in Reformed covenantal thought and practice makes me more suspicious of their rationale than the standard line found in the confessions, catechisms, and church orders. I do not place men above criticism, but their insight and wisdom into the Scripture and covenant are presently more compelling to me.

Additionally, I very much fear a lapse into sacerdotalism. Not even Roman Catholics believe that toddlers should partake of Holy Eucharist, however external, mechanical, and automatic their conception of the church and its ordinances. We are told by paedo communion advocates that the Reformed "hog" the table by forbidding two- and three-year-olds. But the experimental piety of the Reformed has always viewed sacraments in a much less mechanical and automatic way. They are efficacious to those who have the thing signified by a true and living faith. Unworthy partakers of the Supper eat and drink judgment upon themselves. Some may see this as driving off Jesus' lambs.

But the Reformed churches weren't being uncharitable to their covenant children. They brought them to the introductory ordinance, and labored with prayer that one day they would come of their own volition to that ordinance which demands a self-conscious (and self-examined) faith. They steered a safe course between the anti-covenantal Baptists on the one hand, and the anti-conversion high churchers on the other hand. Covenant is important, but God can raise children to Abraham from stones if He must.

Well, I've gone too long, and I had better not neglect my covenant children in the process! Perhaps I'll bow out of discussion for awhile. I welcome your response, Phil.

Yours,
Michael

From: Michael
Phil Tabor,
Here is a rather well expressed summary at the end of an article by Rev. Mark Horne (PCA) in support of paedo communion:

> "According to Hebrews 9.10, the various ceremonial cleansings in the Mosaic economy were 'baptisms' (literal Greek translation). When one became ceremonially unclean one was barred from the sanctuary and, therefore, cut off from the Sacraments. The whole point of being baptized was to regain access to the feast. Our children have been baptized. Our children are not 'unclean, but ... holy' (1 Corinthians 7.14).

> They should not be barred from the feast. To invent reasons for barring the little children from the Real Presence of the Lord Jesus, not only nullifies any professed allegiance to the Regulative Principle of worship, but it brings down upon us the indignation of Christ (Mark 10:14).

> To all of this, the warning in 1 Corinthians 10:27-32 is extremely pertinent. The Corinthians were guilty of permitting some to hog the Table and force others to go hungry and thirsty (10:21, 33). Let us demonstrate that we can discern the Lord's Body by including our children in it.

> Our baptized children ought not be barred from the Lord's Supper."

If you would like to read the full article, here is the link.
http://www.hornes.org/theologia/content/mark_horne/a_
    brief_response_to_rev_richard_bacons_opposition_to_paedocom-
munion.htm
Michael

From: Phil Tabor
Michael,

I think the absence of specific reference to wives and children partaking in the Passover supper has the same explanation as to why only males were counted in the feeding of the five thousand and four thousand. Women and children literally did not count in Hebrew culture. However, that does not mean that when a man counted himself, he did not include his women and children in factoring how much lamb he needed. Quite frankly I would find it incredible, based on the circumstances of the first Passover and the significance of the Passover for all Hebrews, that the women and children would stand by and watch the men feast. The significance of the meal was in preparation of travel. Were not the women and children traveling also? In fact Moses refused to take just the men out in the dessert to feast before the Lord when Pharaoh tried to compromise. And yet, even if the children did not eat, neither did the women and yet we do not exclude them from communion.

In regards to the Last Supper, it does not seem to me that Jesus excluded women and children but rather selectively included only the inner twelve apostles. It does not appear that this was a restriction based on gender or the demands of the Passover, but on his purpose to pass on information to them that was, at that point, for their ears only. In regards to Peter's wife and the wives of the other apostles, no conclusion can be reached as to whether they had come up from Galilee or not (or even if she was alive). Scripture is silent so we cannot come to a conclusion.

I, too, am leery of overturning four hundred years of Reformed tradition. But I also do not see the scriptural argument behind that tradition as conclusive. I do not think that Paul sets forth self-reflection as a prerequisite for those incapable of doing such. Do you believe that the mentally disabled can never receive communion? Do you think that would please God? Scripture is pretty consistent in teaching that the powerless have a special place in God's heart.

One other point that is telling for me. The history of the church for the first thousand years seems to have included paedo communion. The Orthodox church has practiced it consistently to this day. Paedo communion was dropped in the Western church with the rise of the doctrine of transubstantiation. It was part of the process of the concern over spilling the blood of Christ. This concern caused the laity to withdraw from receiving the cup and to refrain from giving the cup to infants. Without the cup, infants could not be given the bread as the practice was to either give the infant just the wine or sop the bread in wine so the infant would not choke on it.

The concern was not that infants and young children were not prepared for communion, but that they were not capable of properly handling the body and blood of Christ.

So, we have a choice, ignore a thousand years of church precedence or four hundred. Neither choice is particularly attractive. In order to choose, I can only go to Scripture and seek out what God's will is regarding children. On the whole, based on the Scriptures I have quoted, it seems to me that he would prefer them to be included, not excluded.

In regards to Reformed groups that allow paedo communion, the following leave the practice to the local congregation:

Reformed Episcopal Church
Confederation of Reformed Evangelicals
Association of Free Reformed Churches

These two small groups practice Paedo communion:

Federation of Reformed Churches
Reformed Heritage Church

I believe this was a hotly debated issue as part of the Reformation. I think Calvin's strong stance may have squelched debate on the issue. I would be interested to know if the issue was discussed in formulating Westminster and if so, how strongly was it endorsed. One of the issues with standards is all issues tend to get the same weight, whether the delegates were a hundred percent behind them or it was a 51/49 decision.

I will speak to some of my Westminster expert friends and see if they can shed some light.

Phil Tabor

From: Phil Ross

Phil Tabor,

Thank you for your response to Michael. You have provided much good food for thought.

But I think that you have underestimated the place of women and children in ancient Hebrew culture. There is a sense in which women and children did not count, but we need to be careful about projecting our modern gender sensitive assumptions onto that culture.

I believe that the ancient Hebrew church practiced biblical headship, and therefore only "counted" families, that is heads of households—men. But it had nothing to do with gender inequity, and everything to do with according family jurisdiction to the head of the household. In other words, the jurisdiction of the church did not enter the family directly but came through the father. So, the head of the house represented the family in the courts of the church.

Again, the model is representative government, and it was modeled in the family so that it would be meaningful in the church.

Phil Ross

From: Michael

Phil Tabor,

Thanks again. I should repeat that I am by no means vigorously denying that children partook of the Passover. That they were present is likely. That the Passover proper and the rest of feasting were identical, and that both adults and infants participated, is not yet clear to me. Further, the following series of articles give another very plausible argument for the contrary:

http://www.fpcr.org/_vti_script/search_this_site.htm0.idq

Even if two- and three-year-olds did participate in the Passover, I think that the command to self-examination would then alter things—perhaps as women were given the equivalent of "NT circumcision" (baptism). As for the mentally handicapped, I would say that it depends on the degree of the handicap. Some cannot even chew or swallow, but God is sovereign, and can regenerate the heart of his people, however far their minds are gone. It is not cruel for the church to withhold the sacrament when it would be just like any other meal to the recipient.

I appreciate your interaction. This has certainly stimulated thought.

Michael

From: Phil Tabor

Phil Ross,

I did not mean to trivialize women (or children). I was making a play on words. My point was that whenever the people are counted, it is the men only that are counted. I believe you are correct as to the reason, although I would not totally discount the existence of gender bias in the culture.

Phil Tabor

From: Kirk v d Swaugh

I believe Phil Tabor is asking all the right questions in regard to this doctrine. These are the same questions I have wrestled with over the past couple of years. In the church which I pastor we spent the Lord's Days of January to April of this year considering the Sacraments. After this extended look I was left with a growing conviction that our children were to be included at the Table. I, too, acknowledge that this goes against the well-documented Reformed practice and as such I tread cautiously. But the logic seems inescapable.

If, borrowing Augustine's words, the Sacraments are "visible words" and as such the Table proclaims the Lord's death until he comes (1 Corinthians 11:26), i.e., the Gospel, why do we not allow the ordinance to do it's work in our midst? When we withhold the cup from these youngest members of our covenant community are we sending the message that the Gospel is not for them? Do we not expend much energy in teaching our kids the message contained in God's written words? Indeed, we do not withhold the Gospel when it comes to the Bible. Why would we withhold the Gospel when it comes to the visible words God has given to us? I know there is the objection of the need for self-examination but such soul searching is vitally involved in every encounter with the Gospel. As such, we end up expecting it of our children when we teach them of Jesus from the Scriptures. We can expect it of them when they approach the Table as they learn that in this ordinance the Gospel is likewise proclaimed.

Grace and peace,

Kirk

From: Phil Tabor

Yesterday we discussed Jesus as the manna from heaven. Today I would like to take some time to reflect on some thoughts associated with this.

What is manna? Manna is the daily bread provided by God for his people. Christ is this daily bread and we are to feed on him daily.

Christ taught his disciples to ask for manna when they pray, "Give us this day our daily bread." This signifies not only a dependence on

God for physical sustenance, but for spiritual sustenance as well. Jesus is our sustenance. It seems to me that the communion bread is a visible reminder of God's faithfulness in answering that prayer for Him to supply our bread. Certainly we all want to encourage our children to pray the Lord's prayer and expect God to answer faithfully. Doesn't it seem strange that we should withhold from the children who are learning this prayer one of the tangible signs of God's faithful response?

And what happened to the manna of the OT? Moses was instructed to collect some in a golden container and place it in the ark of the covenant as an eternal reminder. Also in this ark were the tablets of the law and the rod of Aaron that symbolized the priesthood. The ark was kept in the Holy of Holies where it was separated from the people. The high priest approached the ark once per year, but the people never could. Until Christ died on the cross.

Then the temple curtain was torn from top to bottom and the access to God was opened to all. Christ is our great high priest. But what about the contents of the ark? The author of Hebrews repeatedly reminds us that because of Christ we are in a new covenant in which the law is not written on stone but is written on our hearts. Peter assures us that we are now all priests, the priesthood is shared among all believers. There are no restrictions surrounding a priestly caste. So if the law is given to all, and the priesthood is given to all, what about the manna, which originally was given to all? Is it not clear that this manna in the new covenant should be available to all?

More tomorrow...
Phil Tabor

From: Phil Tabor
One of the questions that must be addressed in considering paedo communion is, "How does God view the children of covenant parents?" In particular, are they viewed as worthy to take the elements or as unworthy? Clearly, if they are viewed as unworthy, then no parent would dare allow their child to participate as it would be allowing them to bring judgment on themselves.

I want to clarify at this point, I am still excluding the issue of the self-examination requirement. That will be addressed soon. I am just considering right now the general status of children in the New Testament as worthy or unworthy of participation in communion.

First, let us consider what we mean by worthy or unworthy. We are not speaking of merit here, for if we speak of merit, none of us is worthy to partake of Christ. But through his grace we who are in covenant are invited to participate. But there are still times and conditions that might make us unworthy.

In Old Testament terms we would speak of clean or unclean. There were specific rules that defined conditions under which a person could not participate in the rites of faith. There were specific actions necessary to restore oneself to cleanliness or worthiness.

In the New Testament the primary way a person goes from unclean/unworthy to clean/worthy is via repentance. The initial act is accompanied by, signified by, and sealed by baptism. But even after that, there is to be a daily seeking forgiveness and repenting of our sins as exemplified in the Lord's prayer, taught by Jesus directly and in parables.

It is my contention, and I believe the clear teaching of the New Testament, that children's worthiness/cleanness is determined not by their own repentance, of which they may be unable to express, but determined by the status of their parents. While this seems a very peculiar idea to us in our humanistic/individualistic culture, it is not a strange idea in scripture and not a strange idea in the eastern church, and not in the western church up until the advent of humanism during the middle ages.

Let us look at the scriptures.

I believe all who have studied Reformed theology are familiar with 1 Cor 7:14:

> "For the unbelieving husband has been sanctified through his
> wife, and the unbelieving wife has been sanctified through her
> believing husband. Otherwise your children would be unclean,
> but as it is, they are holy."

Here we have Paul explicitly stating that the infant child of a single believing parent is holy, that is set apart for God's service, i.e. clean, because of their believing parent. This verse is used to justify infant baptism against those who claim that people cannot be holy/clean prior to an act of repentance and a confession of faith. The issue at hand here is whether this child of mixed parents should be considered a member of the covenant community, and Paul's answer is a clear *yes*.

But Paul's statement does not stand alone. Jesus addressed this as well, though perhaps a bit more indirectly. For example, in Mark 10:13-16 we have this well known story:

> People were bringing little children to Jesus to have him touch
> them, but the disciples rebuked them. When Jesus saw this, he
> was indignant. He said to them, "Let the little children come to
> me, and do not hinder them, for the kingdom of God belongs to
> such as these. I tell you the truth, anyone who will not receive
> the kingdom of God like a little child will never enter it." And he
> took the children in his arms, put his hands on them and blessed
> them.

These were little children, infants most likely, being brought to Jesus by their believing parents. Does Jesus rebuke them and say, "Until they can make a credible confession of faith they cannot come to me?" No, he rebukes the disciples for keeping them away and then says that we all must receive the kingdom of God as these little ones do. These children have an implicit faith in whomever their parents have faith in. If the parents have faith in Jesus, the infant will have faith in Jesus. We can see the implication for us in some other teachings of Jesus.

Jesus says in John 8:42-44:

> If God were your Father, you would love me, for I came from
> God and now am here. I have not come on my own; but he sent
> me. Why is my language not clear to you? Because you are un-
> able to hear what I say. You belong to your father, the devil, and
> you want to carry out your father's desire.

The love of God is implicit in those who have God as their father. Lies and hatred are implicit in those who have the devil as their father.

The offspring are as their parents.

It is this concept that is in mind when Jesus claims, "I and the Father are one." This statement in and of itself was not shocking. The shock came because Jesus was claiming that God was his Father and that he, therefore was God.

We see this concept also in Peter's sermon. In Acts 2:38-39 Peter replied,

> Repent and be baptized, every one of you, in the name of Jesus
> Christ for the forgiveness of your sins. And you will receive the
> gift of the Holy Spirit. The promise is for you and your children
> and for all who are far off-for all whom the Lord our God will
> call.

Again this is a verse that we are familiar with in discussing baptism. We hold that this shows that when parents are baptized their children

are to be baptized as well. The worthiness of the parents for baptism implies the worthiness of the children. It is especially interesting to note
what follows immediately after Peter concludes this speech (Acts 2:42):

> They devoted themselves to the apostles' teaching and to the fel-
> lowship, to the breaking of bread and to prayer.

Who are the "they" that Luke refers to here? Those who believed
Peter's sermon, repented and were baptized. Is it reasonable to assume
that this included their children? If I limit myself to the baptism, most
Reformed folk would say, "Of course." But the passage also speaks of
teaching, fellowship, and prayer. Do we exclude our children from that?
No. But the passage also includes the breaking of bread. Is this just communal meals or is it the Lord's Supper? I suggest it is both. It appears
from the content of 1 Corinthians that in the early church the Lord's
supper was a communal meal. It is only after Paul's instruction to eat a
meal at home to deal with hunger prior to joining for communion that
we see it become what it is today, a snack. It seems arbitrary to suppose
that the children were included in everything but the Lord's supper. Especially since they have not been given Paul's instruction yet regarding
self examination.

Ancient culture and the biblical language recognize a unity between parent and child that modern culture does not grasp. We must
ask ourselves, is it modern culture or the Bible that is wrong in this? As
Reformed believers we have only one choice in answering this question.

There is a unity between parent and child that permeates Scriptural
teaching, and which informs our understanding of household baptisms
as well. When the head of the household believes in the New Testament
it is assumed that all the household believes because of this implicit
unity.

Now, it is not a unity that cannot be broken. Clearly the Bible
speaks of rebellious children and prodigal sons. But these are the shocking exceptions to the norm.

It is the Biblical approach to assume the faith of the child until such
a time as the child is old enough to express rebellion against the faith.
And only in the face of open rebellion are we to excommunicate the
children of believers.

The anti-paedo communion position takes the opposite approach,
just as the anti-paedo baptist position does. It assumes that children are
unworthy until they prove themselves worthy of communion. Likewise
anti-paedo baptists assume the child unworthy of baptism until they can

prove they are worthy. But this is not the method of Scripture. From Old Testament through New Testamewnt, children of believing parents are deemed to be believers themselves unless and until they prove otherwise.

The process of self-examination that Paul brings up in 1 Corinthians 11 is a matter of judging oneself worthy or unworthy. Scripture declares the young children of worthy parents to be worthy. Is it necessary that the child be able to affirm Scripture's claim for Scripture's claim to be true? Of course not.

Now on Monday I will address the issue of self-examination, but I suspect you may see where I am heading already.

Have a great weekend and a blessed Lord's day.

God Bless,

Phil Tabor

From: Phil Ross

Phil Tabor,

You are essentially correct. However, while family unity surely existed in times past, the principle that applies here is the authority and jurisdiction of family, not family unity. The family is a separate sphere of biblical authority, like the church and the state. The children fall under the jurisdiction of the head of the household. The children of covenant families are baptized on the authority and jurisdiction of the head of the household.

Phil Ross

From: Phil Tabor

Let me start with a brief recap of what I have covered so far:

1) We have seen that the Lord's Supper is not just a revision of the Passover but is a new sacrament that is tied by the teaching of Christ to the giving of manna in the dessert and the feeding of the five thousand, both of which events children were included in the eating. Previously we had discussed that it is at least possible that children participated in the Passover feast as well.

2) We discussed that in general, Scripture, and thereby God Himself considers children worthy of inclusion in the life and rites of the church. Both Jesus and Paul speak and act as if children are holy/clean and representative of the faithful condition we all should be in when we come before God.

Today we will look at the requirement set forth by Paul that believers must examine themselves so as not to come to communion unworthily and consider whether this specific command applies to young children at all and if, assuming it does, there is a way for this command to be fulfilled.

Let us turn our attention to what Paul actually says (1 Corinthians 11:17):

> In the following directives I have no praise for you, for your meetings do more harm than good. In the first place, I hear that when you come together as a church, there are divisions among you, and to some extent I believe it. No doubt there have to be differences among you to show which of you have God's approval. When you come together, it is not the Lord's Supper you eat, for as you eat, each of you goes ahead without waiting for anybody else. One remains hungry, another gets drunk. Don't you have homes to eat and drink in? Or do you despise the church of God and humiliate those who have nothing? What shall I say to you? Shall I praise you for this? Certainly not! For I received from the Lord what I also passed on to you: The Lord Jesus, on the night he was betrayed, took bread, and when he had given thanks, he broke it and said, "This is my body, which is for you; do this in remembrance of me." In the same way, after supper he took the cup, saying, "This cup is the new covenant in my blood; do this, whenever you drink it, in remembrance of me." For whenever you eat this bread and drink this cup, you proclaim the Lord's death until he comes. Therefore, whoever eats the bread or drinks the cup of the Lord in an unworthy manner will be guilty of sinning against the body and blood of the Lord. A man ought to examine himself before he eats of the bread and drinks of the cup. For anyone who eats and drinks without recognizing the body of the Lord eats and drinks judgment on himself. That is why many among you are weak and sick, and a number of you have fallen asleep. But if we judged ourselves, we would not come under judgment. When we are judged by the Lord, we are being disciplined so that we will not be condemned with the world. So then, my brothers, when you come together to eat, wait for each other. If anyone is hungry, he should eat at home, so that when you meet together it may not result in judgment. And when I come I will give further directions."

There it is, unmistakable in verse 28, "A man ought to examine himself before he eats of the bread and drinks of the cup."

But we must first ask: examine himself in regards to what? This is not, as some have supposed, a command for general self examination to uncover any hidden sins that may be lurking in our conscience. It is an examination with a specific purpose as given in the following verse. The purpose is "recognizing the body of the Lord."

Now is Paul speaking of recognizing the *elements* as the body and blood of Christ? In context, I think not. He is speaking of recognizing the *congregation* as the body of Christ. We know this because his criticism of their behavior leading up to these verses is very specific. He is criticizing them for not sharing the meal in a loving and compassionate manner. People are bringing their own food and gorging themselves while others go hungry. Some start early before others arrive. This is made clear in verses 33-34, "So then, my brothers, when you come together to eat, wait for each other. If anyone is hungry, he should eat at home, so that when you meet together it may not result in judgment."

The judgment results from these specific issues he has been addressing in regard to the manner of their eating.

Now, I ask, does a young child in church with their family have control over these issues? Does the young child decide when to start eating, what food to eat or not eat and how to share with the congregation? Obviously not. These matters are the concern of and under the control of their parents. These instructions by Paul are not given to children, but to the adults of the congregation, because it is the adults that are misbehaving and the adults that need correction. If children are participating in a problematic manner, it is only because their parents are controlling them.

And it is proper that their parents control their participation, therefore it is the parents that must do the examination of themselves and their household. And of course this role of the parents is a thoroughly biblical role. Joshua proclaims, "As for me and my house, we shall serve the Lord." He polls the adults of Israel about what they shall do, but when it comes to his household, he makes the determination for them.

This is the biblical role of the head of the household. And we Reformed have always acknowledged this. This is why it is the parents that determine that the child shall be baptized, shall come to church, shall be instructed in the ways of the Lord. Scripture is clear that the church is in charge of discipling adults, but parents are responsible for discipling children, though the church should assist in this.

When Paul writes to Timothy and Titus about the requirements of elders, he makes a point that the church should see how they manage their families. This is not just because a good manager is a good manager in any context, but because the management task given to the father within the household has virtually the exact same responsibilities of the task given to elders within the church. If they cannot perform the tasks of teaching, disciplining, and yes, fencing the table, within their own family, how can they be expected to perform these exact same functions in the church?

But what if we spiritualize this passage and expand it to require the individuals to identify whether they have unrepentant sin to deal with first? Well, I personally think that is adding to Scripture, but even here we have an answer from Scripture.

In 1 Corinthians 10:18 Paul compares the participation in the Lord's Supper with the participation in the food given at the alter in the Old Testament. (Also note here Paul expresses concern for unity in the Lord's Supper in 1 Corinthians 10:15-18).

> I speak to sensible people; judge for yourselves what I say. Is not the cup of thanksgiving for which we give thanks a participation in the blood of Christ? And is not the bread that we break a participation in the body of Christ? Because there is one loaf, we, who are many, are one body, for we all partake of the one loaf. Consider the people of Israel: Do not those who eat the sacrifices participate in the altar?

So let us consider the people of Israel. Who is it that ate of the sacrifices and therefore participated in the alter?

Let us take a look at a specific offering brought to the alter, the fellowship offering. My reason for selecting this is because the fellowship offering is the offering given to express the unity of the people, which we have seen is much the focus of Paul's teaching on the Lord's Supper (Leviticus 7:28-34):

> The LORD said to Moses, "Say to the Israelites: 'Anyone who brings a fellowship offering to the LORD is to bring part of it as his sacrifice to the LORD. With his own hands he is to bring the offering made to the LORD by fire; he is to bring the fat, together with the breast, and wave the breast before the LORD as a wave offering. The priest shall burn the fat on the altar, but the breast belongs to Aaron and his sons. You are to give the right thigh of your fellowship offerings to the priest as a contribution. The son

of Aaron who offers the blood and the fat of the fellowship offering shall have the right thigh as his share. From the fellowship
offerings of the Israelites, I have taken the breast that is waved
and the thigh that is presented and have given them to Aaron the
priest and his sons as their regular share from the Israelites."

Now the portion that was not given to the priest was shared by the
person bringing the offering and his family, but for now I want to look
specifically at the portion given as a wave offering to the priest. In
Numbers 18:11 we learn specifically how the priest is to deal with this
wave offering.

"This also is yours: whatever is set aside from the gifts of all the
wave offerings of the Israelites. I give this to you and your sons
and daughters as your regular share. Everyone in your household
who is ceremonially clean may eat it."

Notice that this portion of the food from the alter is to be consumed
by the priest families, their sons and daughters. But there is a catch, they
must be ceremonially clean! They must be worthy. If they eat this unworthily, they will bring judgment upon themselves.

Clearly the priests determine if they are ceremonially clean by self-
examination. But does Moses or the Lord expect their children to self
examine? Certainly not, the priest will determine if anyone in his family
is ceremonially clean or not before allowing them to eat of food from
the alter. If he were unable to do this, then his children would starve,
because all (or at least most) of the priest's food for his family came from
the alter. They had no land of their own to grow it on.

So if we consider the people of Israel, as Paul suggests, and see that
their familial heads were responsible for examining their children and
determining if they were worthy to receive the sacrifices representing
their fellowship with Israel, should not that same principle apply to the
familial heads examining their families to determine worthiness to receive the Lord's Supper?

There is much more I could say and perhaps should say, but I fear I
have gone on too long already. I will now ask for responses and deal
with issues.

God Bless,
Phil Tabor

From: Phil Ross
Phil Tabor,

Good job.
You wrote:

> "Scripture is clear that the church is in charge of discipling adults,
> but parents are responsible for discipling children, though the
> church should assist in this."

Only the last clause troubles me. While this is not germane to your
argument about paedo communion, it is related to the authority of the
head of the household. How is the church to help discipline children?
Please provide scriptural warrant.
Phil Ross

From: Phil Tabor
This thought came up in another discussion on this topic and I
thought it was too good not to share (Matthew 18:1-6):

> At that time the disciples came to Jesus and asked, "Who is the
> greatest in the kingdom of heaven?" He called a little child and
> had him stand among them. And he said: "I tell you the truth,
> unless you change and become like little children, you will never
> enter the kingdom of heaven. Therefore, whoever humbles him-
> self like this child is the greatest in the kingdom of heaven. And
> whoever welcomes a little child like this in my name welcomes
> me. But if anyone causes one of these little ones who believe in
> me to sin, it would be better for him to have a large millstone
> hung around his neck and to be drowned in the depths of the
> sea."

Now, when we come to the communion service we should pray,
"Lord, I want to do great things for your kingdom so humble me and
make me like this little child whom I will not welcome to your table because he is not like me and able to examine himself." Hmm.

This is not meant to sound sarcastic, and I am not suggesting anyone here would pray this prayer. It is just meant to engender thought
and reflection.
God Bless,
Phil Tabor

From: Phil Ross
Phil Tabor,
You wrote:

> "What I struggle with is that I see precious little in scripture that supports the presupposition that children are to be excluded in any way shape or form. And quite a bit that suggests they are and always have been included."

Perhaps the issue is not whether or not children are included in the Sacrament of the Lord's Supper, but *how* they are included.

If we may assume a separate sphere of authority and jurisdiction for families or headship, then we can propose that a child who does not actively receive communion is still included in the covenant by virtue of his or her father's jurisdiction. The father's children are covenant children by virtue of the jurisdiction of covenant headship, whether or not he allows them to actively receive communion. Also, they are not brought into this condition by baptism, but through the jurisdiction of headship. Baptism is a sign and seal of God's grace and of covenantal headship jurisdiction, not its cause.

Since the next level of jurisdiction above the family is the church, where the head of the house submits himself to the jurisdiction of the elders, perhaps the Sacraments (infant baptism and communion) should be understood as marking various boundaries of covenantal jurisdiction. Consider:

Acts 16:15: And when she was baptized, and her household ....

1 Corinthians 1:16: And I baptized also the household of Stephanas, etc.

To what extent was baptism considered to be a household or family ordinance by virtue of headship jurisdiction? To what extent have we bought into the individualism of the Baptists? And brought that individualism into Reformed theology by way of unexamined presuppositions?

Again, one of the primary biblical themes is representative government, modeled in the family through headship, in the church through eldership, and in the state through kingship. All of which sets up and provides meaning for Christ's representative reign through the family, through the church, and through the state.

Thus, the sacraments may not be so much about the condition of the individuals who participate in them, as about the structures of authority and jurisdiction of a covenantal society. In other words, perhaps we should interpret the Sacraments corporately, rather than merely individually.

Phil Ross

From: Michael
Phil Tabor,
Thanks for the thought-provoking discussion, Phil (Tabor). I am especially encouraged that you are averse from strident presumptivism. And again, I appreciated the mild spirit. How much we lose in a right cause when we mix it with our unholy flame!
God bless,
Michael

From: Phil Tabor
Phil Ross,
I think you may be on to something. Would you care to develop the thought expressed in this statement, "In other words, perhaps we should interpret the sacraments corporately, rather than merely individually" further?
Phil Tabor

From: Phil Ross
Phil Tabor,
Certainly, but to do it properly we must develop it together—corporately. My thought is that the Sacraments are not directed at individuals, but at groups. And not just any old groups, but those groups that have biblical warrant—family, church, and state. In this case the state does not appear to have a role in the Sacraments, but the church and family do. We need to discuss sacramental jurisdiction. Baptism and communion are related to church membership. Baptism formally initiates it, and communion formally maintains it. But what is church membership? Is it not willing submission to the jurisdiction of the church. However, such submission to church jurisdiction does not eliminate the authority and jurisdiction of the family, the head of household. Rather, Paul emphasizes the fact that church membership strengthens or enhances headship authority. It seems to me that the reason for this is that headship models the representational government established by Scripture—eldership and kingship.
And what is representational government? Does it mean that I, as the head of a household, have to or get to do everything that elders, as heads of churches, do. No, elders have a different jurisdiction than heads of households. Submission to authority is involved at every level. Simi-

larly, wives have a different jurisdiction than husbands—not worse, nor better, only different. Christ's sacrifice was essentially representational. He represents us before God. The analogies are legion.

The overriding biblical concern is authority. God's authority is established through the authority of Scripture and Scripture establishes the authority of headship, eldership, and kingship. The common factor of each jurisdiction is its representational nature. Individuals are to govern themselves with regard to spiritual things by imitating Christ. In addition, help is provided by family headship, church eldership, and state kingship.

Thus, the essential character of a biblical society is corporate adherence to God's covenant in the family, in the church, and in the state. That adherence is expressed differently in each jurisdiction, according to Scripture. And the sacraments of the church, the essential exercise of biblical authority and jurisdiction, reflect the corporate nature of the covenant.

Help me out.

Phil Ross

From: Phil Tabor

Michael,

I think we will have to agree to disagree and I assure you I recognize that mine is the minority report and hold nothing but good will to you and your faithful approach to the Scriptures.

I think there are basic presuppositions that affect out understanding and without those presuppositions changing, there can be no agreement on this issue.

I see Scripture as holding out the child as the model of covenant membership (i.e. referring to Israel as the children of Israel throughout the Old Testament and Jesus specifically telling us our faith must be as that of a young child) and therefore to be fully included in covenant life and to be assumed faithful until proven otherwise.

I will not presume to summarize your presupposition but will just state that it seems to be contrary to this in significant ways.

Thus, we read Paul differently. You read his statement about self-examination as a prerequisite to all entry to the table, I read it as an admonition to those in need of it and who are able to do so.

An example of how I see it would be if I were to close a meeting by commanding those present to, "Drive carefully lest you get in an accident."

If you assume that everyone who attends the meeting must drive their own car, then you are right in assuming the command applies to all.

If, however, you assume that some people are too young to drive or for other reasons rode with others to the meeting, then you would apply the command only to those who were driving.

You assume that everyone must bring themselves to the communion table, and therefore your reading of Paul is necessary.

I assume that young children can be brought to the table by their parents and therefore my reading is appropriate.

It seems to me that children's participation in Passover is much the same. If you presume they should be excluded, the passages can be viewed to support that, if you assume they should be included, the passages allow that.

What I struggle with is that I see precious little in Scripture that supports the presupposition that children are to be excluded in any way shape or form. And quite a bit that suggests they are and always have been included.

And finally, let me agree with you that we are not to presume our children's salvation based on their being born to us and baptized into the covenant. I also agree that the means is the same for child and adult conversion.

However, I would strongly disagree with any suggestion that the date of their rebirth can be presumed to be after a certain age. The Psalms make it clear that David had faith from infancy. There are countless people raised in the church that have known nothing but faith all their lives. I see no Scripture to suggest there is a magic age of accountability.

But there are some raised in Christian homes who eventually turn from the faith, never to return. But the same can be said for those who are converted and baptized as adults. Some stay and some do not. We cannot presume the salvation of those who come into the church as adults either. So I am not sure how that affects the discussion regarding children.

In any case, thank you all for your patience with me as I have laid out my case, and especially you Michael, for your charity in dealing with me.

God Bless,

Phil Tabor

From: Phil Ross

Phil Tabor,

Good questions. You realize, of course, that you are talking about a thesis sized argument to answer them correctly. But because such a thesis is not in my future, I will poke and stab at your questions.

Ideally, family, church, and state share a common purpose—the glory of God, where *glory* is understood as *jurisdiction*.

Of course there is some overlap of authority between family, church, and state. And at the same time, there are lines of demarcation, but probably not clear enough to suit our modern proclivities. I suspect that these blurred lines of authority/jurisdiction are, by design, for our sanctification. So, I don't expect that we will understand Scripture like an engineer understands blueprints. God is more tolerant than that. I suspect that God's plan is more tolerant that we can abide.

I believe that in the New Testament era the head of the house was baptized into the church, and because of his headship jurisdiction, his household was graciously folded into God's covenant, even baptized at times. Sometimes families were baptized, sometimes individuals were baptized. But baptism always signified the engagement of God's covenant, His representative government in family, church, and state.

Nonetheless, the church membership of his household was not a matter of fiat, but was considered to be the ongoing responsibility of the head. His first job as a new Christian was the education/sanctification of his household in the doctrines of the faith. His household was his responsibility under his family jurisdiction.

They didn't watch TV in the evenings, but more than likely engaged in Christian education as a household. The church membership of his household was an ongoing responsibility, not a sign-on-the-dotted-line-and-you're-done kind of thing. The church membership of his family would unfold over decades, but the church considered them members until evidence suggested otherwise.

Could the elders bring sanctions against a family member. Yes, but they went through the head, not around him.

This responsibility fell to women whose husbands were not Christian. The church graciously considered her children to be sanctified by the wife's authority (over them) and her work to raise them in the nurture and admonition of the Lord.

At what point does the son come out from under the jurisdiction of his father? That question is still with us. I have three teenage sons, and they are so different that their "coming of age" will take place at different times and ages. They do not mature at the same rate. So, there is no definitive answer in Scripture or in life. The joy is in the journey.

Do people join the church as families today? Or as individuals? Well, families usually join together (at the same time) and individuals join as individuals, but only because their families are broken or they are separated from them. Church is a family affair, but in our day families are very broken. So it is harder for us to see that.

What is the basic unit of the biblical covenant? The individual or the family? What was it in Jesus' day? Let me suggest that the basic biblical covenant unit is the covenanted individual, which requires him to be related to others, if not his natural family, his church family. A covenanted individual is a person under authority. The unity of such people requires willing mutual submission to a common authority.

Personal profession plays a key role in sanctification. Normally such profession would first be made within the family. The head of the household would then discuss such a profession with the elders of the church, who would then get involved in the examination because wisdom is found in a plurality of counselors (Proverbs). Making a profession before the gathered church, then, is a part of sanctification. The individual grows through such a public confession, as does the church body.

At the same time personal profession is not some magic talisman that brings people into the church. No, grace alone brings God's people into the covenant body. Personal profession is a both a tool and a measure of sanctification.

We have made church membership something that it was not in the first century. The church was fluid and dynamic in the early days. They did not have the luxury of the kinds of considerations we have. But we cannot go back to their time, nor could they have anticipated ours.

What does this have to do with paedo communion? Everything. The decision to allow a child to receive communion originates with the child. It must be *desired.* The child asks the father because the family ju-

risdiction belongs to him. He consults with his wife, then the elders because church jurisdiction belongs to the elders. And the elders then
work with the father, not usurping his jurisdiction, but honoring it.
When the elders honor headship jurisdiction, they strengthen the head
and the family and the church and their own authority. The elders are
charged with the sanctification of covenant families. It's not so much a
matter of making the rules, but of growing a kingdom, of trying to keep
up with the amazing toleration of God.

We will have to work out our own salvation in fear and trembling.
Phil Ross

From: Phil Tabor
Phil Ross,
Several questions come to mind here. It seems to me that the familial head and the elders share a common purpose, which is making disciples of the people under their care. I am wondering to what extent you
see overlap in this. Do the elders have direct authority over the members
of a household or only through the head?

Do members of a household join the church individually, or *en
masse*?

If *en masse,* then how do we deal with situations such as Paul addresses in 1 Corinthians 7 where you may have an unbelieving husband
as head of the household, but a believing wife who wants to participate
in the church with her children. Paul seems to suggest that she can as
long as she is not forbidden by her husband. From the churches perspective, is she the head of the household in matters pertaining to the
church, i.e., over the children?

At what point does a son come out from under his Father in the
household? When he leaves home to marry (that would seem to be the
answer from Genesis)? What about a man called to celibate service like
Paul? Is a household literally those living in one house, or is it relation-
ally defined?

And when the church performs a sacrament, who is responsible for
fencing? The head of the household, the elder or both? Does the answer
change for adult males within the household?

What role, if any, does personal profession of faith play in all of this?
Phil Tabor

From: Phil Tabor

Phil Ross,

Thanks for the encouragement.

The process of making disciples of Jesus Christ is more than discipline (teaching and correcting), which is why I used the term discipling (making one a disciple). In the great commission Jesus tells us to make disciples, baptizing and teaching. From this we conclude that the administration of the sacraments is part of the discipling process. I think you would agree that the church must administer the sacraments to the child, although the parents bring the child to the sacrament.

In addition, the children sit under the preaching of the church and, in many cases the church provides teaching for children. While I agree that the responsibility for the teaching of the children rests squarely on the shoulders of the parents, it would be poor stewardship not to take advantage of those members of the body who are gifted in working with young ones. See Paul's instruction for older men to work with young men, older women to work with young women outside familial structures.

And finally, it is helpful if the church provides guidance and supporting materials for the parents to use in training up their children. This is part of the churches role in discipling the parents. Again refer to Paul's instruction regarding the experienced and mature helping the inexperienced and/or immature.

Now, which of these issues do you feel needs additional biblical warrant?

Phil Tabor

From: Phil Ross

Phil Tabor,

It seems that you continue to view the sacraments from an individualistic, rather than a covenantal perspective. A covenantal view of communion, for instance, is that the church administers the sacrament to the family, not merely the individual. Thus, communion is to be given to the head of the household, who then gives it to the members of his household as he or she sees fit (in consultation and through the instruction of the elders, to be sure). In fact, I believe that sacramental administration is a primary symbol of biblical authority and jurisdiction, not necessarily personal commitment and/or belief (though it does not preclude these).

The point is that the church honors the jurisdiction of the family through the administration of the sacraments. Just as an Ohio sheriff will honor the jurisdiction of Iowa by not simply arresting an Ohio fugitive who has fled to Iowa, but by soliciting the permission and help of Iowa law enforcement. He does not go directly to the fugitive. Legal jurisdiction must (and is) always honored by going through the appropriate jurisdiction, otherwise the case can be dismissed on technical grounds.

So, yes, the elders can administer sacraments and teach children, but must honor the jurisdiction of the family, the head of the household, who has authority over the family.

One way that family jurisdiction is violated in the contemporary church is through evangelism efforts that are aimed specifically at children, prior to the conversion of the parents (or in the hope of reaching the parents through the children). This is not a biblical practice.

Admittedly, contemporary families are so broken and jurisdictionally dysfunctional that it is difficult for the church to honor a family jurisdiction that families themselves are ignorant of. Nonetheless, the best way to re-institute biblical categories of thought and behavior is to honor them in spite of popular ignorance. Discipling the *ethnos* involves teaching them biblical authority—the authority of the Bible, the state, the church, the family and the conscience.

Note that Jesus commands us to make disciples of the "nations."

> "Go ye therefore, and teach all nations, baptizing them in the
> name of the Father, and of the Son, and of the Holy Ghost"
> –Matthew 28:19

As you know, nations (gr. *ethnos*) means:
1. a multitude (whether of men or of beasts) associated or living together
    1. company, troop, swarm
2. a multitude of individuals of the same nature or genus
    1. the human family
3. a tribe, nation, people group
4. in the Ols Testament, foreign nations not worshiping the true God, pagans, Gentiles
5. Paul uses the term for Gentile Christians

While the term sometimes suggests a multitude of individuals, those individuals were almost always associated with families and extended families. The family structure was not as broken and deteriorated then as it is now. So, we must not project our contemporary experience of decrepit family structure upon Scripture. Rather, we should make every effort to understand family structure as it was in the Old Testament and in the early church—and it was not like it is now.

Sure there were individuals not associated with families that constituted special cases. But the norm involved discipling men—heads of households, who would then disciple their own children until they were of an age to be discipled by another, perhaps at a Synagogue school. But that took place for young men not less than about twelve years old, and even then many such lads would not have attended such a school for a variety of reasons.

Nonetheless, it was understood to be young men or men who were entering adulthood. Children younger than that were the responsibility of the family.

We've been Sunday Schooled for so long that we don't know any better. But we must realize that Sunday School is a modern invention that mimics secular education, not Scripture. Sunday School is a new measure, as are youth ministry, nursery, VBS, etc. (I'll bet that's a can of worms, but nonetheless true!)

Thus, the church administers the sacraments to the family as a symbol of its jurisdiction. The head of the household, then, yields to the authority of the church by allowing his family to participate.

In fact (to take it a step further), I would argue that the unity Christ prayed for in John 17:21, "That they all may be one; as thou, Father, art in me, and I in thee, that they also may be one in us: that the world may believe that thou hast sent me," is more about biblical jurisdiction than our understanding of abstract doctrine or theology. Sure, it's about theology and doctrine, but the foundation of right theology and doctrine is not taking systematic theology from the right seminary, but about biblical authority and jurisdiction—Bible, state, church, family, and conscience. In other words, church sacraments and church unity are functions of biblical jurisdiction. And the reason that Scripture applies to every aspect of life pertains to the ubiquity of its jurisdiction.

Phil Ross

From: Phil Tabor

Phil Ross,

I agree with most if not all of what you say here. As such, I am a little surprised by your first sentence, "It seems that you continue to view the sacraments from an individualistic, rather than a covenantal perspective." How so?

I suspect you are reacting to my statement, "I think you would agree that the church must administer the sacraments to the child, although the parents bring the child to the sacrament."

Do you disagree with this statement? I think perhaps we are dealing with interpretation of process. Do you hold that when parents bring a child to be baptized, the father actually does the baptism? I do not think so, though the father's role is crucial, it is the ordained elder that does the baptism.

Likewise with communion, as the elements are distributed are you suggesting the elders must give the elements to the head of the household who then must pass them out to his family? I would suggest that as a communal covenant meal that it matters little who passes to whom as long as all who are present receive. The head of the household has the authority to withhold the sacrament from members of his household if he deems that necessary.

Likewise the elders may withhold it from individuals or households whom they deem necessary to excommunicate. I see overlapping authority here as in the matter of the sacraments the children are under the authority of both the head of the household and the elders of the church.

In regards to Sunday School, you have a very valid point that there has been historically an attempt to follow the secular models of education, and this is wrong. However, there is a biblical model of identifying giftedness within individuals and making use of that giftedness to achieve the goals of the church and it's families. Thus, while I have real problems with much of the methods and curriculum which I see in many Sunday Schools, especially the lack of any consistent catechetical criteria, I do not have an objection to the church identifying people who work well with young children and setting aside time and materials for them to spend with the children teaching them, augmenting and supporting the goal/responsibility of the parents to teach their children.

Let me be more specific. I have asked at several churches what the goal of their Sunday School program is and have gotten very lame responses. When asked what my child would know at a minimum upon completion of the program, most of them looked at me with a bewildered expression. Now, as a parent I find this very frustrating because I have no idea how to work with such a program. What are it's strengths and weaknesses? Where do I need to augment or how can I reinforce?

Now, I have encountered some churches where they have a well thought out program that a parent can work with. But far too many churches view this as really care-taking time so that parents can either attend worship without being bothered by kids (frightening) or attend their own Bible Study without being bothered by the kids. The giftedness of the teacher is usually judged by a willingness to volunteer to spend an hour with the children without beating them or allowing them to run amok (although in some churches, even this last criteria has been dropped). The idea is that if the kids learn anything it is a bonus. The most important thing is to keep them occupied with "Christian stuff," so the kids do little crafts around a Bible story and when asked what they learned they usually have no answer.

Now, there are some churches that really do identify people gifted in communicating Biblical truth to young children and giving them the resources to do it. And sometimes these people have a real plan and program that they can explain to parents and can be worked with. But my experience is that this is few and far between. But I have seen it enough to know that it can be done, so let us not dismiss the idea just because it is not being done well. Let us refocus the goals and define the better process.

I think the catechisms developed by the various reformed bodies are a great idea. I just wish more churches used them as the basis of their Sunday School program in a way that parents could understand and take advantage in their own efforts to train up their children.

Phil Tabor

From: Phil Ross
Phil Tabor,

I think that we are in essential agreement. But where I would cancel Sunday School and give a catechism curriculum to the parents and have the children in worship, I suspect that you would provide Sunday School with catechism curriculum.

Of course there are specially gifted teachers who can benefit children. But, unfortunately, they are the exception rather than the rule. Thus, I would lobby to not set policy based upon the exceptional cases. Too often we establish policy on the basis of exceptional cases. Policy should be based upon biblical norms, not experiential exceptions.

I was right with you until your last paragraph, where you said, "I think the catechisms developed by the various reformed bodies are a great idea. I just wish more churches used them as the basis of their Sunday School program in a way that parents could understand and take advantage in their own efforts to train up their children."

My concern is not so much with the curriculum of Sunday School programs, but with the existence of Sunday School programs. A good curriculum does not justify an unbiblical program. Those specially gifted teachers do not require Sunday School programs in order to teach.

Would such a church be ignoring the needs of the children? Not at all, not if they concentrated their efforts on meeting the real needs of the head of the household by placing his biblical authority responsibility squarely upon his shoulders, and offering to help. Not to do it with his help, but to have him do it with the church's help. Big difference.

Regarding who administers baptism and/or who serves communion to a minor, we must not ignore the context. Yes, of course, a non-family elder could hold the baby and pour the water. But again, in ancient biblical cultures that elder would likely be related to the baptizee. But, related or not, the elder would be supervised by the head of the household at the baptism of a family member. The elder would be a guest within the jurisdiction of the head of the household. The head of the household might even hold the infant (not give up control and support), while the elder pours.

While there is much overlap of biblical jurisdictions, there are also boundaries that must be respected. Going out of our way to respect those jurisdictional boundaries used to be called politeness and/or manners. Well, it still is called that, but manners and politeness have been in rapid decline for centuries.

And at communion, the elders should (in my opinion) hand the elements to the head of the household, who would then serve his own family. Is this worse than being served by whoever happens to be sitting next to you? Maintaining the symbolism of the structures of biblical authority, especially during the sacraments, is important. It is the symbolic point of the sacraments themselves. It helps to teach that authority is not promiscuous, to borrow one of Calvin's expressions.

When the elders hand the tray to whoever happens to be at the end of the pew, they fail to symbolize the jurisdiction of the family. This practice does not teach, honor, or symbolize the authority of headship. So, I would lobby that on communion day, the head of the household position him- or herself to receive the tray directly from the elder and serve his or her own family. In this way, the hierarchical structure of biblical authority is honored and symbolized at every level. It is often done this way today, particularly with the younger communicants who are prone to spillage. But that's the wrong reason!

It's a little thing. But in love the little things turn out to be quite important.

Phil Ross

From: Phil Tabor
Phil Ross,

I am not sure that people gifted in working with children are so very rare. I think the bigger problem is that they are not given proper direction from church leadership in what to present. The reason I support the catechisms as a basis is because it then becomes easy to coordinate what is going on in Sunday School with what is going on at home. What I favor is kids attending Sunday School and worship. One of the chief values to me for Sunday School is the value of kids hearing the same message from church authority that they hear from home authority. I think it is very beneficial when the kids have to deal with the culture at large to know that these beliefs are not just something Mom and Dad cook up while the kids are in bed, but are the true teachings of the true church. Yes, they should get some of that from the pulpit, but to be quite honest, most preachers talk right over the top of the heads of the kids and that is not necessarily a bad thing as long as they are getting the message through to the adults. We could get into another discussion about the sad state of preaching these days, but let's not go there right now.

In regards to serving the sacraments, we really have very little to go on in regards to communion, but the New Testament example on baptism is pretty clear that it was John and his disciples, then the disciples of Jesus that did the baptisms directly. Oh, how many debates in the church would be resolved if Luke had just given us the details of one household baptism. But I find no suggestion that the parents did the baptizing, but rather the apostles did it. I think it is good for the parent to hold the child if the baptism is by pouring or sprinkling. If it is by immersion, then the elder should be holding the child.

In regards to communion, I think one of the overriding purposes of communion is to identify the body of Christ as one body, one family. I find your call to reinforce boundaries within the body at this time of unity a bit troubling. Is not the person on my left and my right my brother or sister in Christ, regardless of my age and theirs?

I suggest that the place for discernment is before the serving, at which point the elders and heads of households should deal with anyone who should not participate. Once that decision has been made, then I think all should participate as one family, united in Christ and recognizing His authority equally over all. I think that is the message of 1 Corinthians 11, and in fact a majority of 1 Corinthians as a whole. I do not think this negates elder or headship authority, but puts it in the perspective that that authority is in Christ and under Christ.

Phil Tabor

CHRISTIAN MARRIAGE

Thinking About Marriage…

The first thing that you should notice is that the above word is *marriage* and not *wedding*. The deepest concern of the church is for the marriage. Sure, you should have a nice wedding, but more important is the stability and longevity of the marriage.

"Unfortunately in many cases the church has contributed to the divorce problem of our nation by promoting easy weddings," says H. Norman Wright, a pastor and author of several marriage counseling books. Easy weddings ask nothing, provide nothing, and do nothing. The intent of the church is not to make your wedding hard, but to make your marriage meaningful. Like so many things in life, you will get out of it what you put into it.

Marriage is a sacred relationship that was instituted by God. Christians understand that God is love and, therefore, God is positively involved in every marriage. The essence of marriage is a commitment that has its foundation in the faithfulness of God's love. The Pastor ceremonially offers the marriage God's blessing. Those who attend the wedding are the community of support who join in affirming the marriage and offering support and thanksgiving for the new family, created and blessed by God. However, to seriously offer God's blessings means that the marriage must have God's approval. The marriage must conform to the will of God. That means that those who are getting married must aim their marriage at God's purpose for marriage.

If the church offers marriage without any expectation of Christian faithfulness on the part of the couple, the church would be hypocritical —guilty of saying one thing and doing another. The vows of Christian marriage can only work if we make promises we intend to keep—and then keep them. The vows of Christian marriage necessarily involve promises to God and Jesus Christ because of God's active involvement in Christian marriage.

"Marriage is an honorable estate, instituted of God, and signifies the mystical union which exists between Christ and his Church," says the introduction to the traditional wedding service. The honorableness of marriage comes because it is a life-long commitment to your wedding promises.

Public Vows

The wedding vows are more than promises between two individual people. They involve whole communities as the couple lives out their lives together as husband and wife. Marriages literally unite families, and families of families. Consequently, faithfulness to the marriage promise will effect the promise-keeping abilities of entire communities. Marriage is a public promise every bit as much as it is a personal affair. Marriage is *personal*, but not *private*. This is attested to by the public nature of the wedding ceremony.

We all must take care that the institutional and social aspects of marriage and promise-making are not damaged or lost. In reality, the institutional and social aspects of promise making in marriage have deteriorated greatly in the past century, and we in the church need to reclaim and revive them. No promise between people is purely private or individual; rather, every such promise has social consequences. Keeping a promise builds up human society, just as breaking a promise contributes to social disintegration. So the church asks that the promises of marriage be "uttered aloud" and that the ceremony occur "before God and these witnesses," an underscoring of the public nature of marriage.

The Church

The church's ministry to those who marry is similar to its ministry to all: *to provide nurture and support for living out our promises to God and to each other.* Consequently, Christ's church stands ready to help you and your family as you begin to live together—and on into the future. We care about you, about your spouse, about your children, and about the success of your marriage.

The Wedding

The wedding ceremony itself, like all ceremonies of the church, is first and foremost a worship service. The primary purpose of any church service is worship. Your wedding service is no exception. Therefore, what happens at your wedding is important to the church. We want you to have the best possible experience as you enter into your new life together. So, we will do everything that we can to insure a good, worshipful experience for you.

"What therefore God hath joined together, let not man put asunder," says Jesus of marriage in Matthew 19:6. Christian marriage is not merely a legal contract that can be broken or revoked just because someone has their feelings hurt or becomes unhappy. It is a life-long union of a man and woman based on sacred and solemn life-long vows to God and to one another. If the vows are not taken seriously, the marriage will suffer—and the community will suffer as well.

Divorce is a real problem—it always has been. But God is merciful, thanks be to Jesus Christ. People can make a new beginning. Divorce does not mean that you cannot be remarried.

No matter what your experience, when you come to a church to be married it must be with the conviction that you are meant for each other for life, and that as you live into future days and years it will be in harmony, with increasing understanding, respect and love—regardless of the disagreements you will encounter with each other. And you will encounter disagreements!

Your love and commitment to one another will be confirmed and your faith strengthened if you know that the pastor is also confident that your love is based in mutual trust and understanding. In a series of personal sessions with the couple the pastor will help to confirm your understanding of yourself and your potential mate. He will talk candidly with you about biblical marriage responsibilities, about open, honest communication and share with you some insights and practices that will help you to establish a happy and enduring home.

There is much to consider long before you walk down the aisle. Like anything else, a good foundation is important for a long-lasting and meaningful marriage relationship.

Church Involvement

A Christian wedding service presumes that those who are to be united in marriage are active members of a Christian church, that each party has professed Jesus Christ as Lord and Savior. Why? Because a Christian marriage is built upon the support of the worshiping community. No couple can survive the storms of our times without the support of a loving and actively supporting community.

If the bride or groom is not an active member of a Christian church, the pastor will initiate discussion about personal commitment within a Christian community as a prerequisite for a successful marriage commitment. To do otherwise is to belittle the purpose of Christian marriage or a church wedding.

DEFINITION OF MARRIAGE

The definition of terms always determines the shape and conclusion of an argument, case, statement, or policy, assuming that it unfolds logically. Thus, the definition of marriage is the central concern in the debate about so-called *gay marriage*.

However, as soon as the issue is referred to as "gay marriage" its definition is influenced by the preposition "gay." To consider "gay marriage" at all is to assume that there are various types of marriage, "gay marriage" being one of them. But such thinking contradicts common dictionaries, common traditions, common practices, common law, and common sense.

To define a thing requires going to its root or genesis. Where did the thing come from? What is its purpose? What has been its history? And lastly what is the common understanding of the thing in contemporary society?

Marriage finds its origin in the Bible. Of course, people are free to disregard the Bible, but in doing so they disregard the historic traditions of Christianity, Judaism, Islam, and the foundation of America's legal system (at least its first 200 years). In the United States the combined adherence of these religious traditions represents a very healthy majority opinion, should majority opinions count for anything in America. So, if this majority is to discuss the issue of "gay marriage," they should call it by its biblical and historic name—*sodomy*.

The *American Heritage Dictionary* defines "sodomy" as "1. anal copulation of one male with another. 2. Anal or oral copulation with a member of the opposite sex. 3. Copulation with an animal." The same dictionary defines "sodomite" as one who engages in sodomy. The long history of sodomy is dark and full of deceit.

To engage in sodomy is to use a thing (sex) in a manner that is contrary to its fundamental purpose (procreation). Sodomy, then, has no social purpose or function. It is simply an activity of personal sexual self-gratification. And consenting adults are free to engage it in the privacy of their own homes, unless they claim biblical fidelity or children are involved.

The purpose of biblical—and, therefore, traditional—marriage, on the other hand, is procreation within families. Thus, marriage—family—has been called the cradle of civilization. Children are best raised in healthy families composed of a mother and a father who have covenanted together in the promise to remain together for life for the sake of the betterment of their children and their society.

How does biblical marriage contribute to the betterment of children and society? By modeling normal (procreative) sex roles, representative government, and the importance of the integrity of promises and social contracts.

Biblical marriage, however, is not merely a social contract between two people. It involves a contract with God. Similarly, civil marriage (a relatively recent invention) involves a contract with the state. Christian marriages are registered with the state, but civil marriages are not registered with the church. Thus, the state is a party involved in all marriages because the state claims an interest in the welfare of all individuals.

But does the state have an interest in the personal sexual self-gratification of individuals? Recent court decisions have already redefined the family in an attempt to legitimize sodomy. But what interest does the state have in sodomy, since by definition it cannot produce offspring? Granted that the state may have an interest in the health and disease aspects of sexual activity because it threatens individuals. Does the state also consider sodomy to be a legitimate form of birth control? Does the pursuit of happiness guarantee the right to engage in sodomy? And if so, why should children be exempt from such a right if it is endemic to the expression of human character? Does the state have the right to undermine and destroy traditionally biblically-based families?

Families are biologically related social units. Of course, adoption is also a legitimate element of family constitution, but it is the exception rather than the norm. Definitions ought to be based upon norms, while allowing for exceptions, and not based upon exceptions to the norm.

The acceptance of state sanctioned sodomy will drive a serious wedge between biblical government (instituted in part through families) and civil government that will have very serious consequences for society because at the point that the state legitimizes (encourages) sodomy the majority of citizens (those claiming adherence to Christianity, Judaism, Islam, and the historic foundation of the American legal system) will find themselves in an irreconcilable disagreement with their own government. They will be threatened by the fact that their government will actively and intentionally undermine and destroy the very foundations of biblical society—the biblically defined and regulated family.

It almost appears that someone's behind-the-scenes strategy is to cause the American people such distress with their government that they will abide the dismantling (or redefining) of the Constitution. Sodomites have always been political pawns in the game of dismantling nations.

The problem is not the Constitution, but the ongoing failure to abide by it. Similarly, the problem is not the legal definition of marriage, but the failure to abide by it. More broadly, the problem is not the traditional biblical perspective, but the failure to abide by it.

Welcome to the age of American anarchy.

Congregational History

The story of the Bible is the story of God's work in the world. It is His (God's) story that is the fundamental and original understanding of history. It is only in the post-Enlightenment, modern, secular, humanistic world that God has been written out of history (His story without Him). Historians since eighteenth century tell us that history is the story of man, of humanity, and that to suggest God's involvement in history amounts to a confusion of history with religion. But such an idea is a modern invention and is patently false.

It should be obvious that every fact of history must be interpreted in the light of God from a biblical perspective. But God is no less involved in the study of history from a non-biblical perspective. If we believe that God exists, then all of history necessarily relates to Him. And if we believe that God does not exist, then all of history must deny Him. In either case, God plays a central role either as the central actor or as the central thing to avoid.

It is true that history can be written from a variety of perspectives, but again that does not mean that all historical perspectives are equal in validity or trustworthiness. It is incumbent upon Christians to understand the world and its history from the perspective of the Bible not just ancient history, but contemporary history, as well. That is what it means to be a Christian. So, to fail in this regard is to fail to be a Christian in any meaningful sense.

One of the unique things about the history of the Bible is that it has been written without providing a positive view of humanity or of Israel, God's chosen people—nor of the church, or the apostles. The Old Testament is filled with the flaws and foibles of God's chosen people. People are not prone to provide an unflattering view of themselves, yet that is precisely what we find in Scripture. And we find the same thing in the New Testament. None of the biblical writers hide or gloss over human foibles, sins, or shortcomings. Biblical heroes are not cast in a positive light.

The adage of our day is that winners write the history of their exploits and in so doing portray themselves in a positive, favorable light. But that is not what we find in Scripture. The culmination of the Old Testament story is the threat of the destruction of Israel, following in the pattern of Israel's previous destructions. Samaria and the Northern Kingdom was destroyed in 722 B.C. by Assyria, and Jerusalem was destroyed in 586 B.C. by the Babylonians, to name only the major defeats.

The story of the New Testament is the story of Jesus Christ, God's only begotten Son, come to earth to provide for the salvation of His people through the propitiation of His Father by dying for the sins of His people on the cross. In the face of His self-sacrifice for the benefit of His people, we find the Jewish establishment rejecting and denying that Jesus is the long-awaited Christ. The consequence of their denial was the destruction of Jerusalem in A.D. 70 by the Roman army, which threw the newly established Christian church into a world-wide mission on behalf of the resurrected Christ to gather His people for His return in glory.

The Bible is the story of how God uses the events of history to accomplish His will.

His Story

> "We believe in the progressive self-revelation of God to His covenant people through the vehicle of history. All things have a direction toward the consummation of God's good purposes. The culmination of the ages is the manifestation of God in the flesh, Jesus Christ, first in humiliation to accomplish God's eternal redemption and finally in glory to consummate the Kingdom of God. To these fullnesses of time God orchestrates all of history leading up. The Church [Abraham's seed] is the nation of choice through which God has delighted to bless all the nations of the world. ... the Scriptures [are] the progressive self-disclosure of God. All of the Scriptures point to the Lord Jesus Christ, the eternal Son of God, become flesh. And all of the Scriptures need to be interpreted in light of His historical work, death, resurrection, and ascension."
> —from *Biblical Theology and Redemptive Historical Hermeneutics.*

"If you do not know history, you do not know anything. You are
a leaf that does not know it is part of a tree." —Michael Crichton

A Brief History of Congregationalism

Renewal is often the rekindling of a former glory, and the former
success of Congregationalism was indeed great. Yet, history does not
travel backwards.

The majority of contemporary Congregational church members are
not from Congregational backgrounds. Even so, most contemporary
Congregationalists themselves do not know about the long struggles
that mark the history of Congregationalism. Therefore, this essay will
attempt to briefly point out some important markers in the landscape of
Congregational history. Ours is a long history, and quite significant in
the development of the modern church. Consequently, Congregationalists must receive both credit and blame for much in the contemporary
Christian situation.

We will begin our tour of history in the modern era with the New
England Puritans and the development of the Westminster Confession
of Faith, adopted by an act of the English Parliament in the 1640s under
Charles I.

"What does that have to do with us?" you might ask.

Everything.

"Whatever associations the word 'Congregational' may have in the
modern church, Congregationalism was once regarded as the most radically Calvinistic wing of English Puritanism."[1] In other words, Congregationalists took Calvinism very seriously.

Here we find our first difficulty because many modern members of
Congregational churches don't even know what Calvinism is. And if
they do, they most likely have a second hand understanding of the so-
called "five points" of Calvinism, which were *not* developed by Calvin.
Allow me to review.

James Arminius challenged the basic tenets of Calvin in the 1600s.
The Synod of Dort was called to settle the differences between Arminius
and Calvin. The defenders of Arminius presented the Arminian position
by way of five main points. The Calvinists argued against those points,

---

1   All subsequent quotes, unless otherwise noted are from *The Cambridge Platform: A
    New Edition of the Historic Puritan Congregational Church Order*, by Darrell Todd
    Maurina, Editor, 1994.

winning the decision of Dort and establishing the five points of Calvinism. Calvin himself had already died, and was not involved.

The traditional five points of Calvinism were developed in response
to Calvin's enemies in order to refute them. While true and foundational
to Calvin's understanding of Scripture, the five points alone strip the life
out of his biblical understanding and set up a kind of straw man that can
be more easily attacked.

Calvinists themselves found it necessary to school themselves on the
five points in order defend their position. Over time, Calvin became
known for these Five Points, which he himself did not articulate as they
are commonly described. None of the Five Points were unique to
Calvin's teaching, but are found throughout the Bible, the biblical
teachings of the Third Century Church Father, Augustine, and the
Council of Orange, 529 A.D.

But before you begin to think that Congregationalists were radical
because of their Calvinistic theology, you must realize that the vast majority of Protestant churches in existence at the time were Calvinistic. It
was not Calvin's theology that set the Congregationalists apart, it was
their radically consistent application of Scripture to church government
—polity. Congregationalists were convinced that churches should be organized and governed by the dictates of Scripture.

Congregationalists did not organize and govern their churches on
the basis of Calvin, but upon Scripture. They merely cited Calvin to
substantiate their case, as did the Presbyterians and early Baptists. Neither did they conform their biblical understanding to Calvinism. It was
never Calvin first and the Bible second. Rather, they found Calvin to be
in harmony with fundamental biblical truth. Only then did they adopt
him.

Although Congregationalists agreed with the theology of the Westminster Confession, they took exception to its Presbyterian polity. The
Westminster Confession sought to establish regional churches in presbyteries, composed of representatives from several churches in a given
region. The presbytery, then, had the authority to dictate policy and
procedures to local fellowships.

The Congregationalists, while always willing to gather in regional
associations, did not believe that the Bible gave any such authority to regional associations or presbyteries. Rather, they found the Bible to put
all of its authority in the local church itself.

They believed there was no higher biblical authority than the local church, and based their belief on the total depravity of man. Sinful men would always sin and abuse power. They found that the Bible itself limited the power of the church to its local expression. Biblical elders and deacons never had jurisdiction beyond the confines of the local church. Congregationalists have always been cooperative, but leery of authority because of the sinful tendency to abuse it and the human tendency to impose it.

"A number of Congregationalists had been members of the Westminster Assembly, but had not been successful in preventing the inclusion of the hierarchical system of Presbyterianism expressed in Chapters 30 and 31 of the Westminster Confession" (p. iii). At the time the American colonies were part of the Church of England. So, the Westminster Confession found its way to America. But the colonists, leery of the abuse of power that they had suffered at the hands of the Bishops of the Church of England, resisted its simple adoption.

"In May of 1646, a group of Massachusetts ministers asked the Massachusetts General Court (the colonial legislature) to call a special synod of the Congregational churches throughout New England for September 1646 to debate a number of questions which were troubling the Congregational churches regarding baptism and church membership" (p. iii). Congregational churches insisted that those seeking church membership make public profession of their faith, which usually involved an oral statement of repentance from sin and declaration of conversion, and that only children of regenerate, participating members could receive the sacraments, baptism and communion.

Of course, it must be remembered that at the time only Congregational church members were permitted to vote in civil elections. The historical momentum to separate voting privileges from church membership led to a corresponding effort within the church to ease the requirements for church membership. Many people "insisted that as English citizens they had the right to have their children baptized by the local church in their area regardless of whether they were willing to make a public profession of faith or join the church" (p. iii).

Williston Walker, a prominent Congregational historian, "and other historians have generally judged that their primary reason for supporting Presbyterianism was that they could in this way gain civil voting rights" (p. iii). Civil and secular concerns began to shape church polity.

The process of separating the civil government from the church, involved a breaking of the comprehensive theology and discipline of the church. To provide voting rights for more people, the requirements for church membership were eased. The result was that the emerging needs of civil government were gained at the expense of the integrity of Congregational church membership.

To correct the erosion of church polity and to demonstrate general agreement with the theology of the Westminster Confession, the Congregational Synod of Massachusetts adopted the celebrated Cambridge Platform in 1647. "While one with the Presbyterians on matters of Calvinist doctrine and also one with them on their Reformed view that the Bible alone should determine principles of church government, the Congregationalists differed from the Presbyterians primarily on questions of what the Bible teaches about church polity" (p. iv).

While Presbyterians placed church power in the hands of elected elders in Presbyteries, the Congregationalists divided church power between local elders and their congregations. The elders governed the church, but the congregation could veto their decisions if they thought it necessary and had the votes. Likewise, the Congregational elders could veto decisions made by the voting congregation.

As an aside, "at a later date Baptist pastors in the London area followed the lead of the English Congregationalists and produced their own revision of the Westminster Confession" (p .v), known as the Baptist Confession of 1689. The Baptist Confession, the leading document related to the founding of the Baptists in America, is nearly identical in doctrine to the Westminster Confession, and similar to the polity of the Cambridge Platform.

"The return of the monarchy in 1660 practically destroyed organized Puritanism in England in both its Presbyterian and Congregational forms. Those ministers who would not conform to the rituals and polity of the Church of England were ejected from their pulpits and placed under severe restrictions. Presbyterian pastors, banned from meeting in Presbyteries, were forced into practical Congregationalism. Within a generation, the remaining differences had declined to the point that a merger between the two groups was attempted in 1691. By that time, the Presbyterians were willing to abandon hierarchical synodicalism and the Congregationalists were willing to adopt the unobjectionable parts of the Westminster Confession. This union was eventually disrupted due to the liberalizing tendencies and eventual lapse into Unitarianism of many English Presbyterians. In England itself, unlike New England, the Congregationalists became known as 'hyper-Calvinists' while the Presbyterians began to deny the Trinity" (p. v).

Only when we understand that the liberal arguments and perspectives that cause so much struggle in the churches today (1997) are not new, but in fact very old, do we begin to appreciate history. Liberalism is not a modern disease, but an ancient disease in modern disguise. All of its arguments have been addressed and refuted before—much more eloquently than the meager attempts in the modern age. Ignorance of history is one of Satan's most effective weapons.

While one faction of church historians do indeed argue in favor of man-made traditions (Roman Catholics), others emphasize historical study to keep the church from repeating its mistakes (Reformed and Evangelical churches). Satan keeps bringing the same old, tired arguments to the table, but camouflages them with new jargon.

At about the same time the Cambridge Platform (1646) was developed in Massachusetts, a group of Congregationalists met in England with similar concerns. Meeting in the Savoy Castle, they addressed the same concerns by adopting the Westminster Confession, except sections 30 and 31, which they changed to reflect their commitment to Congregational polity. They wrote the famous Savoy Declaration. The Savoy Declaration has been a distinction of the Conservative Congregational Christian Conference (CCCC).

Some of the changes the Savoy Declaration made to the Westminster Confession declare that "there are no officers over the whole body, and that officers in one church do not have the indiscriminate right to exercise their office in other churches" (p. vi). Congregationalists do not believe that Scripture mandates regional bishops. "Pastors may not intrude upon other churches to preach, exercise discipline, or administer sacraments unless so invited; elders or deacons who transfer to another congregation serve as elders or deacons in their new congregation only if duly elected to that office by their new church" (p. vi).

Congregationalists were not opposed to cooperation with other churches, nor were they opposed to synods (regional meetings). Rather, "Congregationalists held that synods were not necessary to the existence of the church but were often helpful due to sin in the church" (p. viii).

Some of the differences between the Presbyterians and Congregationalists are summarized below. Note that the Cambridge Platform and the Savoy Declaration are in agreement in the matters under discussion.

1. The Westminster Confession declared that synods have the right "ministerially to determine controversies of faith and cases of conscience." The Cambridge Platform defined their power more narrowly as to "debate and determine" such cases. The difference is in the authority of synodical decisions.

2. The Westminster Confession declared that synods may "set down rules and directions for the better ordering of the public worship of God, and the government of His Church." The Cambridge Platform limited this right to "clear from the Word holy directions for the holy worship of God and good government of the church," precisely specifying that all such directions must be taken from the Word of God.

3. Rather than "authoritatively determining" cases involving church discipline, a Congregational synod is at most "to give direction for the reformation thereof" and is not permitted "to exercise church censures in way of discipline, nor any other act of church authority or jurisdiction, beyond actions of the Jerusalem Synod (Acts 15)." In Congregationalism, synods don't *decide*, they *recommend*, only local churches can exercise discipline.

4. The Cambridge Platform went further in its language that "the principle ground" of obeying the decisions of a synod is their agreement with the Word of God, "without which they bind not at all."

Many Presbyterians mistakenly believe that Congregationalists don't believe in eldership. They will be surprised to read the chapter in the Cambridge Platform, "Of Ruling Elders and Deacons"—particularly when they find "a description of ruling elders which is substantially the same as that in their own local (Presbyterian) churches." Those who think Congregationalists hate synods and any other type of inter church cooperation or mutual discipline will find Chapter Sixteen, "Of Synods," to be equally jarring. Chapter Fifteen, applying Matthew 18 to inter church discipline, specifying that churches have the right to call a special synod to make a decision about the orthodoxy of a church, and specifying that 'particular churches approving and accepting of the judgment of the Synod, are to declare the sentence of non-communion respectively concerning them,' will be especially interesting to those who believe that Congregationalism allows churches to believe anything they want and is neither capable of nor interested in church discipline" (p. ix-x). So where did all the misunderstandings of Congregationalism come from?

In a word—*liberalism*. The merger mentality of the twentieth century has mixed together a variety of types of churches under the umbrella of Congregationalism. Congregationalism has always required a regenerate balance of power in the church to function properly. That balance is both its strength and its weakness—strong when regenerate and balanced, weak when not. Its strength is its fidelity to Scripture. Yet, Congregationalism has proven to be weak in its ability to resist the historical momentum of regional powers and liberal perspectives of developing denominationalism.

Consequently, the confusion of Congregationalism is historical. For instance,

> "from the earliest days of Congregationalism, there have been
> two views of the authority of elders in the local church. One
> view, commonly known as Barrowism, held that rule was placed
> by Christ in the elders. A second view, commonly known as
> Brownism, taught that the members themselves exercised pri-
> mary church rule."

At issue was not final authority, but the governance of the local church. Did the Elders rule with congregational approval? Or did the congregation govern itself by popular vote? What is the role of leadership in the church? What is the proper relationship between the governors (officers, elders, deacons) and the governed (other members)?

> "For the first 150 years of Congregationalism, most Congrega-
> tionalists defined their polity as the view that Christ placed ruling
> authority, not in a Pope (Roman Catholicism), not in the bishops
> (Episcopalianism), not in a presbytery (Presbyterianism), not in
> civil government (Erastianism), but in the elders of the local
> church" (p. x).

The difference between Congregationalism and Presbyterianism of that time pertained primarily to the authority of the Presbytery.

The issue of church government comes to a head when elders abuse their authority. What recourse does Congregationalism provide in such a case? Catholics can appeal to the Pope, Episcopalians to the bishops, Presbyterians to the presbytery, but Congregationalist can appeal only to the local congregation.

> "The system adopted by the Cambridge Platform prescribed that
> in ordinary situations no church act could be completed without
> the consent of both the congregation and the elders."

This provided a veto of sorts for both the elders and the congregation.

In actual practice, consent was given to the elders by the silence of the congregation. Most of the time the congregation acted only to ratify or challenge the decisions of the elders. Recommendations and suggestions could be made to the elders at congregational meetings, but usually the congregation waited for the elders to come to them with specific proposals for them to ratify. This protected the church from the enthusiasm of quick or rash actions.

Over time Congregationalists developed a high view of ruling elders. In fact, they set qualifications so high that it was difficult to find any applicants. Many churches ended up with only one ruling elder, some had none. As the number of elders diminished in Congregational churches, the importance of their function in the life of the church also dissipated. This unfortunate turn of circumstances provided a kind of *fall* from the strength of Congregationalism as it was originally conceived.

Some Congregationalists then began to argue for not having elders at all. Having eliminated elder rule altogether, other Congregational churches developed a Deacon/Trustee form of government. Before long, the boards of deacons began to take on many of the former spiritual roles of the elders.

> "The boards of trustees—originally a civil office to control the
> meeting house and handle financial administration—increasingly
> assumed the functions of a diaconate. ... But the prominent Puri-
> tan pastor, Cotton Mather, warned that the elimination of ruling
> elders would result in either the evil of rule by democratic con-
> gregational meetings or the evil rule by dictatorial pastors" (p. xi).

By the late 1700s Mather's prediction bore fruit. In many Baptist and Congregational churches, ruling elders almost entirely died out. In many cases, still today it can be observed that many Baptist (fundamentalist or independent) churches have dictatorial powers delegated to the pastors, and many Congregational churches are ruled by the whims of democratic all-church meetings.

Contrary to popular opinion, historic Congregationalism did not encourage or support democratic governance of the church. Rather, historic Congregationalism supported elder rule with congregational veto, a balance of power between the rulers and the ruled.

The 1801 Plan of Union, an agreement between Congregational and Presbyterian churches to do joint missions in the Old Northwest Territory of the Great Lakes, again brought Congregationalists and Presbyterians together into what some called "Presbygational" church polity. While these churches were generally more tolerant about the inner workings of local church government, they reintroduced elder rule into Congregationalism—which, in turn, set an anti-elder faction into motion.

> "The Congregational historians Henry Martyn Dexter and Williston Walker conducted something of an anti-elder campaign in periodicals and church history books, arguing that the Cambridge Platform had erred in its view of elders and that the turn to pure democracy was an improvement" (p. xii).

That "improvement" encouraged and strengthened modern liberalism that is dominant today among Congregational churches (and others).

In the years following 1865 (the end of the Civil War), a series of mergers with a number of denominations brought churches of widely differing backgrounds into Congregationalism. The result being that "among modern conservative Congregational churches, it can accurately be said that 'Congregationalism,' as a term, is not used to describe a form of local church government; it is used to describe a method of inter church relations" (p. xii).

Today congregationally governed churches include all churches that have an independent polity, churches that do not answer to a higher ecclesiastical authority. But not all independent churches are Congregational churches. Rather, Congregational churches today, while maintaining a fierce independence, cooperate with other like-minded churches for mission, education, and advice. The key factor is that their cooperation is of a non-binding type.

Congregational churches seek fellowship with other churches, but shun the lordship of one church or one body over another. Rather, Congregationalists believe that all born again Christians should be equally guided by the presence and power of the Holy Spirit. However, for the sake of church government, more mature Christians are elected to rule, yet their decisions are subject to ratification or cancellation by the ruled.

The key to making Congregational churches function correctly (as God intends His churches to function) requires that each church member be a born again, believing, and Spirit-guided Christian. Where members fall short of this high calling, Congregational churches fail to function according to the biblical model. Confusion, dissension, and fruitlessness often result.

Successful Congregational churches (unified in truth and Spirit) maintain a high view of Scripture (God's Word is infallible and sufficient), a high view of worship (not high liturgy, but worship in the power and presence of the Holy Spirit), a high view of the church (active participation in the life of the church), and a high view of calling to personal discipleship.

THE HALFWAY COVENANT
Half-Asked Questions, Half Assessed Answers

Classical Congregationalism had barely been hatched when its demise began. Expectations for church membership had always been strict among Congregational churches, in keeping with Christ's demands upon the faithful. The high-water mark had been set by the Cambridge Declaration (1649), which stated:

> The doors of Christ's churches on earth do not stand so wide open that all sorts of people, good or bad, may freely enter as they desire. Those who are admitted to church membership must first be examined and tested as to whether they are ready to be received into church fellowship or not. ... These things are required of all church members: repentance from sin and faith in Jesus Christ. Therefore repentance and faith are the things about which individuals must be examined before they are granted membership in a church, and they must profess and demonstrate these in such a way as to satisfy rational charity that they are genuinely present.
> —from *The Cambridge Platform*, rev. ed. by Peter Murdy, 1998, 10:2.

The Cambridge Platform had been written to address issues of church polity and membership. At the time, the Congregational churches in America had a near monopoly on religious expression. That monopoly was short-lived but real. The Synod actually took place in the Massachusetts legislature. The Cambridge Platform came out of the high point of Congregationalism in America. However, as we will see, the Congregational churches were sabotaged by their apparent success.

All church members had to testify to their own regeneration and manifest evidence of the same in their lives because the church was understood to be a regenerate community on earth. The concern was to maintain the purity of the church in this regard. Yet, with this strictness also came a generous mercy that was expressed in the following statement from the Cambridge Platform:

> The weakest measure of faith is to be accepted in those who desire to be admitted into the church, because weak Christians, if sincere, have the essence of the faith, repentance, and holiness which are required in church members. Moreover, these weak Christians have most need of the church's ordinances for the con-

firmation of their faith and their growth in grace.
—Cambridge Platform, 10:3.

Christian faith is not a matter of mere boldness, but of genuine sincerity. Not all Christians are bold in the faith, but all must sincerely profess the faith.

However, within a generation of the writing of the Cambridge Platform came the publication of the Halfway Covenant (1662). The Halfway Covenant attempted to reduce the qualifications for baptism and membership in the church, and represents a significant downgrading of the purity of regenerate Congregationalism. The Halfway Covenant was adopted in order to allow certain people to retain a limited measure of membership privileges without meeting the full measure of personal qualifications. In short, the church became a respecter of persons (see James 2:9).

The problem arose when parents who had themselves been baptized into the church, but who had never been able to confirm their own baptism with a testimony of personal regeneration, brought their children for baptism. Prior to this time infant baptism had been extended only to the children of confessing and regenerate members because only the regenerate would (or could) raise their children in the true wisdom and admonition of the Lord. But now apparently unregenerate parents wanted their children to be baptized.

No doubt there was some peer pressure that influenced the situation. Both the Roman Catholic Church and the Church of England baptized the children of nominal Christians. Some nominal Christians then sought the same from the Congregational churches. They were unaware of the importance that regenerate purity played in the life of Congregational churches.

This very issue then became a major factor in the rejection of infant baptism by many Christians. It brought the issue of infant baptism to the fore among mainline churches. The problem of church purity and infant baptism is admittedly knotty and does not avail itself of any simple solutions. There are, however, two solutions that are obvious and easy, but must be rejected from the outset. One easy solution is to baptize all who request it as the Church of England does. The other is condemn infant baptism as erroneous. While both of these solutions provide immediate relief from the tension and complexity of the problem, neither is in accordance with Scripture. Both tend to eliminate the baby with the bath water.

The Halfway Covenant was an earnest attempt to solve this knotty problem with a compromise. Unfortunately the compromise was flawed as well. The Halfway Covenant follows:

> I do heartily take and avouch this one God who is made known to us in the Scripture by the name of God the Father, and God the Son even Jesus Christ, and God the Holy Ghost to be my God, according to the tenor of the Covenant of Grace; Wherein he hath promised to be a God to the Faithful and their seed after them in their Generations, and taketh them to be his People, and therefore unfeignedly repenting of all my sins, I do give up myself wholly unto this God to believe in, love, serve and Obey Him sincerely and faithfully according to this written word, against all the temptations of the Devil, the World, and my own flesh and this unto death. I do also consent to be a Member of this particular Church, promising to continue steadfastly in fellowship with it, in the public Worship of God, to submit to the Order, Discipline and Government of Christ in it, and to the Ministerial teaching, guidance and oversight of the Elders of it, and to the brotherly watch of Fellow Members: and all this according to God's Word, and by the grace of our Lord Jesus Christ enabling me thereunto. Amen.   —Halfway Covenant, 1665

Upon first reading we modern Christians may have some difficulty even seeing the problem. In many respects the Halfway Covenant provides a stronger statement than a great many contemporary churches demand. We might be tempted to envy the faithfulness of those who, failing to meet the full measure, settled for a half measure.

In addition to the statement itself, the Halfway Covenant was subscribed to without a formal declaration of personal regeneration. It is a statement of faith that did not issue from membership candidates, but which was imposed upon them (contrary to Congregational practice!). A personal declaration was to be made during the membership examination process, but when it was not forthcoming, the Halfway Covenant was imposed. The statement is not faulty for what it contains, but for what it replaces—a confession of personal regeneration.

The Halfway measures were as much about the membership process as about the statement of faith. Manfred Kohl said that

> the formal recognition as church members of those who were not consciously regenerated and not under full covenant obligation tended to relax the strict Puritan standard and to weaken the appeal of the churches to the popular imagination. Slowly but

surely a process of secularization began to take place, and before
the end of the first century of American Congregationalism a democratization of its churches was evident in the obliteration of
the distinction between the 'saints of the visible congregation'
and members of the parish at large, both groups now having a
voice in church government. —*Congregationalism In America*,
Manfred Kohl, Congregational Press, 1977, p. 21

Williston Walker said of the Halfway Covenant:

So too "owning the covenant" was, in the view of the originators
of the Halfway Covenant practice, a solemn personal acceptance,
as far as it lay in a man's power unaided by divine grace, of his
place in the visible Kingdom of God, and a formal declaration of
his intention to do his best to lead a Christian life by association
in worship and discipline with the recognized people of God.
—*The Creeds and Platforms of Congregationalism*, Williston
Walker, 1977, p. 278

In other words, the Halfway Covenant introduced a salvation that
could be accomplished by human effort or commitment! It represented a
major departure from the Reformed doctrine of the church as developed
in Congregationalism. Remember, it had been the Congregationalists
who endeavored to apply nothing but pure biblical standards to every
area of church polity and life. Indeed, Congregationalism is a high calling! But it is the biblical calling established for all Christians.

The process of the secularization of American Christianity is further
illustrated in Roger Finke and Rodney Stark's book, *The Churching of
America, 1776-1990* (Rutgers University Press, 1977). Their research
shows that in 1776, nearly a century after the Cambridge Declaration,
Congregationalists represented 20.4 percent of the total number of national religious adherents. While that number was down considerably
from the previous century, the decline in Congregationalism gained
momentum during the following century. By 1850 Congregationalists
represented only 4.0 percent of the total.

While classical Congregationalism was never intended to make
church government into a system of democratic rule, that's exactly what
happened. The confusion between what I have called classic Congregationalism and democratic Congregationalism continues today. It is an issue that requires a discernment that may only be available to the regenerate. The distinguishing factor is that pure Congregationalism requires
the decisions and votes of regenerate members yielded to Christ, where

democratic or popular Congregationalism simply requires the decision and votes of members, regenerate or not, spiritually discerning or not. It becomes an issue because the qualifications for membership have deteriorated. Democratic Congregationalism has resulted in a decision making process that is fraught with political struggle, and worldly maneuvering.

Similar trends existed in all of the older mainline denominations. Episcopalians slid from 15.7 percent to 3.5 percent during the same period. Presbyterians went from 19.0 percent to 11.6 percent. These three denominations alone represented 55.1 percent of religious adherents in 1776, but only 19.1 percent in 1850. Yet interestingly, during the same period the Methodists grew from 2.5 percent to 34.2 percent!

These figures clearly represent a trend. But what accounts for it? If we look at the situation from a theological perspective the earmarks of the popular, secular democratization of the churches stands out clearly. The theology of the Congregationalists, Episcopalians, Presbyterians (and many Baptists as well) was Reformed Calvinism. These denominations differed from one another in some details and practices, but agreed in the basic contours of the Christian faith.

The Methodists, however, were Arminian. John Wesley edited a periodical titled *The Arminian Magazine* for many years. Clearly, the theological trend was from Calvinism to Arminianism, from a church membership (and by implication a theology of salvation) that was wrought by God alone, toward a membership (and by implication a salvation) that resulted from works, where human commitment became the ground of both salvation and church membership. Arminianism contributed to secularization because it shifted the burden of salvation from God to man.

Williston Walker sums it up well:

> Indeed, there is a reason to believe that in many places admission to the covenant came to be looked upon much as signing a temperance pledge has been frequently regarded in our day,—as a means by which large bodies of young people might be induced to start out in the right path in life.   —Walker, p. 279.

Reforming Synod of 1679-80

The Reforming Synod of 1679-80 attempted to address the spiritual downgrade that occurred in the churches following the Half-Way Covenant debacle. Pastors and people began to believe that they were undergoing divine judgment as a result of the increasing faithlessness in the churches.

> "The sense of alarm regarding the state of New England engendered by the decline of visible piety, was greatly intensified by a series of disastrous events which seemed to the men of that age divine judgments" (Walker, 411).

Indian wars broke out anew, fires burned many homes, an increase in shipwrecks was experienced which in turn reduced supplies, an epidemic of small-pox ravished the pilgrims, the Stuart government increased its acts of aggression against the colonies, which included a concerted effort to bring Episcopacy to the Puritan commonwealths. These disasters and others convinced the clergy that America was under God's judgment.

Increase Mather led the charge to call "a synod as the best means for securing the spiritual improvement of New England" (Walker, 413). The clergy were convinced that these things were the expression of God's judgment against New England. As they looked to the Reformation as a model for spiritual renewal they came to believe that they were required to repent publicly, to both confess wrongs committed and to renew their covenant with God. Furthermore, they believed that such renewal would not be effective until

> "Magistracy, Ministry, Churches and people rise up together, in their proper places and order, unto the work" (Walker, 415).

A petition was drawn up and submitted to the Massachusetts General Court, May 28, 1679. The petition made no effort to change the Cambridge Platform or the Savoy Declaration, yet Walker suggests that the legislature itself may have been critical of the implied failure of those documents to bring about their intended results. The petition itself sought to inquire into the nature of the evils that had provoked God's judgment so that necessary reforms could be made. At this point in history, it should be noted, the Congregational churches stood in the same situation as the Church of England had, in that Congregational churches were the only established churches recognized by the Massachusetts government.

The Savoy Declaration was the uncontested statement of doctrinal conformity, and the Cambridge Platform served as the statement of church polity.

> "The New England churches still stood, as a body, with uncriti-
> cising loyalty on the basis of the Puritan theology of England as it
> had been in the first half of the seventeenth century" (Walker,
> 421).

The Massachusetts court heartily sympathized with the prevailing doctrine and thought present at the Reforming Synod, and approved all that was said and done. However, in the spirit of Congregationalism

> "the Court wisely refrained from commanding its use by the
> churches" (Walker, 422).

Consequently, the churches were free to renew or not renew their covenant. The fact that Walker would consider this action wise reveals either his lack of understanding or lack of commitment to classic, Reformed doctrine. For without court imposed action, lethargic churches were allowed to remain lethargic. Churches that were drifting into Unitarianism and Arminianism were allowed to ignore the orthodox statements of doctrine and policy that were the heritage of the Reformation, in the spirit of Congregationalism! These churches were often involved legal trusts that committed them to their historic theological position.

By refusing to hold churches to their legally binding established trusts, this action (or lack of action) brought many churches to openly oppose Reformation theology. In addition, they opposed Unitarian and Arminian theology as well. No clear theology could be maintained by the majority where opposing theologies were allowed coexistence. It is not possible to be both Trinitarian and Unitarian, nor is it possible to believe in the sovereignty of God and the sovereignty of man at the same time. Theological confusion is the natural result of such a position (or non-position).

The Reforming Synod of 1679-80 had a political understanding that is much divorced from our contemporary understanding. The Massachusetts reformers stated that they did not read in the Scriptures or in history that any significant religious reformation had ever taken place "except the Magistrate did help forward the work" (Walker, 426). In other words, they believed that it was necessary to have the support of those in political power, or at least to have a significant political element of such support.

Thus, genuine reformation success in our own day must buck this biblical and historical trend of governmental support, or the political tide in our own day will continue its downward slide. The Synod drew up several questions that their reforming efforts would seek to answer. To help us understand that the battles we fight today are not new but ancient, we will briefly examine these questions.

> "What are the Evils that have provoked the Lord to bring his Judgments on New-England?" (Walker, 426).

There is no doubt that they believed that the circumstances they suffered were the result of God's judgment. The answers to this question speak for themselves.

> "There is a great and visible decay of the power of Godliness amongst many Professors in these Churches" (Walker, 427).

In particular they cited "secret worship," what we call private, personal prayer and devotion. Secondly,

> "The Pride that doth abound in New-England testifies against us" (i.e., against the churches, Walker, 427).

That pride manifested as "a refusing to be subject to Order according to divine appointment" (ibid.). The Scripture reference cited in support here was Numbers 16:3, alluding to Korah's rebellion against the authority of Moses. The implication points to the diminishing authority and respect of clergy, another phenomena present today. In addition, the pride that they saw manifested as "contention," haughty dress, and a lack of pursuing Christianity seriously (ibid.).

Other causes of God's judgment were that "church fellowship and other divine Institutions (were) greatly neglected," a lack of discipline "extended toward the Children of the Covenant," and improper worship described as "humane inventions" and "Will-worship" (Walker, 428). The list reads as if it were our own modern litany of concerns—irreverent behavior during worship, Sabbath breaking, a lack of family prayer and Scripture reading, etc. What was the source of these difficulties?

> "Most of the Evils that abound amongst us, proceed from defects as to Family Government" (Walker, 429).

The burden of responsibility was placed upon the parents for failing to pass on the faith to their children, and in particular upon fathers who are biblically charged with that responsibility. In some respects, the reformers said that the sins of the fathers were being visited upon the children. What sins? "Intemperance"—alcoholic consumption, "company keeping with light and vain persons," gambling, idleness, promise breaking, "inordinate affection to the world" making religion subservient to worldly interests, and a general unwillingness to engage in genuine, personal, religious reform.

Next the reformers asked what could be done "so these Evils may be Reformed" (Walker, 433). The first answer given insisted that those who were concerned with reform should set an example for others regarding the previously mentioned sins. Fathers, mothers, pastors, and reformation leaders must be above reproach in their own personal faithfulness.

Secondly, they believed that churches and individuals needed to re-subscribe or renew their commitment,

> "to declare our adherence unto the Faith and order of the Gospel, according to what is from the Scripture expressed in the Platform of Discipline" (Walker, 433).

The Platform of Discipline was an allusion to The Cambridge Platform. They believed that they should hold fast to the theology of the Protestant Reformation, and in particular to the Savoy Declaration.

Thirdly, the Reformers took aim at the laxity that had infected the local church membership process. People that sought to join a church should

> "be not admitted unto Communion in the Lord's Supper without making a personal and publick profession of their Faith and Repentance" (Walker, 433).

Note the several elements of the process. Confession must be both personal and public. By "personal" they meant that each prospective member must have personal understanding of Reformed doctrine (biblical teaching). In addition, each prospective member must pledge himself to it publicly. However, they were not simply interested in an abstract knowledge of doctrine, for they also insisted that there be public profession of faith (doctrine) and of repentance (or what we sometimes call spiritual experience). Again, they were not speaking of religious experience generally, but specifically of the experience of the prospective member regarding his own repentance of sin. This position regarding church membership provided a simple reiteration of The Cambridge Platform, Chapter Twelve, "Admission of Members into the Church."

Fourthly, in order for reformation to be effective

> "it is necessary that the Discipline of Christ in the power of it
> should be upheld in the Churches" (Walker, 433).

By "discipline" they meant not only excommunication and other censures of members, but the self-imposed exercise of Christian behavior based upon a classic, Reformed understanding of theology.

> "It is a known and true observation, that remissness in the exer-
> cise of Discipline, was attended with corruption of manners
> (morals), and that did provoke the Lord to give men up to strong
> delusions in matters of Faith" (Walker, 433).

To be deluded in matters of faith required a false understanding of theology, an understanding that opposed the basic tenets of the Savoy Declaration, that being their standard.

Next, they required that every local church have a

> "full supply of officers, according to Christ's Institution. The Lord
> Christ would not have instituted Pastors, Teachers, Ruling Elders
> (nor the Apostles have ordained Elders in every Church (Acts
> 2:14, 23; Titus 1:5) if he had not seen there was need of them for
> the good of his People; and therefore for men to think they can
> do well enough without them, is both to break the second Com-
> mandment, and to reflect upon the wisdom of Christ, as if he
> did appoint unnecessary Officers in his Church" (Walker, 434).

The reformers lamented the loss of teaching elders in the churches, such persons being responsible for the teaching of Reformed theology and doctrine which served as the foundation of healthy church life. Today we further lament the loss of elders in many Congregational churches as well. Even those churches that still maintain elders have seriously diminished the qualifications, duties, and expectations for office.

The Massachusetts reformers further recommended that no laws be passed by the Commonwealth "but that there is Scriptural warrant for" (Walker, 435). For them, all laws—church or state—must have biblical warrant. Remember that Massachusetts was a biblically covenanted community at that time. The role that education played in the propagation of the faith was also addressed. They insisted that all schools be founded upon and teach biblical principles in order to maintain and support their common covenant.

> "The interest of Religion and good Literature have been wont to rise and fall together" (Walker, 435).

How far we have departed from these reforming efforts! Remember also that modern government is no longer biblically covenanted.

In spite of all the reforming work proposed they were well aware that there could be no success in their efforts unless the Lord blessed them. Without God Himself leading and guiding their every step, they were bound to fail in their own efforts to bring reform to the Colonies. Thus they prayed and plead that God "would be pleased to rain down righteousness" upon them, in "both ordinary and extraordinary manner(s)" (Walker, 435). The Confession of 1680, produced in Massachusetts, was "so nearly identical with the doctrinal part of that adopted at the Savoy Synod in 1658" (Walker, 439) that Walker omitted printing it. Rather, he simply referred readers to the Savoy Declaration. The differences were thought to have been merely matters of organization and administration, not doctrine. What has not been clearly understood is the relationship between doctrine and organization, or philosophy and administration. Indeed, differences in administrative and organizational structures are rooted in doctrine or philosophy.

The next significant effort to renew the churches came about as the result of the doctrinal shift occurring throughout New England, a shift from the Calvinism of the Reformers to both an Arminian and Universal (or Unitarian) understanding of Scripture growing in popularity among many. While both Arminian and Unitarian theologians existed—and indeed were in the process of capturing crucial positions in higher education and seminaries, both positions represented a common or uneducated and unregenerate revolt against the biblical principles of the Reformation. But these insights get ahead of the story.

HEADS OF AGREEMENT

The Heads of Agreement resulted from the effort to unify the Congregational and Presbyterian churches in the midst of their decline. They believed that the two denominations agreed doctrinally, but differed organizationally.

> "Their great point of divergence was in regard to the existence or non-existence of a national church" (Walker, 441).

Following the Act of Uniformity of 1662 some two thousand Puritan pastors were driven out of their churches in England. The Act of course was issued by England's Parliament, yet we must not forget that at that time New England was an English Colony. That Act forbade the organization of Presbyterianism, which had presented itself as an alternative to the Episcopacy of the Church of England. Congregationalism or Independency had always been an unrecognized and illegal form of church organization in England, though at times it was more or less tolerated. However, with the Act of 1662 it became

> "evident that, hunted as they were, the most strenuous Presbyterians were in a position practically similar to that of Congregationalists" (Walker, 443).

Because Puritan pastors were on the run, the movement to unite the two denominations "was purely ministerial, and one in which the churches, as distinguished from their pastors, had no share" (Walker, p. 444). Thus the effort to establish independent Congregational churches was not a movement of the laity to create democratically governed churches, but was a movement by the clergy to establish biblically governed churches against the encroachment of the state into church affairs.

In the Presbyterian system the hierarchical government of the church extended beyond the local church and was anchored in the regional Presbytery. Whereas in the Congregational system the government of the church did not extend beyond the local church. Any attempted union of these two systems needed to downplay the significance of this important difference. Those who were critical of the unification effort charged the Heads of Agreement with "great Ambiguity" (Walker, p. 446). The Heads were obscure at important points because they were open to more than one interpretation. Union would require a certain amount of ambiguity because the differences involved doctrinal and philosophical positions that could not be (and have never been) reconciled.

The resulting Heads of Agreement were generally supported by Congregationalists because an ambiguity of interpretation was possible that allowed a kind of non-binding authority to be given to Presbyteries or regional associations of churches. The Presbyterians, however, required more. Thus, they were deprived of the kind of effective authority upon which their system depended. Walker confirms that "the leading features of the Heads of Agreement are thus essentially Congregational" (Walker, p. 448). This fact deserves more careful consideration among many current independent churches, in that it establishes a loose form of cooperation and connectedness among churches.

Curiously, a disagreement ensued between Congregationalists and Presbyterians, not about church authority or structure, but about the Reformed doctrine of imputation and redemption. This disagreement, a central tenet of Scripture, dealt with the procedure and effect of the application of Christ's righteousness to the salvation of the sinner. The disagreement appeared to divide the clergy on other than denominational lines.

> "The Congregationalists seem to have been no more pleased with the supposed Antinomianism of Dr. Crisp than the Presbyterians; but Dr. Williams was one of the Presbyterians who had seemed to them most filled, as the historian of the quarrel puts it, with 'a *prejudiced Spirit* against the Government of the Congregational Churches, and the Order wherein they walk'" (Walker, p. 451, emphasis original).

Thus, the English efforts toward union were aborted earlier than the American efforts.

The Heads of Agreement, written in London, reiterated the importance of doctrine and experience regarding church membership, insisting

> "that none shall be admitted as Members, in order to Communion in all the special Ordinances of the Gospel, but such persons as are knowing and sound in the fundamental Doctrines of the Christian Religion, without Scandal in their lives; and to a Judgment regarded by the Word of God, are persons of visible Godliness and Honesty; credibly professing cordial subjection to Jesus Christ" (Walker, p. 457).

Church members must evidence knowledge and experience of what was considered to be classic Reformed doctrine, with apparent and obvious Godliness and personal integrity. To whom must these evidences be given? To the leaders—pastor, elders, deacons—and to the congregation. The Heads also insisted on duly qualified and ordained church officers. Balancing the administrative power of churches the Heads supported the Cambridge Platform division of power between the governors and the governed.

> "In the administration of Church Power, it belongs to the Pastors
> and other Elders of every particular Church (if such there be) to
> Rule and Govern; and to the Brotherhood to Consent, according
> to the Rule of Christ" (Walker, p. 458).

Two other points of interest can be mentioned. The Heads insisted that all who professed Christ "join themselves as fixed members of some particular church" (Walker, p. 458). Such fixed church members were not free to church hop or church shop, but "ought to continue steadfastly with the said Church" (ibid.). Any transferring or changing of churches required that the sending church issue a "recommendation" to the receiving church regarding the individuals involved. Some churches still do this today, but it is haphazard and sloppy in that individuals under censure from one church are often received into membership in another without consultation regarding the nature of the censure.

Finally, the Heads of Agreement, were in accord with Reformed doctrine, insisting not on the organizational or administrative concerns, but with the

> "Doctrinal part of the [Thirty-Nine] Articles of the Church of
> England, or the Confession, or Catechisms, Shorter or Larger,
> compiled by the Assembly at Westminster, or the Confession
> agreed on at the Savoy, to be agreeable to the said Rule" (Walker,
> p. 462).

SAYBROOK PLATFORM

The Saybrook Synod, meeting in Connecticut in 1708, produced the most important confessional document in New England. It amounted to a fifteen-point statement of ecclesiastical polity that reaffirmed the Savoy Declaration and the Heads of Agreement. The articles provided for regional "consociations" of churches with powers of oversight of the local congregations. It also created ministerial associations in each region, with powers to examine ministerial candidates on doctrine and morals. Thus, it marked a significant step toward Presbyterianism. But we must note that the congregational churches felt the need for additional help and power beyond the local church to keep churches from diverging in matters of doctrine. Consociations were intended to help stem the doctrinal drift experienced everywhere.

Walker suggests that the Halfway Covenant was the fruit of Arminian influence among the churches, and that Unitarianism was the fruit of the Halfway Covenant (Walker, p. 284). It is an interesting and insightful observation because the decline of Congregationalism appears to have been the result of doctrinal attacks by both Arminians and Unitarianists. However, the issues of concern were presented as church membership and administrative issues not doctrinal issues. Consequently, Walker (and to some extent Congregationalism itself) bypassed discussion of the doctrinal issues by framing the concerns as administrative issues regarding church membership.

For instance, the Halfway Covenant dealt with the baptism of infant children of people who were not church members or lapsed church members, and the Unitarian Controversy, in addition to issues regarding the Trinity and divinity of Christ, proclaimed that the atonement was universally efficacious and applied to all people. Both issues attacked and undermined the traditional doctrinal positions of "Unconditional Election" and "Limited or Particular Atonement." What is missing in Walker and other literature at the time is a discussion of these particular doctrinal issues and their relationship to the situation. Walker alludes to the doctrinal conflict, but says nothing of substance about it.

On February 5, 1799, the Hartford North Association issued a statement identifying the Saybrook Platform as "not Congregational, but contains the essentials of the church of Scotland, or Presbyterian Church in America, particularly as it gives decisive power to Ecclesiastical Councils; and a Consociation consisting of Ministers and Messengers or a lay representation from the churches (and) is possessed of substantially the same authority as a Presbytery" (Walker, p. 514). The identification of the Saybrook as Presbyterian appears to have resulted in the wholesale rejection of its doctrinal basis as well as its polity by Congregationalists.

The baby had been thrown out with the bath water. Thus, Walker goes on to say that "even before the adoption of this (Hartford North Association) declaration the Saybrook system had ceased to have the special sanction of the law. (Thus) the revision of the statutes which followed the Revolution, in 1784, silently repealed the legal authority of the Saybrook establishment by omitting all reference to it" (Walker, p. 514-15). The legal protection of Congregational polity appears to have resulted in the demise of its Reformed doctrine, while Arminianism and Unitarianism gained increasing momentum in traditional Congregational churches over the following decades.

The effort to shore up doctrinal concerns by establishing a system of strong ecclesiastical regional government that was a main feature of the Saybrook Platform "essentially modified the Congregationalism of America" (Walker, p. 516). The modification that followed Saybrook allowed Congregational churches increasing freedom to repudiate Reformed doctrine without objection as a matter of independent polity. The doctrinal unity of Congregationalism was dealt a mortal blow as churches became completely free to pick and choose to believe whatever doctrine they liked, without regard for the prevailing views of other Congregational churches or their own historic theology, and in the wake of fewer and fewer Reformed church leaders.

By the time this historical movement produced the Constitution of the National Council of Congregational Churches and the Oberlin Declaration (1871) the concern to maintain Reformed doctrine had been eclipsed by the concerns for church unity. Thus, said Walker, the National Council's

> "statement of faith, adopted at Oberlin (where Charles Finney
> served as President from 1851-66), are valuable as illustrating the
> catholicity of spirit which has accompanied this growth of de-
> nominational consciousness. In matters of doctrine the constitu-
> tion is more important for what it does not affirm than for that
> which it declares. Though nowhere expressly stated, the under-
> standing at Oberlin at its adoption, and the interpretation since
> usually put upon it, is that it holds out the olive branch of de-
> nominational fellowship to brethren of Arminian sympathies, and
> is but a further illustration of that desire not to limit Congrega-

tional brotherhood to those who hold exclusively to the system known as 'Calvinism.'"

Thus, in the Congregationalism of the National Council two theological systems, antithetical at every point, were brought into a kind of administrative unity. James Arminius opposed Calvinism at five points. Unlike Calvin he believed that people were not totally depraved; he believed that election to salvation was conditional upon the individual's reception of God's decree; he believed that Christ's atonement was universally effective and potentially applied to all people everywhere; he believed that people could resist God's call and lose their salvation; and he believed that people could not be sure of their own salvation until they actually arrived in heaven.

At each of these foundational points of biblical understanding Arminius took exception to Calvin's teaching. And now these two systems of interpretation and belief would become bed-fellows under the umbrella of Congregationalism in an effort to maintain denominational unity. However, the proposed unity could not possibly have been doctrinal unity or a unity engendered by a common understanding of Scripture, but could only have been a man-made administrative unity that valued denominationalism over biblical doctrine.

At the same time it appears that Walker either did not perceive this situation or chose to ignore it in his comprehensive history of Congregationalism. For he concludes his work with these words. "The Gospel (that the National Council) presents is essentially the same that the fathers set forth as the basis of their faith, but it holds that Gospel to be intended for all men and to be wide enough in its provisions of redemption for the needs of the whole human race" (Walker, p. 584). However, such a statement, such a belief, amounts to the wholesale repudiation of Reformed theology and historic Congregationalism.

REFLECTION

The reformation and renewal efforts that began with the Synod of 1679-80 identified the need for doctrinal renewal, but were unable to establish that renewal among the churches in any effective way. They knew that the inherited doctrines of the Protestant Reformation were being undermined and obviated. They identified the source of this disintegration to be an increase of sin and apathy on the part of succeeding generations. The children of those who had established the Puritan theocracy[2] in the wilderness were not as enthusiastic or committed to the vision as the founders had been. Their grandchildren were even less concerned.

The rise of Arminianism and Unitarianism occurring throughout New England over the same period also played a significant role. Both of these aberrant theologies had established themselves within the Congregational churches, and others. Factions and sects multiplied as churches struggled with theological disparities. The effort to allow these theological differences to coexist within Congregationalism—the perspective that Walker appears to have supported—surely effected the rise of Christian apathy. How do vying theologies produce apathy? People grow tired of arguing, tired of trying to bridge an unbridgeable gap. Efforts to harmonize these systems have not produced satisfactory results. The best that can be said is that this chapter of Congregationalism resulted in a lack of theological concern upon the part of most church members. Explain it however you please, but the result has been widespread apathy among Congregational churches, and many others others as well.

Unable to harmonize these vying systems, and unwilling to choose between them, church members have simply abandoned the effort to do either. The early part of the twentieth century produced the Social Gospel, in part no doubt because the waning energies and concerns of the church needed to be focused somewhere, and they could not endure the tensions of irresolvable theological conflict. Thus, all subsequent efforts toward unity have shied away from the major tenants of these theological systems because they could not be reconciled.

It would appear then that a more faithful effort toward reformation and renewal must take this history into account. Genuine reformation has always been a function of theology, not administration. If the Con-

---

2   This is not to be confused with an ecclesiocracy, which is leadership by church authorities. Theocracy is leadership by God.

gregational efforts erred anywhere, they erred by trying to create an administrative solution to a theological problem. They endeavored to hold together administratively what they could not hold together theologically.

Thus, contemporary efforts will no doubt be more fruitful as they endeavor to wade into these theological disparities and like Elijah of old bring God's people to the ancient issue of faltering between two opinions. "If the LORD is God, follow Him; but if Baal, follow him" (1 Kings 18:21). The Lord has always insisted that certain choices are required by those who would remain faithful to His Word.

May the Lord Himself show us the way. And may we more and more depend upon Him to do exactly that.

CHARLES FINNEY

Friend of Foe?

The most successful advocate of Arminianism in America was not Jacobus Arminius (1560-1609), but Charles Finney (1792-1875). Because *The Works of Arminius* (Baker Book House, reprinted 1996) are highly intellectual and academic—bordering on the arcane, few people have (or will) read them. Arminius, a young boy when Calvin died, was concerned about the division in the Church brought about by the Protestant Reformation. He proposed to mend the theological breach between the Roman Catholic Church and

Charles Finney

the Protestant Reformation by correcting several perceived errors in Calvin's theology. Positively stated, he attempted to reassert Catholic theology into Protestantism, *sans* the Pope. His purpose was to bring Protestants back to what he thought to be a true belief—a catholicity held previously by the Roman See. He thought Protestantism to be in error, and hoped to help correct it. However, he succeeded most in further fracturing an already fractured church.

Charles Finney began working in a law office in Adams, New York, and after a limited formal education was later admitted to the bar. He began to attend religious services conducted by a Presbyterian friend, George Gale, who then discipled Finney in Reformed Presbyterian doctrine. At first Finney bristled at Presbyterian dogma, but after studying the Bible himself he was converted in 1821. Turning from his work in law, he began to preach, and received Presbyterian ordination in 1824 without having attended seminary or having any formal theological training. His ordination, of course, required full assent to all the doctrines of Reformed theology, which he did not hold.

The Great Awakening of the 1740s had stimulated several variant styles of revival, among them was what became known as New Lightism. The driving forces of New Lightism were several New England Congregational preachers who supported the Great Awakening and its apparent emphasis upon an instantaneous or sudden conversion experience that included highly emotional and mystical elements. Many Congregationalists were moderates in this regard, and some people include Jonathan Edwards among these moderates.

Other of these New Lights became radical separatists and were vehemently critical of the established Reformed churches. They assumed that the Reformed Calvinist beliefs of the established churches had caused them to become highly ineffective, even dead to the Word of God. These same preachers were adamant about the absolute separation between church and state. The New Lights employed New Measures in their revivals, measures that sparked a great controversy among Congregationalists.[3]

From every indication it appears that Finney came in contact with the New Lights, and adopted much of their theology into his own. However, the theology of the New Lights was opposed to the theology of his Reformed Presbyterian ordination at every point. After struggling with various theological issues and with his Presbytery, Finney fled to Congregationalism. And it was as a Congregationalist that Finney accomplished his most influential work.

In 1835 Finney became professor of theology at Oberlin College, Ohio, at that time a new Congregational college. Associated with that school for the rest of his life, Finney served as its president from 1851-1866. There Finney taught and refined his theology.

Finney's theology is difficult to categorize because it does not fit the normative patterns of theology. It is organized and presented much more like a work in philosophy than theology, with a significant emphasis upon morality. Trained as a lawyer, Finney was a practical tactician whose work in the application of revival techniques is practically unrivaled, and widely praised.

However, from an evangelical perspective Charles Finney said some rather disturbing theological things. Without a doubt Finney's aim was to overturn the established doctrines of Reformed theology. His teaching and practice went against them at every point.

The preeminent doctrine upon which the Protestant Reformation stands or falls, said Luther, is the doctrine of justification by faith alone, sometimes called salvation by grace alone through faith alone in Christ alone. These Reformed "solas" (Latin meaning *alone*)— *Sola scriptura* "Scripture alone," *Sola fide* "faith alone," *Sola gratia* "grace alone," *Solo Christo* "Christ alone," *Soli Deo gloria* "to the glory of God alone"—became the rallying cry of the Reformation, and shaped the very heart of

---

3   See *Asahel Nettleton: Life and Labors*, by Bennet Tyler & Andrew Bonar, Banner of
      Truth, reprint 1996. Nettleton, another Congregational minister, was one of Finney's
      most adamant opponents.

Protestantism. As such, we will look at what Charles Finney said about the doctrine of justification.

To understand Finney's doctrine of justification we must understand the framework for moral government that he posited, not political government but theological government. He was concerned about how God was able to govern the world and at the same time preserve human morality. He understood morality to require human freedom. Without a free will, he posited, people cannot be moral. This idea, however, originates in moral philosophy, not in the Bible.

Finney learned from his studies in law that governors can issue pardons, but judges cannot. Judges, on the other hand, may acquit, but not pardon. The differences have to do with guilt and pardon. A governor's pardon acknowledges the guilt, but cancels the punishment even though the charge remains. Whereas the judge's acquittal alone eliminates the guilt because it nullifies the charge against the defendant. Thus, Finney's concept of justification involved a pardon but not an acquittal; it was not forensic—meaning: not in the domain of the law or of a judge.

Finney taught that God acts as a governor rather than a judge when He pardons sin. The theological difficulty with Finney's doctrine of justification is that both the guilt and the charge of sin remain, while the punishment alone is abated by God's forgiveness. Thus, forgiven sinners are understood to continue life on a kind of probation that has been granted for good behavior. This probation is understood as a function of God's grace. However, every new sin then requires a fresh justification (pardon), and places the Christian under the constant threat of condemnation for unforgiven or ongoing sin. Finney understood that God dangled that threat over the heads of sinners as a motivation for good behavior. Finney's concept of justification then requires ongoing and strict obedience to God in order to be effective.

However, this understanding of justification belongs to Roman Catholcism. If it is true, the whole of the Protestant Reformation has been for naught! Could it be that Finney's theology, which comes part and parcel with the practice of his revival techniques, has served to further undermine Protestantism itself? Exactly what did Finney say? He began one of his lectures on justification by telling us "what gospel justification is not."

Gospel justification is the justification of sinners; it is, therefore, naturally impossible, and a most palpable contradiction, to affirm that the justification of a sinner, or of one who has violated the law, is a forensic or judicial justification. ... sinners to be forensically pronounced just, is impossible and absurd.

> I find it important to distinguish between the ground and condi-
> tions of justification and to regard the atonement and work of
> Christ not as a ground, but only as a condition of gospel justifica-
> tion.[4]

Here Finney said that Christ did not secure salvation for anyone in particular, but only met a general condition for a potential salvation that would be offered to all, but which required sinners to meet certain conditions before it would take effect. That is, each sinner must secure his own salvation from his own resources, from his own decision, commitment, etc.

Finney said that "repentance is also a condition of our justification" (p. 366), which means that God's justification of sinners is conditioned upon their repentance, that it depends upon the right behavior of the sinner, which in turn means that sinners cannot be saved until they prove themselves worthy. He continues, "It is self-evident that, until the sinner breaks off from sins by repentance or turning to God, he cannot be justified in any sense" (p. 366).

However, this completely overturns the heart of Protestant theology. The Protestant Reformers said that it is the power of God alone that enables sinners to turn from their sin, and that power (will power not free will) is given as a gift of grace. The Reformers maintain that it is God's commitment to his people that guarantees salvation, not the commitment of individuals to God. God's commitment is strong and able, while man's is weak and unable.

Finney expands his thinking by saying that "faith in Christ is, in the same sense, another condition of justification" and even "that perseverance in obedience to the end of life is also a condition of justification" (p. 366). Where the Reformers said that people were saved by the faithfulness *of* Christ, Finney said that people were saved by their own faithfulness *in* Christ. Where the Reformers said that Christians could persevere in faithfulness because of Christ's strength, Finney said that their perseverance depended upon their own strength. The Reformers said that Christians are faithful because of their justification, Finney said that they are justified because of their faithfulness. Again, the difference is the

---

4   Finney, Charles. *Systematic Theology*, Expanded Edition, Bethany House Publishers, reprint 1994, p. 360.

classic distinction between the Protestant understanding of justification and the Roman Catholic understanding.

Finney believed that sinners must put an end to their sinfulness before they can be justified. "It certainly cannot be true, that God accepts and justifies the sinner in his sins," wrote Finney. He continued to argue "that present, full, and entire consecration of heart and life to God and His service, is an unalterable condition of present pardon of past sin, and of present acceptance with God" and "that the penitent soul remains justified no longer than this full-hearted consecration continues" (p. 368).

In addition, Finney taught that preachers should focus on the interior decision of sinners, but never mentioned that they should preach about the action of God in Christ at the cross. "A prime object with the preacher must be to make present obligation felt. ... Sinners ought to be made to feel that they have something to do .... Religion is something to do, not something to wait for .... A change of heart is the sinner's own act."[5]

It cannot be clearer that Finney believed that the justification of sinners is conditioned upon their own beliefs and actions, and that the maintenance of that justification is in their own hands. According to Finney salvation depends upon the mindset and actions of individuals. Salvation is understood by Finney to be a possibility whose actuality depends upon the individual, rather than a certainty that has been initiated and completely satisfied by Christ on the cross. Finney himself understood that the classical Reformed Protestant understanding of salvation was other than what he taught, that Reformed Protestant theology "is certainly another gospel from the one I am inculcating" (p. 369).

Taking specific aim against the Westminster Confession, to which he had sworn allegiance at his ordination—and therefore against the Savoy Declaration of the Congregational churches, Finney argued that justification "is not founded in Christ's literally suffering the exact penalty of the law for (sinners), and in this sense literally purchasing their justification and eternal salvation." Appealing to the natural understanding of man he suggests that justification cannot proceed "on the ground that Christ has fully and literally paid your debt. To represent the work and death of Christ as the ground of justification in this sense, is a snare and stumbling-block" (p. 373).

---

5   Finney, Charles. *Revivals of Religion*, Moody Press, 1962, as quoted in Reformation & Revival Journal, Vol. 6, No. 4, 1997, p. 123).

Pointing out the capstone of his argument he said, "Neither is the atonement, nor anything in the mediatorial work of Christ, the foundation of our justification" (p. 375). Again and again he takes up the Roman Catholic/Arminian argument against the biblical doctrine of justification by faith alone taught by the Reformers. Agreement with Finney regarding justification amounts to the nullification of the Protestant Reformation.

But, you might say, Finney offers so many useful and practical means for bringing about revival. Indeed, Finney's revival measures have proven to be very effective in bringing many people to commit themselves to Christ. However, where the basis of their commitment is grounded in Finney's understanding of justification—the heart of Finney's theology, it is not compatible with historic Protestantism. It is a commitment to a person's own ability to become and remain faithful to the demands of Christ. It is a noble sentiment, but a folly proven by Scripture itself.

The Pharisees and Sadducees, maintained a similar commitment to the Old Testament law, but their commitment to such personal holiness based upon obedience to God only served to harden their hearts against the gospel of Christ. They were unable to achieve or sustain the righteousness demanded by God, and their failure led to the destruction of the Temple, Jerusalem, and the whole of the Old Testament enterprise of personal righteousness through obedience and ceremonial sacrifice.

Nonetheless Finney's immediate success at bringing many people to revival services and into church membership grew and spread into many, many Congregational churches and others. Finney appealed to the immediate and measurable success in what we have come to know as "church growth techniques." But the growth that he brought into the Protestant churches was, at its heart, utterly opposed to historic Reformed Protestantism. Is it any wonder that over the years since Finney there has been increasing conflict, disarray, and dissent within and among modern Protestant churches?

C.I. SCOFIELD

Fruit of the Root

The name of C.I. Scofield is not usually associated with liberalism, yet Scofield's roots lie at the heart of the post 1865 Congregationalism where Charles Finney made his home. Finney's Congregationalism promoted a doctrine of polar opposites, as previously indicated.

The 1865 Statement of Faith of the Congregational churches, brought the two mutually exclusive theological systems of Calvin and Arminius into a kind of harmony, and did it by fiat. The purpose behind such a statement of faith was, no doubt the reconstruction of America, which had been torn asunder by the Civil War. While the hoped for purpose or end may have been honorable, the actual means severed theology from both reason and history.

C. I. Scofield

What did Scofield share with liberalism?

Oswald T. Allis put his finger on it more than half a century ago. Writing in the Evangelical Quarterly (January, 1936), he proposed that Dispensationalism shares the fundamental error that is made by the so-called "higher criticism." It is now obvious that the higher criticism movement placed itself and its proponents above Scripture in order to critique Scripture's structures and sources. That process has been very destructive of the "high view" of Scripture that is foundational to the historical, orthodox doctrines of the faith. Despite the apparent differences between Scofieldism and higher criticism they share a foundational tenet.

> "Higher Criticism divides Scripture up into documents which differ from or contradict one another. Dispensationalism divides the Bible up into dispensations which differ from or even contradict one another; and so radical is this difference as viewed by the extremist that the Christian of today who accepts the Dispensationalist view finds his Bible (the part directly intended for him) shrunk to the compass of the Imprisonment Epistles" (Allis, *Evangelical Quarterly*, Jan., 1936).

Both tear apart the unity of Scripture by cutting and pasting either Scripture itself (as does higher criticism) or biblical history (as does Dis-

pensationalism) to suit their theories. The methods of both undermine biblical unity, albeit different aspects of biblical unity. While higher criticism cuts the Bible into pieces and destroys its unity, so Dispensationalism cuts biblical history into pieces and destroys its unity. And interestingly enough, both share the same roots—theologically, historically, and denominationally. There are two concerns here: 1) dispensationalism as theology, and 2) Scofield, the man. Since the theology comes from the man, let's consider the man first.

Scofield The Man

Genealogical data has been gathered about the Scofield family from the records of various Congregational churches in New York State. Cyrus Ingreson Scofield was born in Michigan on August 19, 1843. His birth place is important because he was later awarded the Confederate Cross of Honor. His mother died the year he was born, probably from delivery complications. His father remarried shortly thereafter.

When the Civil War began, 1861, Cyrus, seventeen-years-old, was visiting his sister in Tennessee. Records show that he then enlisted in the 7th Regiment of the Tennessee Infantry on May 20, 1861. While it was irregular—even illegal according to regulations, it was not unusual for teenagers to join the Confederate army. He simply listed his age as twenty-one. Curiously, he never returned to his birth place in Michigan, though he traveled the world.

Suspicion being what it was during the Civil War, official word finally reached Company H of the 7th Tennessee in August, 1862, that an "alien" was in their midst. A man from Michigan had joined the Confederate army. An order was issued to release Private Scofield. However, the 7th Tennessee was about enter a significant engagement of the enemy at Antietam. When Scofield later indicated that the Cross of Honor was awarded for his service at Antietam, no one noticed that Southerners refer to it as the battle of Sharpsburg. If you know anything about Civil War buffs today, you will know that such an apparently minor point still makes a major difference.

It should also be noted that the Confederate Cross of Honor was not an award given by the Confederate government. Rather, it was given to Confederate war veterans by the United Daughters of the Confederacy beginning in 1900, thirty-eight years after the Sharpsburg/Antietam battle. Nor is there any evidence that the young Scofield was converted or effected by the revival that swept the Confederate army, in that he admitted that he was ignorant of things Christian at the time.

By September,1862, Scofield had been discharged from the Confederate army by his own request. Four years later, September 21, 1866, he married Leontine Cerre before a justice of the peace in St. Louis. A civil wedding was his only option because the Cerre family was Catholic, and he was not. We can only assume that the lack of a religious ceremony was not a problem for Cyrus. Their first child, Abigail Leontine Teresa Scofield, was born July 13, 1867, in St. Joseph, Missouri, across the state from St. Louis. Abigail was baptized in St., Joseph's Cathedral, St. Joseph, Missouri. Their next child, Marie Helene, was born October 4, 1869, in St. Louis and baptized the same month at St. Therese de Avilla Church in St. Louis. Following that baptism, the Scofields moved to Atchinson, Kansas.

Kansas Politics

Cyrus worked for John J. Ingalls, a Kansas lawyer and politician, prior to his admission to the Kansas bar. The only case that he is known for sure to have worked on was a large land grant case that involved some holdings of his wife's family, the Regis Loisel case. It involved thousands of acres of land which eventually became available for settlement. Plots could be purchased from Scofield in Atchinson.

Scofield's entry into politics occurred at approximately the same period of time as his work on the Regis Loisel case. The 1872 Kansas elections were particularly volatile. Charges of corruption against the Republican incumbent were voiced, and in the politicking that followed, Scofield nominated John J. Ingalls for Congress. Following a dramatic discovery and exposure of campaign bribery by the incumbent, Ingalls won, taking his seat in the 43rd Congress.

March 11, 1873, John J. Ingalls submitted a petition to President Grant recommending Scofield for the position of United States District Attorney for the District of Kansas. Acceptance of the appointment made Scofield, at twenty-nine, the youngest District Attorney in the country. At his oath of office, June 8, 1873, Scofield solemnly swore that he had

> "never voluntarily borne arms against the United States since I
> have been a citizen thereof, that I have voluntarily given no aid,
> countenance, counsel or encouragement to persons engaged in
> armed hostility thereto ...that I have not yielded a voluntary sup-

port to any pretended government authority, power of constitution, within the United States, hostile or inimical thereto...."

This oath of office is particularly troubling because some twenty-seven years later he received the Confederate Cross of Honor for service at Sharpsburg.

On December 14, 1873, the Daily Times of Leavenworth carried a story that stated that an affidavit existed in which Scofield had been paid a sum of money to keep a certain man from being brought to trial. Joseph Canfield said that "if that report could be substantiated, Scofield's description of the 'Loisel case' to the Dispensational constituency, through Luther Rees, was unprincipled."[6] The fact is that Scofield re-signed his position as District Attorney December 20, 1873, just six months after taking office.

Emeline Scofield Papin, Cyrus' sister, drew up her will November 7, 1877, bequeathing equal share of her substantial estate to her siblings, Cyrus, Laura, and Victorine. But she stipulated that if Cyrus and Leon-tine were not living together, the share for Cyrus must be shared equally with his wife. Emeline took care to address a situation that she thought might occur. That same year the St. Louis City Directory listed Cyrus I. Scofield as a practicing lawyer.

Interestingly, the Circuit Court of St. Louis had on its docket Case 0 44252, Jephtha H. Simpson vs. Cyrus I. Scofield, Emeline E. Papin, and C.F. Betts. It seems that Cyrus had used a $200 note, signed by Emeline, to pay a debt. When Mr. Simpson tried to cash the note, Eme-line refused to pay. Her response to the petition served on her by a deputy of the County Sheriff's Office stipulated that she never signed any such note. Cyrus could not be found.

Another endorsed promissory note for $900 made to the order of Emeline E. Papin (like a check made to Emeline and endorsed by her) made its way to courts on April 1878, as well, Case 46333. Similarly, Emeline denied ever signing it, and Cyrus could not be located. At a May 6 hearing the case was dismissed by the plaintiff. It is not known if restitution was made.

A similar situation of a note made with Emeline's endorsement is found in the Court Docket 45326, August 14, 1877. And again, Emeline denied ever signing such a note. An article in the November 7, 1879, is-sue of the Republican, a St. Louis newspaper, confirms that Scofield had

---

6   Canfield, Joseph. *The Incredible Scofield and His Book* (Ross House Books, Val-lencito, CA, 1988.

been arrested and charged with forgery, but that the case had been dropped.

Forward With Moody

Late in 1879 D.L. Moody was making final arrangements for a St. Louis evangelistic campaign, and the name of C.I. Scofield suddenly became known in a subgroup that was utterly remote from any he had ever known, as he later reported to have worked in that campaign. The usual story was that Scofield had finally been saved from the demon drink and was a changed man. Nothing is impossible with the Lord! Tom McPheeters is credited with presenting Christ to Scofield, who was reported to have accepted Christ in McPheeters' law office during this period. It also appears that Leontine and her children had remained in Atchinson. They were not with Cyrus in St. Louis during these years.

Scofield's early theological training came under the Rev. James H. Brookes, pastor of the Walnut Street Presbyterian Church, St. Louis. Brookes was a friend and student of John Nelson Darby, the Plymouth Brethren leader. "J.N. Darby is usually regarded as the founder of Dispensationalism."[7] Scofield's biographer, Charles Trumbull, stated that Scofield was ignorant of things Christian up to 1879, the year he assigned to his conversion.

In July, 1880, Scofield joined Pilgrim Congregational Church in St. Louis. About this same time, the St. Louis Association of the Congregational Churches issued him a license to preach. He immediately organized the Hyde Park Congregational Church and continued to serve it until 1882.

A story that was printed in both the Atchinson Patriot and later in the Daily Capital (August 27, 1881) reported that

> "the last personal knowledge that Kansans have had of this peer
> among scalawags, was when about four years ago, after a series of
> forgeries and confidence games he left the state and a destitute
> family and took refuge in Canada. For a time he kept under-
> cover, nothing being heard of him until within the past two years
> when he turned up in St. Louis, where he had a wealthy wid-
> owed sister living who has generally come to the front and
> squared up Cyrus' little follies and foibles by paying good round
> sums of money. Within the past year, however, Cyrus committed
> a series of St. Louis forgeries that could not be settled so easily,

---

7   *The New International Dictionary of the Christian Church*, Zondervan, 1978.

and the erratic young gentleman was compelled to linger in the St. Louis jail for a period of six months."

While this story may be part fabrication with the intent to slander, it suggests that there are some indiscrepancies in the life and story of C.I. Scofield. At the very least we know that, after several filings, a decree of divorcement was issued to Leontine Scofield on December 8, 1883, in Atchinson, Kansas, Case 2681. At this point, Scofield was four-years-old in his Christian life and had been ordained into the Christian ministry by Congregationalists, who apparently knew nothing of Leontine or Scofield's children.

A year prior to his divorce (1882) he received a call to First Congregational Church, Dallas, Texas. At first many Texas Southerners in the community viewed him as a Northerner. But when they learned of his involvement in the Confederate Army, he was widely accepted as a brother, though they couldn't understand why he would preach in a Yankee church. Nonetheless, an Ordination Council had been held for Scofield as part of the first meeting of the North Texas Congregational Association held at First Congregational Church in Dallas on October 17, 1883. The Dallas church grew quickly from 17 to 250 in just a few years.

On March 11, 1884, he married Hettie Van Wark, just three months after his divorce was official. While it is burdensome to read and comprehend the various dates given, it should be obvious of their importance because much of Scofield's paper trail does not square with his own stories about his life.

Noel Paul Scofield was born December 22, 1888 in Michigan. Emeline Papin died October 25, 1889, and as her will stipulated payments of one-sixth the estate were paid to Cyrus and Leontine, his divorced wife.

Higher Calling

Scofield broke into print in 1888 with a booklet titled, *Rightly Dividing the Word of Truth*, which presented his developing dispensational understanding. It was printed by Loizeaux Brothers of New York, a Plymouth Brethren printing company. He immediately began to teach and preach at various Bible conferences. "He was primarily concerned with the Prophetic Bible Conference which was to reshape a significant part of American Protestantism."[8] He was also a regular presenter at the Niagara Bible Conferences, where his theology was honed.

---

8   Canfield, p. 114.

In 1890 he began publishing a monthly magazine, *The Believer*, in order to 1) bear testimony to a "body of truth being neglected," 2) aid Bible study, and 3) correct the "nearly complete effacement of the line separating the Church from the world." He also began his Comprehensive Bible Correspondence Course in the same year. Scofield became President of the Board of Trustees of Lake Charles College, a Congregational school in Lake Charles, Louisiana. In addition, he was also head of the Southwestern School of the Bible in Dallas, forerunner of Dallas Theological Seminary. In 1886 he became the Superintendent of the American Home Missionary Society for Texas and Louisiana, a Congregational mission society. All of this extra work demanded much of Scofield's time, thus his church provided an annual five-month paid vacation to facilitate it.

Luther Rees, a graduate of Scofield's Bible classes, had been filling the pulpit during Scofield's long vacations. Rees was ordained at First Congregational Church in 1892. A pamphlet titled, *Jesus Christ as Preacher*, the sermon given at Rees' ordination ceremony, bears the heading "Sermon preached by Dr. C.I. Scofield." This is the first known instance of Scofield's use of the title, "Dr." However, there is no indication anywhere that he ever received any doctorate from any school, not even an honorary doctorate. For that matter there is no evidence that he ever attended or graduated from any institution of higher learning, neither in law nor in religion. Its not that such degrees are all that important, but that he claimed to have something he did not have.

In Rees' ordination sermon "Dr." Scofield said that people "are amazed when (they) turn back to the preaching of Finney and find that the very substance of it was stiff doctrine. But because it was *God's* (italics in original) doctrine, men fell in thousands at the feet of Jesus, so in our day we find Spurgeon and Moody, preachers of the dear old doctrines."[9] But, as previously discussed, Finney's doctrines were 180 degrees from Spurgeon's, and did not represent the old, tried and true biblical teaching. Nonetheless, Scofield revealed that his own teaching belonged to Finney's school of thought.

In 1895 D.L. Moody returned to Dallas for more evangelistic meetings. Moody had come to Dallas in 1866 at Scofield's invitation, so it was not surprising that he was a featured speaker at the Moody event. Scofield had also been invited by Moody to preach at Moody's home

---

9   Canfield, p. 136.

church, Trinity Congregational Church, in East Northfield, Massachusetts.

Trinity Congregational Church issued a call to Scofield late in 1895. He was able to maintain his demanding conference schedule by maintaining his long vacations at East Northfield as he had at First Church in Dallas. Thus, he was instrumental in founding the influential Niagara Conference in July, 1901.

Literati Extraordinaire

The other act of 1901 that has escaped public attention was his admission into the Lotos Club in New York City. The Lotos Club, an exclusive social literati club, sponsored and mentored various kinds of artists. Article I, Section II of its Constitution reads,

> "The primary object of this Club shall be to promote social intercourse among journalists, artists, and members of the musical and dramatic professions, and representatives, amateurs, and friends of Literature, Science, and the Fine Arts: and at least one third of the members shall be connected with said classes."[10]

Not the usual domain of Fundamentalist Christians.

Scofield's participation in the Lotos Club is beyond denial. The 1912 *Who's Who in America* lists the Lotos Club as Scofield's address. A letter written in 1905 to A.C. Gaebelin was written on Lotos Club stationery. According to *The New International Dictionary of the Christian Church*, Gaebelin had been a pastor in New York City, "where he began a remarkable ministry to the Jews." Apparently, he wrote and published his particular, dispensational understanding of prophecy all over the world, but focusing particularly on the Middle East. It is also interesting to note that Samuel Untermeyer, a notorious criminal lawyer, was on the Literary Committee of the Lotos Club at the time of Scofield's induction. Canfield tells us that Untermyer was particularly interested in The Zionist Movement. Coincidence? Perhaps. But what in the world was Scofield doing in the Lotos Club?

According to Gaebelein, Scofield first suggested the idea of a reference Bible to him at a Sea Cliff Conference meeting, at a wealthy resort in New York. Gaebelein suggested that he (Gaebelein) "should speak to a number of brethren about the publication of the Reference Bible and sound them out as to their support."[11] Alwyn Ball, a New York real es-

---

10 Canfield, p. 173.
11 Gaebelein, as quoted in Canfield, p. 175.

tate man, was approached. Gaebelein reported, "He fairly bubbled over with joy, and fully endorsed the plan; and, better than that, Mr. Ball pledged a considerable sum of money to assist the project."[12]

Others were contacted and similar support was expressed. He discussed the idea with Francis Fitch, who had published Scofield's Bible Correspondence Course. The principle work of Fitch, a member of the Plymouth Brethren, was the publishing of New York Stock Exchange lists. Fitch, who had worked with Scofield before, was concerned that such a project was beyond the abilities of Scofield. Gaebelein reported that Fitch said, "I know he (Scofield) can never finish such a work."[13] As it turned, out Fitch was convinced and lent his support to the project, but did not publish the Reference Bible.

Contrary to popular opinion among Fundamentalists, Scofield's work was not popular among many Christians at the time. Rather, his popularity was limited to a small group of Bible prophecy students, many of whom were quite wealthy.

Scofield resigned the East Northfield pulpit in 1903. Ill health and a busy schedule kept him from his pastoral duties. Nonetheless, Cyrus and Hettie traveled to Europe in 1904 to work on the *Reference Bible*. They met with Robert Scott, a publisher in London who suggested that none other than Oxford University Press ought to publish the Reference Bible. When Scofield replied that he had no contacts at the Oxford Press, Scott arranged a meeting with Henry Frowde, the head of the home division of Oxford University Press. Work on the *Reference Bible* was to progress on this trip. Several large-page, wide-margin notebooks were purchased. The plan was to paste the text of the entire Bible page by page into these notebooks, and his reference notes would then be added as he worked them up. Boxes of these notebooks traveled with the Scofields all over Europe and the Middle East.

Upon returning, Scofield again suffered illness. Writing on Lotos Club stationery, Scofield wrote to Gaebelein suggesting that Gaebelein work on the Reference Bible. That note reads, "By all means follow your own views of prophetic analysis. I sit at your feet when it comes to prophecy, and congratulate in advance the future readers of my Bible on having in their hands a safe, clear, sane guide through, what to most is a labyrinth."[14]

---

12 Canfield, p. 175.
13 Ibid.
14 Canfield, p. 188

Trumbull (Scofield's biographer) stated that Scofield "covered the whole field of such scholarship, whether friendly or unfriendly to the Bible." Anyone who knows the depth and breadth of such an effort knows that it requires a lifetime of intense study. That level of study does not appear to be a characteristic found in Scofield's life.

Scofield acknowledged the influence of two scholars whom he admired, and to whom he was introduced through his association with the Oxford Press. Wescott and Hort had advanced a new theory about New Testament sources, which laid the ground for the proliferation of modern Bible translations. But curiously, the work of Wescott and Hort utterly opposed the King James Version of the Bible, labeling it as faulty and error prone.

Scofield signed the contract with Oxford University Press in New York on June 5, 1907. The oddity of a major, world-wide press signing a contract with a little known, sectarian preacher grows with one's knowledge and experience of what it takes to get published. Oxford University Press is not known for its support of Christian causes, particularly sectarian or Fundamental causes. It's an academic press.

The 1908 annual report of First Congregational Church in Dallas included a report by Scofield, who had returned as senior pastor. Denominational difficulties were reported as "the Fundamentalist-Modernist controversy was reaching the simmering stage."[15]

Magnam Opus

When the *Scofield Reference Bible* was officially released on January 15, 1909, Scofield was in Dallas presiding over a church business meeting. Again, it seems odd that there is no record of any celebration of such an historic event at the Oxford headquarters in New York. The business of that meeting in Dallas was the withdrawal of First Church from the Lone Star Association in light of the Association's Modernist tendencies. Scofield approved of the withdrawal, and severed his own connection with Congregationalism in 1910.

Scofield sent copies of his new Reference Bible to each of his daughters in Kansas. Obviously, he had not forgotten them, but evidence shows that he had little contact with them or financial support for them as they grew into adulthood. He wrote to his daughter Helene on September 30, 1909. "When I get rich I am going to have 3 homes—one in a winter apartment on Washington Heights, N.Y. City, one at Crest-

---

15 Canfield, p. 202.

wood, one at Sorrento, Italy.... I shall have a large lecture room in the Carnegie Institute, & hold forth to all & sundry who may come for biblical instruction say 3 afternoons & 3 evenings in the week. At Sorrento & Crestwood I shall write books—*un peu*—but mostly loaf and invite my soul."[16] Hardly the values usually attributed to Fundamentalists!

1910 brought the publication of *Addresses on Prophecy*, by C.I. Scofield, published by A.C. Gaebelein. In that book Scofield asks,

> "Is it not so much wealth, luxury, power, pomp, and pride that have served to deflect the church from her appointed course...? The church, therefore, has failed to follow her appointed pathway of separation, holiness, heavenliness and testimony to an absent but coming Christ; she has turned aside from that purpose to the work of civilizing the world, building magnificent temples, and acquiring earthly power and wealth, and in this way, has ceased to follow in the footsteps of Him who had not where to lay His head."

The 1911 Who's Who in America, Vol. 7, listed:

> SCOFIELD, Cyrus Ingerson, clergyman; b. Lenawee Co., Mich., Aug. 19, 1843, and reared in Wilson Co., Tenn; S. Elias and Abl (Goodrich) S: pvtly fitted for coll., but univ. studies interrupted by breaking out of Civil War; m. Hettie van Wart, of Ypsilanti, Mich., July 14, 1884, Pvt. Co. H. 7th Tenn. Inf. May 1861 to close of Civil War; served in Army of Northern Va. under Gen. Lee, and awarded Cross of Honor for valor at battle of Antietam; admitted to Kan. bar, 1869, mem. Kan. Ho. of Rep. form Atchinson and Nemaha cos., 1870-1; apptd U.S. atty. for Kan. by President Grant, 1873. Converted to Christian religion at St. Louis, 1879, ordained Congregational ministry, 1883, pastor First Ch., Dallas, Tx., 1882-1895, Moody Ch. Northfield, Mass. 1895-1902 and First Ch., Dallas, 1905-7. Has lectured extensively on Bible subjects in Europe and America. Mem. S.A.R. Colonial Founders, Soc. Colonial Wars, Club Lotos, Author Rightly Dividing the Word of Truth, 1885, Addresses on Prophecy 1909, The Doctrine of The Holy Spirit, 1906, Lectures on Galatians, 1907 Editor, Scofield Reference Bible 1910, Bible of 1911, 1911 (sic). Head of Scofield Corr. Bible Sch. Home, "Crestwood," Ashuelot, N.H., and Lotos Club, New York. Office 156 5th Ave., New York.

---

16 Canfield, p. 224.

There are several inaccuracies and omissions in this listing, which could have only come from Scofield himself because *Who's Who* gathers information from the individuals themselves. There is no mention of his first wife, Leontine, or his daughters, Abigail and Marie Helene, nor of his divorce, nor of his Son by Hettie, Noel, or of his "law practice" in St. Louis.

In 1915 Scofield began writing for *The Sunday School Times*, the same year he organized The Community Church of Douglastown, New York. His Bible Correspondence Course was taken over by Moody Press and remains part of Moody's ministry today. A revision of *The Scofield Reference Bible* was published in 1917 because of several glaring errors. Gaebelein contributed significantly to that update.

In 1920 Charles Trumbull, a well respected religious journalist and Yale graduate, interviewed Scofield for a series of articles on his life and work for The Sunday School Times. Oxford University Press later printed them as *The Life Story of C.I. Scofield*, which until Canfield's book (1988) was the only published biography of Scofield. Canfield has unearthed much more information about Scofield than has been previously published, and discovered many errors and contradictions in Trumbull's biography—errors and contradictions that a nationally known, Yale journalist should not make—the likes of which are not found in any of Trumbull's other published works.

In a letter dated May 3, 1921, from Scofield to his daughter Abigail, he confesses some measure of continuing love for Leontine and his daughters by her, though he admits that he never gave any proof of it. The letter demonstrates that, though he never visited or supported his Atchinson family, he never forgot them. But neither did he mention them to his Christian friends or reading public. During the same month he wrote and signed his last will and testament. Neither Abigail nor Marie Helene were mention and neither shared in his estate.

Final Reckoning
He died July 24, 1921. His funeral was held in the First Baptist Church near Flushing because the Douglastown Community Church had no building. People from around the world noted his passing, but there was no one from Atchinson, Kansas, at his funeral.

His entire estate was bequeathed to Hettie and Noel. There was no mention of his daughters by Leontine, or of his first wife, Leontine. Nothing was mentioned about giving anything to any Christian ministry, nor any educational, social, or charitable establishment. Nothing. Nor did his will mention anything about his faith or the Lord. Apparently, there is little information at all about the royalties of the *Scofield Reference Bible*.

While working on an unpublished dissertation on the life of Scofield, William BeVier contacted Noel, Scofield's surviving son, in 1960. However, no information about his father has ever come from Noel. Noel responded to BeVier's request, "Regret to advise you I cannot give you the data requested and please do not bother me in the future." Canfield reports that "neither Noel, his wife, nor the granddaughter played any role in the Dispensational movement or its evangelical successor."[17]

The life of Scofield through the eyes of Canfield, whose research is well documented, is truly incredible. But what can we make of the theology that Scofield championed through is best selling Reference Bible. We have already seen that it is built upon an Arminian foundation and borrowed heavily from the Plymouth Brethren theologian, J.N. Darby.

Dispensationalism

Dispensationalism teaches that there have been a variety of dispensations or administrations throughout history. At the heart of the differing dispensations have been different methods or ways that God has dealt with His people. According to Scofield, a dispensation is "a period of time during which man is tested in respect of obedience to some specific revelation of *the will of God*."[18] Scofield listed seven dispensations: *Innocence, Conscience, Human Government, Promise, Law, Grace,* and the *Kingdom*.

Dispensationalism's unique contribution to theology is the belief that God treats or judges people differently in each dispensation. God's treated people differently during the dispensation of *Conscience* than He did during the dispensation of *Innocence*, different during the dispensation of *Promise* than during *Human Government*, different during the dispensation of the *Grace* than the *Law*. This view is, however, contrary to historic, orthodox Christianity (what has been understood to be historic, orthodox Christianity until the Modern Age, that is!).

The older view taught that God always treated or judged people by the same criteria because God is just and never changing. Particularly,

---

17 Canfield p. 297.
18 Douglas, p. 303, italics original.

the churches of the Protestant Reformation championed this view when they called the Church of Rome to Reformation. The Protestant churches turned away from the innovations and changes brought about by Rome. They not only went back to the Old Testament, but they returned to the original sources to study it.

The danger inherent in Dispensationalism is that people will believe that only certain parts of the Bible are relevant to them because they live in a particular dispensation. Too often such people believe that they can dispense with God's law, that the whole of the Old Testament law no longer applies because we live in a dispensation of grace. However, the founders of Protestantism—Luther, Calvin, Knox, Owen, etc.—proclaimed that salvation was by grace alone, start to finish, cover-to-cover. Salvation has always been by grace. Abraham was saved by grace, as was Noah and Moses and Isaiah, etc.

The thing that people don't realize is that Dispensationalism is a relatively new theology that was popularized by Scofield and his *Reference Bible*. How did it become so popular? It is easy to understand, and was made readily available through Oxford University Press, a very liberal publisher.

And yet, C.I. Scofield continues to be held in high esteem by many, many Fundamentalists today. Yet, we cannot simply blame Scofied or Finney for their errant theology. Rather, the blame lies at the feet of the pastors and churches who were "taken in" by their "success."

Polity

What is a church?

The church is not a 501(c)(3) not-for-profit organization. The Internal Revenue Service (IRS) does not define a church, God does. The church is the people of God.

The church exists in and through Jesus Christ, and is a distinctive biblical reality. At the same time it is continuous with ancient Israel, the seed of Abraham and God's covenant people. The new covenant under which the church lives (1 Cor. 11:25; Heb. 8:7-13) is a new form of the relationship in which God says to His chosen community, "I will be your God, and you shall be My people" (Jer. 7:23; 31:33; cf. Ex. 6:7).

Under the new covenant, the Old Testament priests, sacrifices, and sanctuary have been superseded by the mediation of Jesus (Heb. 1-10). Believers in Christ are the seed of Abraham and the people of God (Gal. 3:29; 1 Pet. 2:4-10).

Secondly, the limitation of the old covenant to one nation (Deut. 7:6; Ps. 147:19, 20) is replaced by the inclusion in Christ on equal terms of believers from every nation (Eph. 2; 3; Rev. 5:9, 10).

Thirdly, the Spirit is poured out on the church, so that fellowship with Christ (1 John 1:3), ministry from Christ (John 14:18; Eph. 2:17), and foretastes of heaven (2 Cor. 1:22; Eph. 1:14) become realities in the experience of the church.

The unbelief of most Jews (Rom. 9-11) and the majority of Gentiles in the church is depicted by Paul as God's breaking off the natural branches of His olive tree (the historical covenant community) and replacing them with wild olive shoots (Rom. 11:17-24). The new covenant does not exclude Jews, and Paul taught that their general rejection of the church will one day be reversed (Rom 11:15, 23-31).

The New Testament teaches that the church is the fulfillment of the Old Testament hopes and patterns, brought about by Jesus Christ. The church is:

- the family and flock of God (John 10:16; Eph. 2:18; 3:15; 4:6; 1 Pet. 5:2-4),
- His Israel (Gal. 6:16), the body and bride of Christ (Eph 1:22, 23; 5:23-32; Rev. 19:7; 21:2, 9-27), and
- the temple of the Holy Spirit (1 Cor. 3:16; cf. Eph. 2:19-22).

The church is a single worshiping community, permanently gathered in the true sanctuary, the heavenly Jerusalem (Gal. 4:26; Heb. 12:22-24) and the place of God's presence. The church is one, although the worshiping community consists of the church militant—those who are still on earth, and the church triumphant—those who have died and entered glory. On earth, the church appears in its local congregations, each one is a microcosm of the church as a whole. According to Paul the one church universal is the body of Christ (1 Cor. 12:12-26; Eph. 1:22, 23; 3:6; 4:4), but so is each local congregation (1 Cor. 12:27).

The church on earth is one in Christ despite the great number of local congregations and denominations (Eph. 4:3-6). It is holy because it is consecrated to God corporately, as each Christian is individually (Eph. 2:21). It is catholic (meaning 'universal') because it is worldwide. Finally, it is apostolic because it is founded on apostolic teaching (Eph. 2:20). All of these four qualities may be seen (Eph. 2:19-22).

There is a distinction to be drawn between the church as people see it and as God alone sees it. This difference is the historic distinction between the "visible church" and the "invisible church." *Invisible* does not mean that it cannot be seen, but that its exact boundary is not known to us. Only God knows (2 Tim 2:19) which members of the earthly congregations are inwardly truly born again, and so belong to the church as an eternal and spiritual fellowship. Jesus taught that in the organized church there would always be people who seemed to be faithful, not excluding leaders, who were nevertheless not renewed in heart and would be exposed and rejected at the Judgment (Matt. 7:15-23; 13:24-30, 36-43, 47-50; 25:1-46). There are not two churches, one visible and another hidden in heaven, but one church only, known perfectly to God and known imperfectly on earth.

Christians must "therefore ... be even more diligent to make your call and election sure" (2 Pet. 1:10). Personal assurance of faith is gained and revealed by six marks of the Spirit:

- conviction of sin
- a lively faith
- holiness of life
- private prayer
- personal study and
- reverence for God's Word.

Inasmuch as they practice these things Christians will grow in personal assurance of their faith. The lack of these marks is cause for concern.

The New Testament assumes that all Christians will share in the life of a local congregation, worshiping in the body, accepting its nurture and discipline (Matt. 18:15-20; Gal. 6:1), and sharing its ministry and witness. Christians who refuse to join other believers disobey God and spiritually impoverish themselves (Heb. 10:25).

Covenantal Church

> In studying divine covenants in general, one is treading through understanding God's Redemptive Plan throughout history. This is a matter of Eternal Salvation. It answers the question: How may a sinful man approach God? (Exodus 3:5).   —Witsius

> God has had one purpose and plan for mankind ever since the Fall: to restore a people for Himself from fallen humanity through Messiah Jesus   —Fred Klett, Mongerism.com

CHURCH GROWTH

> And the glory which thou gavest me I have given them; that they
> may be one, even as we are one. — John 17:22

> The phrase "Give glory to God" (Jos. 7:19, Jer. 13:16) is a He-
> brew idiom meaning, "Confess your sins." The words of the Jews
> to the blind man, "Give God the praise" (John 9:24) are an adju-
> ration to confess. They are equivalent to, "Confess that you are
> an impostor," "Give God the glory by speaking the truth;" for
> they denied that a miracle had been wrought.
> —Easton's Bible Dictionary

> For we do not dare to rank or compare ourselves with some of
> the ones commending themselves. But they, measuring them-
> selves among themselves, and comparing themselves to them-
> selves, are not perceptive. But we will not boast beyond measure,
> but according to the measure of the rule which the God of mea-
> sure distributed to us, to reach even to you. For we do not over-
> stretch ourselves as though not reaching to you. For we also came
> to you in the gospel of Christ; not boasting beyond measure in
> the labors of others, but having hope that the growing faith
> among you will be increased according to our rule, to overflow-
> ing; to preach the gospel in that beyond you, and not to boast in
> another's rule in things made ready. But he who glories, let him
> glory in the Lord. For not he who commends himself is ap-
> proved, but he whom the Lord commends.
> — 2 Corinthians 10:12-18

"Remember, everything we do gets hijacked by marketing." That was the warning Sun Microsystems Inc. Chief Researcher John Gage had for developers working on emerging grid computing standards at the Global Grid Forum in Seattle in June, 2003. His comment reflects a general truth about what might be called "marketing creep," the tendency toward the domination of marketing as the ultimate concern of every organization, including the church.

Church Growth, or the application of business marketing principles to the church, has been a thriving business for many, many years. I have studied and pondered the ways, means, issues, and applications for much of that time. But something has troubled me about the effort to market Christ's church. A dissonance in the pit of my stomach caught my attention early on, but identifying the source and nature of the my concern has proven to be difficult.

After all, I want the Lord's people to reach out to lost sinners with the love of Christ. I don't want churches to keep their proverbial lights under a bushel basket. We need to share our faith for the greater expansion of Christ's church and the glory of God. These are all good things. The aim and purpose of church marketing or church growth appears to be a good thing. But is it?

I'm sure you can hear my hesitation about this noble effort to increase God's Kingdom and Christ's church. But please know from the outset that my hesitation is not related to the expansion of Christ's church in the modern world. Lord knows, we need to capitalize on everything that will move the Kingdom forward. This article is not against evangelism or church growth.

Having worked in the area of secular marketing for a couple of years now, an insight and perspective about the problem with modern Church Growth and the Movement it inspired has finally jelled in my brain. The issue may be hard for you to see, it has certainly been hard for me to get a clear fix on it. Please bear with me.

I attended my first Church Growth workshop in 1982. There we learned how churches have failed to extend the most rudimentary business oriented hospitality to visitors. Visitors were described as potential customers for the services that churches should provide to their members. We learned about name tags and signage, parking and accessibility, friendliness and follow-up. In short, we learned to treat visitors and members like customers, and to better provide for their needs.

Honestly, at that time the people from the churches in attendance at that seminar were astonished by the lack of what might be call today a customer-centered approach to worship, the main attraction or venue for generating additional members, additional customers or more business. How could the churches be so out of touch with the people they professed to love and serve? We all went home with new resolve to become more visitor- or customer-centered in our worship and programs.

The initial insight about name tags and signage, parking and accessibility, friendliness and follow-up was well received, as it should be. There's nothing inherently wrong with these concerns.

As the Movement continued to develop momentum it began to apply its principles more and more widely, even to the content and choreography of the worship service itself. As marketing principles became more widely used in worship planning and execution, I became more and more disillusioned. But I could not put my finger on the nature of my concern.

The small churches that I served as pastor increasingly saw Church Growth principles as potentially answering many of their small church concerns. Noses and nickels became increasingly important to the governing boards, particularly as they saw so many of their own young people abandon them and turn to modern churches that employed customer-centered marketing principles to every aspect of church life. Everything in such churches was done from the perspective of customer friendliness and ease of use. After all, these principles have clearly established themselves as engines that can—and have—grown phenomenal businesses and churches. Who can argue with success?

Nonetheless, some dissonance remained for me. I was not willing to turn the church over to the marketing department, whether it be denominational, local, or parachurch. Something smelled wrong about it, but what was it?

Then it came to me in a flash.

Church members (or visitors) are not customers to the church, any more than family members (or children) are customers to their respective families. The church is not a business, it's a family. Now, that does not mean that business and marketing principles cannot be successfully and effectively applied to churches. They can! But how they are applied makes all the difference in the world. There is nothing wrong with name tags and signage, parking and accessibility, friendliness and follow-up in and of themselves. Nor is there anything wrong with new church music.

However, the church is a service organization, not a sales organization. The purpose of the church is not to serve its members, but to serve the Lord Jesus Christ. Members are not to be the objects of service, but the vehicles of service. The difference involves a shift in philosophical or theological perspective.

If the old adage that the "customer is always right" is true, then church members are not customers, nor are church visitors. Rather, God is the only real customer of the church. God is the only Person who is *always right*. And God is the One to receive the service, whether it's a worship service, a prayer service, or service to the community. It is done for the Lord, not primarily or directly for His people. We are to satisfy God, not ourselves or our church visitors.

This insight about church practice comes from the study of the Bible and its use and interpretation through the centuries. The traditional understanding of church practice was that the church is to be God-centered, not man-centered or woman-centered. God is the object of our service, not ourselves or each other—nor even the wider community.

With that fundamental insight the application of marketing or business principles can indeed be applied to the activities and practices of churches. But such application must always take a back seat to the prior concerns of God's Word, historically understood and practiced.

In fact, the concern for church history is essentially a business marketing principle itself. Businesses keep records, and reports are made from those records. Any business worth its salt will know how it has performed in the past, so that it can endeavor to make improvements. And no business will simply abandon its past practices, but will only make well-planned, small, incremental adjustments to its activity or practice. History is a key element for business success, and is an essential element of Christianity.

The essential insight here is that the worship and life of the church are not to be centered around the needs of its members, visitors, or the wider community, but around service to God as defined in the Bible. The people who attend worship are not themselves to be served. Rather, we worship as a service to God, just as we pray as a service to God, and reach out to a lost world in the service of God.

However, the bulk of the Church Growth Movement and its materials do not reflect this attitude. Rather, the Movement has succumbed to "marketing creep." Marketing dominates the Church Growth Movement, and has eclipsed the biblical call to faithfulness. Faithfulness, not broad community appeal, is the highest priority of Christians and their churches.

"Church Growth" has become the byword for evangelism everywhere today. The Church Growth model is almost universally applied, regardless of theology or denomination. All church activity is measured in Church Growth categories.

The Church Growth model for evangelism involves the application of secular business practices to the church. We see an emphasis upon the pastor as CEO and business management practices applied to every aspect of church life. Just as business conforms every activity to its bottom line—increased market share, maximization of profits, etc. Churches now conform every activity to the bottom line defined by the Church Growth model. Increasingly, that bottom line pertains to "noses and nickels."

The problem is that the Church Growth model is not a biblical model, and it is failing to actually grow churches. Nowhere in Scripture did the disciples set out to "start a church" as we think of churches today. The primary concern of the New Testament disciples was to help people get right with God, not to start new churches or grow existing ones. The focus was on God, not upon themselves.

Today's churches have been captured by modern, secular institutionalism. The values and practices of the business world have become the values and practices of churches. But this should not be!

Our emphasis upon informal Christianity[1] is intended to restore biblical values and practices to the churches. We believe that biblical fidelity trumps church growth as a measure of faithfulness. Getting right with God, not self-aggrandizement, is the mission of the church.

This is not to say that growth is bad or unbiblical, it is not. But church growth is secondary to biblical fidelity.

Pseudo-Gospel

"The dangers inherent in the church growth movement are many, and the crucial issue in assessing those dangers is whether we are talking about becoming Christians or about building institutional membership. The greatest danger in the movement may be that it obviously succeeds. If one tailors the church to identify with its culture and engages in the pseudo-gospel of 'possibility thinking,' promising to assuage guilt with the minimum of pain and connecting that promise with marketing techniques, there will be success. The question is whether the result will bear any similarity to the church."[2]

---

1   Ross, Phillip A. *Informal Christianity—Refining Christ's Church*, Pilgrim Platform, Marietta, Ohio, 2007.
2   Elliott, Ralph H. *Dangers of the Church Growth Movement*, http://www.missional-networking.org/2013/05/28/dangers-of-the-church-growth-movement/.

Biblical Governance for Christian Churches and Nonprofits

John Carver has developed an excellent corporate board model that he has trademarked as Policy Governance® (www.policygovernance.com). The model is brilliant and Carver applies it to every sort of board —governmental, private, corporate, and religious.

The model is to be commended to all but one type of board—Christian boards. Why should Christian boards be different than other kinds of boards? Because Christian governance is different than all other forms of governance. By definition, to be Christian is to be governed by Christ as He is revealed through Scripture.

Boards that govern Christian organizations must, as Carver himself insists, begin by identifying the proper ownership authority, ascribing to the CEO complete authority over the organization, and then setting policy from the widest possible means limitations to increasingly narrow limitations until any reasonable interpretation of policy is acceptable to the board. The board, however, governs on behalf of the proper owner(s), thus all policies must be acceptable to the owner(s), as well. For Christian churches and nonprofits that means that all governance policies must conform to the historic Christian principles of the Bible.

How will Christian governance differ from other types of policy governance? Christians understand that God Himself is the owner of all things, and especially of His churches and the various ministries that purport to be Christian. This means that Scripture must be the foundation upon which all Christian governance is built. In fact, it means that Christian governance is actually nothing more and nothing less than Christian stewardship, wherein a steward manages on behalf of another. Thus, Christians are not free to determine governance policy, but must first and foremost understand, translate, communicate, and institute the governing policies of Scripture. In this regard, however, much of Carver's insights and ideas will apply, although their application must always be based upon and constrained by Christian biblical principles.

This issue comes into play because Dr. Carver suggests that churches, denominations, and para church ministries should define their ownership as being composed of members and/or benefit recipients. However, in order to maintain conformity with Scripture in the matter of ownership, we must understand that members and/or benefit recipients are nowhere in Scripture defined or understood to be owners of churches and/or ministries. All faithful Christians will agree that God alone is the owner of His churches and their ministries, and that God's people are called to be faithful stewards. Stewards are more akin to staff than owners. Are Christians free to graft secular governance policies onto biblical institutions? Of course not, not if we intend to be faithful. Because Dr. Carver has missed this fundamental understanding of Scripture and the nature of Christian institutions we need to proceed with caution in regard to any adaptation of Policy Governance® to biblical institutions. However, at it's root, it is my observation that the Policy Governance® model is not secular at all, but actually biblical in origin—though Dr. Carver does not appear to recognize the biblical roots of his model. How so? Allow me to explain.

According to Scripture, the ownership of a Christian Church is necessarily God Himself.[3] The Christian Church is not a creature of the state, nor a state created corporation. The existence of the Christian church precedes the development of the state sanctioned corporation, and therefore cannot be considered to be a creature of the state. Such consideration can exist only through a confusion of definitions.

The church can be considered to be a creature of the state only through the violation of Article One of the Bill of Rights of the United States Constitution, which would automatically nullify any such relationship. Separation of church and state means that the state cannot govern the church, nor can the church govern the state. They are separate jurisdictions. The point is that Christian churches are not fundamentally 501(c)(3) corporations, but are corporate bodies owned and governed by Jesus Christ. While God owns everything,[4] it is particularly important for His people to acknowledge His ownership of His churches[5]. Dr. Carver has said that to distribute ownership between God and His people (members and/or benefit recipients) amounts to a confusion of ownership in the Policy Governance® model. And he is right.

However, from a biblical perspective God's people cannot be considered to be owners in any sense. They are stewards who manage resources for another.[6] Furthermore, the traditional teaching of Original Sin mitigates against such confusion between ownership rights (those who are self-directed) and stewardship obligations (those who are directed by another). The story of the Fall of humanity in Genesis 3 is the story of just such confusion by Adam and Eve. Thus, God—Father, Son

---

3   Genesis 1:1.
4   Psalm 50:10.
5   Matthew 28:18.
6   Titus 1:7.

and Holy Spirit—is the only rightful owner of a Christian church and/or Christian ministries.

In order to be faithful to Scripture, Christian denominations, local churches, and/or Christian para church ministries must begin their policy determination with Scripture, because, as Carver teaches, maintenance of the "larger bowl" policies must always take precedence over "smaller bowl" policies. The global ends question is: What benefit for what people at what cost? While God's purpose is to save His people, they are not saved for their own benefit, but for God's purposes.[7] And God's ultimate purpose (His universal end) is His own glory.[8]

The next smaller biblical ends policy (global end, if you will) is human fruitfulness, reproduction, and dominion under God's leadership.[9] Thus, dominion is a function of stewardship, of managing the earth according to God's plan.

The cost for achieving the benefit (salvation) has already been paid by Jesus Christ. Thus, a global biblical ends statement for a Christian church might be something like: a) Salvation for God's people through Jesus Christ; b) families living in grateful obedience to God's Word; c) families worshiping and serving God according to God's will (Scripture). Smaller "bowls" would further explicate some of the fruits of the Spirit that are to be produced by saved Christians,[10] describing what such fruits look like. For instance, d) people who manifest love, joy, peace, patience, kindness, goodness, faithfulness, gentleness, and self-control. To lose sight of the fact that God is the owner of the church is to invite servants and stewards—staff—to make ownership policy. And, while it is done all the time in all sorts of churches, it is a big mistake. If God is not the owner, then the stewards of the church are not obligated to accomplish His will. And if He is, they are.

The CEO of the Christian Church is Jesus Christ Himself, not the pastor.[11] Don't think this is overly impractical or idealistic. It is not. Jesus left a detailed list of instructions and policies. The first order of Christian churches is to do what the Lord has commanded in Scripture in our

---

7   Mark 1:43-44.

8   Leviticus 9:6; Psalm 21:5, 24:7, 57:5, 71:8, 79:9, 106:47, 108:5, 115:1; Matthew 25:31; Mark 8:38; Luke 21:27; John 1:14, 2:11, 5:44, 8:54; Romans 3:23, 5:2, 6:4, 15:7; Revelation 7:12, etc. It must also be noted that not all people will be saved by God because some people go to hell (Matthew 5:22, 5:29-30, 10:28, 23:33; Luke 12:5; 2 Peter 2), and hell, damnation and the destruction of evil also serve the glory of God.

9   Genesis 1:28; 1 Titus 6:13-17, Revelation 1:6, etc.

10 Matthew 7:20-21; Galatians 5:19-23.

11 Matthew 28:18.

own lives, in our own families, in our own churches and in our own nation. The biblical model of church governance is not inadequate, though many people fail to understand (or like) it. The problem is not in the biblical model, but in our failure to abide by it.

The means limitation policy of Christian churches has been given firstly through the Ten Commandments. God's will is to be accomplished everywhere by many and various means, but some means have been proscribed. Further, such means limitation policies apply not only to the CEO (Jesus Christ), but are proscribed for all of God's people (His staff).

Jesus Himself fulfilled all the requirements of God's law (the Ten Commandments), which qualified Him alone to be CEO of His churches, and as in the Policy Governance® model He has been given all authority.[12] He has accomplished (purchased) the salvation of His people so that they are free from the consequences of their sin, and can freely engage obedience to His Word (Scripture) to the best of their ability without the fear of failing or of damnation. Why is this important? People are limited by their fears, so the Lord took away the ultimate fear for His people—hell and damnation. People will perform better if they focus on accomplishment rather than the fear of failure.

The New Testament further refines and explicates the biblical means limitation policy.[13] Such means limitation policies might be written as a) no association with anyone guilty of sexual immorality or greed; b) no association with idolaters, revilers, drunkards, or swindlers; c) no manifestation of bitterness, wrath, anger, clamor, slander and/or malice; d) no conversation or entertainment that employs or regards sexual immorality, impurity, anger, wrath, hypocrisy, envy, malice, slander, obscene talk, passion, evil desire, impurity and/or covetousness, e) no lying or intentional deceit of any kind among self-professing Christians, etc.

Thus, the job of the elders (governors) is to understand and communicate biblical policy to the people of the churches. And the fact that there are a variety of opinions about what the Bible says or means does not mean that God's Word is confused or insufficient. It only means that people are confused and insufficient. Thus, God's people must rely upon Bible study, prayer, fellowship (the counsel of the Church Militant), and

---

12   Matthew 28:18.
13   For example, see 1 Corinthians 5:11; Ephesians 4:31, 5:3, Colossians 3:5-10; 1 Peter 2:1, etc.

history (the counsel of the Church Triumphant) to aid their understanding of and obedience to God's Word, if they intend to be faithful.

Pastors, elders, and deacons can indeed apply much of the wisdom of Policy Governance to their operations. For instance, elders and pastors can make much use of the ends/means distinction, and focus on the biblical ends to be accomplished by the Christian churches.[14]

In addition, church members can realize that they are not church owners. While they may be property owners, the church is not the property. Elders and pastors can similarly realize that they are not owned by the congregation, but by Jesus Christ Himself. And because of that ownership they are responsible to God for the accomplishment of His last will and testament—Scripture.

A very important application is that church elders can also speak with one voice. In fact, they must speak with one voice in order to demonstrate the unity of the church. In as much as they do not speak with one voice they do not model the unity of the church. Unity, not diversity, is a biblical end for Christian churches.[15] Obviously there is a wide diversity of people who are members of Christ's churches, but as members of the Body of Christ they are not to celebrate their diversity,[16] but are to develop their unity in Christ.[17]

DR. BIERY'S RESPONSE

A response to this article: Responding to Issues Raised Concerning Ownership, Biblical Governance for Christian and Nonprofits, by Richard M. Biery, M.D., with contributions from Rev. David Mustine, and Olan Hendrix, June, 2005.

Responding to Issues Raised Concerning Ownership, Biblical Governance for Christian and Nonprofits, by Richard M. Biery, M.D., with contributions from Rev. David Mustine, and Olan Hendrix, June, 2005

Occasionally one hears that Policy Governance,® as some have come to understand it after reading something about it, does not apply to Christian organizations. They sometimes raise what they believe are Scriptural issues based around God's ownership of Creation and His Church. These observers make several valid points which deserve being addressed, but they also have confusion or misunderstanding over other

---

14 Ephesians 4:11-14, Revelation 19:7.
15 Ephesians 4:3, 4:11-14; 1 Peter 3:8.
16 1 Corinthians 12:4-6.
17 Philippians 1:27, 2:2.

points, or at least those points need further development. Since these concerns from time to time arise, we have addressed them in this article.

Background

Policy Governance was originally developed to address and improve nonprofit governance. However, the model became increasingly recognized to be robust and applicable to all classes of governing boards. With its vital concept of ownership, which possesses legal reality in many organizational types, such as membership organizations, federations, and for-profit corporations it also provides a moral basis for understanding ownership and accountability in other nonprofit organizations and ministries that do not have clear (or any) legal ownership. This has proven to be an extremely important and powerful concept and is where everything starts.

Policy Governance has been received with interest, if not enthusiasm, by large numbers of Christian organizations, both evangelical and mainline, and by many students of management and leadership who are Christians, some having served for decades as senior leaders. Many have taken advanced training in Policy Governance to enable them to better lead their boards, or teach other boards. Policy Governance is used (or alleged to be used) by several dozens if not hundreds of Christian organizations, ranging from organizations and churches of confessional tradition to those of liberal tradition to organizations and churches of evangelical and fundamentalist traditions such as Bible Churches. Why? What features of Policy Governance make it so appealing to such a broad range of Christendom?

Students of Policy Governance have observed for some time that Policy Governance has within it (is based on) values or principles that comport with Biblical virtues, and that it enables governing boards to govern accordingly, giving clarity to their values, permitting them, as no other governing tradition has before, to achieve a rigor in governance and oversight, to govern with integrity, to diligently honor their fiduciary responsibility, and clarify their moral accountability to those counting on them to govern well, especially those investing in them with their giving, prayers and efforts. This is a remarkable achievement for a model. It is alleged that Augustine once said all truth is God's truth. A model that has and provides such integrity seems to meet the criteria of which Augustine was talking.

Response

In fact, it is to this last point (to whom is the board accountable?) that the first, and perhaps major, objection is raised, the question of ownership. This is the concept and principle that Carver has called ownership. Ownership, in a Policy Governance context as applied to nonprofits (non-membership) and religious organizations, is the often ill defined group of people to whom the board owes some duty of steward- ship and the consequent moral accountability for the organization, espe- cially that duty to see that the organization accomplishes the purpose for which it was created and/or for which people currently support it and invest in it. Ownership, in this usage, is commonly seen as those who contribute (as investors) in some form, donations, prayer, time, etc., (but not "funders" in the usual sense of the word). These, generally faithful, contributors do so because of their support for the ends, the vision, of the organization. Ownership is not, contrary to what some mistakenly say, the beneficiaries, although people may, of course, be both beneficia- ries and owners. Nevertheless, the two ideas (and the purpose and value each receive) are quite different. These kinds of owners are often re- ferred to as the "moral ownership" when the accountability is not for reasons of legal ties. In any case, ownership in Policy Governance, whether religious or secular, is always temporal and composed of people. We'll come back to that point because it is important.

Before we go on, in order to prevent confusion, there is one impor- tant sense that God's ultimate and "only" ownership could be under- stood, and that is that Church authority derives from God. It does not derive from human government or other human organizational cre- ation. Consequently, for example, the U. S. Constitution guarantees that the government does not have the right to "establish" or intervene in the religious enterprise of the people, their beliefs and religious practices. The Church is not subject to the political will of secular government. This is sometimes confusing because government does have certain non-religious authority over the organizational entities that the Church (people and their choice of organization) creates (discussed later).

Christian organization boards will always certainly acknowledge God or Christ as their ultimate owner (and the ultimate owner of their membership's resources as well, of course (Luke 16)). However, the chain of stewardship and its accountability doesn't ignore the temporal moral ownership and simply pass from God directly to a board (or worse, some leader), leaving other accountabilities out. The board is accountable to both its moral ownership and to God. If someone argues that, "God alone is the owner of His churches and their ministries," this is a puzzling and untrue statement, either spiritually or legally. It would be true if one said "ultimate owner." But it is dangerous to claim that God alone is the owner without acknowledging any moral accountability to some other group for the way the organization is run. It is an invitation to abuse of power, avoiding valid human investment and consequent accountability, (which happens with disturbing frequency by Christian leaders who claim to answer to no one but God and end up abusing the trust they have been given and ignoring it).

Recognizing a temporal moral ownership to which the board subordinates itself as a servant of God and steward goes far in preserving the integrity of the board and the executive. Policy Governance boards recognize this. Let abuse or fraud creep in and the board will quickly learn a lesson in temporal accountability. Dr. Carver readily acknowledges this stewardship role of the board. Because others are also stewards of what God has given them and that they give it to an organization to further steward those gifts, whatever they are, does not nullify the concept that, from the point of view of the recipient organization, the donors or "investors" are temporal moral owners as the term is used in Policy Governance.

Ownership is essentially different from being a beneficiary such as a student, patient, client, attendee, or whatever we call the recipients of organizational largess—those that receive the benefits of the "products" created by the organization. Christian leaders generally have no trouble understanding this concept. Even when ownership and beneficiary are mixed in the same person, such as in the case of church members, the two concepts can be separated. When wearing one hat the questions and concerns are different than when one wears the other hat. Church boards using Policy Governance meet with members as owner-members concerning, for example, a vision for the whole and the desired purpose of that local church, what results it should create in people's lives and in the community, and church leadership meets with specific recipient groups for input on "products" of their specific interest such as children's or youth programs, missions, singles group, etc.

To understand this question of ownership better, a useful approach is the idea that organizations produce two types of values, one for the owners, the reason why the owners created and continue to "invest" in the organization, and one for the beneficiaries, which may be training, medical care, inspiration, counsel, evangelism, shelter, entertainment, etc. Moral owners, such as donors, generally contribute because they believe in the purpose of the organization and want to share in its ministry. The value for them, in this case intangible, is one of the spirit and gratification regarding what the organization is accomplishing and, for Christians, an eternal investment and reward. The value for beneficiaries is often tangible, temporal, and personal. It, too, of course, could have eternal consequences, but not in the same sense. Owners tend to have a big picture and long term view of the organization. Beneficiaries experience the organization's "product" as personal, fairly immediate, and focused. They are much less interested (as beneficiaries) in the big picture or the long term as long as their needs are met. In the case of a congreationally led church or membership organization both values are occurring in the same people. The members are both temporal owners and beneficiaries of their church's activities.

Certainly Christians acknowledge God's ultimate ownership of both humanity and all of creation, and they strive to live according to Biblical precepts. (We are obviously generalizing.) And Christian leadership, biblically, should strive to govern with a sense of accountability to God. Furthermore, Christian ministries are usually deemed, at least morally, as instruments of the Church at large—para church, although not necessarily tied to any given church. This leads to the conclusion by many Policy Governance boards that they include a moral accountability to at least the larger family of believers they include in this group. Since Christ is the Head of the Church, they also acknowledge an accountability to Christ, while not denying their accountability to other believers. This does not mitigate the value or validity of the concept of temporal ownership. In fact, it is dangerous, as noted by many expert observers, if an organization's leadership (either its board or its CEO) sees only God as the owner and acknowledges no temporal accountability. Such a view is an invitation to corruption and abuse of authority. History has amply demonstrated it. One needn't look far. (C.f. for example, *Churches That Abuse*, Ronald M. Enroth, Zondervan, 1992) Recognizing temporal accountability to a conceptual ownership (not just beneficiaries), whatever we call it, results in responsible behavior by leadership, including the board.

Concerning the Church and churches. This is a term which is can easily become subject to equivocation. The Church Universal is one concept and the church at Main and Central is another. In fact, the word can refer to a building or a group of people who worship together and claim a common faith. To discuss the church, then, calls for careful use of terms. Although Christ is the Head of the Church (ownership implied, cf. Col. 1), the most common Biblical metaphor for the Church Universal is the Bride of Christ, not something owned by Him. He called his disciples "friends" and, metaphorically, friends of the bridegroom, interestingly enough. (Of course, they are also His creatures.) Nevertheless, there must still be local fellowships called churches. Today those fellowships own property, conduct programs, pay salaries, and have legal duties besides spiritual duties. As such, they are indeed creatures of the state as well of the Kingdom. The state created the corporate category (eleemosynary) under which that church is recognized (and protected) and it has a tax number. It is not taxed, as such, but it does have certain tax requirements on it including the duty to pay payroll taxes. No more need be said. The state constitutionally must stay out of the religious beliefs and business of the church but not out of its safety (building and fire codes), the safety of its children (child abuse protections), and any abuse of its financial trust, etc. If those entities, those fellowships of believers, are congregationally based and autonomous, (though they may owe allegiance to a larger group such as a denomination), they are governed in some manner by a board in much of the western world. This board has an ownership to which it is accountable.

Concerning Ends
Taken from R.M. Biery paper on "What is Biblical About Policy Goernance?" 2002.

Policy Governance recognizes that all organizations (indeed, all designed systems) have a purpose outside of themselves. This idea of purpose is teleological, and a well-recognized term expressing the notion of teleology is "end." (From the Greek, *teleos,* and used repeatedly in the New Testament in reference to purpose, or completion.) Carver purposefully selected "Ends" for this class of policy. "End" is used frequently within Christian literature. For example, mankind has an "end" established by God. Solomon, in the book of Ecclesiastes in the last chapter, tells us what that end is. We also find the term used in regard to mankind in commonly used catechisms.

Furthermore, an additional Biblical principle is that the owner, (in the case of mankind—God), has the right to determine the purpose or end. Policy Governance recognizes this principle and builds it into the process. No other form of governance we know does this. Under Policy Governance the board is expected to find out and know the thinking of the ownership in areas relevant to ends, particularly. This is called "connecting with owners," and the board considers it in policy formulation, since the board is steward for the ownership, albeit a wise and knowledgeable one, but neither is it an autonomous one. The board of Christian organization has a responsibility to know both the mind of its temporal owners and the Mind of its ultimate Owner to the extent it can know His Word and seek His wisdom.

R. M. Biery, M.D. 2005[18]

RESPONSE TO BIERY

This is a response to *Responding to Issues Raised Concerning Ownership, Biblical Governance for Christian and Nonprofits*, by Richard M. Biery, M.D., with contributions from Rev. David Mustine, and Olan Hendrix, June, 2005, who responded to my article on Christian Governance.

It appears that Dr. Biery is responding to an article that I wrote. He quotes without credit from my article on Christian Governance, "God alone is the owner of His churches and their ministries."

First of all, I believe that Policy Governance® is applicable to Christian organizations, but that it requires an adjustment or particular focus for it to be biblically faithful. This statement alone suggests that Carver's Policy Governance is not in and of itself biblically faithful. And it is not. Biblical faithfulness requires acknowledgment of God's sovereignty and the implications thereof. Carter makes no such acknowledgment, neither explicitly nor implicitly. Rather, he credits several secular writers as providing the essential foundation for his system, and is unaware of the biblical foundation he is building upon. Yet, simply building upon a biblical foundation is no guarantee of biblical fidelity. The Judaizers built on biblical foundations but failed to be faithful (Romans 9:6).

The issue of biblical faithfulness and the determination of what constitutes such faithfulness is itself a point of contention. For instance, the Unitarian Universalist Association (UUA) is (I believe) the only denomination that recommends Policy Governance® for its member churches. But the UUA, by its own definition is not Christian in any traditional sense. Following in its wake, other churches are endeavoring to use Policy Governance® principles, most of which would be categorized as Lib-

---

18 http://www.broadbaker.com/ArtRespnstoIssuesConcerningOwnership-Biblical.htm

eral. (See *Christianity and Liberalism*, by J. Gresham Machen, 1921, public domain.)

The point I attempted to make in my previous article is that for faithful Christians biblical principles must trump Policy Governance® principles. Said another way, biblical principles have priority over Policy Governance® principles. The points at which they are in conflict are no doubt another area of discussion. I suggested in my previous article that the idea of ownership is an area that Policy Governance may easily differ with the dictates of Scripture. The area of organizational ownership provides a clear example of how organizations can give a theological nod to the "ultimate" ownership of God, and proceed to ignore the practical implications of biblical principles through Policy Governance.®

Before you think that I am being unfair to those who use Policy Governance® in a Christian organization because I accuse them of being philosophically or theologically inconsistent, let me say that such inconsistency is not limited to such a small circle of people. The practice of logical inconsistency is not new with the advent of Policy Governance®. It has a long and distinguished history. (See the work of Cornelius Van Til who has traced this kind of logical inconsistency through the history of Christianity in his groundbreaking books.) Jesus Himself acknowledged the reality of such inconsistency in Matthew 7:21-22, Matthew13:15 and Matthew 15:18 (quoting from Isaiah 29:13). The fact that this kind of logical inconsistency is rampant today, in the church and out, makes discussion difficult and complex in spite of the fact that biblical truth is itself not difficult to understand.

Let me repeat myself, Policy Governance® has application to Christian organizations, but to remain faithful to Scripture some adjustments must be made. And the first of those adjustments has to do with the issue of organizational ownership. Since Christians in fellowship are an expression of the church, the issue is: who owns the church? I agree with most of what Dr. Biery has said about ownership regarding God as the ultimate owner and the potential abuse of authority. But the abuse of authority is not unique to Christianity, all authority can be abused, whether by an executive, a board of directors, or even civil government —Christian, Muslim, or Atheist.

A Google® search using "critique of policy governance" will bring up a list of articles with varying objections to Policy Governance. (For instance, *The Exercise of Power*.[19]) Among the critics of Policy Gover-

---

19 http://www.ftlcomm.com/ensign/desantisArticles/2000_200/desantis230/CarverMa-

nance are those who accuse it of setting up the CEO to abuse the sweeping authority accorded to him/her by Policy Governance boards. My point is simply that Christianity is not the source of the abuse of authority, sin is. And only Christianity faithfully engaged can remedy sin. By the same token, the issue of the abuse of authority is one of the primary issues that feeds the devolution of civil society in our day. Because corporate structure has historically followed the organizational principles of Congregationalism (my own church background), corporations and other organizations who have charters, officers, boards, and by-laws are essentially Congregational in polity. And the single most destructive error of Congregational churches is its failure to understand and abide by biblical authority.

In the same way that the CEO can abuse his/her authority in the organization s/he is responsible for, the board can abuse its powers of oversight, using those powers to inappropriately to seek their own gain, break laws, and/or act immorally. While one of the strengths of Policy Governance® is its emphasis and treatment of accountability, the wrong understanding of accountability definitions and structures—and particularly to whom one is ultimately accountable to—can still lead to a lack of accountability.

Again, my point is that Christian organizations have not cornered the market in the abuse of authority. In fact, with some adjustments Policy Governance® can help to reclaim a proper understanding of authority and accountability. But it must be understood that all authority is founded on biblical authority because God is the original author (authority) of humanity, social order, and history. The perspective that I am arguing for (and I believe that Dr. Biery and may I agree on this) is that biblical principles and values must actively engage policy development and deployment for Christian organizations. The critical issues involve the definition of said principles, values, and the methodology of their employment. (Dr. Biery and I may even discover that we have much agreement about these matters, as well.)

Nonetheless, I must press the point. The danger of people thinking of themselves as owners or even co-owners of Christian organizations is that Carver insists that the board is obligated to accomplish the purposes set by the owners. When people—in particular the board—understand themselves to be owners or co-owners they tend to believe that they then hold the power (or some of the power) to determine the ends and

---

ch.htm

purposes for which the organization exists. My point is that such determination belongs to God alone. And so, I cry with the historic Protestant Reformers, "*Sola Scriptura, Solus Christus, Sola Gratia, Sola Fide* and *Soli Deo Gloria.*" As stewards we are relatively free to determine how to accomplish God's purposes, but not to alter those purposes themselves.

Often purpose and methodology are intimately related. And a change in methodology will often produce a change in purpose. Great care must be taken to honor and maintain God's purposes for His church. This is the issue, and I am arguing that too many churches take too many liberties at exactly this point, policy governed or not.

In other words, God is not merely the "ultimate" owner, but He is the "immediate" owner as well. The suggestion that God is the "ultimate" owner suggests the theology of Deism, not Christianity. Deism is the belief that God exists but is not involved in the world. It maintains that God created all things and set the universe in motion and is no longer involved in its operation. Such a theology denies the sovereignty of God and substitutes the sovereignty of humanity by suggesting that God allows people to do whatever they think best. In contrast, traditional, biblical Christianity understands human freedom to have its highest expression in the accomplishment of (and obedience to) God's will.

This is the issue of authority that must be explicitly addressed and exercised by those organizations that intend to be faithful to Scripture. Therefore, prior to a discussion of how Carver's Policy Governance® applies to biblically faithful governance of Christian organizations there must be some common understanding of what it means to be faithful to Scripture because the principles of biblical fidelity must take precedence over the principles of Policy Governance® in church related organizations. At the same time, it will be discovered that there are many areas that the principles of Policy Governance® do provide helpful clarity and appropriate application for Christian organizations.

Biery says that "Policy Governance, whether religious or secular, is always temporal and composed of people." I agree. All human authorities must be held accountable to other human beings. Christian Governance is also always temporal and composed of people, but it is not *merely* temporal. It is also eternal. And in a similar vein, Jesus Christ is a person—not only *was* He a person when He walked the earth, but He *is* an eternal Person of the Holy Trinity (a point that is denied by Unitarians, by the way). Biery's point is that people must be accountable to other people. I agree.

But at the same time, people are not *merely* accountable to other people. They are also accountable to God, to history, to law, etc. Can living people be accountable to dead people? Yes, according to current law people can be accountable through corporate and legal structures like wills and trusts to someone who is deceased. My point is that living people can be accountable to more than other living people—and limiting accountability merely to other people in denial of immediate accountability to God and history encourages the failure to learn from and incorporate the values and principles of history and Scripture.

Biery's treatment of the relationship between church and state is too shallow—yet understandably so. This is a side issue that I brought up in my previous article as an example of how biblical authority differs from so-called secular authority. He says that "the U. S. Constitution guarantees that the government does not have the right to 'establish' or intervene in the religious enterprise of the people, their beliefs and religious practices." I agree. However, the establishment of 501(c)(3) taxable status for religious organizations constitutes a violation of the Establishment Clause of the First Amendment because it establishes civil government tax laws for churches. That is the central protection of the Establishment Clause and constitutes an encroachment of civil authority into the jurisdiction of church authority because, as Biery acknowledges, it subsumes church authority under civil authority.

And in fact, that law impinges directly upon the preaching (and therefore the doctrine and theology) of churches in that it forbids certain political topics from the pulpit in order to maintain that tax status. Technically, the law was not passed by Congress, but by the IRS, so the letter of the Constitution is acknowledged at the same time the spirit of the Constitution is denied. This is another example of that logical inconsistency mentioned earlier.

However, this does not mean that religious organizations are "above" the law. Churches that violate the law and endanger and/or abuse people must be held responsible. Church jurisdiction is not immune to the civil jurisdiction any more than the civil jurisdiction is immune to church jurisdiction. There are areas where these jurisdictions will impinge upon one another and discretion is required for adjudication. Complete separation is impossible.

But that is far beyond the scope of our present concern. For our purposes, we need to acknowledge that churches must comply with civil law. It is the extent of the jurisdiction of civil law that is in question. Nonetheless, we all must "Render to Caesar the things that are Caesar's, and to God the things that are God's" (Mark 12:17). Paul repeats this sentiment in Romans 13:1, "Let every person be subject to the governing authorities. For there is no authority except from God, and those that exist have been instituted by God."[20]

Biery's conclusion that Policy Governance® as a structure builds in the idea that the board must know the ends and purposes of the owner(s) is true enough, as far as it goes. Policy Governance® does do this. However, that fact in and of itself is no guarantee that those who practice Policy Governance® will in fact faithfully honor the purposes of the founders and/or owners. If you need an example of this, ask yourself whether any organizations have ever gotten away from the original purposes of their founders. This is such a commonplace fact of modern society that it might be better to ask what long standing organizations have not done this. And when its done it begins in the board room.

Take Yale or Harvard Universities, for instance. Both were founded for the purpose of providing educated clergy for faithful Protestant Reformed Christian churches. They were both founded as bastions of orthodox Protestant theology. Where are they now? Are they faithful to the vision of their founders? No, they produce far more atheists and agnostics than Christians. The same pattern of the abandonment of founding principles has swept through modern society, and much of it occurs in the name (but not in the spirit) of historical and theological fidelity. In other words, it is common today for organizations to claim to be faithful to their founders while undermining and disregarding the very faith they claim.

These organizations have always been accountable to their boards. That fact is indisputable. But what they have not been accountable to is God and history. It is precisely because of the effectiveness of Policy Governance® that makes it both appealing and dangerous. Authority is clearly identified and empowered, decision making is streamlined, and organizations are equipped to do what they do much more effectively by using Policy Governance.® That is not in doubt.

---

20 Note that religious organizations are not mandated to become governmentally sanctioned 501(c)(3) tax exempt organizations. Such a designation is voluntary and not required by the IRS or any department of the Federal Government. This is a huge issue. For further study see: www.hushmoney.org.

The issue I am trying to raise is that it is not good to give an organization that is already going in the wrong direction the power to accomplish the wrong ends more effectively. I enthusiastically agree with Dr. Biery that the obligation of the religious board is to "know both the mind of its temporal owners and the Mind of its ultimate Owner to the extent it can know His Word and seek His wisdom."

However, after twenty-five years of ministry I must confess that religious boards are awash in the worldly concerns of fundraising and property management, and all too often fail to "know His Word and seek His wisdom" in the board room. Fundraising and property management are not the central concerns of Scripture, nor do they reflect the core values and principles of Scripture. Boards focus on them because they are relatively easy to accomplish, are immediate, demanding and pressing, and are measurable. Whereas the high ideals, values, and principles of Scripture provide a much more difficult row to hoe, much less to measure. But they are the true ends for which Christ's church should exist. Difficulty is not an excuse for poor performance. Nonetheless, poor performance is preferable to excellence in the accomplishment of the wrong ends.

Inasmuch as the governing bodies of Christian churches and church related organizations focus on worldly ends, they encourage the adoption of worldly ends by their members and future leaders. And that is exactly what we see when we take a long view of the historical development of Christian churches in America over the last two centuries. As worldly values have crept into the church and her governing bodies churches have increasingly chased after worldly ends and the "practical" means dictated by the world for their accomplishment. (I am advocating biblical principles, not "other worldly" ends and means.)

Furthermore, I contend that this is a central concern for Policy Governance® because Policy Governance® has taken its central insights from Scripture (though Carver has not acknowledged the extent of his debt to Scripture). Thus, Policy Governance® in general should conform to the (greater, larger, wider, higher) ideals, values, and principles of Scripture prior to, and in the midst of, the practice of governance. "Governance" is another word for "leadership." And the fundamental characteristic of church leadership is faithfulness, not polity or the mechanics of governance.

Policy Governance® is in fact a highly effective method of organizational governance. And precisely for that reason, greater attention must be given to consistent biblical faithfulness prior to and during the exercise of Policy Governance® lest the very effectiveness of Policy Governance® become the source of greater demise by more efficiently leading churches and ministries further and faster away from God's central purposes.

Seeker Friendly

"This 'seeker' or sinner-friendly church growth movement theology suggests that the Church needs to be conformed to the image of the world. But the Apostle Paul writes that we (and the world) are to be conformed to the image of Christ (Romans 12:2). Christ is a rock of offense to the world and we are trying to make Him appealing to the world. Decorate and disguise Christ and then you can reach 'unchurched Harry and Mary' and draw people into the Kingdom? Entertain people into repentance? Whatever happened to the scriptural commandment "come out from among them, be ye separate?" (2 Corinthians 6:17).

> Christ was willing to become publicly humiliated (not decorated), scourged, disgraced, shamed, pulverized beyond recognition for us. But the seeker-friendly movement seems to suggest that we have to apologize for the gospel in order not to offend anyone. The Church in Symrna was one of only two churches in Revelation which Christ commended and had NOTHING against. Why? Because they were faithful even to the point of death (Revelation 2:10). These saints were willing to be (and were) martyred. At the end of time we see again saints who 'loved their lives not unto death' (Revelation 12:11). In fact, even in the Twentieth Century there have been more saints martyred than since the foundation of the Church."[21]

The Practice of Christianity in the Local Church

The practice of Christianity apart from a proper theological foundation, firmly rooted in the Word of God written, builds on uncertain ground. The success of Christ's Church depends upon the clear, explicit articulation of the historic biblical gospel.

God's Governance, Not Man's

Congregationalism is often misunderstood to be a kind of church democracy where everyone has a vote and the church is governed by majority rule. While this description is true to an extent, it is a blatant misrepresentation of the deeper truth of the Congregational model of church government. Christ's church is not governed by majority rule,

---

21 Sundquist, James. *Church Growth Movement, Part I, Biblical Christianity or the Church of Laodicea?*, 2003.

but by Jesus Christ. Congregationalism conforms to God's will as long as church decisions conform to God's rule.

This, however, does not mean that Congregationalism is without human leadership. Churches are to be governed by pastors, elders and deacons with the blessing and approval of the congregation, in conformity to Scripture.

Equality Before God

One of the primary tenets of Congregationalism is that all believers are of equal status before God. In regard to this, three things must be observed and followed for Congregationalism to remain true to the gospel.

First, we must honor the principle that only born-again believers are actually members of Christ's Body, the Church—universal and triumphant. Regeneration is a necessary criteria for church membership. In as much as members are not regenerate, the church falls into corruption. Unregenerate people are not led by the Holy Spirit. Where the majority of church members are unregenerate, they are given to mob rule, and are able to out vote the leadership of the Holy Spirit. This is not only a potential danger, but has happened many times in history. However, the danger of the abuse of authority does not out weigh the need to maintain sensitivity to the Spirit's leadership.

Second, it must be recognized that the equal status of believers before God does not mean that all believers have the same function and authority in the church. Status is not the same as function or authority. Nor does function or authority confer superior or inferior status upon some of God's people. Equality before God is not a matter of power, but pertains to sin, guilt, repentance, forgiveness, and humility. We are all equally guilty and equally forgiven of sin before God.

The equal status of believers before God means that each church member must be in complete and, therefore, equal submission to God and His ordained agencies—primarily to Scripture, but where men have an authority given by Scripture, then to those men, as well. But remember, Christ's authority turns leaders into servants.

The biblical model (Ephesians 5 and 6) is: elders and deacons in submission to Christ, husbands in submission to elders and deacons (in the Lord), wives in submission to husbands (in the Lord), children in submission to parents (in the Lord). All are to be equally submitted to Christ through an ordained authority. Where this submission is not in evidence, the Body of Christ—the Church—is corrupt. That is, it is rusty and cannot function properly.

Equal status before God is reflected in Congregationalism by the practice that each church member has equal voice and vote. The Holy Spirit is equally able to reach and lead each regenerate member. The principle of the wisdom of Proverbs is maintained "in the multitude of counselors" (Proverbs 11:14). Yet, the assumption and necessity is that each member is regenerate and their counsel is Spirit-led.

Another danger within Congregationalism is the temptation to disregard the ordained structures of authority and function (the spiritual leadership of elders, deacons, and husbands) because of a misunderstanding of the believer's equal status before God. Again, equal status does not justify the disregard of family or church authority. Nor does God-given authority justify its abuse. Equal status does not mean equal function.

It must also be a matter of understanding and practice that God's ordained authority operates by inspiration and not by domination. God's leaders serve, they do not lord over others (Matthew 20:25-26). All biblical submission must be submission to Christ through a regenerate, ordained authority, i.e. elder, deacon, born-again husband.

Third, the purpose of Congregational polity is to encourage, support, and follow the leadership of the Holy Spirit. In other words, Congregational churches are not to be led by majority vote, as if the church members are in a political contest. Rather, each born-again church member is to study God's Word, seek the leading the of Holy Spirit, and only then to vote his or her biblically informed conscience in matters of arbitration.

Division in the Body (the Church) indicates the failure to adequately seek the Lord's will regarding the matter causing division. Rather than move forward on the basis of a divided vote regarding some issue, the church should enter into further prayer and Bible study regarding the matter. Division in Congregational churches should not be a call for action, but must be seen as a call for additional spiritual discernment. To force a vote or call for action in the face of division is a sign of corruption because it ruptures the integrity of the body (the Church). Of course, this practice can only work where the church is truly regenerate.

Born Again

More than simply vote on a matter, Congregationalists must be ready and able to biblically and theologically justify their position—to convince others or to be convinced by others, because it is in the process of biblical and theological justification of the concerns at hand that Congregational polity calls upon the leadership of the Spirit. Consequently, only when those who have voting privileges are regenerate—in a personal relationship with Jesus Christ, and actually seek and obey the leadership of the Holy Spirit—does the Spirit actually lead. The failure of any one aspect of Congregational polity can diminish the leadership of the Holy Spirit and open the church to potential error and corruption.

Because belief determines behavior, errors of belief result in lapses of moral and organizational behavior. Congregationalism is a very effective means of allowing the church to be led by the Spirit, but it also falls easily into error unless each church member actively and honestly pursues the leadership of the Holy Spirit in his or her own life.

Head Of The Church

Jesus Christ is the real head of each local church—not the pastor, not the elders, not the deacons, not the majority vote. The church functions correctly only when the pastor, elders, deacons, and members are in full submission to Jesus Christ, God's Word.

If Jesus Christ is not your personal head (Lord) and the head (Lord) of your family in both theory and practice, you are neither regenerate nor Spirit-led. Christ's leadership begins in the family, and must be evidenced in the family (Ephesians 5:22-ff) before it is granted in the church.

Right Foundation

Congregationalism is rooted in the theology of the Protestant Reformation. The clarity and comprehensiveness of that theology is the key to its success. The only effective foundation of any local church is a clear, orthodox (right) expression of biblical theology. Theology requires knowledge and understanding of God. Theology is the first fruit of a personal relationship with the Lord. In personal relationship we come to know the Lord. When churches (God's people) stray from classic, biblical Christianity they produce the fruit of error—sin and heartache.

Our beliefs guide our conscience, and our conscience guides our behavior. Immoral and ungodly behavior evidence a misinformed conscience. And a misinformed conscience is reformed by orthodox (right) belief, right doctrine. The church becomes dictatorial when it focuses upon the enforcement of moral behavior because real morality is always self-imposed by one's own conscience, not imposed by others. Therefore, the church's correct area of function is the teaching of orthodox (right) belief or biblical doctrine. Errors of practice and behavior are indications of errors in belief.

Fallacies of Contemporary Churches

Sunday School is not found in Scripture, but is an example of the church following the lead of the culture. Sunday School works against the integrity and jurisdiction of the family by undercutting the father's responsibility to bring up his children in the love and admonition of the Lord. Sure, fathers are largely irresponsible. But the way to encourage their responsibility is not to usurp their authority. Rather, the church should insist that they engage their authority by exercising their responsibility for the spiritual leadership of the family.

Youth Groups tend to provide impressionable teenagers with the immature counsel of their peers, rather than providing counsel and godly models of faithful adults. Like most youth oriented programs and instruction, youth groups tend toward immaturity and irresponsibility. Popularity tends to command the attention of the participants.[22]

Pastoral divorce, not divorce among the clergy, but the successive divorces that clergy and their families model by moving from church to church, sets a tone of covenantal infidelity among believers. If church membership involves a covenant with God and other church members, it is comparable to marriage. The Bible teaches that marriage is to be a life-long relationship. The marriage grows mature by working through difficulty, not by avoiding it. The same is (or should be) true of church membership. Most of the time a pastor leaves his church and covenants with another he is committing spiritual divorce among God's people. The same is true for lay people who go from church to church, but the pastor has more responsibility in that he tends to set the model for be-

---

22   See *Critique of Modern Youth Ministry*, by Christopher Schlect, Canon Press, Moscow, Idaho.

havior in his church. Should a pastor remain with single church for his whole ministry? Life-long relationships are the biblical norm for covenants.

THE CAMBRIDGE PLATFORM

A declaration of principles of church government and discipline, forming a constitution of the Congregational churches. It was adopted by a church synod at Cambridge, Mass. in 1648, and remains the basis of the temporal government of the churches. It had little to do with matters of doctrine and belief. The Congregationalists of Connecticut later subscribed (1708), in the Saybrook Platform, to a more centralized church government, resembling Presbyterianism.

CHAPTER I

Of the form of church government; and that it is one, immutable, and prescribed in the word.

1. Ecclesiastical polity, or church government or discipline, is nothing else but that form and order that is to be observed in the church of Christ upon earth, both for the constitution of it, and all the administrations that therein are to be performed.

2. Church government is considered in a double respect, either in regard of the parts of government themselves, or necessary circumstances thereof. The parts of government are prescribed in the Word, because the Lord Jesus Christ, the King and Lawgiver in his church, is no less faithful in the house of God, than was Moses, who from the Lord delivered a form and pattern of government to the children of Israel in the Old Testament; and the holy Scriptures are now also so perfect as they are able to make the man of God perfect, and thoroughly furnished unto every good work; and therefore doubtless to the well ordering of the house of God.

3. The parts of church government are all of them exactly described in the Word of God being parts or means of instituted worship according to the second commandment, and therefore to continue one and the same unto the appearing of our Lord Jesus Christ, as a kingdom that cannot be shaken, until he shall deliver it up unto God, even to the Father. So that it is not left in the power of men, officers, churches, or any state in the world, to add, or diminish, or alter any thing in the least measure therein.

4. The necessary circumstances, as time and place, etc., belonging unto order and decency, are not so left unto men, as that, under pretense of them, they may thrust their own inventions upon

the churches, being circumscribed in the Word with many general limitations, where they are determined with respect to the matter to be neither worship itself, nor circumstances separable from worship. In respect of their end, they must be done unto edification; in respect of the manner, decently and in order, according to the nature of the things themselves, and civil and church custom. Does not even nature itself teach you? Yea, they are in some sort determined particularly—namely, that they be done in such a manner as, all circumstances considered, is most expedient for edification: So as, if there be no error of man concerning their determination, the determining of them is to be accounted as if it were divine.

CHAPTER II

Of the nature of the catholic church in general, and in special of a particular visible church.

1. The catholic church is the whole company of those that are elected, redeemed, and in time effectually called from the state of sin and death unto a state of grace and salvation in Jesus Christ.

2. This church is either triumphant or militant. Triumphant, the number of them who are glorified in heaven; militant, the number of them who are conflicting with their enemies upon earth.

3. This militant church is to be considered as invisible and visible. Invisible, in respect to their relation, wherein they stand to Christ as a body unto the head, being united unto him by the spirit of God and faith in their hearts. Visible, in respect of the profession of their faith, in their persons, and in particular churches. And so there may be acknowledged a universal visible church.

4. The members of the militant visible church, considered either as not yet in church order, or walking according to the church order of the gospel. In order, and so besides the spiritual union and communion common to all believers, they enjoy moreover a union and communion ecclesiastical, political. So we deny a universal visible church.

5. The state of the members of the militant visible church, walking in order, was either before the law, economical, that is, in fami-

lies; or under the law, national; or since the coming of christ, only congregational (the term independent, we approve not): therefore neither national, provincial, nor classical.

6.   A congregational church is by the institution of Christ a part of the militant visible church, consisting of a company of saints by calling, united into one body by a holy covenant, for the public worship of God, and the mutual edification of one another in the fellowship of the Lord Jesus.

CHAPTER III

Of the matter of the visible church, both in respect of quality and quantity.

1.   The matter of the visible church are saints by calling.
2.   By saints, we understand:
     1.   Such as have not only attained the knowledge of the prin-ciples of religion, and are free from gross and open scandals, but also do, together with the profession of their faith and repentance, walk in blameless obedience to the Word, so as that in charitable discretion they may be accounted saints by calling, (though perhaps some or more of them be un-sound and hypocrites inwardly), because the members of such particular churches are commonly by the Holy Ghost called "saints and faithful brethren in Christ"; and sundry churches have been reproved for receiving, and suffering such persons to continue in fellowship among them, as have been offensive and scandalous; the name of God also, by this means, is blasphemed, and the holy things of God defiled and profaned, the hearts of the godly grieved, and the wicked themselves hardened and helped forward to damnation. The example of such does endanger the sanc-tity of others, a little leaven leavens the whole lump.
     2.   The children of such who are also holy.
3.   The members of churches, though orderly constituted, may in time degenerate, and grow corrupt and scandalous, which, though they ought not to be tolerated in the church, yet their continuance therein, through the defect of the execution of dis-cipline and just censures, does not immediately dissolve the be-ing of a church, as appears in the church of Israel, and the churches of Galatia and Corinth, Pergamos and Thyatira.

4. The matter of the church, in respect of its quantity, ought not to be of greater number than may ordinarily meet together conveniently in one place; nor ordinarily fewer than may conveniently carry on church work. Hence, when the holy Scripture makes mention of the saints combined into a church estate in a town or city, where was but one congregation, it usually calls those saints "the church" in the singular number, as "the church of the Thessalonians," "the church of Smyrna, Philadelphia," etc.; but when it speaks of the saints in a nation or province, wherein there were sundry congregations, it frequently and usually calls them by the name of "churches" in the plural number, as the "churches of Asia, Galatia, Macedonia," and the like; which is further confirmed by what is written of sundry of those churches in particular, how they were assembled and met together the whole church in one place, as the church at Jerusalem, the church at Antioch, the church at Corinth and Cenchrea, though it were more near to Corinth, it being the port thereof, and answerable to a village; yet being a distinct congregation from Corinth, it had a church of its own, as well as Corinth had.

5. Nor can it with reason be thought but that every church appointed and ordained by Christ, had a ministry appointed and ordained for the same, and yet plain it is that there were no ordinary officers appointed by Christ for any other than congregational churches; elders being appointed to feed not all flocks, but the particular flock of God, over which the Holy Ghost had made them overseers, and that flock they must attend, even the whole flock; and one congregation being as much as any ordinary elders can attend, therefore there is no greater church than a congregation which may ordinarily meet in one place.

CHAPTER IV
Of the form of the visible church, and of church covenant.

1. Saints by calling must have a visible political union among themselves, or else they are not yet a particular church, as those similitudes hold forth, which the Scripture makes use of to show the nature of particular churches; as a body, a building, house, hands, eyes, feet and other members, must be united, or else (remaining separate) are not a body. Stones, timber, though

squared, hewn and polished, are not a house, until they are compacted and united; so saints or believers in judgment of charity, are not a church unless orderly knit together.

2. Particular churches cannot be distinguished one from another but by their forms. Ephesus is not Smyrna, nor Pergamos Thyatira; but each one a distinct society of itself, having officers of their own, which had not the charge of others; virtues of their own, for which others are not praised; corruptions of their own, for which others are not blamed.

3. This form is the visible covenant, agreement; or consent, whereby they give up themselves unto the Lord, to the observing of the ordinances of Christ together in the same society, which is usually called the "church covenant" for we see not otherwise how members can have church power over one another mutually. The comparing of each particular church to a city, and unto a spouse, seems to conclude not only a form, but that that form is by way of covenant. The covenant, as it was that which made the family of Abraham and children of Israel to be a church and people unto God, so is it that which now makes the several societies of Gentile believers to be churches in these days.

4. This voluntary agreement, consent or covenant—for all these are here taken for the same—although the more express and plain it is, the more fully it puts us in mind of our mutual duty; and stirs us up to it, and leaves less room for the questioning of the truth of the church estate of a company of professors, and the truth of membership of particular persons; yet we conceive the substance of it is kept where there is real agreement and consent of a company of faithful persons to meet constantly together in one congregation, for the public worship of God, and their mutual edification; which real agreement and consent they do express by their constant practice in coming together for the public worship of God and by their religious subjection unto the ordinances of God there: the rather, if we do consider how Scripture covenants have been entered into, not only expressly by word of mouth, but by sacrifice, by handwriting and seal; and also sometimes by silent consent, without any writing or expression of words at all.

5. This form being by mutual covenant, it follows, it is not faith in the heart, nor the profession of that faith, nor cohabitation, nor baptism.

    1. Not faith in the heart, because that is invisible.
    2. Not a bare profession, because that declares them no more to be members of one church than another.
    3. Not cohabitation: Atheists or Infidels may dwell together with believers.
    4. Not Baptism, because it presupposes a church estate, as circumcision in the Old Testament, which gave no being to the church, the church being before it, and in the wilderness without it. Seals presuppose a covenant already in being. One person is a complete subject of baptism, but one person is incapable of being a church.

6. All believers ought, as God gives them opportunity thereunto, to endeavor to join themselves unto a particular church, and that in respect of the honor of Jesus Christ, in his example and institution, by the professed acknowledgment of and subjection unto the order and ordinances of the gospel; as also in respect of their good communion founded upon their visible union, and contained in the promises of Christ's special presence in the church; whence they have fellowship with him, and in him, one with another; also in the keeping of them in the way of God's commandments, and recovering of them in case of wandering, (which all Christ's sheep are subject to in this life), being unable to return of themselves; together with the benefit of their mutual edification, and of their posterity, that they may not be cut off from the privileges of the covenant. Otherwise, if a believer offends, he remains destitute of the remedy provided in that behalf. And should all believers neglect this duty of joining to all particular congregations, it might follow thereupon that Christ should have no visible, political churches upon earth.

CHAPTER V

Of the first subject of church power; or, to whom church power doth first belong.

1. The first subject of church power is either supreme, or subordinate and ministerial. The supreme (by way of gift from the Father) is the Lord Jesus Christ. The ministerial is either extraordi-

nary, as the apostles, prophets and evangelists; or ordinary, as every particular Congregational church.

2. Ordinary church power is either power of office—that is, such as is proper to the eldership—or power of privilege, such as belongs to the brotherhood. The latter is in the brethren formally and immediately from Christ—that is, so as it may, according to order, be acted or exercised immediately by themselves; the former is not in them formally or immediately, and therefore cannot be acted or exercised immediately by them, but is said to be in them, in that they design the persons unto office, who only are to act or to exercise this power.

CHAPTER VI

Of the officers of the church, and especially of pastors and teachers.

1. A church being a company of people combined together by covenant for the worship of God, it appears thereby that there may be the essence and being of a church without any officers, seeing there is both the form and matter of a church; which is implied when it is said, "the apostles ordained elders in every church."

2. Nevertheless, though officers be not absolutely necessary to the simple being of churches, when they be called; yet ordinarily to their calling they are, and to their well being; and therefore the Lord Jesus Christ, out of his tender compassion, has appointed and ordained officers, which he would not have done, if they had not been useful and needful for the church; yea, being ascended up to heaven, he received gifts for men, and gave gifts to men; whereof officers for the church are justly accounted no small parts, they being to continue to the end of the world, and for the perfecting of all the saints.

3. These officers were either extraordinary or ordinary: extraordinary, as apostles, prophets, evangelists; ordinary, as elders and deacons. The apostles, prophets, and evangelists, as they were called extraordinarily by Christ, so their office ended with themselves; whence it is that Paul, directing Timothy how to carry along church administration, gives no direction about the choice or course of apostles, prophets or evangelists, but only of elders and deacons; and when Paul was to take his last leave of the church of Ephesus, he committed the care of feeding the

church to no other, but unto the elders of that church. The like charge does Peter commit to the elders.

4. Of elders (who are also in Scripture called bishops) some attend chiefly to the ministry of the Word, as the pastors and teachers; others attend especially unto rule, who are, therefore, called ruling elders.

5. The office of pastor and teacher appears to be distinct. The pastor's special work is, to attend to exhortation, and therein to administer a word of wisdom; the teacher is to attend to doctrine, and therein to administer a word of knowledge; and either of them to administer the seals of that covenant, unto the dispensation whereof they are alike called; as also to execute the censures, being but a kind of application of the word: the preaching of which, together with the application thereof, they are alike charged withal.

6. And for as much as both pastors and teachers are given by Christ for the perfecting of the saints and edifying of his body; which saints and body of Christ is his church; and therefore we account pastors and teachers to be both of them church officers, and not the pastor for the church, and the teacher only for the schools: though this we gladly acknowledge, that schools are both lawful, profitable, and necessary for the training up of such in good literature or learning as may afterwards be called forth unto office of pastor or teacher in the church.

CHAPTER VII
Of ruling elders and deacons.

1. The ruling elder's office is distinct from the office of pastor and teacher; the ruling elders are not so called to exclude the pastors and teachers from ruling, because ruling and governing is common to these with the other; whereas attending to teach and preach the Word is peculiar unto the former.

2. The ruling elder's work is to join with the pastor and teacher in those acts of spiritual rule, which are distinct from the ministry of the Word and sacraments committed to them; of which sort these be as follows:

    1. To open and shut the doors of God's house, by the admission of members approved by the church; by ordination of officers chosen by the church and by excommunication of

notorious and obstinate offenders renounced by the church, and by restoring of penitents forgiven by the church.

2. To call the church together when there is occasion, and seasonably to dismiss them again.

3. To prepare matters in private, that in public they may be carried an end with less trouble, and more speedy dispatch.

4. To moderate the carriage of all matters in the church assembled, as to propound matters to the church. To order the season of speech and silence, and to pronounce sentence according to the mind of Christ with the consent of the church.

5. To be guides and leaders to the church in all matters whatsoever pertaining to church administrations and actions.

6. To see that none in the church live inordinately, out of rank and place without a calling, or idly in their calling.

7. To prevent and heal such offenses in life or in doctrine as might corrupt the church.

8. To feed the flock of God with a word of admonition.

9. And, as they shall be sent for, to visit and pray over their sick brethren.

10. And at other times, as opportunity shall serve thereunto.

3. The office of a deacon is instituted in the church by the Lord Jesus; sometimes they are called helps. The Scripture tells us how they should be qualified: "Grave, not double-tongued, not given to much wine, not given to filthy lucre." They must first be proved, and then use the office of a deacon, being found blameless. The office and work of a deacon is to receive the offerings of the church, gifts given to the church, and to keep the treasury of the church, and therewith to serve the tables, which the church is to provide for; as the Lord's table, the table of the ministers, and of such as are in necessity, to whom they are to distribute in simplicity.

4. The office, therefore, being limited unto the care of the temporal good things of the church, it extends not to the attendance upon, and administration of the spiritual things thereof, as the Word, and sacraments, and the like.

5. The ordinance of the apostle, and practice of the church, commends the Lord's Day as a fit time for the contributions of the saints.

6. The instituting of all these officers in the church is the work of God himself, of the Lord Jesus Christ, of the Holy Ghost. And therefore such officers as he has not appointed, are altogether unlawful, either to be placed in the church or to be retained therein, and are to be looked at as humane creatures, mere inventions and appointments of man, to the great dishonor of Christ Jesus, the Lord of his house, the King of his church, whether popes, cardinals, patriarchs, archbishops, lord-bishops, arch-deacons, officials, commissaries, and the like. These and the rest of that hierarchy and retinue, not being plants of the Lord's planting, shall all be certainly rooted out and cast forth.

7. The Lord has appointed ancient widows (where they may be had) to minister in the church, in giving attendance to the sick, and to give succor unto them and others in the like necessities.

CHAPTER VIII
Of the election of church officers.

1. No man may take the honor of a church officer unto himself but he that was called of God, as was Aaron.

2. Calling unto office is either immediate, by Christ himself—such was the call of the apostles and prophets; this manner of calling ended with them, as has been said—or mediate, by the church.

3. It is meet that, before any be ordained or chosen officers, they should first be tried and proved, because hands are not suddenly to be laid upon any, and both elders and deacons must be of both honest and good report.

4. The things in respect of which they are to be tried, are those gifts and virtues which the scripture requires in men that are to be elected unto such places, viz.: That elders must be "blameless, sober, apt to teach," and endued with such other qualifications as are laid down: 1 Tim. 3:2; Tit. 1:6-9. Deacons to be fitted as is directed: Acts 6:3; 1 Tim. 3:8-11.

5. Officers are to be called by such churches whereunto they are to minister. Of such moment is the preservation of this power, that the churches exercised it in the presence of the apostles.

6. A church being free, cannot become subject to any but by a free election; yet when such a people do choose any to be over them in the Lord, then do they become subject, and most will-

ingly submit to their ministry in the Lord, whom they have chosen.

7. And if the church have power to choose their officers and ministers, then, in case of manifest unworthiness and delinquency, they have power also to depose them; for to open and shut, to choose and refuse, to constitute in office, and to remove from office, are acts belonging to the same power.

8. We judge it much conducing to the well being and communion of the churches, that, where it may conveniently be done, neighbor churches be advised withal, and their help be made use of in trial of church officers, in order to their choice.

9. The choice of such church officers belongs not to the civil magistrates as such, or diocesan bishops, or patrons: for of these, or any such like, the scripture is wholly silent, as having any power therein.

CHAPTER IX
Of ordination and imposition of hands.

1. Church officers are not only to be chosen by the church, but also to be ordained by imposition of hands and prayer, with which at the ordination of elders, fasting also is to be joined.

2. This ordination we account nothing else but the solemn putting a man into his place and office in the church, whereunto he had right before by election; being like the installing of a magistrate in the commonwealth. Ordination therefore is not to go before, but to follow election, The essence and substance of the outward calling of an ordinary officer in the church does not consist in his ordination, but in his voluntary and free election by the church, and his accepting of that election; whereupon is founded that relation between pastor and flock, between such a minister and such a people. Ordination does not constitute an officer, nor give him the essentials of his office. The apostles were elders, without imposition of hands by men; Paul and Barnabas were officers before that imposition of hands. The posterity of Levi were priests and Levites before hands were laid on them by the children of Israel.

3. In such churches where there are elders, imposition of hands in ordination is to be performed by those elders.

4. In such churches where there are no elders, imposition of hands
    may be performed by some of the brethren orderly chosen by
    the church thereunto. For, if the people may elect officers,
    which is the greater, and wherein the substance of the office
    does consist, they may much more (occasion and need so re-
    quiring) impose hands in ordination; which is the less, and but
    the accomplishment of the other.

5. Nevertheless, in such churches where there are no elders, and
    the church so desire, we see not why imposition of hands may
    not be performed by the elders of other churches. Ordinary
    officers laid hands upon the officers of many churches; the pres-
    bytery at Ephesus laid hands upon Timothy an evangelist; the
    presbytery at Antioch laid hands upon Paul and Barnabas.

6. Church officers are officers to one church, even that particular
    over which the Holy Ghost has made them overseers. Insomuch
    as elders are commanded to feed not all flocks, but the flock
    which is committed to their faith and trust, and depends upon
    them. Nor can constant residence at one congregation be nec-
    essary for a, minister—no, nor yet lawful—if he be not a minis-
    ter to one congregation only, but to the church universal; be-
    cause he may not attend one part only of the church to which
    he is a minister, but he is called to attend unto all the flock.

7. He that is clearly released from his office relation unto that
    church whereof he was a minister, cannot be looked at as an
    officer, nor perform any act of office in any other church, unless
    he be again orderly called unto office; which, when it shall be,
    we know nothing to hinder; but imposition of hands also in his
    ordination ought to be used towards him again: for so Paul the
    apostle received imposition of hands twice at least from Ana-
    nias.

CHAPTER X
Of the power of the church and its presbytery.

1. Supreme and lordly power over all the churches upon earth
    does only belong to Jesus Christ, who is king of the church, and
    the head thereof. He has the government upon his shoulders,
    and has all power given to him, both in heaven and earth.

2. A company of professed believers, ecclesiastically confederate, as
    they are a church before they have officers, and without them;

so, even in that estate, subordinate church power under Christ delegated to them by him, does belong to them in such a manner as is before expressed, Chap. V. Sec. 2, and as flowing from the very nature and essence of a church; it being natural unto all bodies, and so unto a church body, to be furnished with sufficient power for its own preservation and subsistence.

3. This government of the church is a mixed government (and so has been acknowledged, long before the term of independency was heard of); in respect of Christ, the head and king of the church, and the Sovereign Power residing in him, and exercised by him, it is a monarchy; in respect of the body or brotherhood of the church, and power from Christ granted unto them it resembles a democracy, in respect of the presbytery and power committed unto them, it is an aristocracy.

4. The Sovereign Power, which is peculiar unto Christ, is exercised:

    1. In calling the church out of the world into a holy fellowship with himself.

    2. In instituting the ordinances of his worship, and appointing ministers and officers for the dispensing of them.

    3. In giving laws for the ordering of all our ways, and the ways of his house.

    4. In giving power and life to all his institutions, and to his people by them.

    5. In protecting and delivering his church against and from all the enemies of their peace.

5. The power granted by Christ unto the body of the church and brotherhood, is a prerogative or privilege which the church does exercise:

    1. In choosing their own officers, whether elders or deacons.

    2. In admission of their own members; and therefore there is great reason they should have power to remove any from their fellowship again. Hence, in case of offense, any brother has power to convince and admonish an offending brother; and, in case of not hearing him, to take one or two more to set on the admonition; and in case of not hearing them, to proceed to tell the church; and as his offense may require, the whole church has power to proceed to the public censure of him, whether by admonition or excom-

munication: and upon his repentance to restore him again unto his former communion.

6. In case an elder offend incorrigibly, the matter so requiring, as the church had power to call him to office, so they have power according to order (the counsel of other churches, where it may be had, directing thereto) to remove him from his office, and being now but a member, in case he add contumacy to his sin, the church, that had power to receive him into their fellowship, has also the same power to cast him out that they have concerning any other member.

7. Church government or rule is placed by Christ in the officers of the church, who are therefore called rulers, while they rule with God; yet, in case of mal-administration, they are subject to the power of the church, as hath been said before. The Holy Ghost frequently—yea, always—where it mentions church-rule and church government, ascribes it to elders; whereas the work and duty of the people is expressed in the phrase of "obeying their elders," and "submitting themselves unto them in the Lord." So as it is manifest that an organic or complete church is a body politic, consisting of some that are governors and some that are governed in the Lord.

8. The power which Christ has committed to the elders is to feed and rule the church of God, and accordingly to call the church together upon any weighty occasion; when the members so called, without just cause, may not refuse to come, nor when they are come, depart before they are dismissed, nor speak in the church, before they have leave from the elders, nor continue so doing when they require silence; nor may they oppose or contradict the judgment or sentence of the elders, without sufficient and weighty cause, because such practices are manifestly contrary unto order and government, and inlets of disturbance, and tend to confusion.

9. It belongs also unto the elders to examine any officers or members before they be received of the church; to receive the accusations brought to the church, and to prepare them for the churches hearing. In handling of offenses and other matters before the church, they have power to declare and publish the counsel and will of God touching the same, and to pronounce sentence with the consent of the church. Lastly, they have

power, when they dismiss the people, to bless them in the name of the Lord.

10. This power of government in the elders does not any wise prej-udice the power of privilege in the brotherhood; as neither the power of privilege in the brethren, prejudices the power of government in the elders, but they may sweetly agree together; as we may see in the example of the apostles, furnished with the greatest church power, who took in the concurrence and con-sent of the brethren in church administrations. Also that Scrip-ture do declare that what the churches were to act and to do in these matters, they were to do in a way of obedience, and that not only to the direction of the apostles, but also of their ordi-nary elders.

11. From the premises, namely, that the ordinary power of govern-ment belonging only to the elders, power of privilege remain-ing with the brotherhood, (as the power of judgment in matters of censure and power of liberty in matters of liberty,) it follows that in an organic church and right administration, all church acts proceed after the manner of a mixed administration, so as no church act can be consummated or perfected without the consent of both.

CHAPTER XI
Of the maintenance of church officers.

1. The apostle concludes that necessary and sufficient maintenance is due unto the ministers of the Word from the law of nature and nations, from the law of Moses, the equity thereof, as also the rule of common reason. Moreover, the Scripture does not only call elders laborers and workmen, but also, speaking of them, says that "the laborer is worthy of his hire;" and requires that he which is taught in the word, should communicate to him in all good things, and mentions it, as an ordinance of the Lord, that they which preach the gospel, should live of the gospel, and forbids the muzzling of the mouth of the ox that treds out the corn.

2. The Scriptures alleged requiring this maintenance as a bounden duty, and due debt, and not as a matter of alms and free gift, therefore people are not at liberty to do or not to do, what and when they please in this matter, no more than in any other

commanded duty and ordinance of the Lord; but ought of duty to minister of their "carnal things" to them that labor among them in Word and doctrine, as well as they ought to pay any other workmen their wages, and to discharge and satisfy their other debts, or to submit themselves to observe any other ordinance of the Lord.

3. The Apostle, Gal. 6:6, enjoining that he which is taught communicate to him that teaches "in all good things," does not leave it arbitrary, what or how much a man shall give, or in what proportion, but even the latter, as well as the former, is prescribed and appointed by the Lord.

4. Not only members of churches, but "all that are taught in the Word," are to contribute unto him that teaches in all good things. In case that congregations are defective in their contributions, the deacons are to call upon them to do their duty; If their call suffices not, the church by her power is to require it of their members; and where church power, through the corruption of men, does not or cannot attain the end, the magistrate is to see that the ministry be duly provided for, as appears from the commanded example of Nehemiah. The magistrates are nursing fathers and nursing mothers, and stand charged with the custody of both tables; because it is better to prevent a scandal, that it may not come, and easier also, than to remove it, when it is given, it's most suitable to rule, that by the church's care each man should know his proportion according to rule, what he should do before he do it, so that his judgment and heart may be satisfied in what he does, and just offense prevented in what is done.

CHAPTER XII
Of the admission of members into the church.

1. The doors of the churches of Christ upon earth do not by God's appointment stand so wide open, that all sorts of people, good or bad, may freely enter therein at their pleasure; but such as are admitted thereto, as members, ought to be examined and tried first, whether they be fit and meet to be received into church society or not. The Eunuch of Ethiopia, before his admission, was examined by Philip, whether he did believe on Jesus Christ with all his heart. The angel of the church at Ephesus is com-

mended for trying such as said they were Apostles, and were not. There is like reason for trying of them that profess themselves to be believers. The officers are charged with the keeping of the doors of the church, and therefore are in a special manner to make trial of the fitness of such who enter. Twelve angels are set at the gates of the temple, lest such as were "ceremonially unclean" should enter there into.

2. The things which are requisite to be found in all church members, are repentance from sin, and faith in Jesus Christ; and therefore these are the things whereof men are to be examined at their admission into the church, and which then they must profess and hold forth in such sort as may satisfy "rational charity" that the things are indeed. John Baptist admitted men to baptism confessing and bewailing their sins; and of others it is said that "they came and confessed, and showed their deeds."

3. The weakest measure of faith is to be accepted in those that desire to be admitted into the church, because weak Christians, if sincere, have the substance of that faith, repentance and holiness, which is required in church members; and such have most need of the ordinances for their confirmation and growth in grace. The Lord Jesus would not quench the smoking flax, nor break the bruised reed, but gather the tender lambs in his arms, and carry them gently in his bosom. Such charity and tenderness is to be used, as the weakest Christian, if sincere, may not be excluded nor discouraged. Severity of examination is to be avoided.

4. In case any, through excessive fear or other infirmity, be unable to make their personal relation of their spiritual estate in public, it is sufficient that the elders, having received private satisfaction, make relation thereof in public before the church, they testifying their assents thereunto; this being the way that tends most to edification. But whereas persons are of greater abilities, there it is most expedient that they make their relations and confessions personally with their own mouth, as David professes of himself.

5. A personal and public confession and declaring of God's manner of working upon the soul, is both lawful, expedient and useful, in sundry respects and upon sundry grounds. Those three thousand, before they were admitted by the apostles, did

manifest that they were pricked at the heart by Peter's sermon, together with earnest desire to be delivered from their sins, which now wounded their consciences, and their ready receiving of the word of promise and exhortation. We are to be ready to "render a reason of the hope that is in us, to every one that asks us;" therefore we must be able and ready upon any occasion to declare and show our repentance for sin, faith unfeigned, and effectual calling, because these are the reason of a well grounded hope. "I have not hidden thy righteousness from the great congregation."

6. This profession of faith and repentance, as it must be made by such at their admission that were never in church society before; so nothing hinders but the same way also be performed by such as have formerly been members of some other church, and the church to which they now join themselves as members may lawfully require the same. Those three thousand, which made their confession, were members of the church of the Jews before; so were those that were baptized by John. Churches may err in their admission; and persons regularly admitted may fall into offense. Otherwise, if churches might obtrude their members, or if church members might obtrude themselves upon other churches without due trial, the matter so requiring, both the liberty of the churches would thereby be infringed, in that they might not examine those, concerning whose fitness for communion they were unsatisfied; and besides the infringing of their liberty, the churches themselves would unavoidably be corrupted, and the ordinances defiled; while they might not refuse, but must receive the unworthy which is contrary unto the Scripture, teaching that all churches are sisters, and therefore equal.

7. The like trial is to be required from such members of the church as were born in the same, or received their membership, or were baptized in their infancy or minority by virtue of the covenant of their parents, when being grown up unto years of discretion, they shall desire to be made partakers of the Lord's Supper; unto which, because holy things must not be given unto the unworthy, therefore it is requisite that these, as well as others, should come to their trial and examination, and manifest their faith and repentance by an open profession thereof, before

they are received to the Lord's Supper, and otherwise not to be admitted thereunto. Yet these church members that were so born, or received in their childhood, before they are capable of being made partakers of full communion, have many privileges which others (not church members) have not; they are in covenant with God, have the seal thereof upon them, viz: baptism; and so, if not regenerated, yet are in a more hopeful way of attaining regenerating grace, and all the spiritual blessings, both of the covenant and seal; they are also under church watch, and consequently subject to the reprehensions, admonitions and censures thereof, for their healing and amendment, as need shall require.

CHAPTER XIII

Of church members, their removal from one church to another, and of letters of recommendation and dismission.

1. Church members may not remove or depart from the church, and so one from another as they please, nor without just and weighty cause, but ought to live and dwell together, forasmuch as they are commanded not to forsake the assembling of themselves together. Such departure tends to the dissolution and ruin of the body, as the pulling of stones and pieces of timber from the building, and of members from the natural body, tend to the destruction of the whole.

2. It is, therefore, the duty of church members, in such times and places, where counsel may be had, to consult with the church whereof they are members about their removal, that, accordingly, they having their approbation, may be encouraged, or otherwise desist. They who are joined with consent, should not depart without consent, except forced thereunto.

3. If a member's departure be manifestly unsafe and sinful, the church may not consent thereunto; for in so doing they should not act in faith, and should partake with him in his sin. If the case be doubtful and the person not to be persuaded, it seems best to leave the matter unto God, and not forcibly to detain him.

4. Just reasons for a member's removal of himself from the church, are:

    1. If a man cannot continue without partaking in sin.

2. In case of personal persecution: so Paul departed from the disciples at Damascus; also, in case of general persecution, when all are scattered.

3. In case of real, and not only pretended want of competent subsistence, a door being opened for better supply in another place, together with the means of spiritual edification.

4. In these or like cases, a member may lawfully remove, and the church cannot lawfully detain him.

5. To separate from a church, either out of contempt of their holy fellowship, or out of covetousness, or for greater enlargements, with just grief to the church, or out of schism, or want of love; and out of a spirit of contention in respect of some unkindness, of some evil only conceived or intended in the church, which might and should be tolerated and healed with a spirit of meekness, and of which evil the church is not yet convinced (though perhaps himself be) nor admonished; for these or the like reasons, to withdraw from public communion in word or seals, or censures, is unlawful and sinful.

6. Such members as have orderly moved their habitation, ought to join themselves unto the church in order where they do inhabit, if it may be; otherwise, they can neither perform the duties nor receive the privileges of members. Such an example, tolerated in some, is apt to corrupt others, which, if many should follow, would threaten the dissolution and confusion of churches, contrary to the Scripture.

7. Order requires that a member thus removing, have letters testimonial and of dismission from the church whereof he yet is, unto the church whereunto he desires to be joined, lest the church should be deluded; that the church may receive him in faith, and not be corrupted in receiving deceivers and false brethren. Until the person dismissed be received into another church, he ceases not by his letters of dismission to be a member of the church whereof he was. The church cannot make a member no member but by excommunication.

8. If a member be called to remove only for a time where a church is, letters of recommendation are requisite and sufficient for communion with that church in the ordinances and in their watch; as Phoebe, a servant of the church at Cenchrea, had a

letter written for her to the church at Rome, that she might be received as becomes saints.

9. Such letters of recommendation and dismission were written for Apollos, for Marcus to the Colossians, for Phoebe to the Romans, for sundry others to other churches. And the apostle tells us that some persons, not sufficiently known otherwise, have special need of such letters, though he, for his part, had no need thereof. The use of them is to be a benefit and help to the party for whom they are written, and for the furthering of his receiving among the saints, in the place whereto he goes, and the due satisfaction of them in their receiving of him.

CHAPTER XIV
Of excommunication and other censures.

1. The censures of the church are appointed by Christ for the preventing, removing and healing of offenses in the church; for the reclaiming and gaining of offending brethren; for the deterring of others from the like offenses; for purging out the leaven which may infect the whole lump; for vindicating the honor of Christ and of his church, and the holy profession of the gospel; and for preventing of the wrath of God, that may justly fall upon the church, if they should suffer his covenant and the seals thereof to be profaned by notorious and obstinate offenders.

2. If an offense be private, (one brother offending another) the offender is to go and acknowledge his repentance for it unto his offended brother, who is then to forgive him; but if the offender neglect or refuse to do it, the brother offended is to go, and convince and admonish him of it, between themselves privately, if there upon the offender be brought to repent of his offense, the admonisher has won his brother; but if the offender hear not his brother, the brother offended is to take with him one or two more, that in the mouth of two or three witnesses every word may be established, (whether the word of admonition, if the offender receive it; or the word of complaint, if he refuse it,) for if he refuse it, the offended brother is by the mouth of the elders to tell the church, and if he hear the church, and declare the same by penitent confession, he is recovered and gained; and if the church discern him to be willing to hear, yet not fully convinced of his offense, as in case of heresy, they

are to dispense to him a public admonition; which, declaring the offender to lie under the public offense of the church, does thereby withhold or suspend him from the holy fellowship of the Lord's Supper, till his offense be removed by penitent confession. If he still continue obstinate, they are to cast him out by excommunication.

3. But if the offense be more public at first, and of a more heinous and criminal nature, to wit, such as are condemned by the light of nature; then the church, without such gradual proceeding, is to cast out the offender from their holy communion, for the further mortifying of his sin, and the healing of his soul in the Day of the Lord Jesus.

4. In dealing with an offender, great care is to be taken that we be neither over strict or rigorous, nor too indulgent or remiss: our proceeding herein ought to be with a spirit of meekness, considering ourselves, lest we also be tempted, and that the best of us have need of much forgiveness from the Lord. Yet the winning and healing of the offender's soul being the end of these endeavors, we must not daub with untempered mortar, nor heal the wounds of our brethren slightly. On some, have compassion; others, save with fear.

5. While the offender remains excommunicate, the church is to refrain from all member like communion with him in spiritual things, and also from all familiar communion with him in civil things, further than the necessity of natural or domestical or civil relations do require; and are therefore to forbear to eat and drink with him, that he may be ashamed.

6. Excommunication being a spiritual punishment, it doth not prejudice the excommunicate in, nor deprive him of his civil rights, and therefore touches not princes or magistrates in respect of their civil dignity or authority; and the excommunicate being but as a publican and a heathen, heathens being lawfully permitted to come to hear the Word in church assemblies, we acknowledge therefore the like liberty of hearing the word may be permitted to persons excommunicate that is permitted unto heathen. And because we are not without hope of his recovery, we are not to account him as an enemy, but to admonish him as a brother.

7.   If the Lord sanctify the censure to the offender, so as by the grace of Christ, he does testify his repentance with humble confession of his sin, and judging of himself, giving glory unto God, the church is then to forgive him, and to comfort him, and to restore him to the wonted brotherly communion, which formerly he enjoyed with them.

8.   The suffering of profane or scandalous livers to continue in fellowship, and partake in the sacraments, is doubtless a great sin in those that have power in their hands to redress it, and do it not. Nevertheless, in so much as Christ, and his apostles in their times, and the prophets and other godly men in theirs, did lawfully partake of the Lord's commanded ordinances in the Jewish church, and neither taught nor practiced separation from the same, though unworthy ones were permitted therein; and inasmuch as the faithful in the church of Corinth, wherein were many unworthy persons and practices, are never commanded to absent themselves from the sacraments, because of the same; therefore the godly, in like cases, are not to presently separate.

9.   As separation from such a church wherein profane and scandalous livers are tolerated, is not presently necessary; so for the members thereof, otherwise unworthy, hereupon to abstain from communicating with such a church in the participation of the sacraments, is unlawful. For as it were unreasonable for an innocent person to be punished for the faults of others, wherein he has no hand, and whereunto he gave no consent; so is it more unreasonable that a godly man should neglect duty, and punish himself; in not coming for his portion in the blessings of the seals, as he ought, because others are suffered to come that ought not; especially considering that he neither consents to their sin, nor to their approaching to the ordinance in their sin, nor to the neglect of others, who should put them away, and do not; but, on the contrary, heartily mourns for these things, modestly and seasonably stir up others to do their duty. If the church cannot be reformed, they may use their liberty, as is specified, CHAP. XIII. Sect. 4. But this all the godly are bound unto, even every one to do his endeavor, according to his power and place, that the unworthy may be duly proceeded against by the church, to whom this matter does pertain.

CHAPTER XV

Of the communion of churches one with another.

1. Although churches be distinct, and therefore may not be confounded one with another, and equal, and therefore have not dominion one over another; yet all the churches ought to preserve church communion one with another, because they are all united unto Christ, not only as a mystical, but as a political head; whence is derived a communion suitable thereunto.

2. The communion of churches is exercised sundry ways.

    1. By way of mutual care in taking thought for one another's welfare.

    2. By way of consultation one with another, when we have occasion to require the judgment and counsel of other churches, touching any person or cause, wherewith they may be better acquainted than ourselves; as the church of Antioch consulted with the Apostles and elders of the church at Jerusalem, about the question of circumcision of the Gentiles, and about the false teachers that broached that doctrine. In which case, when any church wants light or peace among themselves it is a way of communion of the churches, according to the Word, to meet together by their elders and other messengers in a Synod to consider and argue the points in doubt or difference; and, having found out the way of truth and peace, to commend the same by their letters and messengers to the churches whom the same may concern. But if a church be rent with divisions among themselves, or lie under any open scandal, and yet refuse to consult with other churches for healing or removing of the same, it is matter of just offense, both to the Lord Jesus and to other churches, as betraying too much want of mercy and faithfulness, not to seek to bind up the breaches and wounds of the church and brethren; and therefore the state of such a church calls aloud upon other churches to exercise a fuller act of brotherly communion, to wit, by way of admonition.

    3. A third way, then, of communion of churches, is by way of admonition; to wit, in case any public offense be found in a church, which they either discern not, or are slow in proceeding to use the means for the removing and healing

of. Paul had no authority over Peter, yet when he saw Peter not walking with a right foot, he publicly rebuked him before the church; though churches have no more authority one over another, than one apostle had over another, yet, as one apostle might admonish another, so may one church admonish another, and yet without usurpation. In which case, if the church that lies under offense, does not hearken to the church which does admonish her, the church is to acquaint other neighbor churches with that offense, which the offending church still lies under, together with their neglect of the brotherly admonition given unto them. Whereupon those other churches are to join in seconding the admonition formerly given; and if still the offending church continue in obstinacy and impenitency, they may forbear communion with them, and are to proceed to make use of the help of a Synod or counsel of neighbor churches, walking orderly (if a greater cannot conveniently be had) for their conviction. If they hear not the Synod, the Synod having declared them to be obstinate, particular churches approving and accepting of the judgment of the Synod, are to declare the sentence of non-communion respectively concerning them; and thereupon, out of religious care to keep their own communion pure, they may justly withdraw themselves from participation with them at the Lord's Table, and from such other acts of holy communion, as the communion of churches otherwise does allow and require. Nevertheless, if any members of such a church as lies under public offense, do not consent to the offense of the church, but do in due sort bear witness against it, they are still to be received to wonted communion, for it is not equal that the innocent should suffer with the offensive. Yea, furthermore, if such innocent members, after due waiting in the use of all good means for the healing of the offense of their own church, shall at last (with the allowance of the counsel of neighbor churches,) withdraw from the fellowship of their own church, and offer themselves to the fellowship of another, we judge it lawful for the other church to receive them (being otherwise fit) as if they had been orderly dismissed to them from their own church.

4. A fourth way of communion with churches, is by way of participation; the members of one church occasionally coming unto another, we willingly admit them to partake with them at the Lord's Table, it being the seal of our communion not only with Christ, not only with the members of our own church, but also of all the churches of the saints; in which regard we refuse not to baptize their children presented to us, if either their own minister be absent, or such a fruit of holy fellowship be desired with us. In like cases, such churches as are furnished with more ministers than one, do willingly afford one of their own ministers to supply the place of an absent or sick minister of another church for a needful season.

5. A fifth way of church communion is by way of recommendation, when a member of one church has occasion to reside in another church; if but for a season, we commend him to their watchful fellowship by letters of recommendation; but if he be called to settle his abode there, we commit him, according to his desire, to the fellowship of their covenant by letters of dismission.

6. A sixth way of church communion, is in case of need to minister relief and succor one unto another, either of able members to furnish them with officers, or of outward support to the necessities of poorer churches, as did the churches of the Gentiles contribute liberally to the poor saints at Jerusalem.

3. When a company of believers purpose to gather into church fellowship, it is requisite for their safer proceeding and the maintaining of the communion of churches, that they signify their intent unto the neighbor churches, walking according to the order of the gospel, and desire their presence and help, and right hand of fellowship; which they ought readily to give unto them, when there is no just cause of excepting against their proceedings.

4. Besides these several ways of communion, there is also a way of propagation of churches; when a church shall grow too numerous, it is a way, and fit season to propagate one church out of another, by sending forth such of their members as are willing to remove, and to procure some officers to them, as may enter

with them into church estate among themselves; as bees, when the hive is too full, issue forth by swarms, and are gathered into other hives, so the churches of Christ may do the same upon the like necessity and therein hold forth to them the right hand of fellowship, both in their gathering into a church and in the ordination of their officers.

CHAPTER XVI
Of synods.

1. Synods, orderly assembled, and rightly proceeding according to the pattern, we acknowledge as the ordinance of Christ; and though not absolutely necessary to the being, yet many times, through the iniquity of men and perverseness of times, necessary to the well being of churches, for the establishment of truth and peace therein.

2. Synods being spiritual and ecclesiastical assemblies, are therefore made up of spiritual and ecclesiastical causes. The next efficient cause of them, under Christ, is the power of the churches sending forth their elders and other messengers, who being met together in the name of Christ, are the matter of a Synod; and they in arguing, debating and determining matters of religion, according to the Word, and publishing the same to the churches it concerns, do put forth the proper and formal acts of a Synod; to the conviction of errors, and heresies, and the establishment of truth and peace in the churches, which is the end of a synod.

3. Magistrates have power to call a Synod, by calling to the churches to send forth their elders and other messengers to counsel and assist them in matters of religion; but yet the constituting of a synod is a church act, and may be transacted by the churches, even when civil magistrates may be enemies to churches and to church assemblies.

4. It belongs unto Synods and councils to debate and determine controversies of faith and cases of conscience; to clear from the Word holy directions for the holy worship of God and good government of the church; to bear witness against mal-administration and corruption in doctrine or manners, in any particular church; and to give directions for the reformation thereof; not to exercise church censures in way of discipline, nor any

other act of church authority or jurisdiction which that presidential synod did forbear.

5. The Synod's directions and determinations, so far as consonant to the Word of God, are to be received with reverence and submission; not only for their agreement therewith, (which is the principal ground thereof, and without which they bind not at all), but also, secondarily, for the power whereby they are made, as being an ordinance of God appointed thereunto in his Word.

6. Because it is difficult, if not impossible, for many churches to come altogether in one place, in all their members universally; therefore they may assemble by their delegates or messengers, as the church of Antioch went not all to Jerusalem, but some select men for that purpose. Because none are or should be more fit to know the state of the churches, nor to advise of ways for the good thereof, than elders; therefore it is fit that, in the choice of the messengers for such assemblies, they have special respect unto such; yet, inasmuch as not only Paul and Barnabas, but certain others also were sent to Jerusalem from Antioch, and when they were come to Jerusalem, not only the apostles and elders, but other brethren also do assemble and meet about the matter; therefore Synods are to consist both of elders and other church members, endued with gifts, and sent by the churches, not excluding the presence of any brethren in the churches.

CHAPTER XVII
Of the civil magistrate's power in matters ecclesiastical.

1. It is lawful, profitable and necessary for Christians to gather themselves together into church estate, and therein to exercise all the ordinances of Christ, according unto the Word, although the consent of the magistrate could not be had thereunto; because the apostles and Christians in their time did frequently thus practice, when the magistrates, being all of them Jewish or pagan, and most persecuting enemies, would give no countenance or consent to such matters.

2. Church government stands in no opposition to civil government of commonwealths, nor any intrenches upon the authority of civil magistrates in their jurisdictions; nor any whit weakens their hands in governing, but rather strengthens them, and furthers the people in yielding more hearty and conscionable

obedience unto them, whatsoever some ill affected persons to the ways of Christ have suggested, to alienate the affections of kings and princes from the ordinances of Christ; as if the kingdom of Christ in his church could not rise and stand, without the falling and weakening of their government, which is also of Christ; whereas the contrary is most true, that they may both stand together and flourish, the one being helpful unto the other, in their distinct and due administrations.

3. The power and authority of magistrates is not for the restraining of churches or any other good works, but for helping in and furthering thereof; and therefore the consent and countenance of magistrates, when it may be had, is not to be slighted, or lightly esteemed; but, on the, contrary, it is part of that honor due to Christian magistrates to desire and crave their consent and approbation therein; which being obtained, the churches may then proceed in their way with much more encouragement and comfort.

4. It is not in the power of magistrates to compel their subjects to become church members, and to partake of the Lord's Table; for the priests are reproved that brought unworthy ones into the sanctuary; then it was unlawful for the priests, so it is as unlawful to be done by civil magistrates; those whom the church is to cast out, if they were in, the magistrate ought not to thrust them into the church, nor to hold them therein.

5. As it is unlawful for church officers to meddle with the sword of the magistrate, so it is unlawful for the magistrate to meddle with the work proper to church officers. The acts of Moses and David, who were not only princes but prophets, were extraordinary, therefore not inimitable. Against such usurpation the Lord witnessed by smiting Uzziah with leprosy for presuming to offer incense.

6. It is the duty of the magistrate to take care of matters of religion, and to improve his civil authority for the observing of the duties commanded in the first, as well as for observing of the duties commanded in the second table. They are called gods. The end of the magistrate's office is not only the quiet and peaceable life of the subject in matters of righteousness and honesty, but also in matters of godliness; yea, of all godliness. Moses, Joshua, David, Solomon, Asa, Jehoshaphat, Hezekiah,

Josiah, are much commended by the Holy Ghost, for the putting forth their authority in matters of religion; on the contrary, such kings as have been failing this way, are frequently taxed and reproved of the Lord. And not only the kings of Judah, but also Job, Nehemiah, the king of Nineveh, Darius, Artaxerxes, Nebuchadnezzar, whom none looked at as types of Christ, (though were it so there were no place for any just objection) are commended in the book of God for exercising their authority this way.

7. The objects of the power of the magistrate are not things merely inward, and so not subject to his cognizance and view; as unbelief, hardness of heart, erroneous opinions not vented, but only such things as are acted by the outward man; neither is their power to be exercised in commanding such acts of the outward man, and punishing the neglect thereof, as are but mere inventions and devices of men, but about such acts as are commanded, and forbidden in the Word; yea, such as the Word does clearly determine, though not always clearly to the judgment of the magistrate or others, yet clearly in itself. In these he of right ought to put forth his authority, though oft times actually he does it not.

8. Idolatry, blasphemy, heresy, venting corrupt and pernicious opinions, that destroy the foundation, open contempt of the Word preached, profanation of the Lord's Day, disturbing the peaceable administration and exercise of the worship and holy things of God, and the like, are to be restrained and punished by civil authority.

9. If any church, one or more, shall grow schismatical, rending itself from the communion of other churches, or shall walk incorrigibly and obstinately in any corrupt way of their own, contrary to the rule of the Word; in such case, the magistrate is to put forth his coercive power, as the matter shall require. The tribes on this side Jordan intended to make war against the other tribes for building the altar of witness, whom they suspected to have turned away therein from following of the Lord.

FINIS

Issues

The concern here is not the noun but the verb. The action of *issuing* suggests going, coming, or flowing out. Synonyms are *egress* and *emergence*. Think of issuing orders. Think of one's children as one's issue. To get at the root meaning of the word it may be helpful to consider an archaic but important definition.

Definition

Webster tells us that the word *issue* used to suggest a final outcome that usually constituted a solution (as of a problem) or resolution (as of a difficulty); and a final conclusion or decision about something arrived at after consideration. *Issue* was thought of as the end of a process or the conclusion of an effort or line of thinking. For example, "I hope that his enterprise would have a prosperous issue," in the sense that the enterprise, endeavor, or idea would produce children or fruit of a particular character.

Issue is a product of character or genetics. The biblical term is *kind* (Genesis 1:11), in modern parlance—*species*, which suggests a common form, character, or type. Applying this to the plural noun *issues*, then, our subject or topic is the fruit of an idea, a philosophy, a line of thinking, or a particular worldview.

Example

People ask, "Where do you stand on the issues?" Then they will usually list several issues of concern to them, for instance, abortion, homosexuality, gay marriage, war (either in general or a specific engagement), drugs, taxes, etc. The concern about issues is a concern about the application of a person's faith, philosophy, ideas, and/or worldview.

An application is always a derivative concern. The application of a particular thought, idea, or worldview issues forth in the articulation and/or establishment of policy. In other words, *policy* is the fruit of a mindset, a philosophy, a theology, a point of view, and/or a worldview. Policies are the application of a particular line of thinking. Thus, the question of issues is a question of policies.

Cascade

Particular policies are the result of a cascade of ideas, rules, and/or values. The Latin root of the word *cascade* is *casus*, and means *fall*. Thus, the meaning of *cascade* is a steep, a hill, or edge where a thing can fall from. Once a thing is falling, it is out of its own control, and is caught up in an inevitable outcome, a cascade. Think of a waterfall. When a swimmer nears a waterfall and gets caught in the cascade, he cannot extract himself from the inevitable conclusion of going over the fall. He becomes part of the cascade. Thus, a cascade determines the result or outcome of a particular thing.

More generically, a cascade involves a series wherein something is arranged or occurs in a succession of stages such that each stage derives from or acts upon the product of the preceding stage. Think dominoes. Think slippery slope, as when one is on the slippery slope all subsequent motion is down hill or toward a particular conclusion. Resistance is futile. Such is the nature of a cascade.

A cascade is a logical and necessary process that concludes at a particular endpoint or outcome through the application of a particular rule or a particular set of rules.

By Design

The current rage in the world of web design is something called Cascading Style Sheets (CSS). A style sheet is a set of instructions that are implemented by a computer and applied to a range of situations downstream (so to speak) without the need for the repetition of the instructions. A Style Sheet is a set of hierarchical rules that, once stated, will always be applied in a specific order without restatement. And one of the frustrating things about CSS designing is that sometimes a particular rule is being applied, but the source instruction for that rule is difficult to determine because it is upstream and far removed from the immediate situation or code context. Once one understands the order of the cascade, the rule can be determined. Such is the nature of a cascade.

The secret to using Style Sheets effectively is understanding the order of the cascade.

THEOLOGICAL CASCADE

The concern in this section is an explication of what I call *theological cascade*, the order, rules and issues of thoughts, values, and ideas. The biblical cascade under consideration, the order of the cascade, is that theology determines (or produces) philosophy, and philosophy determines (or produces) ethics, and ethics determines (or produces) policy, and policy determines (or produces) behavior or action.

The cascade can be mapped as follows:

1. Theology
   2. Philosophy
      3. Ethics
         4. Policy
            5. Behavior/Action

And because the connections are necessary by definition, the cascade flow can be followed in both directions—upstream and downstream, once one understands the underlying structure of the cascade. However, in the real world people are seldom aware of such a cascade in which they live and move, though cascades are real. Both a conscious person and an unconscious log will go over a waterfall once they are in the flow of the cascade. According to the Bible, all people are caught in a particular cascade—the Fall (Genesis 3).

Of course, God has sent Christ with a specific rule that will alter the Genesis 3 cascade. Designers can think of Jesus Christ as an inline style tag (rule) that is attached to a particular piece of code (a person). Inline style tags (rules) trump the cascade and force the immediate application of the rule. They stop the cascade flow regarding a particular code element.

It has been said that ideas have consequences. Those consequences are the issues (the progeny or fruit) under consideration. Issues are consequences of thought systems, both intended consequences and accidental or unforeseen consequences. Particular issues come out of particular points of view, particular beliefs, and particular values. Our worldviews define and produce issues. Issues are the products of worldviews. Our intent is to show the connections between issues and worldviews, between belief and behavior.

EMERGENCE

Fads have become the engines that drive culture in the 21st Century. Corporations chase fads in order to profit from them in various ways. Corporations also create fads as a means of marketing their products. The ideal marketing program is the establishment of a cult following such as Harley Davidson has done in the motorcycle world.

The latest (1990s) fad to hit the church scene is known as "The Emergent Church." So, what exactly is the emergent church? It's hard to tell because it is still emerging. Nonetheless, careful examination of the roots of "emergent theory"[1] will reveal the driving spirit behind the fad.

The term *emergent* was coined by the pioneer psychologist G. H. Lewes who wrote:

> "Every resultant is either a sum or a difference of the co-operant forces; their sum, when their directions are the same—their difference, when their directions are contrary. Further, every resultant is clearly traceable in its components, because these are homogeneous and commensurable. It is otherwise with emergents, when, instead of adding measurable motion to measurable motion, or things of one kind to other individuals of their kind, there is a co-operation of things of unlike kinds. The emergent is unlike its components in so far as these are incommensurable, and it cannot be reduced to their sum or their difference" (Lewes 1875, p. 412) (Blitz 1992).

The concept behind the term has been in use since at least the time of Aristotle. John Stuart Mill and Julian Huxley are just some of the historic luminaries who have written on the concept. The alert Christian will note that the sources of emergent theory are not biblical or Christian. Rather, they are Godless in nature and Liberal and/or Socialist in character. The historical roots of emergent theory reveal that it is antithetical at every point to Scripture and Christianity.

> "In philosophy, emergence is often understood to be a much stronger claim about the etiology (cause) of a system's properties. An emergent property of a system, in this context, is one that is not a property of any component of that system, but is still a feature of the system as a whole. Nicolai Hartmann, one of the first

---

1   Meehl, Paul E. & Sellars ,Wilfrid. "The Concept Of Emergence," *Minnesota Studies in the Philosophy of Science*, Volume I: *The Foundations of Science and the Concepts of Psychology and Psychoanalysis* (University of Minnesota Press, 1956), pp. 239-252. http://www.ditext.com/sellars/ce.html.

modern philosophers to write on emergence, called this a *catego-rial novum* (new category).

Systems with emergent properties or emergent structures may appear to defy entropic principles and the Second Law of Thermodynamics, because they form and increase order despite the lack of command and central control. This is possible because open systems can extract information and order out of the environment.

Emergence helps to explain why the *fallacy of division* is a fallacy. According to an emergent perspective, intelligence emerges from the connections between neurons, and from this perspective it is not necessary to propose a "soul" to account for the fact that brains can be intelligent, even though the individual neurons of which they are made are not."[2]

Note that this explanation attempts to provide philosophical explanation for the emergence of new categories of being, what is considered to be the creation or development of novel categories, levels, or entities of being where no such category, level, or entity existed previously. In other words, the *emergent theory* is ultimately attempting to explain what the Bible calls *creation* from a Godless, evolutionary, or materialistic perspective. It attempts to explain the origin and appearance of mind and soul without reference or recourse to God or to Scripture. The root and the goals of the emergent theory are *not* insignificant.

The Emergent Church

As for church, *Emergent* is a name that is being used at the moment to describe the church's response to the current emerging culture, and the peculiar aggregation of believers being called up out of this culture to follow Jesus back into it.

"Emergent" as it is used in *"emergent theory"* is a name given to the phenomena (sic) of how new organizational structures progress from low-level chaos to higher level sophistication without a hierarchical command structure. Emergent theory explains how birds change direction, how slime mold moves, how ant colonies are built and how Amazon.com knows so much about us. The process involves constant communication and feedback among the lowest level of organization, pattern recognition, local action affecting global behavior, and takes into consideration the element of unpredictability in a chaotic system. Solomon was wise in suggesting that we observe the ways of the ant and be

---

2   http://en.wikipedia.org/wiki/Emergence

wise (Proverbs 6:6). And the emerging church has been wise in allowing the vocabulary from emergent behavior to give a window of insight to the traditional church....

New churches among the emerging culture generally have an organizational structure that is best described as "emergent." Emergent organizations (ant colonies, slime mold) organize from below rather than top-down, they depend on feedback for adaptation, show decentralized thinking, and respond locally in a way that affects the global situation. In writing about the "Character of the Emergent Church," Kester Brewin sees emergent systems as being "open systems, adaptable systems, learning systems, having distributed knowledge, and modeling servant leadership" (From *The Complex Christ: Signs of Emergence in the Urban Church*).

"Our minds may be wired to look for the pacemakers, but we are steadily learning how to think from the bottom up" (Steve Johnson, *Emergence*).

Emergent behavior is a good way to describe how new churches are responding to a complex world of chaotic unpredictability and multiple possibilities. One of the defining features of emergent churches is that they are usually started with no predetermined ideal of what they will mature into or what size and shape they will become, since they will also be shaped by the culture they transform. Another word for this is "missional." Unpredictability opens the possibility for a miraculous intervention and retooling by God during the process, as long as structures are simple, and communication is constant.[3]

One of the things that concerns me most about the so-called *emergent church* is the character of some of the organizations that are actively involved in shaping it. Consider my seminary *alma mater*, whose logo (2002) appears to the right.

PACIFIC SCHOOL *of* RELIGION

BERKELEY, CALIFORNIA

Pacific School of Religion (PSR) is undoubtedly the most radically Liberal seminary in America that still claims to be Christian. However, its close association with the Unitarian Universalist Association (UUA) and the Swedenborgian movement suggest that it has long since left any version of orthodox Christianity. PSR also hosts the The Center for Lesbian and Gay Studies in Religion and Ministry and has been, if not the

---

3   Source: LeRon Shults Blog, http://leronshults.typepad.com/my_weblog/2007/02/deconstructive_.html.

earliest, at least one of the most significant institutions promoting the acceptance of homosexuality is society and in Christianity. These facts give me great pause, and my subsequent conversion to historic, biblical Christianity since graduating from PSR continue to weigh heavily upon my spirit. If nothing else, the Lord has given me through my conversion an unusual understanding of the spirit, forces, philosophies, and theology of this movement.

So, what does this have to do with the emergent church? PSRs new motto is "Equipping historic and emerging faith communities for ministries of compassion and justice." PSR has positioned itself to be a driving force in the emergent church. Caution: steep decline ahead!

The emergent church is not a new phenomenon that is arising from some advanced state of society, as if it were some sort of new evolutionary entity or institution. Rather, it appears to be more akin to Ephesian 4:14: "...tossed to and fro by the waves and carried about by every wind of doctrine, by human cunning, by craftiness in deceitful schemes." The appearance of what is being called the *emergent church* is a fruit of a particular kind of theological cascade.

The following article has been reproduced to provide an example of how the Emergent Theory has been developed and incorporated by those who are hostile toward Christianity. Note how the Emergent Theory is being used to further prop up the materialistic Theory of Evolution as a new attempt to explain "spontaneous generation."

EMERGENT EVOLUTION

> If Random Evolution is associated with old-style (reductionist) materialism, scientism, and strict Darwinism, Emergent Evolution is the natural outgrowth of new style materialism, Pantheism, Holism, systems theory, ecology, Gaia theory, and other more developed paradigms.
>
> Emergent evolution agrees with Materialism and Materialistic Pantheism in considering the physical universe as the substratum of existence. But it also sees this reality as able to unfold higher levels of organization that transcend it and that are not defined by its limitations, or predictable by its laws. To give a trivial example, Life emerges (evolves) out of Matter. But life cannot be explained or defined according to physical or chemical laws that are otherwise very capable of explaining inanimate matter. Life represents something totally new. It has emerged out of matter but it constitutes a new grade of organization, a "symmetry break" so to speak. In a sense, life is a "singularity" as far as inanimate matter is

concerned, it is a whole new grade of organization, functioning, expression.

And in the same way mind emerges out of life, and represents a whole new grade of organization that cannot be explained in merely biological or metabolic terms.

I personally consider the emergent paradigm to be an extremely profound yet at the same time simple, obvious, common-sense way of explaining the universe. Moreover it provides a way to link both science and materialism on the one hand, and metaphysics and spirituality on the other. Thus we find materialistic thinkers like James Lovelock and Lynn Margulis propounding an emergent theory of life and planetology (the Gaia hypothesis). They came upon this from a materialistic perspective, yet it is a hypothesis that goes beyond materialism (even if its founders are dead against the intuitive New Age and Neo-pagan interpretations, and I am sure would not be at all pleased to see what had become of their superb theory even on the present site ;-).

Coming to Emergent Evolution from the other direction, metaphysical and spiritual thinkers like Teilhard de Chardin and Sri Aurobindo see evolution as an emerging out of matter of higher qualities, culminating in the spiritual culmination that Teilhard terms the Omega Point and Sri Aurobindo Supramentalisation. Although both Teilhard and Aurobindo advocate a teleological stance, what they say is also pure Emergent paradigm. Carl Jung is another great visionary who seems to hold an emergent theory of evolution (the Collective Unconscious and then Consciousness evolving out of the original nonconscious biological and elemental substratum), even if he does not articulate it such a specific or clear manner.

And straddling and incorporating both camps are those like Erich Jantsch, who's incredible book on systems theory and cosmic evolution, the *Self-Organizing Universe*, is, to my mind at least, one of the most fascinating and inspiring works of science ever written.

All of which gives us a map of the cosmos and cosmic evolution as a process that is dynamic not static, meaningful not purposeless, yet in keeping with both the spiritual and the materialistic perspectives.

Source: Kheper website, over 1500 pages, dedicated to a new scientific and esoteric evolutionary paradigm concerning the nature of existence and its infinite metamorphoses, and the transformation of the Earth and the planetary consciousness to a post-singularity state of Supramental (Infinite Truth-Consciousness) divinization.

Marriage Amendment
On the Horns of a Dilemma

President George W. Bush has called for an amendment to the Constitution in order to stop the encroachment of those who want access to the various federal and state benefits that are accorded to married couples. Those benefits include various financial arrangements that were originally provided to encourage and sustain marriage in the United States, i.e., common ownership of property, insurance beneficiary defaults, taxation as a common unit or household, and default inheritance rights.

Those who are calling for marriage rights between same sex couples see it as a matter of equal rights, as a continuation of the civil rights movement and the fight against arbitrary discrimination against various classes or groups of people.

> "To discriminate socially is to make a distinction between people on the basis of class or category without regard to individual merit. Examples include racial, religious, sexual, disability, ethnic, height-related and age-related discrimination. Distinctions between people which are based just on individual merit (such as personal achievement, skill or ability) are not discriminatory" (Wikipedia).

This definition of discrimination is an expansion of the Civil Rights Movement of the 1960s, which was itself the continuation of the emancipation of slaves following the Civil War, and contains the same seeds of conflict.

There are significant problems with this definition and the effort to eliminate all social categorization. This effort is the philosophical continuation of an historical movement known as the Levellers. This movement grew out of a secular misunderstanding of the Book of Acts and common property ownership, and is intent upon bringing about worldwide communism as the fundamental structure of human organization or society. But that is not the subject of this article, though this history provides the context for proper understanding of the same sex marriage issue. Here we are concerned simply with the definition of marriage.

Currently, civil marriage laws fall under the jurisdiction of the various states, not the federal government. Although, part of the federal union of the states requires that each state respect the marriage laws of the other states. The Defense of Marriage Act, which defined marriage for purposes of federal law as the legal union between one man and one woman as husband and wife, passed the House of Representatives by a vote of 342 to 67, and the Senate by a vote of 85 to 14 in 1996. Similar defensive marriage laws were also passed in 38 states and express an overwhelming consensus in our country for protecting the traditional (and in the case of the United States—Christian) institution of marriage.

The *modus operandi* of the various groups working to establish equal marital rights for same sex couples is to force all issues and disagreements into federal courts in order to play out the already established equal rights protection language in existence throughout the various elements of the federal government. The recent passage of same sex marriage laws in Massachusetts will bring the issue to federal jurisdiction for a settlement that applies to all states. Thus, while the issue of marriage is presented as a personal morality issue—with an emphasis on biblical morality on one side, and an emphasis on civil rights morality on the other—the as yet unspoken issues pertain to both state rights within the federal union and the continuing expansion of federal jurisdiction across the board.

There are two ultimate resolutions regarding the present concerns about marriage. One is to establish a Constitutional law that defines marriage nationally, the other is to eliminate the civil financial benefits that are currently associated with marriage. Neither resolution will benefit American society. Rather, the United States is in the process of being impaled on the horns of a dilemma that will result in disembowelment. This result is not unexpected because it is the goal of both Marxists and Leveller ideologies.

The problems with the establishment of a Constitutional amendment to define marriage pertain to the separation of church and civil governments (or state). How so? In every society and civilization marriage is associated with churches and religion because marriage is understood to have divine authority and associations. Thus, for the civil government to enact legislation pertaining to the definition of marriage is an encroachment of civil government into the jurisdiction of church or religious government. Were this Constitutional Amendment to pass, civil government would then establish the social foundation of churches and/or religions—and in particular, Christianity.

In order to see this more clearly, one needs only look at the language of the proposed Amendment, which reads "Marriage in the United States of America shall consist only of the union of *a man and a woman*" (emphasis mine). The problem with this definition is that it eliminates the role of God, church, and religion with regard to marriage.

Traditionally, Christianity defines marriage as a three strand cord consisting of husband, wife, and God. God is absolutely foundational to Christian marriage because it is God who provides the covenantal (or legal) foundation for marriage. Christian marriage is not merely a contract between two people, nor merely a contract between two people and a community. According to Scripture, it is a covenant with God that establishes the rights and duties that exist between a husband, a wife, and their children. This marriage covenant legitimates the issue of children.

The husband and wife make specific pledges or promises to one another, and they covenant with God to honor those pledges and promises. Scripture includes instruction regarding family inheritance rights and obligations. Part and parcel of the legitimization of family bonds are matters of property and inheritance rights. God provides the authorization and foundation of marriage, and will provide sanctions for dishonoring His covenant. In fact, the model of the Christian gospel itself is inextricably bound up with property and inheritance rights. The kingdom of God is the promised inheritance of the redefined family of born again believers. Inheritance policy is critical to the gospel of Jesus Christ.

The problem is that the currently proposed Constitutional Marriage Amendment writes God out of the commonly recognized definition of marriage in America. Such an act will have serious long-term negative consequences for American society in that marriage will no longer seek nor be worthy of God's blessings or protection, and will utterly change the structure of American society. Such a change will have serious financial and social repercussions. We may argue the merits or demerits of the change, or the nature of the change, but structural change itself will be the inevitable result.

If the Marriage Amendment is passed, the primary foundation of Christian churches, which is the Christian family and the marriages that constitute Christian families, will accrue increasing disdain and discrimination in the wider culture. Why? Because the foundational covenant with God that establishes Christian marriage will not be recognized by civil governments. This will result in increasing ignorance of the biblical roots of the marriage covenant, which will be increasingly ridiculed as unnecessary—or worse, as contrary to the well-being of civil governments by those who oppose Christianity. This in turn will encourage another form of discrimination—Christian discrimination—in the effort to correct the Christian discrimination against same sex marriage.

This is important because the only biblically legitimate role, and the traditional role of civil government regarding marriage, is to recognize the social legitimacy of marriage, not to define or grant it. Marriage is not a right granted by civil government, but is a privilege, with ensuing rights and responsibilities, that is granted by God alone. Why? Because God claims ownership of the issue of marriage—the children produced by the marriage union. The concern is that the authority that legalizes (or defines) marriage has legitimate ownership rights of the children produced. Thus, it is not the church that legalizes marriage, but it is God Himself who defines and legalizes Christian marriage. And it is certainly not the civil government that defines or legalizes marriage.

The role of the civil government is to simply recognize the legality of marriage, and by doing so the civil government recognizes God's ownership of the issue (children), with all of the biblical rights and duties pertaining thereunto. Thus, it is a very serious thing to write God out of the definition of marriage as recognized by civil governments.

Thus, a better approach to the resolution of unequal civil rights pertaining to marriage would be for the civil government to disestablish all financial benefits pertaining to marriage and to treat all individuals equally with regard to employment and taxation. All civil laws pertaining to financial benefits related to marriage should also be eliminated as a matter of equal treatment of all individuals. This will also harm the institution of marriage in America, but it will not redefine the institution.

Granting legality, rights and/or duties regarding marriage is not the prerogative of the civil government. In fact, all laws regarding marriage by the civil government constitute the encroachment of civil government into the jurisdiction of religion. The civil government should not be in the business of legitimizing marriage because marriage is traditionally and biblically under the jurisdiction of church (or religion). That is the source of the problem. The state (civil government) continues to usurp the biblically mandated authority and jurisdiction of the church.

The removal of the special financial benefits granted by civil government to married couples will go a long way toward the resolution of the current problem by removing the special financial benefits accorded to married couples by civil governments. Unfortunately, it will also contribute to the continuing degradation of marriage and family in American society because marriage will no longer be financially encouraged across the board.

WHAT'S WRONG WITH CURRENT MARRIAGE LAWS?

In a recent article (*Marriage Equality*,[4] the following scenario was suggested: the person you love is injured in an automobile accident and is barely clinging to life in the hospital, but you cannot visit him or her because you are not married. It is then suggested that the cure for this problem is to change the marriage laws. "In this moment of tragedy you cannot be with the person you love because of one simple reason: you are gay."

But wait a minute! The problem is not the gayness of some couples, nor the institution of marriage. The problem is HIPAA.

The real problem is a health care issue rather than a gay or marriage issue. Why is the easiest solution to the problem not amending HIPAA? Isn't it HIPAA that stops the visit? It is. Isn't HIPAA a much more recent law? And shouldn't the remedy use the least extensive means to remedy the problem? Why does HIPAA trump marriage? And since the entire structure of U.S. health care is in the midst of the most serious and extensive overhaul in history, why not amend HIPAA to include visiting rights for civil unions rather than change the oldest institution in history? No one would argue against amending HIPAA to include civil unions.

I agree with Nick Benson who wrote, "It is time to change the law in Ohio and uphold the rights of all of our people." But it is most certainly *not* necessary to change the definition of the most universal and longest standing social custom—marriage—simply to provide equal rights for civil unions. And since tax laws change every year anyway, why not amend the tax laws to provide the same benefits for civil unions that are provided for married couples. It is simply unnecessary to engage in the most divisive political fight in the history of the U. S. to solve this simple problem.

I also agree with Nick when he writes, "Our founders were wise in that they wanted limitations on government's ability to infringe upon fundamental rights." Our most fundamental rights are not given by civil government, they are given by God. The role of civil government is not to provide such rights, but to protect them. And marriage was established by God. Neither the U. S. Federal government nor the state of

---

4   12/21/2011, http://www. theanchornews.net/index.php

Ohio established the institution of marriage. Nor do they have the right or the responsibility to change it. Civil government has no jurisdiction to amend or alter the definition of marriage, and any such effort constitutes the encroachment of civil government into religious affairs—beliefs, which is a violation of the separation of church and state.

Nick admits that same sex union or homosexuality is a function of religious belief when he wrote, "Just as the freedom of religion has been viewed as a protection against government sanctioning of religion, it is also a form of protection for those who wish to practice their own beliefs unobstructed." And the beliefs that are here indicated are the beliefs that allow for same sex unions or homosexuality. Therefore, just as the civil government has no jurisdiction over religious beliefs, it has no jurisdiction over marriage beliefs.

For most people, marriage and religion go together. That's why people get married in churches. So civil government should also protect those whose marriage beliefs are not religious by allowing civil unions as entirely equal to marriage in the eyes of the law. But for civil government to define marriage in any way exceeds its jurisdiction. For the Federal government or any state government to define marriage at all would constitute the establishment of a religious belief, even if that belief issues from agnosticism or atheism.

Because agnosticism and atheism are particular beliefs about God they are religious in nature. "Belief in God" and "no belief in God" (or "belief in no God") are both theological positions or beliefs, and civil government has no business establishing any belief about God. And if your beliefs about gay marriage are religious, civil government still has no business establishing any belief about God—period.

CONSTITUTIONAL CLARITY

Consider the following:

> "During the debate over ratification of the Constitution, many mainline Christians howled at its silence on religion. The Presbytery of Massachusetts and New Hampshire groused to George Washington, 'we should not have been alone in rejoicing to have seen some explicit acknowledgment of THE TRUE ONLY GOD, AND JESUS CHRIST whom he has sent, inserted somewhere in the Magna Charta of our country.' Washington demurred. 'I am persuaded, you will permit me to observe, that the path of true piety is so plain as to require but little political direction,' he said. 'To this consideration we ought to ascribe the ab-

sence of any regulation respecting religion from the Magna
Charta of our country.'

Reflected in this debate, two competing themes combined to
compose the dissonant music of early American politics. The first
theme, sounded in New England from the time of the Puritans,
posited the ideal of a Christian Commonwealth. Uplifted by the
imperatives of Christian morality, the government would be a
shining city on a hill, fulfilling God's mandates and receiving his
aid.

The second theme, codified in Thomas Jefferson's Declaration
of Independence, arose from Enlightenment France. Rather than
that of Christian Commonwealth, it posited the ideal of individual freedom. Jefferson dreamed of establishing an Empire of Liberty, whose government sacredly would protect each individual's
God–given freedom of conscience.[5]

Seldom do we find such a clear explanation of the central concern
that has animated American politics during the more than two hundred
years of its existence. There have been two competing religious worldviews that were written into the Constitution. This debate has been expressed over the years as to whether or not the United States is or has
ever been a Christian nation.

The above quotation shows the two sides: the Puritan or biblical
worldview versus the Enlightenment or French worldview. So, which
do you think is the American original?

I understand that the quote I selected is incomplete. What I found
interesting was the admission that there were clearly two sides to the issue: the Enlightenment side and the Christian side. This is seldom acknowledged by the enemies of Christianity. While the details of these
positions are numerous and can be confusing, the basic division is correct and reflects the long history of both sides, from the Renaissance to
the current era.

From a Christian perspective the Constitutional debates occluded
the most important ingredient in the recipe for human government,
probably because they assumed it—the Christian church. Note the absence of any reference to the Christian church in the debates. It is quite
odd that the most powerful social institution of their own time appears
to play no role in human government as envisioned by the founders.

---

5   From the Unitarian Universalist Association webiste: http://www.uua.org/visitors/uu-
     perspectives/55665.shtml

Am I wrong about this? If so, point me to the references, other than the proverbial separation clause.

Of course church and civil governments are to be separated. They have different jurisdictions. The Founders all knew and understood this because they were students of Calvin. About ninety percent of all Protestant Christianity at the time was Calvinistic, and Calvin set the standard for Protestant church theology and order in early America. Calvin's importance in this debate cannot be overemphasized, not the man, obviously. He was long dead—but his work. Those who were members of churches understood this and submitted themselves to church government. And those who were not members were not members precisely because they refused to submit themselves to church government. Indeed, this was the genesis for the proliferation of Protestant denominations—and it still is.

The point is that from that Calvinist Christian perspective, church government played the critical role between the federal (civil) government and the individual (conscience), not the state (civil) government. Thus, by substituting "state government" for "church government" in the debates the actual role of church government was constitutionally defined to play no significant role in government, other than an amorphous "inspiration" to do the "right" thing. Individuals in the newly construed U.S. would be governed by this amorphous religious and largely undefined morality without teeth because the "real" struggle was defined as being between the newly conceived federal government and the existing states government.

I don't want to make light of the relationship between the national and state governments, it is very important. However, by placing the focus of the enduring debate in the civil realm, and occluding the role of the church and its role in moral development, the moral or religious realm slowly collapsed from neglect over the following centuries. Of course, the Founders mostly understood morality from a Christian perspective, and lived it. But as Washington said, our government is explicitly for people who understand and practice morality from a Christian perspective, and will not work without this key element.

Well, over time and through neglect Christian morality in society generally has been lost—central and key elements of that morality have even been lost by most Christians! The foundational institutions of family and church have been collapsed. And our government isn't working as it was designed. And to resurrect the Constitution apart from the necessary foundation of the Christian church and Christian family life is an invitation to a totalitarianism of a different stripe. What is missing is personal moral restraint, and the civil government cannot produce that. It is the job of the church to teach and encourage morality.

While Jefferson thought that a Constitutionally mandated religion or morality would be an expression of tyranny (I agree), the greatest tyrannies that haunt the pages of history have Constitutionally mandated no religion. They have been intentionally and explicitly atheistic. So, Jefferson had the right concern, but he pointed it in the wrong direction. Jefferson tore civil government from the fabric of the existing American culture that was primarily based upon the Christian church. He separated civil government from the environment for which it was designed.

He was undoubtedly driven to do this because of the various abuses of authority in the churches. There have always been plenty of such abuses, and they will undoubtedly continue until the Lord returns. But over time Christianity has actually matured—oh, how I hope that individual Christians will catch up with the historical maturity of Christian history! Apparently, the bulk of our contemporary churches and their members prefer personal ignorance to the maturity of historic faithfulness.

And so now, we have federal, state, and local governmental abuses in abundance because Jefferson didn't want Jesus Christ to impinge upon his precious desire for freedom from religious moral authority. Are the abuses of civil government any better than ecclesiastical abuses? More people will be hurt by a faulty federal government than a faulty church. And, in order to get the federal government right, we need to first get the church right (the foundation). Getting the church right will contribute greatly to getting the federal government right. But getting the federal government right without consideration for the church will simply continue to produce more errors and problems.

Promise Breaking

"Despite ongoing negotiations with its unions, United Airlines has told the bankruptcy court that the 'likely result' will be a decision to terminate all of its pension plans. That would precipitate the biggest pension default in history, more than twice the size of the Bethlehem Steel Corporation default in 2002. The move is expected to destabilize the already struggling airline industry, prompting other old-line carriers like Delta to eventually follow suit to maintain competitiveness." – Christian Science Monitor

Am I so far gone that I don't see things right anymore, or does the federal government through the auspices of the bankruptcy courts establish that lying is an acceptable business practice as long as it is done on a grand enough scale. What other conclusion can be drawn?

The argument in favor of institutional deceit (allowing corporations to simply renounce their legal obligations) is undoubtedly that United Airlines is so large and so important to our economy (read: national security) that to allow it to fail would be tantamount to economic disaster. The problem with this argument is that an economy cannot function apart from just weights and measures (Leviticus 19:36, Proverbs 16:11), otherwise known as trust and honesty.

Trust and honesty are foundational to all economies, foundational to the whole idea of money. A dollar bill is nothing more than a promissory note. It is a promise. Credit and credit cards are also instruments of promise. This means that financial transactions are fundamentally promises. It means that culture or society rests on the integrity of promises, and when the reliability of promises—particularly institutional and legal promises—diminishes, the very fabric of society weakens. At the point of institutional unreliability, the fabric will tear and financial destabilization and social panic if not collapse will follow.

When government subsidizes deceit and promise breaking, it undermines the stability of the very society it governs. Everything that devalues promise-keeping produces social and economic instability. Thus, to prop up a failing business (any business!) through governmental intervention is to credit the failure to the government, and institutionalize or legitimize deceit and fraud. Note that if United Airlines is allowed to default on its pension obligations, other airlines will follow suit.

What lessons can be learned? First, it is not someone else's responsibility to save for your retirement, not even the government's. To give that responsibility to someone else is to give away your future. Second, government should be about the institutionalization of truth and honesty, preferably by example.

CULTURE, LIFESTYLE & RELIGION

Think of culture and your mind fixes on the arts and music—highbrow tastes. Think of lifestyle and, if homosexuality doesn't crowd everything else out, your mind fixes on material goods and buying cool stuff. Think of religion and your mind fixes on dismal, dour, old people carping about the state of the world.

Interesting that these words conjure up such different definitions and reactions because they actually mean the same thing – the tastes, values and practices of a particular people.

Culture comes from cultivation, the art of growing things. Gardens are cultivated to produce flowers or fruit. Are civilizations, societies or groups of people cultivated? You might say that some are and some aren't, suggesting that cultivation requires discipline and expertise. We usually think of cultivated people as educated people, people of knowledge and experience.

And such people are usually successful. They have money and are able to choose their lifestyle, which is often composed of fine things related to art and music—highbrow things, expensive things. So, we understand that culture and lifestyle are naturally related. But religion? It just doesn't fit into the same category as culture and lifestyle. Or does it?

The essential meaning of religion is to bind. Religious people are bound to God, bound by God's moral dictates, and bound together in fellowship with one another. Limitation and constraint are at the heart of religion. And that's why religion is not popular today. People reject all limitation and constraint because they believe that being human essentially means being free, free of constraints and limitations. Freedom is the cause of the day. People think that religion is opposed to freedom because of its limitations and constraints.

But such thinking is nonsense. The political freedom that Americans enjoy today is a product of former American Christianity. Christianity cultivated the ideas and political structures of freedom for centuries in America. Our freedom is the fruit of Christian culture, it grows in the soil of Christianity.

Have you ever watched children play in an unstructured environment? We don't see much of this anymore because today children's lives are so structured. When I grew up we played basketball in the alley with some friends. Today, kids only play on a real court with uniforms, coaches, referees and tournaments—or they don't play at all. Same thing with football, baseball, etc. Children's lives today are much more structured than they used to be.

But if you ever get a chance to see children playing in an unstructured environment you will see them organize themselves into teams, begin playing and invent rules as they go. Rule invention comes about because of some injustice, someone cheats or takes unfair advantage of another. At some point someone gets hurt, and a rule is made.

The point is that play requires rules just as life requires laws. Without rules and laws play and life deteriorate into the exercise of power and oppression—the strong oppress the weak, the rich oppress the poor, the smart oppress the dumb, etc. Oppression offends our innate sense of justice, fairness. It isn't fair that some people oppress others. All people should be free from oppression. And so rules, laws, limitations and constraints must be put in place to insure that the weak are not oppressed by the strong, that the poor are not oppressed by the rich, and that the dumb are not oppressed by the smart.

A sport without rules, referees and coaches quickly turns into chaos. Games are played best when the rules are strictly observed. The same thing is true of life. Thus, religion—God's limitations and constraints—allows life to be lived to the fullest extent by all people. That is, all people who observe God's limitations and constraints. Those who ignore God's limitations and constraints find themselves in the penalty box.

God is very much in the business of creating and developing Christian culture, Christian society. He is not just discipling or cultivating individual Christians. He is also cultivating Christian nations—not a one world Christian government, but nations that observe God's limitations and constraints in order to establish and preserve maximum freedom for all people.

It's Not The Sex, It's The Integrity

Elliot Spitzer, New York State Attorney General, was caught with his pants down (New York Times, March 10, 2008). So, what's the big deal. Sex is everywhere. Should we just get used to it?

First, the fact that immorality is everywhere does not make it moral (right). Morality is not a function of popularity, it is a function of righteousness. (It is the right word. Look it up.)

Allow me to try to provide a biblical overview of sex. The control and discipline of sexual energy and sexual activity is an engine of civilization. Sex is not simply about two people getting glassy-eyed. The connection between sex and civilization is not the sexual act itself, but the nature of the traditional marriage relationship that legitimizes or legalizes the act. Marriage is the key to a proper biblical understanding, not the sex. And traditionally, marriage and sex have been held together in an exclusive union by religious and social mores—not just Christian, but biblical Christianity makes the best defense of sex being exclusively limited to marriage. It is woven into the legal system of virtually every society.

And what is so special about marriage, particularly Christian marriage? The promise to be faithful to one's marriage partner, the promise to do what you say you will do, that's what. Society is built upon promises. Money is a promise, as are checks, bank notes, credit, etc. It's all about promises. Promises are the building blocks of civilization. In Christianity this line of thinking is called covenant theology. The basic idea is that kept promises (good promises) are good for civilization and broken promises (bad promises) are a kind of corruption or rot of the fabric of civilization. Broken promises undermine and destroy civilization. They also make our money worth less, which is also bad for civilization.

Promise keeping is a kind of habit. The bad thing is that the breaking of one promise makes it easier to break another, etc., *ad infinitum*. The more promises that a person breaks, the easier it is to continue breaking promises. There's a momentum both personally and socially to promise keeping and to promise breaking. The one leads to a healthy civilization and the other leads to an unhealthy civilization. One increases life, the other increases death, to put it starkly.

The traditional teaching is that sex is reserved for marriage, period. Prostitution (promises for hire) and its variants always involve breaking promises. The idea of prostitution applies to more than sex. For instance, the definition includes: "One who sells one's abilities, talent, or name for an unworthy purpose." A prostitute has no honor in the same way that a mercenary has no honor, no integrity. Prostitution destroys honesty, honor and integrity, which are the currency of promises, which in turn are the building blocks of civilization. My assumption is that honor and integrity are good things, and that they are good for society.

Why is a person's sex life a concern of the community? Why is sex not simply a private matter? Because it has the potential to create lives, and those lives are the concern of the community, of society. The fact that birth control technology has interfered with the relationship between sex and children doesn't mean that that relationship has been broken. While all sex does not produce children, all children are produced by sex, even so-called test tube babies. The relationship between sex and children (making babies) cannot be separated, except in our imaginations.

Sex is always promissory or contractual, relating to or part of a binding legal agreement. The bind always involves promises. Marriage sex is promissory because of the marriage. Prostitution is promissory because money is exchanged and money itself is nothing more than promises. Kids and consenting adults often promise not to tell, other consenters tell and marriage promises break. Sex often ruins friendships because it requires more than friendship, it requires legitimization. And legitimization is a function of the community.

So, how a person performs in the bedroom (not regarding sex, but marriage) is the business of the community because it provides an indication of one's promise keeping abilities. This is particularly important for political leaders, whose public careers are built on their promise keeping abilities. So, failure in the bedroom increases the likelihood that other promises will be broken. It's an indication of promise keeping weakness, which is also know as lying, cheating, and being unfaithful.

So, yes, Chelsea (Clinton), dad's (Bill Clinton) performance is not a private matter, particularly when the Oval Office is mistaken for the bedroom. It is our business.

CHRISTIAN CONTEXT: SHORT SHEETED

Richard Hughes in a recent article, "The Christian Right in Context, Part 1: The Long View" (Huffington Post, 11/8/2010) puts conservative Christianity in the context of liberalism. His essay oozes with the liberal righteousness of supposed objectivity, but is blindly ensnared in the religious philosophy of dualism. Hughes' views are not objective.

Yes, I too have a bias, and my bias is for Trinitarian Christianity. Rather than hide my bias, or pretend that it is objective, I put it on the table for all to see. Serious discussion of religious and philosophical matters requires no less, and genuine discussion of such issues will take a giant step forward as others admit and examine their own presuppositions.

I have not read Bellah's book, *The Broken Covenant*, either. However, I am familiar with Bellah's work and perspective, and will put this on my reading list. But my concern is not initially with Bellah, but with Hughes. Allow me to examine the words and perspective of his article.

Evidence of Hughes' bias begins here: "the Christian Right has so successfully eaten away at the core, bedrock values that shaped this nation at its founding." I am not arguing against the insight that genuine Christianity and American nationalism are incompatible, but am simply pointing out Hughes' underlying commitment to American nationalism at the expense of genuine Christianity.

He suggests an irony in the assertion of the Christian right that has been pointing out the erosion of American values by blaming others —"liberals, secularists and humanists"—rather than acknowledging its own role in that erosion. Hughes' assumption is that American nationalism and genuine Christianity actually agree in their liberalism, secularism, and humanism, and that the Christian Right has been rocking the boat of this cozy relationship, as if real Christians should be celebrating it in the first place.

What he failed to notice is that liberalism, secularism, and humanism are antithetical to biblical Christianity precisely because they deny the central thing that makes Christianity unique among world religions —the Trinity. Part and parcel of that denial is the corresponding denial of the divinity of Jesus Christ, which is the central element of the Trinity that makes the Trinity applicable to humanity and this world. Christianity is not primarily a philosophy from which general principles can be extracted and applied as a formula for better living. Christianity is personal. At the center of the faith is the divine Person of Jesus Christ who has come to renew humanity with a "piece" of Himself so as to

bind individuals and the God of the Bible in personal and covenantal relationship, as a means of establishing human sustainability in this fallen
world.

Hughes pits a philosophical threesome—liberalism, secularism and
humanism—against the largely reactionary and misguided philosophy of
conservative Christianity. The important thing to see is what isn't acknowledged or articulated—the theology of Trinitarian Christianity. It
is important to see it because it stands in opposition to and as a corrective for both the liberal and the conservative perspectives. While both
liberalism and conservatism appear to struggle against one another, they
compete to dominate society with one or the other expressions of a
monotheistic perspective. They are fighting about whether the dominant American monotheism should be liberal or conservative, but they
agree that monotheism should dominate.

Christianity differs. While Christianity is monotheistic, its
monotheism is trinitarian rather than unitarian. And this fact highlights
the long religious struggle that has been raging, not only in this great
nation but throughout the even longer history of the world. That long
religious war is primarily a war of ideas, but occasionally it unfaithfully
breaks out in violence as one side or the other attempts to force its perspective on an unwilling populace.

Hats off to Hughes and Bellah for acknowledging that the central
dispute in American politics is religious. It takes some courage to face
this fact because by and large the American monotheistic and nationalist
effort has been to deny and suppress this fact because of its volatility.
This has been a particularly useful strategy for the Left wing of the
American nationalist movement, also known as liberals, secularists and
humanists. The Right wing of the American nationalist movement, the
Religious Right, has been more willing to engage in religious discussion
because they have endeavored more effectively to paint Christianity in
the right colors. The Left wing of American nationalism has been fighting back recently by adding more disparate colors from the rainbow.

The monocular limitation of both political colorings (perspectives)
comes through the realization that both are more expressions of American nationalism than of biblical Christianity. Both the Liberal and the
Conservative viewpoints center on American nationalism in the name of
God, but with the denial of God's Trinitarianism in Christ. By and
large, the Liberals tend to deny the Christ part, and the Conservatives
fail to understand the Trinitarian part.

This situation is made more confusing by the fact that the religious Right is itself in the grip of philosophical and religious internal dualistic struggle between the monotheism of the Right and the monotheism of the Left. Christians, right and left, have failed to consider a full-orbed trinitarian solution because they don't understand the Trinity. The Right is warring within itself as to whether it is essentially Christian or Libertarian, trinitarian or unitarian. This struggle evidences the same contours as the larger struggle between Conservatism and Liberalism nationally.

And the limitations of philosophical dualism hides the Third Rail of Christianity—the divinity of Jesus Christ—from the field by presenting various false, dichotomous choices of a Left/Right continuum. All expressions of a Left/Right philosophical or religious continuum are necessarily dualistic because they only contain two poles: Left and Right. All considerations and perspectives are understood, comprehended and mapped onto (forced into) the Left/Right continuum, to the denial of the Third Rail—Jesus Christ. All considerations and perspectives of the false Left/Right dichotomy deny, denigrate or attempt to destroy the full dimensionality of reality that can be seen and understood from a full-orbed biblical, Trinitarian Christian perspective.

Granted, that trinitarianism is about a thousand times more complex than dualism, but the complexity is essential to the truth, beauty, and actual objectivity of the reality in which we as human beings live. However, seeing the third dimension (the truth of God in Christ) is not a function of intellect or education, but of realization. Because Christ is real, He must be seen and understood as real. Thus, denial, denigration, and deceit about Christ amounts to denial, denigration, and deceit about the fullness of reality, and engenders a kind of blindness to important biblical subtleties like the difference between God's dominion and political domination.

Hughes also accurately suggests that the three major conflicts in American history were embodied in the Revolutionary War, The Civil War, and the 1960s Cultural Revolution. The Revolutionary War created a unitarian or deist document known as the American Constitution by attempting to create a political compromise between Unitarians and Trinitarians (Deists and Christians). That compromise has been in conflict ever since, even though at the same time it has utterly changed the world for the better.

The next time the American experiment broke down was during the Civil War, which was essentially a religious war between the mainline Unitarians in the North and the Calvinistic Trinitarians in the South. It was as much about states rights as it was about slavery, and the contours of the struggle are variegated. The South argued for a weak federal government to support an equitable balance of power, and the North argued that the federal government could sometimes play its trump card of political dominance. The South was wrong about slavery, but right about states rights and the balance of power. And the North was right about slavery and wrong about its political dominance. Of course, this is an over simplification, but it makes the point with broad strokes.

The Unitarians prevailed in that conflict and imposed their theology upon the nation as the *American Civil Religion* (another Bellah title) by working to embed unitarianism (the perspective not the religion) into the national legal and educational systems. The trinitarians (orthodox Christians) have struggled to clarify the theological confusion generated by the Constitutional compromise, as evidenced by the long-standing and hotly contested disputes about the "real character" of the American Founders. Additional confusion has resulted because the compromise has been perpetrated in the general spirit of Christianity, but not in the Trinitarian truth of Christianity. Thus, Trinitarians have continued to articulate and press their case regarding the Christian roots of the Constitution, while the unitarians have continued to argue for the universality (unitarianism) of those roots.

The American Cultural Revolution of the 60s began the third unitarian push for dominance with a bold step to completely overturn the values of traditional (trinitarian) Christianity through the imposition of a Unitarian version of Christianity. At least that is the character of the current American struggle as seen from a trinitarian Christian perspective. The conflict burns brighter by the day. I'm convinced that resolution will require the acknowledgment of deepest aspects of the conflict, the religious aspects. So, I'm grateful for Hughes' willingness to put it on the table, but frustrated that he seems to think his position is the objective view.

Hughes says that "when proponents of the Christian Right claim that the Founders were uniformly Christian, they are clearly wrong." He is right about this. They were not all Christians, Trinitarians. Some were Deists, who share the philosophical foundations of Unitarians. At the time, the Founders themselves were caught up in what is known in American church history as the Unitarian Controversy that was raging in what we today call the Mainline denominations. It still is.

That ancient controversy has actually been raging since Nimrod built the tower of Babel in an effort to dominate the world by scaling heaven. The roots of this historic, ongoing conflict were imposed in the Constitution itself by the intentional elimination of all Christian references and an unacknowledged premise of the truth of Unitarian principles but dressed in Christian language. The compromise struck in Philadelphia in 1776 vaguely implied some Christian rootage without directly mentioning Christianity or Christ or the Bible in the Constitution. This allowed Christians (Trinitarians) to believe in the Christian rootage of the Constitution, and the Deists (Unitarians) to ignore or deny it at the same time. That discussion has continued unabated ever since.

Hughes clearly sums up the heresy of the Constitution: "the Declaration of Independence grounded the religious meaning of the American experiment not in a God exclusively revealed in the biblical text, but in 'Nature and Nature's God.' That is, in the God all humans can know and understand through nature, quite apart from the biblical revelation." Unitarians, liberals, secularists, and humanists believe that they can understand God apart from the Bible and apart from Jesus Christ. Indeed, the god of the Constitution by this very admission is not the God of the Bible. This is huge! The proverbial cat is out of the bag and on center stage.

Trinitarian Christians must not feed the dualism that attempts to hold in union the unitarianism of the Christian Left with the unitarianism of the Christian Right in the name of American nationalism or American Christian nationalism. And neither can any claim on the mantle of global internationalism be made without bringing this same philosophical and theological conflict to the international stage.

Indeed, the current international conflict that is raging between the Christian West and Islam is cut from the same cloth. The unitarianism of Islam cannot abide the trinitarianism of Christianity. Many people have wondered how Western liberals are able to tolerate and even join forces with Muslims, given Islam's apparent conservative religious beliefs and virulent opposition to liberal policies. The answer is that both Islam and liberalism share a unitarian understanding of reality (or God) and deny the divinity of Christ (or the trinitarianism of reality). Thus, both seek to impose monotheism upon the world, and differ only about who will be in charge. Neither understands how Spheres of Sovereignty (a term coined by Abraham Kuyper, the 19th Century Dutch politician, journalist, statesman, and theologian) actually works, and accuse trinitarians of wanting to do what unitarians want to do—impose their "truth" on all. But it is a false accusation engendered in trinitarian ignorance.

Hughes then grounds the American Christian right on the Second Great Awakening. Charles Finney would be one of the chief representatives of the Second Great Awakening. And again Hughes correctly identifies the theology of the American Christian right as in fact being grounded in the Second Great Awakening. But he fails to note that such theology was branded a Christian heresy in the 17th Century Protestant church. The fact of this Arminian heresy has been broadly ignored and this theology has then gone on to dominate modern Evangelicalism. He's right about that, too. And this insight is a very unsettling sentiment, so the majority of Christians have pushed it into the recesses of denial and ignorance.

Nonetheless, clarification of our actual present and historic, philosophical and religious situation is essential for the determination of a way forward. As a biblical, trinitarian Christian I believe Jesus' teaching that the truth will set us free. As such, anything less than the trinitarian truth of the Bible in the light of Christ will drive us into a blind bind. Lord, have mercy!

CHRISTIAN CONTEXT: REJECTING CHRIST

Richard Hughes continues his series of articles in the Huffington Post, *The Christian Right in Context: Building a Christian America*, with a clear statement of his bias. By saying that "There have always been Christians who have resisted religious pluralism and diversity," he assumes that religious pluralism and diversity are the sine qua non of biblical Christianity, as if the emphasis of biblical Christianity and Progressive Liberalism are of the same root. But they are not. Consider the First Commandment: "You shall have no other gods before Me" (Exodus 20:3). Nonetheless, Hughes works to braid Christianity and multiculturalism into a single strand that comports with a liberal spin of American history.

By thanking the Constitution that rabid, fundamental, even Al-Qaeda-like Christians could not impose their narrow-minded and archaic practices—not mere views but the imposition of ancient biblical law—upon America by "coercion or the force of law," he reveals his disgust with and lack of understanding of genuine Christianity. Therefore, he argues, Christians had to use the only weapon left to their disposal—persuasion—to try to accomplish their dastardly desires. It is not that Christianity, nor I, have anything against persuasion per se, but that Hughes paints it as the last means available for Christians to use to try to "force" their neighbors to give up common sense, rather than the Christians' first and only means of ordinary evangelism. Indeed, persuasion is even the very means of governing this great democratic republic that our American Founders gave us. Political debate is about persuasion. Yet, he insinuates that Christians are not to engage in persuasion in the public square!

He cites three historic efforts by Christians to use persuasion in the public square and brands them all as religious revivals: the Second Great Awakening (1800s–1830s), the Fundamentalist Controversy (1920s–1930s) and what I will call the Reagan Revolution (1980s–today). The oversimplification of this historical approach to American history boggles the mind. That a serious academic would conflate fact and opinion so carelessly in order to ride a favorite hobby horse (liberalism) at the expense of historical accuracy speaks volumes about the world in which we currently live—and the state of academia.

The truth is that much good and much evil came from the Second Great Awakening, which was fueled by a historically heretical theology. So, to call it "Christian" is only partly true because it freely used Christian nomenclature but eschewed Christian orthodoxy. It produced a mixed crop of genuine Christian faithfulness and genuinely Christian social institutions, but at the same time strengthened the heresies of humanism and liberal social institutions.

Hughes writes that as a consequence of the Second Great Awakening "many now viewed allegiance to the Christian faith, embodied in a Protestant denomination (it made no difference which one) as part and parcel of American patriotism." This is most certainly true, but it does not represent a good thing with regard to Christianity, but rather provides evidence for the apostasy of those who held (and continue to hold) such an idea as an element of Christian faith. While there is nothing wrong with being a Christian and being a Protestant, much is wrong with conflating the two loyalties. Hughes' analysis is fine as far as it goes, but it is significant because he fails to apply it equally to the political Left. What he fails to say screams from the page.

He is saying that the Christian Right has no right claiming that civil government should be a tool for the Christianization of America. He goes on to argue that the values of the Christian Right should not steer the state. However, he also argues that there were other consequences of the Second Great Awakening that concerned social justice and poverty, which must be understood as Christian or biblical values, as well. These Social Gospel values are now being trumped by the political Left as objective values that must be inculcated by civil government. What began in the Christian church, various institutions of social care (hospitals, orphanages, elder care, etc.), have been co-opted or usurped from the voluntary participation by Christians and church institutions to the mandatory imposition of these same things through the tax funded structures of civil government by the political Left.

Let me see if I understand him correctly: when the Right gets involved in civil government, it poses a problem to liberty, but when the Left gets involved, it is an expression of universal responsibility. I'm not arguing against the values of social justice and charity on behalf of the Right because the Right is not opposed to justice or charity. Rather, the issues are who should provide it and who should receive it?

Granted that slavery should have never been part of America, but it was very much a part of the Old World. So, when Old World people came to America they brought it with them. But it was not just white Europeans who supported slavery. African tribalism regularly enslaved other African tribes, and Muslims have always supported slavery. The impetus to abandon slavery came from Christians, not African tribes-people or Muslims. And Hughes rightfully acknowledges this fact by re-minding us that it issued from zeal of the Second Great Awakening for social reform.

Where the European Reformation worked for church reform, the Second Great Awakening worked for social reform. And because the Second Great Awakening also opposed the Calvinistic established Amer-ican churches, it turned to the only other vehicle of social reform avail-able—civil government. Thus, the social reformers who inherited the zeal of the Second Great Awakening—the Social Gospel Movement—shifted the responsibility for various social institutions like hospitals, or-phanages, retirement care, etc. from the churches (and families) to the civil government. Thus, what was rightfully and traditionally a function of church and family has increasingly become a tax burden for civil gov-ernment. This shift of social responsibility from church to state is the fruit of the theological heresies of the Second Great Awakening.

Why make such a shift? Because more and more Americans had abandoned their churches and/or families in pursuit of the American Dream. The early Western Frontier was no place for families, and with-out the social support of family life and responsibility, historic churches had difficulty taking root in the society. The American religious wars spurned by the Second Great Awakening produced new churches for the New Light (Lite) Christians who had a passion for being passionate, but who at the same time ground up traditional family and church rela-tionships to produce various sorts of "spiritual" affinity groups, orga-nized around ideas rather than kinship.

The "core meaning of America: liberty and justice for all" has not been undermined by Fundamentalism, as Hughes suggests, but by the cancerous growth of civil government. What has been undermined by Fundamentalism is not the core meaning of America, but the core meaning of Christianity: faithfulness and charity. And the instrument of that undermining has been the unprecedented growth of civil govern-ment at the expense of self-government, family government and church government. The error of the social justice doctrine is the overemphasis of civil government by the underemphasis of the other institutions of government. It lacks the biblical balance of multiple jurisdictions.

Hughes goes on to say that "industrialization that occurred both during and after the Civil War contributed to unthinkable levels of grinding poverty in cities throughout the northern part of the United

States." To say that modern industrialization brought poverty to America is most certainly false. The reality is far more complex. Nonetheless, American industrialization brought the greatest growth of economic wealth and development that the world has ever known. This, however, does not mean that there was no poverty in America. But the shape of the larger, more general curve of economic development does not illustrate human poverty, but wealth and individual advancement.

It also facilitated corporate greed and the abuse of workers as cost cutting measures were instituted in order to develop gargantuan American companies. However, to suggest that corporate greed is synonymous with Christianity or capitalism is absurd. The categorization that "'Christian America' rejected (the) efforts of the working poor and found the unions as threatening as the immigrants themselves" is again full of bias and false innuendo. Because most people were Christian at the time the majority of people in any group were Christian, but that does not mean that whatever the group did was an expression of faithful Christianity. Labor unions were undoubtedly begun by people who professed Christianity, as were the bulk of corporations. But those same labor unions who organized to protect their wages and working conditions, those whose have inherited the labor unions themselves, were threatened by immigrants.

Churches were not threatened by immigrants! This was a time of unparalleled evangelism. Christianity was busy welcoming immigrants into their congregations and/or helping to support new churches. Christianity has always been an evangelical movement that is passionate for growth and development. So, to suggest that Christians were threatened by immigration is nonsense. Sure, there were differences of belief and behavior. But Christians as a group have more in common with one another than they do with unbelievers, and the majority of immigrants were from Christian countries.

The "radically new world view, predicated on evolutionary assumptions, (that) began to undermine both the ideal and the reality of a 'Christian America' involved the nationalization of public (read: governmental, tax funded) education. The central engine of this Darwinian worldview was public education, which had become an instrument of civil government. Prior to this time, public education was synonymous with Christian education. Public education was begun by Christians to serve Christian purposes. Thus, public education became a divisive wedge in American society, dividing children from their parents and unbelievers from believers.

Darwin's theory of evolution functionally replaced God as the source of life itself. It undercut the very first verse of the Bible and cast a serpentine shadow onto all of God's Word in the name of science and progress. Science itself was literally changing the very environment in which people lived, as if science had godlike powers of creation. The newness and great successes of science swayed many Christians and their ministers to rethink their most basic beliefs about the Bible and God. Science, in its infancy, seemed to contradict the Bible. Reconciliation and harmonization would need to wait for the maturity of science and technology, when Newtonian Physics would give way to Quantum Mechanics and Nuclear Physics. Yet, Hughes seems to be stuck in the conundrums of an infantile science.

Many of those new understandings that had their genesis in the early 20th Century came from Sigmund Freud, an atheist Jew who was a self-confessed hater of God and the Bible. The revolutions in psychology that were produced by Freud and his followers were not new light into the human condition and treatment, but were actually resurgent shadows of darkness and despair from the pre-Christian past. Freud introduced deviant sexuality as the cure for moral repression of sin—and called it progress. And if that isn't unbelievable enough, the really unbelievable thing is that people believed him. In the name of human maturity and development Freud augured for the advent of adolescent sexual morality and the release of the passions that threaten civilization itself in the name of progress.

Hughes' acknowledges that the "Second Great Awakening was in sync with the spirit of its age," which if you know anything about the Bible is not a good thing. That a Christian revival would promote the spirit of the age as opposed to the Spirit of Christ, and would do so in the name of Christ, is horrifying—but true. The spirit of the age was that the kingdom of God and the establishment of American democracy were synonymous. Again, the fact that well-meaning Christians would even think that such conflation of church and state was itself a Christian ideal is disturbing.

The Bible has always taught the separation of church and state. Even in ancient Israel the kingly and priestly casts were separate. But what is more disturbing is that Hughes blames Fundamentalism for standing against such heresy. On the one hand, Hughes argues for the separation of the Right from the state, but not the separation of the Left from the state.

The optimism of the Second Great Awakening was built on the antinomianism of the spirit of the age and its love of sin—in the name of Christianity, of course! And the pessimism of the Fundamentalists was actually the reassertion of the biblical doctrine of sin in the face of ram-pant social depravity. Unfortunately, Fundamentalists did—and still do—pine for the past. Unlike Shariah-minded Muslims who want to return to the morality of a 7th Century Persia, too many theonomy-minded Christians want to return to the morality of a more progressive 17th Century Europe. But when compared with the progressives of today, who want to return to the morality of an early Sodom (sometime prior to the birth of Isaac, which was 1712 B.C.E.), the Fundamentalists seem practically reasonable. Unfortunately, history does not flow backward. And besides, the good-old-days never actually were as good as anyone remembers them.

Hughes goes on to suggest that one of the significant differences between the Second Great Awakening and the Fundamentalist Move-ment was that the Second Great Awakening worked to unite the coun-try while the Fundamentalist Movement worked to divide it. It is true that religion both unites and divides. It unites believers and divides them from sinners. Religion (common beliefs and assumptions about reality) is the only thing that unites people. And sin is the primary thing that di-vides people. The most basic Christian understanding is that the world is awash in sin and Christ came to save people from it. Thus, the world is awash in separation and division, but Christ came to unite people by separating them from their sin.

The Second Great Awakening moved Christian values into the public square and created social institutions to support them. As a result, more people experienced the love and care of Christ. But the theology of the Second Great Awakening was insufficient to tie the blessings of Christ to the Person of Christ. So, people (unbelievers and confused be-lievers) began to think that they could extract social principles from the Bible and apply them helter skelter to society apart from Christ, as if Christ didn't need to be personally involved in the giving of His bless-ings. In other words, unrepentant people got a taste of Christian social service and liked it. They liked it so much that they brought those social services under the wing of civil government so they could be paid for with taxes and so that everyone, regardless of belief or repentance, could enjoy the blessings of Christian social service.

The Fundamentalists, on the other hand, reasserted the theology that teaches that Christ's blessings go with right belief and repentance, because right belief and repentance are the very things that animate Christians to service. And without them, neither the call nor the passion for service exist. And without the service, the blessings dry up. We see this today as we reap the fruit of the application of biblical social principles apart from personal relationship with Jesus Christ. That fruit manifests as people wanting the benefits of biblical social principles but not the responsibilities of right belief, repentance and service. People want to be blessed, but they don't want the only God who actually bestows blessings. The fruit is the entitlement mentality that is driving the world to the brink of financial ruin.

CHRISTIAN TRINITARIAN POLITY

One of the major conflicts within Christianity concerns polity or the form of denominational church government. The three historic forms of Christian polity are episcopal, presbyterian and congregational. Episcopalian polity is top-down hierarchy and includes Catholics, Anglicans and others. Presbyterian polity is led by regional groups of ministers called Presbyteries and have a regional, representative style government. Congregationalism is independent or locally governed and is usually associated with democratic control. Adherents from all three argue that their particular form is the biblical form, and all trace their origins to the New Testament. There are shelves of volumes describing and defending each position.

After many years of study and reflection on church polity, I find that Scripture itself is not as clear as we want it to be on this matter. As with baptism, Scripture simply does not supply the clarity we want regarding either the best mode of baptism—immersion, pouring or sprinkling, or the best mode of church government—episcopal, presbyterian or congregational. Convincing arguments can be made for each mode, and each has its own weaknesses and strengths.

What we know for sure is that Scripture is true and can be trusted regarding things like the modes of baptism and church polity, and that the various modes all have ardent defenders who are able to provide solid biblical arguments for each. This leads to the conclusion that all are indeed biblical, and therefore useful for God's people, but all have limitations regarding their appropriateness with regard to the context and circumstances of their use. This is not an argument of relativity that undermines the ultimate truth of the Bible. But it is an argument that incorporates the doctrine of the Trinity in the body of Christ, the church.

The church is alive. It is a dynamic, living entity that is subject to the realities and vicissitudes of time. Churches grow and mature—and decay. Consequently, because churches can be in different stages of growth and maturity, one rigid view of polity cannot provide optimal church governance across the board. Rather, it may well be that Scripture provides variations in church polity in order to satisfy the needs of churches in various stages of maturity. How might this play out?

One church may require an episcopal polity because of the immaturity (understood as a paucity of mature Christians) of the greater society in which it is planted. Another church in a more mature society may find that a presbyterian polity is better because it uses the greater levels of maturity of its members in leadership. And a church in a mature Christian society may find that congregational polity is best suited because it is planted in a mature Christian society. Thus, depending on the condition and needs of particular churches and the degree of genuine Christianization of the society in which they are planted, this or that polity may be more suitable to a particular situation.

In broad brush, we find that the New Testament churches had been planted in the pagan Roman Empire and required an episcopal polity to keep them on track for genuine growth in Christ. Later, the Reformation found that a presbyterian polity was better suited because of the growing maturity of Christendom (Christian Europe) at that point in history. Later, as the Christian church was planted on the shores of America, it found itself (or thought that it found itself) in a society of mature, responsible Christians and opted for congregational polity. Those first Christians who emigrated to America tended to be quite mature in their faith across the board.

Thus, depending on the context of the church and the genuine Christianization of the society in which it is planted, God found it optimal to provide a variety of church polities, each of which could carry and convey the gospel of Jesus Christ. This, of course, is a far too simple analysis and will break down if pressed. It simply suggests a tendency or trend and must not be taken to provide consistent analysis in every situation.

We get into trouble when we suggest that all churches must have the same particular form of church government because that is not the model we find in Scripture. The adherents of each form of polity find that Scripture teaches their particular polity. This, then, suggests that God's understanding of Christian unity or church government is not political uniformity. Church unity is not a matter of all churches having the same kind of polity, nor is it a matter of all churches believing in doctrinal uniformity. Our differences are beneficial. They contribute to our continued growth and maturity in Christ. Paul said that we would always have divisions among us, and that such divisions are necessary for the recognition of genuine truth (1 Corinthians 11:18-19).

Insanity

U.S. Rep. Gabrielle Giffords was shot along with a bunch of other people on Saturday (1/8/2011), as the shooter, 22-year-old Jared Lee Loughner, fired into the crowd. By all appearances Loughner was a psychologically disturbed individual who acted alone. He had a previous grievance with Giffords.

People want to know why Loughner shot Giffords. Not twenty-four hours into it, various pundits have suggested that the toxic political atmosphere of contemporary American politics caused this distraught young man to "cross the line" and commit murder. The suggestion that conservative talk radio is the source of the toxic political atmosphere is patently absurd. People forget that America was forged out of war and violence, and has struggled to hold together viciously opposed political perspectives for more than 200 years. This is neither the first nor the most bitter season of toxic American politics.

But the most offensive aspect of the charge against talk radio is the suggestion that the whistle blower (talk radio) is the source of the problem (toxic politics). The fact that talk radio is critical of the administration does mean that talk radio is responsible for toxic political atmosphere. As my mother used to say, "It takes two to tango." The fact that one side is loud and boisterous and the other is soft and measured does not mean that the loud side is spewing poisonous ideas and the soft side is not.

At the root of the problem is the lack of political civility. Discover what has drained civility from American society and you will have the culprit. Of course, this assumes that America used to have common civility. Did it? When I grew up we were told that religion and politics were not subjects for polite conversation. Really? Why not? Well, the reason was that these topics revealed various social divisions and those revelations made people angry.

Okay. But who got angry? Do Christians get angry when people disagree with them? Is that anger biblically justified? Did Christ teach us to dis those who disagree with us? Did He teach that we are to shove our ideas down people's throats whether they like it or not? No, He didn't. So, people who get mad when discussing religion and politics are not faithful Christians. At best they are poor models of Christian behavior.

And such people probably don't want others to know that they are hypocrites, if they describe themselves as Christian. People who are not confessing Christians, and who are involved in public discourse, probably don't want others to know that they are not Christian, either—because adherence to Christian values has always been the default position of American politicians. To a great degree Americans still don't trust politicians who are not confessing Christians.

So, two groups of people don't want discussion of religion and politics—hypocritical Christians and non Christians. And one way to discourage discussion (of any kind) is to become angry at certain topics. Lot's of people engage this method of controlling conversation. It is behavior that is learned by children in a permissive society. Children can often control their parents by having a tantrum when they don't get what they want. This practice often continues into adulthood, though refined for adult audiences.

Display of Character

People make all kinds of claims about themselves, about who they are. But when people are under duress, their real character comes to the fore. How people cope with difficulty and stress reveals their true character.

The Middle East has put itself into the spotlight (Green Revolution), particularly in Cairo, Egypt, of late in the effort to change their situation. It appears that protests began as a genuine expression for democratic reform. And such reform is long overdue, as most countries in the area have been run by powerful dictators for several decades—probably for eons if the truth be known. Democracy has never been part of the Middle Eastern DNA. Nonetheless, it appears that there is such a movement in that direction today. However, that spirit is fledgling at best, and it is not the only spirit that is stirring.

Islamic Jihad has also been active since Mohammad walked the desert sands. In fact, Jihad is the means that Mohammad gave to Islam for its growth. Of course, there are two forms of Jihad: the inner Jihad of spiritual maturity, and the social Jihad of domination that naturally results from Islam's main tenet—surrender. Thus, Jihad is the *modus operandi* for Muslims. It is what they do as a religious discipline. It informs Muslim character.

And what we see in the midst of the Middle East protests is the revelation of Muslim character, informed and disciplined by the Qur'an. The central thing that almost all, if not all, of the protesters share is their Muslim faith, liberal or conservative, secular or extreme. They are ninety-some percent Muslim, mostly Sunni. Wahhabi is a branch of Sunni. So, what we see as they come under stress and duress is generic Muslim character as it engages Jihad, the discipline of the Qur'an.

The impact of the Islamic uprising that is sweeping across the Middle East will impact America. Of this there can be no doubt. But the how and what of that impact is yet to be seen. I suspect that it will call into question the success of the American Experiment.

De Toqueville thought that the American Experiment was about democracy, and in a sense it is. From this perspective the American Experiment asks, "Can 'The People' determine their own destiny? Can people govern themselves?" That's what democracies are—self-governing societies. But this is only half the picture.

The other half is about what America was before 1776, and what brought Americans together constitutionally. It's about whether the

U.S.A. is or ever was a Christian nation. Of course, that's debatable, as we have seen for all of our two hundred plus year history. But whether the U.S.A. was founded as an explicitly Christian nation, it was and still is most assuredly a nation of Christians. Currently, about eighty percent of Americans identify themselves as Christian, and this is the lowest percentage in our history. If we consider those who live by Christian values, but don't espouse Christianity, the number would be even higher. Few would argue that the U.S.A. was not founded upon a Christian foundation.

However, the Founders thought it necessary to bring all Americans into the Great Experiment. To do that, they needed to compromise by not explicitly referencing Jesus Christ or the Bible in the founding documents. And this compromise is what makes the American Experiment an experiment in democracy rather than an experiment in Christian government.

Thus, the Experiment is not merely a democratic experiment, but it is equally an experiment about whether America can be governed without reference to Jesus Christ or the Bible. For most of American history, the experiment produced tremendous results by any measure. Indeed, there has never been a nation like the U.S.A. in the history of the world. The U.S.A. has forever changed world history. And for most of American history, Christianity informed American character and values. Of course, there has always been a struggle in America to hold to our Christian roots.

As with the Founders, there were many powerful voices that mitigated against Christianity and her values. That struggle came to a head in the 1960s and those who opposed Christianity took the upper hand as the Second American Revolution swept the land—and the whole of Western Civilization. Since that time the cultural elites have worked hard to turn America away from her Christian roots and values by caricaturing Christianity in the worst possible light and redefining it on the basis of that light.

Church Failure

Robert D. Putnam and David E. Campbell wrote an article, "Walking away from church," for the LA Times (10/17/2010) summarizing their recent book, *American Grace*. It seems that churches might want to hear what their research has uncovered.

> "As recently as 1990, all but 7% of Americans claimed a religious affiliation, a figure that had held constant for decades. Today, 17% of Americans say they have no religion, and these new 'nones' are very heavily concentrated among Americans who have come of age since 1990. Between 25% and 30% of twentysomethings today say they have no religious affiliation—roughly four times higher than in any previous generation."

It is no surprise that young people are leaving the church (or faith or Christianity) in droves. The question is: why is this happening? Obviously, it is a function of secularization. Contemporary society and government believe that secularization provides the greatest hope for world peace and a host of other social "benefits." But what exactly does secularization mean? The dictionary defines it as "The activity of changing something (art or education or society or morality etc.) so it is no longer under the control or influence of religion." And what is the primary instrument that is used to bring about this change? Public education. That's why it effects the young more than the old. Public education is getting better at what it does.

Current sociological evidence provides proof that the secularizing efforts of public education over the past couple of decades are paying off because the younger generations are more secularized than the older generations. Think about this for a moment. Public education is intentionally and successfully undermining the traditional religious beliefs and values of America. The government extracts taxes in order to "educate" our children away from traditional Christian values.

Putnam and Campbell, on the other hand, theorize that the reason is politics rather than education. They think that it is the conservative politics of Evangelical churches that are disaffecting the youth, that the young are opposed to conservative politics. They suggest that people have "adjusted their religion to fit their politics," and that conservatives are more guilty of this than liberals. The fact that too many people are Republican or Democrat before they are Christian cannot be denied. But it seems to me that the guilt should be equally shared.

What particular social issue seems to drive the drift into secularization? Homosexuality.

> "The fraction of twentysomethings who said that homosexual re-
> lations were 'always' or 'almost always' wrong plummeted from
> about 75% in 1990 to about 40% in 2008. ... the association be-
> tween religion and politics (and especially religion's intolerance
> of homosexuality) was the single strongest factor in this porten-
> tous shift."

Gregory Paul disagrees with their analysis in another LA Times article, *What's really hurting Christianity in America*. He agrees with
their findings that

> "The nonreligious are far and away the fastest-growing group,
> with nonbelievers having tripled as a portion of the general pop-
> ulation since the 1960s and nonreligious twentysomethings dou-
> bling in just two decades."

Paul argues that

> "Where Putman and Campbell go off track is in their second
> claim: that aversion among young Americans to the religious
> right is the primary secularizing force, and that skeptical youth
> may flock back to the churches if the latter embrace a less strident
> tone. This is almost certainly incorrect."

He identifies that secularization is a global, transnational phenomenon. And that "Because hard-right Christianity has never been a major
force outside the United States, it cannot be a leading cause of Western
secularization." He cites studies that suggest that where socialism is most
entrenched religious commitment is not. Where the civil state meets all
of the bodily needs of a population, that population does not look to
God for anything.

"Another factor behind Western secularism is the growth of the
popular corporate-consumer culture." When people are caught up in
popular corporate-consumer culture, they have no time for God because
they are busy with their gizmos and gadgets. "The now dominant corporate-consumer culture has driven the religious right into a shrinking
parallel culture that most young Westerners see as pathetically square"–
uncool, not hip, unpopular.

So, the second most powerful factor that steals the minds of children
is the profit-driven corporate-consumer culture. We must not miss the
fact that this culture is corporate, that it is being primarily driven by

global corporate profits, and those who covet such profits, small corporations that emulate the big dogs.

I suspect that the recent concern for jobs, driven by the recent global economic fleecing, I mean crisis, will drive both public and higher education to serve the desires of the corporate-consumer culture in the hope of creating jobs. Indeed, that process has already begun. So, we can look for an increase in global socialization (as opposed to mere national socialism) to be the primary cultural force in the 21st Century, driving secular education and job training for a global culture that is increasingly hostile to religious belief.

What can Christians do to stem the tide? Get your kids out of public education, and shun the drive for global corporate-consumer culture. The best and only effective tool for this will be serious biblical education. Learn the truth about the Bible and teach it to your family. In addition, I suspect that the only viable institution that has any chance to counter the corporate-consumer cultural momentum of globalization is the local church. Real Christians need to recapture local churches.

LANGUAGE ITSELF IS RELIGIOUS

The purpose of language is the communication of ideas. Except for Zen Buddhism, which is founded upon the idea that ideas are not real and there is nothing to communicate. But people being what they are, want to know more about Zen Buddhism and seek out a Zen Master to explain to them that ideas are not real and that there is, therefore, nothing to communicate. And it is such a compelling idea that schools and training centers arise to produce certified Zen Masters. If anything, Zen Buddhism proves that humanity so requires a religious perspective that it makes a religion out of the denial of religion. It makes a god out of the denial of God.

How can this be? Why does this happen? It happens because human beings speak, and because speaking issues out of thinking. And thinking is accomplished with the building blocks of words and ideas. We learn to speak by hearing speech. Words and ideas are, therefore, self-authenticating. If it seems like this line of reasoning seems circular it is because this line of reasoning is circular. Ultimately, all reasoning is circular because the completion of the circle of words and ideas provides the logical proof of the original assertion. Real creative thinking always begins with a raw, unsubstantiated assertion. Ideas grow out of such raw assertions.

These words are not intended to be confusing, but to clarify the reality that all speech is necessarily religious, or if you prefer—spiritual. Language always and necessarily issues from the idea of God. This is true both historically and philosophically. It cannot be otherwise. This is the absolute Truth upon which all other truth rests. Choose any idea from history or philosophy and you are already embroiled in communication through words.

Quaran Burning

Serious public religious discussion is all but impossible these days. It seems that to hold any serious religious belief is to offend those who don't hold that particular belief. And the more seriously you take your faith, the more offensive it is. How has American civil society come to this horrible place? Why can't people have serious but courteous religious discussions where the participants are not hell-bent on spinning every nuance in their own favor? How did we get here? Public education.

We have been educated into this position by our public education system and universities. It is because this phenomenon of intolerance is so widespread that we must look to an equally widespread source. When we follow the money, it leads to public education. Things were not always this way. The change has occurred over the past 40-50 years.

The problem we are experiencing is religious ignorance. We are a religiously ignorant people and that ignorance makes us fearful of philosophical/theological differences. People are afraid of what they don't understand. How has this ignorance come about? Younger people do not have the experience to know how things used to be. The ignorant don't understand what they don't know. For the most part younger people only know how things are now. They don't know what they haven't been taught.

If you were born after about 1965 you will have no personal experience with what I am talking about because your entire life and your experience in public education and college has been inculcated from a perspective that is significantly different than those who were born and educated earlier than that. However, the issue is not a matter of age, but of history and education.

The American revolution of the 1960s has proven to be quite successful in changing the world.[6] And at the same time the general or common philosophical, religious, and political views and ideas about the world have also changed. But here's the fly in the ointment: the cultural revolution of the 60s intended to teach peace and mutual toleration, but

---

6   http://www.newsweek.com/2010/07/15/the-real-life-mad-men-behind-the-60s-ad-revolution.html
     http://www.amazon.com/Turn-60s-Folk-Rock-Revolution/dp/087930703X
     http://60ssexualrevolution.com/
     http://psychedelicadventure.blogspot.com/2010/01/electric-kool-aid-lsd-60s-psyche-delic.html
     http://www.pbs.org/opb/thesixties/topics/revolution/index.html

the actual result has been continuous war, increased crime and violence, the multiplication of drug abuse, personal and social identity crises, and the dumbing down of the population. The fruit, now ripe, has been a decided decrease regarding the toleration of other people and any opinions that differs from liberal immorality. It seems that the more our schools and universities teach peace and toleration, diversity and multiculturalism, the less of it there actually is.

On the ninth anniversary of 9/11, the destruction of the World Trade Center by Islamic terrorists, we have a small Christian church in Florida that is going to hold a public Quaran burning. Why are they doing this? The church pastor, Terry Jones, says that the purpose is to reveal the character of Islam. How will it do this? The burning is intended to make Muslims angry in order to show how they handle anger. Already, we see that protesting Muslims tend to handle anger like immature children who throw a temper tantrum when they don't get their own way. Except these are adults with guns.

On one level it is a bad idea to intentionally make people mad. But on another level, how people handle anger and frustration does in fact reveal a lot about their character and maturity. On the one hand it seems insane to inflame violent people. But on the other hand, it serves to identify to the watching world exactly which people are insane enough to engage in violence and hatred against those who disagree with or anger them.

The Christian Bible teaches that people are to love their enemies and to fight them with random acts of kindness and service for their own genuine good in order to win them over to the love and teachings of Jesus Christ.[7] The Koran, on the other hand, teaches no such thing—quite the opposite, in fact. And that is why Muslims do what they do when they are angered.

> "The Koran contains at least 109 verses that call Muslims to war with nonbelievers. Some are quite graphic, with commands to chop off heads and fingers and kill infidels wherever they may be hiding. Muslims who do not join the fight are called 'hypocrites' and warned that Allah will send them to Hell if they do not join the slaughter."[8]

This kind of violent teaching and behavior must not be permitted in the public arena because it is dangerous. Burning Korans publicly, on

---

7   http://www.bible-topics.com/Enemies.html
8   http://www.thereligionofpeace.com/Koran/023-violence.htm

the other hand, may be stupid and insensitive, but it is not dangerous in and of itself. In America, we are free to do such public protests as burning our own American flag, or the Bible, or other books as acts of free speech. We understand that those who engage in such public antics are trying to make a political point.

And what point are these Koran burners trying to make? That Islam is an inherently dangerous religion when it is taken seriously. The more seriously Islam is taken, the more dangerous it is for non-Muslims because it does not teach religious toleration. It teaches religious and political domination. We can talk about whether Christianity teaches the same kind of things later, but for now it is important to understand—regardless of what any other religion teaches—that the Koran is itself internally and inherently violent and is opposed to the kind of political freedom we enjoy in America.

The toleration of serious Islam in America may, if Islam is successful in its stated intentions, impose Shariah law to the whole world, bring about the end of American religious and political toleration. Shariah law is not tolerant of other religions, but calls for conversion to Islam or the death of other religious adherents who fail to convert. Yes, it allows for both Jews and Christians to coexist with Muslims as a special case. But it mandates that Muslims treat Jews and Christians as *Dhimmi*, second class citizens subject to special taxes and disparaging treatment, as part of that coexistence.[9] The intention is to diminish Judaism and Christianity as much as possible, while tolerating their existence, until the whole world is converted to Islam.

For some unpublicized reason almost every major media outlet and elected politician in the world refuses to acknowledge these simple, plain facts about Islam in contradiction to the overwhelming evidence that Islamic peace is the peace that comes from political and military domination by intimidation, extortion, and violence. Indeed, intimidation, extortion, and violence are the instruments of both Islamic evangelism and it's peace.

Rather than burn the Koran it would be much more beneficial to reveal as objectively as possible exactly what the Koran teaches about things like religious toleration, the treatment of Jews, Christians (*Dhimmi*), and those perceived as enemies. Don't burn your Koran, read it for Christ's sake.

---

9   http://www.whatthewestneedstoknow.com/

WHEN THE KETTLE CALLS THE POT BLACK

Glenn Beck's recent Restoring Honor rally has unleashed a Jinni from the proverbial bottle. It is significant that he has stood in the public square like no one else could at this point in history and called for a national revival of Christian morality. All sane Americans can agree about the need for a renewed sense of morality among both the American leadership and the populace. If only we could quit hurling epithets at one another, and actually read the Bible we just might find the long lost American unity that is needed for a time like this. Fat chance! I've always been a dreamer like Rev. King, trying to focus on the content of character rather than the color of the party.

However, Beck has dumped a HUGE problem on the steps of the Lincoln Memorial. That problem begins with the fact that Beck does not have the credentials to call Obama on his faith. Beck cannot speak for the Christian church because he is a Mormon. Being a Mormon makes Beck a heretic according to all of the broadly accepted ecumenical creeds of historic Christianity. Historic orthodox Christianity is necessarily Trinitarian according to our inherited documents and traditions. And Mormonism is not, which puts it outside the pale of Christian orthodoxy. Because Beck cannot see this distinction, he cannot possibly see what actually makes people Christian. The fact that he talks the talk but remains a Mormon is hugely problematic.

However, the real issue is not the Christian faith of President Obama, but the Christian faith of American Christianity. The real issue is the contemporary orthodoxy of the mainstream churches. Obama's faith is true to his church, the United Church of Christ, which is the largest branch of historic Congregationalism in America. And Congregationalism was the first truly American denomination. It was founded on American soil. The other branches of Christianity were at that time transplants from Europe.

There it is! That is the elephant in the room that no one dares mention—American Christian theological orthodoxy. The social diversity police have been active over the past fifty years undermining the very idea of orthodoxy, as if any and every attempt to define or understand Truth or righteousness constitutes an act of terrorism against the constitutionally protected right to sin. The very idea of Christian theological orthodoxy chills the spines of everyone regardless of their religious sentiments. Atheists, agnostics, Christians, Pagans and adherents of other religions all tremble at the idea of discussing, much less actually deciding on any standard of Christian theological orthodoxy.

The subject conjures up visions of Christian Inquisitions and Crusades of the past. Never mind that such inquisitions and crusades were ill-conceived political escapades that were never part of any version of faithful biblical Christianity, but were episodes in history where the church(es) themselves had been hijacked by godless people in the churches and out. There have always been people in the churches who have claimed to be Christian, but who were nothing of the sort, and who have tried to represent Christianity, but have only muddied the water. Read Jude. From the very beginning of the church,

> "certain people have crept in unnoticed who long ago were designated for this condemnation, ungodly people, who pervert the grace of our God into sensuality and deny our only Master and Lord, Jesus Christ" (Jude 1:4).

This has always been the case. Always.

This fifth column infiltration into the church by unorthodox leaders is why Christianity has had to develop various creeds that define what constitutes Christian orthodoxy. It is also the source of most of the un-biblical crap that has been done in the name of Christianity. Thankfully, we do not have to reinvent that wheel. But we do need to put our shoulders to it. Every faithful Church has historically accepted the Ecumenical Creeds, an umbrella term that refers to the Nicene Creed, the Apostles' Creed, and the Athanasian Creed. The acceptance of these creeds, while not universal, is fully American. The Christian unity that the American Founding Fathers accepted was in harmony with these Ecumenical Creeds.

Thus, it is to these creeds alone to which faithful orthodox American Christians can and must appeal today, if we are to be true to our own histories. And such historical fidelity is an important Christian virtue. If American Christians are to find theological unity today, it can come only from these historic creeds. This, of course, does not mitigate against the Protestant motto or solas: *Sola Scriptura* (Scripture Alone), *Solus Christus* (Christ Alone), *Sola Gratia* (Grace Alone), *Sola Fide* (Faith Alone) and *Soli Deo Gloria* (God's Glory Alone). The failure to gather around this version of Christian orthodoxy will likely amount to the failure of Protestant Christianity, which is the root of the American experiment, and will likely bring about the ultimate failure of the American experiment itself. Such failures are not beyond the pale of possibility, and such failure will bring severe consequences to life as we know it. Indeed, this is the target of the enemies of the gospel and the American experiment.

And make no mistake, there are many powerful people and forces (principalities) working to accomplish these failures. The enemies of the gospel have never been better armed or prepared, nor has Christ's church ever been more unprepared for such a struggle. Nonetheless, it is upon us, ready or not. The need of the hour is a simple but true standard of Christian fidelity. The American Christian standard must be identified, claimed, and raised. This discussion must be engaged. Lord, have mercy.

But we must not engage this discussion in terms of the lives or faithfulness of individual Christians themselves, but in terms of the life and faithfulness of Jesus Christ. Christians do not tout themselves as the ideal to which to aspire to. Rather, we tout Jesus Christ as the standard. He is the model and the judge, not we. Faithful Christians freely admit that they are sinners and have failed miserably to be what Christ has called them to be. And anyone who says differently is either misinformed, self-deceived, lying, or all of the above. We must rise above and stop the reciprocal name calling and character assassination that dominates the airwaves and pixels of the Internet and come to terms with biblical theology, the "Queen of the Sciences." Why? Because theology like philosophy is the study of the values and virtues that animate human identity and behavior. The problems that threaten to overwhelm us are all animated by faulty values, worldviews, virtues, and isms that issue out of poor theology and bad philosophy.

However, we cannot afford to hand this theological/philosophical task over to the so-called experts. Such an avoidance of personal responsibility for our own beliefs and values is the problem, and giving our theological responsibilities to anyone else cannot help. Christ does not require anything but simple faithfulness in God's Word and the efficacy of Christ's sacrifice (Ephesians 2:8). Oh, there is much more to know and learn, but apart from simple trust in the Lord everything else is unknowable and unlearnable.

To the best of my knowledge there is not today any serious Christian or church in existence that believes that Christians should return to the errors of the Inquisition or the Crusades. And those who make such accusations are being neither honest nor fair, whether out of ignorance or spite. Such a suggestion is at best a ruse and distraction. History moves forward, not backward. Christ beckons us forward, not backward. We cannot return to some envisioned Golden Era of the past. In all likelihood, the past never was what we think it used to be. And even if it was, the water that flowed in that stream is no longer there.

All parties to this discussion will immediately see the problem that hamstrings the Christian churches from the getgo: there is no broadly accepted contemporary orthodox Christian standard of unity to which to appeal in our day. Christians have been too busy over the past 200 years fighting among themselves to field any serious candidates for a suitable standard of American Christianity. And that fight is not likely to abate any time soon.

Therefore, it is incumbent upon individual American Christians of every stripe to acknowledge that the struggles that have been occurring in their churches are not struggles between fellow Christians who disagree, but are struggles akin those that Jude experienced. Ungodly people have become leaders in the churches and are not faithful to Christ or Scripture. Oh, they may think themselves to be Christian, but are not (Matthew 7:17-27). Consequently, in far too many cases unfaithful leaders have been corrupting the churches from the inside for a long, long time and for a variety of reasons and in a lot of different ways to the point that today most American Christians themselves can't distinguish between the baby and the bath water. So, focusing on the corruption and the problems it creates will likely be of little help.

In light of this, Beck's call for a return to Christian morality in American society is at best premature because Christian morality cannot return to American society until it returns to American Christianity. Beck's call for renewal should not be aimed at the political process, at least not yet. Rather, for now it must be aimed at the churches. "For it is time for judgment to begin at the household of God" (1 Peter 4:17). It is time to apply the Gideon principle to the churches. The churches will be stronger if they stop colluding with God's enemies. Yes, God has real enemies! Read your Bible.

The church has always been the rudder of American culture, and it still is. The culture has been following the morality of church for at least 200 years. And it still is – and that's the problem! So, to turn the ship of American culture, pressure must be applied to the church, to the rudder. To turn a ship, the rudder must first be in functional order and then be pressed hard and fast against the momentum of the ship. The rudder, the local church(es) must first be turned in another direction in order to turn the ship.

Christians must reassess their understanding of the Bible, confess their errors and the errors of past saints in order to reground their churches on the Rock of Jesus Christ according to an honest and intelligent reading of the Bible. Pray for God to direct the Captain of the ship to set the best course and give the order. But do not neglect to pray for its accomplishment—and soon. Lord, have mercy.

Wait A Minute!

According to Martiga Lohn in the recent Marietta Times article, "Some liberal groups push to exploit Target backlash" (8/14-15/2010), "A national gay rights group is negotiating with Target officials, demanding that the firm balance the scale by making comparable donations to benefit candidates it favors." Two things slap me in the face about this sentence.

First, homosexual groups actively lobby for particular candidates while Christian churches are forbidden by tax law to do so?! Isn't all sexual behavior really just a personal religious preference? One God says this way only, and other gods say no one cares.

Second, exactly how is "negotiating" with business owners "demanding" donations to particular political candidates different from extortion? Isn't this reminiscent of Al Capone, minus the guns of course? Then again, how is any political persuasion different than bribery and extortion?

What exactly does it mean when we say that "politics" is involved? The dictionary says that politics involves intrigue to gain power, where intrigue is a crafty and involved plot to achieve one's own (usually sinister) ends.

The only option to political discussion and persuasion that doesn't engage bribery and extortion is religious and moral persuasion. Who is it, again, that wants to separate religion and politics?

Did you know that the Greek word that is translated as "church" (ekklesia) in the New Testament referred to the principal assembly of the democracy of ancient Athens during its Golden Age (480–404 BCE)? It's enough to make you wonder what's really going on in America.

GULF CRISIS

Perhaps the Lord has decided to treat us according to Romans 1, as if He is saying, Okay. You want oil and money? I will give you up "in the lusts of (your) hearts to impurity" (Romans 1:24). In our lust for oil and money, we are now drowning in oil and money. God gives people what they want, and when people want what God does not recommend, the consequences of disobedience follow.

But those consequences do not usually follow directly or immediately. And this is a function of God's grace. God continues to provide grace to allow His people time to repent and grow in His grace (2 Peter 3:9). There is a sense in which the causality of God operates at a kind of quantum level. Clearly, the world is much more complex that any of our ancestors could ever believe. Spiritual cause and effect relations are not like pool balls on a billiard table, but their complexity causes us to analyze them more like statistical quantum trends.

God tends to be socially gracious until faithfulness is statistically overwhelmed by unfaithfulness. And as God's grace is increasingly ignored in a society it is replaced by His judgment. God not only treats people as individuals, He also treats people corporately. Why? Because our identity as human beings is both individual and corporate. We are individuals, but as individuals we live in societies and our societies provide the context for our individuality.

Do not doubt that God's judgment is absolutely just and specific, it is! However, our comprehension of that justice and its specificity falls far short of God's, and the result is that it appears to us that God's judgment shares some characteristics with what we call quantum theory. So, we don't perceive, for instance, that God punishes this particular sinner for that particular sin, at least not usually. Rather, it appears to us that God indulges sinners more than what seems fair or just, and that like Job we find it difficult to account for how God treats people individually.

However, we can observe that as nations become increasingly engulfed in sin, increasingly horrible things begin to happen—tornadoes, forest fires, earthquakes, financial collapse, disease, crime, etc. It is beyond our analytical abilities to discover a one-to-one correspondence between particular sins and particular judgments, but it is not so difficult to see the larger trend. This, I believe, is our current situation, which conforms to the expectations of Deuteronomy 28, and Luke 2:34-35.

The fact that God has given grace through Christ apart from the law does not mean that God's law has been nullified. As Revelation testifies, the potential for God's judgment is an undeniable reality. Indeed, it is the context against which the gospel of Jesus Christ stands as good news. The good news is real, and when it is ignored and/or denied, it fades into the background and leaves the context, which is God's judgment against sin.

Too Large To Succeed

In college I learned about "economies of scale." The bottom line is that the larger the run of units produced by a company, the smaller the cost per unit. One practical result is that those who can afford to place larger orders get them at increasingly less cost per unit. So, Walmart can always have lower prices because it buys in larger quantities than anyone else. And those lower prices tend to put the smaller companies that sell the same thing out of business.

Another result of economies of scale is that, while the profit per unit shrinks, the profit per company increases. The larger companies make less per unit but sell more units. The cost efficiencies allow the larger companies to make more profit. However, the total profit aggregate in the society is divided between fewer people. The higher prices of the smaller companies produce profits for those companies. So the price savings for the end consumer also produce larger profits for fewer companies. So, the market efficiencies tend to accumulate wealth in fewer hands.

Economies of scale provide a monetary incentive for companies to grow and merge, and if unchecked, to ultimately to dominate the market. Monopolies develop when no one can compete with the efficiencies of a giant corporation in a particular market segment. Monopolies tend to quench competition, which is an engine of capitalism.

Another problem that occurs with economies of scale is that the end result of global corporations is that the ecological footprint of such corporations can become too large for the environment in which it exists. If money is power, and it is, then the aggregation of power creates an ecological danger to the environment. The recent BP oil spill in the Gulf is an example (2010). Such drilling is only possible because of giant corporations. Big projects mean big risks and anything that goes wrong can have big consequences.

Think of a grape vine. Would it be better for a grape farmer to grow a field of regular grapes or one super large grape that could produce ten times as much grape juice as the existing field? Human greed suggests that the greater yield is better. But that is not the way that nature works. If the farmer had only one super huge grape, that grape could be more at risk because anything that threatened the quality of the grape would effect the entire yield. The super grape would have a grape footprint too large for the natural environment to sustain. And if something happened and the grape went rotten, the rot could swamp the environment.

God's nature does not use the same principles of growth that our modern, global, computer based economy uses. Where the global economy requires the efficiencies and precisions of economies of scale, God's nature uses abundance and redundancy. Though nature has her efficiencies, her focus on abundance and redundancy seems a bit excessive.

TAKE IT BACK

When people get serious about taking America back from the Liberals, they will need to go back in history to see when and how our constitutional republic was lost. It will be discovered that Barack Obama is not responsible for turning America in to a socialist nation. That project began centuries earlier with a vision of what America was created to be that has a long established historical lineage. Obama just moved that agenda forward a giant step.

That vision has always been disputed. The division has always been between those who understand that the argument that civil government is "of the people, by the people and for the people" is a biblical position,[10] and those who reject it substitute a socialist (godless) definition, not far different from the Marxist vision of a classless society or democracy of the people.

The political methodology that passed the recent Healthcare Reform bill was worked out 30-50 years earlier in America's Mainline churches. If you are not familiar with it, you might read Gary North's, *Crossed Fingers: How the Liberals Captured the Presbyterian Church*, Institute for Christian Economics, 1996. The process that was perfected in the American Churches is now being applied to the American government.

Reversing the process will be difficult because Liberals have been in charge of public education curriculum for at least a hundred years. Most Americans have already been indoctrinated into believing that the values of Liberalism are America's values. Today, most Americans simply accept those values to be "normal." People don't know any better anymore. Ordinary people do not have access to curriculum selection in the public schools, so whatever paltry influence conservative reformers may garner there will simply be too little and too late.

The most accessible and effective area for conservative reform is exactly the same area that the Liberals used—the Christian churches. But, where the Liberals used duplicity and deceit to weasel their way into positions of church authority, conservatives must use honesty and integrity to recapture the churches. For the most part America's Mainline churches have been abandoned by conservatives, or perhaps I should say that the churches have been purged of conservative Christians.

---

10 This phrase was first used by John Wyclif regarding his translation of the Bible in the mid-1300s, long before Lincoln borrowed it.

The effort to reclaim American Christianity must be done in the Spirit of Jesus Christ. That means that conservatives must themselves first be captured by Jesus Christ. Conservatives must first be mastered by Christ in order to master God's Word, and as they do that the very power of God Himself will be unleashed as the true light of the world. Jesus Christ will train His people to be who He has called them to be, and to reengage the mission He has given His church. This is the revival Christians seek!

Revival begins by reclaiming Christianity, and Christianity is conservative, not libertarian. The fact that the conservative movement has been captured by secular libertarian ideology is part of the problem. Interestingly, the real source for "classical liberalism" is biblical Christianity. We must come to better understand Scripture so that we can see that in some areas Christ is conservative and in others He is liberal. But in every area He is faithful, and we must liberally conserve the faith once delivered (Jude 3).

There is no better training ground for Washington reform than the effort to put local churches back on track. Most of the problems that plague our government today stem from the civil takeover of various church and family responsibilities. The churches abdicated power and authority to the civil government in disobedience to Scripture and in spite of the biblical mandate for the separation of church and state jurisdictions. So, the most natural way to get things back on keel is to return those responsibilities to churches and families.

The civil government has no business in health care or retirement, period. Care and healing have always been responsibilities of church and family. Civil government gladly took them on because 1) churches and families abandoned them, and 2) a lot of money can be made in these areas. Churches and families can be funded for these purposes with the same money that the government intends to use, with uncollected taxes. Churches call it tithing. Families call it saving.

Actually, churches and families will have to take back these responsibilities for at least two reasons. First, because government has spent the money collected for retirement. Social Security is not a savings account. And second, because the 50 million[11] abortions since Roe v. Wade in 1973 have reduced the number of workers contributing to the Social Security system. There's not enough money in Social Security, nor

---

11 Right To Life estimate, http://www.nrlc.org/abortion/facts/abortionstat-s.html

enough workers to sustain it. By mandating it, Washington hoped that new inductees would keep the Ponzi scheme afloat. So far, not bad.

But one day it will crash because the recently passed healthcare bill has no serious provisions for reducing the runaway costs of healthcare. The new money will mostly pay for the new inductees. Waste may be reduced, but not the spiraling costs. The problem never was the lack of healthcare, it has always been the cost of healthcare. And the government's solution leaves the central problem unsolved. The letter (government regulation) kills, but the Spirit (Christ's churches) give life (2 Corinthians 3:6).

REVALUATION OF DEBT

I could title this post "The Jubilee Factor" because it is a simple observation about the teaching of the biblical Jubilee and how it speaks to the current world financial crisis. So, what is the Jubilee?

The Jubilee year (Leviticus 25:11-13) is the year at the end of seven cycles of Sabbatical years, and had a special impact on the ownership and management of land in the territory of the kingdoms of Israel and of Judah. My purpose is not to get into a detailed analysis of the biblical data, but to simply note that the fundamental idea of the Jubilee was the revaluation of debt (property) every so often.

The biblical authors seem to have been aware of the tendency for property and money to end up in the hands of a few people who are particularly blessed with financial skills. And unless this tendency was ameliorated it would cause social problems like tyranny and abuse. The Bible is careful to balance the various social concerns, and money provides a concern that can easily dominate everything else. And when it does, the Bible calls such an unbalance: greed. So, the Bible recommends resetting the economy every fifty years as a way of avoiding various kinds of problems, undoubtedly much like the financial problems our world is currently facing.

That's my brief take on the idea of biblical Jubilee. Rather than getting caught up in the details, I'm looking at it as a general principle of economic balance.

Our current financial crisis reflects world economies that are out of balance. What do I mean? I mean that income and outgo must remain in balance. I'm not arguing for a closed economic system because economies can grow and shrink. While balance does involve rightly dividing the economic pie, the pie itself is not a fixed element. It is a dynamic element.

Nonetheless, as the old adage goes: when your outgo exceeds your intake, then your upkeep will be your downfall. There are many root causes related to the recent financial crisis, but here I want to highlight the primary personal or individual economic perspective. We will set aside the systemic causes and concentrate on the end user.

As the crisis hit, the resources of the end user were diminished, whether by the crash of the Stock Market, the failure of a corporation, the loss of a job, etc. At any given time Joe Citizen has a certain amount of income and a certain amount of outgo, the largest share of which in our current situation is debt related. The average citizen spends about half of their income on home and automobile payments. The specific amounts of those payments is fixed for the life of the loan.

When financial crisis hits, income is reduced but outgo is not. Thus, upkeep becomes downfall. When the problem is a systemic market crash like we current have, it is the value of one's assets that is reduced by the crisis. And since ours is a debt economy where market valuation is a function of debt, the actual value of the dollar varies with the market. For the most part, changes in market value (the Dow Jones Average, etc.) translate into changes in the valuation of the dollar. For instance, one day I have x amount of stocks, and the next day I have x+y amount of stocks. The only thing that actually changed was the valuation of the dollar. Though I have more dollar value, that dollar value is a measure of the same company. Stock is only worth more because someone is willing to pay more for it. And while that does increase the dollars involved, those dollars are inflated. Making money on the Stock Market is a matter of cashing in inflated dollars before they lose their perceived value.

So, when financial crisis hits, income is reduced because the inflated value of the stock is widely discovered and no one is willing to buy the stock at the inflated value. Thus, the value of the shares deflates. The result is that the investor has less dollars.

However, the debt side of the economic balance does not change. Income is reduced by forces outside of personal control, but debt remains the same for the life of the note. This means that debt as a measure of outflow increases relative to income. The dollar value of the market is deflated, but the debt value of the market remains stable. The ratio of debt to income increases and unless something re-balances the end user's balance sheet, debt will overcome income and result in bankruptcy or foreclosure.

There are two classic solutions to the problem: increase income and/or decrease outgo. But however the problem is solved, balance must be restored. Granted that poor management is often the problem in that a faulty debt to income ratio is established—and much of our current situation can be faulted at the personal financial management level. Nonetheless, if a systemic solution like a "stimulus package" is engaged, adjustments to both sides of the equation must be made if balance is to be restored.

The "stimulus package" solutions so far used (Quantitave Easing) do not restore balance for two reasons: 1) all stimulus money has gone to corporations not to people in an effort to maintain the existing economic unbalances in the markets, and 2) all stimulus payments have gone to the income side of the ledger of corporations.

The problem that crashed the markets was bad dept packaged and distributed into complex investment portfolios in ways that hid the bad debt. It is like diluting gold with lead, but selling it as gold. As long as people don't know about the dilution, they can be tricked into paying full gold prices for lead-laced gold. And the crooks who perpetrated the dilution "make" money. But actually they don't "make" money they deflate the value of the dollar but cash in on it before other people know about the devaluation. It is crooked and cheating and should be against the law because it ultimately harms society.

The problem is that too much of the rising market value of the past forty years has been a function of this kind of market inflation (or dollar devaluation). The value of the market rises at the same time that the value of the dollar falls. Of course, some of the market growth has resulted from market expansions worldwide and does represent wealth increase. This kind of growth has real substance behind it, unlike the inflated growth of dollar dilution that does not.

If the value of debt floated with the value of the dollar like the value of the market floats with the value of the dollar, economies would remain in balance. In other words, if debt payments decreased as income decreased, there would be much less bankruptcy and foreclosure. But when the value of assets decreases while the value of indebtedness remains constant, the balance that is required for market stability is lost.

Consequently, a market Jubilee revaluation of indebtedness may be in order. How could it work? On the principle of Matthew 6:12: "forgive us our debts, as we also have forgiven our debtors." In our world every debt is a source of income for someone else. So, when we forgive our debtors, we accrue a personal financial loss or at the least we write off potential income, depending where the debt is in the payment schedule. The point is that forgiveness of our debtors translates into a decrease in the value of our personal portfolio. Forgiveness is costly, but it is surely better than bankruptcy.

Eighth Day

Can God count?

Sunday-1, Monday-2, Tuesday-3, Wednesday-4, Thursday-5, Friday-6, Saturday-7, Whatday?-8

> Leviticus 23:39: On the fifteenth day of the seventh month, when you have gathered in the produce of the land, you shall celebrate the feast of the LORD seven days. On the first day shall be a solemn rest, and on the eighth day shall be a solemn rest.

> Numbers 29:35: On the eighth day you shall have a solemn assembly. You shall not do any ordinary work...

The Hebrews celebrated a Feast called the Feast of Tabernacles, or Feast of the Ingathering, which lasted seven days. This is a thanksgiving feast in which Israel acknowledged the Fall harvest and God's provision for them. It is a happy celebration and a time of joy and rejoicing. Another feature of the feast was the illumination of the Temple.

The pilgrims who came to the Temple would bring lights and torches. In addition, the golden lamps stands would be lit. This prophetically looked forward to the coming of the Messiah. Jesus the Messiah identified Himself as that saving light in John 8:12:

> "Then Jesus spoke again to them, saying, I am the Light of the world. He who follows Me shall not walk in darkness, but shall have the light of life."

Two things characterized the Feast of Tabernacle from the other feasts. One was the illumination of the Temple and the other the pouring of a vessel of water into a basin that was located at the base of the altar. First the golden vessel of water was filled at the pool of Siloam and taken to the altar. Then another golden vessel would be filled with wine and they both would be poured together into the basin. The mixed water and wine would flow down a conduit which carried the water to the Brook of Kidron located across from the eastern wall.

This was ritual prayer for the Fall rains upon which Israel depended. Second it pictured the coming of the Messiah and His kingdom in which the Holy Spirit would be poured on Israel and on believers of all nations. This ritual of water pouring continued for six days and concluded the Feast of Tabernacles. This last day was called the "Day of the Great Hosanan" (Hoshannah Rabbah). The word "Hoshannah" means "save now," and when applied to the feast became "Hosanna" which looked forward to the coming of the Messiah.

The root word of solemn assembly in Hebrew means to shut up or enclose (עצר). Hence the Hebrew name Shemini Atzeret. Because Shemini Atzeret is the last of the year's holidays, it is also referred to as the final revelation. The number 8 is the only positive Fibonacci number, aside from 1, that is a perfect cube.

In the New Testament, Jesus Christ was resurrected from the dead on the eighth day (Matthew 28:1). He came "when the fullness of time was come...made under the law" (Galatians 4:4). The fullness of time under the law according to God's time clock is seven days (days 1-7), the number seven meaning completion. The series is complete in seven. In Biblical gematria (numerology), the numerical value of the name Jesus in Greek is 888. The numerical value of the name Yahweh in Hebrew is 26 or 2 + 6 = 8. A Jewish baby is circumcised unto the Lord 8 days after his birth. David was the eighth son of Jesse.

The eighth day is hidden, not having place within the boundaries of the seven day week. It is not something that can be quantified or marked on a calendar, but stands outside of ordinary time. It is the day of God's fulfilled Sabbath rest in Christ, the day of Christ's resurrection.

Leviticus 23:39 speaks of two Sabbaths. The Sabbath of the first day and the Sabbath of the eighth day. God has ordained not one Sabbath of rest, but two. It is not a rest that is entered into once a week, but is the eternal rest of God in Christ that is outside of time but permeates every day. It is celebrated and remembered on the eighth day, Sunday.

Jesus said: "The sabbath was made for man, and not man for the sabbath: Therefore the son of man is Lord also of the sabbath" (Mark 2:27, 28).

True rest with God, true spiritual peace, is found only in Jesus Christ. Because sin separates us from God. Only through the death of Christ and reconciliation through His blood can peace with God be found. Jesus is Lord of the sabbath because He came to establish that rest and impart it unto His people by faith. Therefore it is written, "For we who have believed do enter into rest" (Hebrews 4:3). The fact that work is not done on the Sabbath teaches that our own works can never bring us into God's rest because ours are always works of sin. The law then drives people to Christ, who is the Lord of the Sabbath, to find righteousness and salvation in Him by faith.

For he has somewhere spoken of the seventh day in this way: "And God rested on the seventh day from all his works." And again in this passage he said, "They shall not enter my rest." Since therefore it remains for some to enter it, and those who formerly received the good news failed to enter because of disobedience, again he appoints a certain day, "Today," saying through David so long afterward, in the words already quoted, "Today, if you hear his voice, do not harden your hearts." For if Joshua had given them rest, God would not have spoken of another day later on. So then, there remains a Sabbath rest for the people of God, for whoever has entered God's rest has also rested from his works as God did from his. Let us therefore strive to enter that rest, so that no one may fall by the same sort of disobedience. (Hebrews 4:4–11)

The rest spoken of does not refer to the seventh day sabbath, it refers to the Eighth Day Sabbath of Christ. It is His Day, His peace, His rest, His unity. And the way you enter in is by faith. Faith in the grace, reconciliation, and love of Christ. It is the Day of the light of the Son.

THE NECESSITY OF EISEGESIS

The first difficulty regarding the proper explanation and use of eisegesis pertains to overcoming the improper use of it. The word is usually contrasted with exegesis, which means reading meaning out of a text. So, eisegesis is then said to mean reading one's own interpretation or meaning into a text. Indeed, both are possible, and in fact both are unavoidable. The inevitability of eisegesis is the central tenet of Postmodernism, which actually denies the possibility of pure exegesis and opts for pure eisegesis or the necessity of subjective reading and the impossibility of objective reading.

The reality of human understanding is much less pure than either the Modernists or Postmodernists have believed because it acknowledges that human beings exist in a subjective/objective continuum. People are necessarily both individual and social beings at the same time. People are both subjective and objective, and neither are completely one or the other. Our subjectivity bleeds into our objectivity and visa versa. It cannot be avoided.

People always and necessarily bring themselves, their thoughts and ideas, to whatever they read. All reading happens from a particular perspective. Reading is the process of taking information into ourselves. Understanding a thing means finding an appropriate place for it in our own personal mental taxonomy. To understand a thing means to make it our own. Thus, we take what is objective to us and bring it into our subjectivity, and when the thing is still recognizable to others after it has passed through our subjectivity, we are said to know it.

This is an important insight because it means that knowledge is always and necessarily social. Human knowledge is always a social construct. So, if we know a thing in a purely private way or in a way that no one else knows the same thing, then while we may think that we know the thing, others will not think we do. Knowledge, meaning and definitions are always and necessarily social. So, when an individual knows a thing, his knowledge must resemble the accumulated subjective knowledge of others in the aggregate. And the acme of that accumulated subjective knowledge is called objective knowledge. Thus the path to objective knowledge leads through the subjectivity of others. The two things, subjectivity and objectivity, are related in such a way that you can't have one without the other.

WHO IS RESPONSIBLE

The responsibility for the deplorable condition of the churches and our families in our day must rest squarely upon us and our churches. Too many churches themselves are guilty of pandering to the world, to the values and activities that draw people away from Christ—and doing so in the churches! Too many Christians are guilty of neglecting their own personal discipleship. Too many adult Christians are not actively involved as a student under a teacher, nor are they teaching Christianity to anyone else, not even their own children.

This gaping hole in the fabric of Christianity provides the greatest opportunity for Christian renewal, revival, and reformation of our time. We must abandon the desperation that seeks the return of some imagined Great Awakening of the past or some other grand spiritual drama that fans the flames of passion and excess. Rather, we must stake our claim to the slow, deliberate, consistent, and comprehensive commitment to the ordinary study of God's Word. We must learn it right and teach it right to our own children, regardless of their age (or ours). The burden is upon parents and grandparents because people learn by teaching. The burden of leadership was given to elders, not simply those who hold a particular church office, but to those who have been wizened by time in Christ. And conversely, we haven't learned a thing until we can teach it. Christians are to practice this teaching on their own children (1 Timothy 3:4-5).

So, when does the responsibility of parenting begin? It begins long before the birth of a child. And when does the responsibility of parenting end? It does not end because your children are always your children. Sure, as adults our own children often don't like or appreciate our advice about their beliefs and behavior in the light of Scripture. They didn't like it any better when they were young! Age is not a factor because people are never too old to learn. They may be too stubborn, but never too old.

No one ever outgrows their need for parental love, nor do parents ever escape the responsibilities of parenthood. The parent/child relationship is eternal. Parents remain parents and children remain children regardless of age or time. Of course people grow and mature, and growth changes the relationship—but it does not end it. Parents have the responsibility to teach and disciple their children. Yes, it gets harder as they get older. That's why the Bible recommends that discipline be firmly established when children are young. But whether or not that happens, parents are not relieved of their spiritual responsibility for their children—young or old.

The Fourth Commandment is valid all our lives, "Honor your mother and your father" (Exodus 10:12, Matthew 19:19). The relationship between parents and children is an eternal relationship. It has eternal joys, eternal consequences, and eternal responsibilities. Both parents and children are involved in the relationship, and both have duties and responsibilities. When should we stop teaching our children or honoring our parents? Never. When should our responsibilities as parents or children end? Never. The relationship changes over time, of course. It is different when our children are small than when they are tall, different again when they are adults with families of their own. But it always exists, even in death. A dead father is still a father.

I know that nobody wants to be a meddling mother-in-law or an interfering grandfather. But where in the Bible does God relieve parents of their responsibility to teach their children? Nowhere. Sure, it's difficult, it's awkward, it's usually uncomfortable. It is no easier or less awkward when the children are young. If you avoided it while they were young, that is exactly why you avoided it—because it's hard. The point is that Christian relationships and responsibilities do not end at 18, or 21, or 35, or any age. We are in it forever because God is in it forever.

This is not an invitation for grandparents to teach their grandchildren things that contradict the children's own parents. Christ is aiming at a united front between grandparents and parents in order to sustain the idea of parental authority. Rather, this is an invitation to for grandparents to teach their own children, even when those children are adults. If not us, who? If not now, when?

GRATITUDE

> "Therefore, as you received Christ Jesus the Lord, so walk in him,
> rooted and built up in him and established in the faith, just as you
> were taught, abounding in thanksgiving" (Colossians 2: 6-7).

If you are rooted in Christ, then the nourishment that you draw from Him will show up in your fruits, in your actions and behaviors. If your actions and behaviors do not reflect the love and discipline of Christ, you need to check your roots, check your fundamental beliefs and values, check your relationship with Jesus Christ. When people are not rooted in faithfulness, when they have not been built up in Christ or established in the faith, when people have not been taught the Bible, they cannot abound in thanksgiving. You can't get blood from a turnip! Nor can people abound in thanksgiving apart from being rooted, built up (*epoikodomeō*—reared or taught) and established (stabilized) in Christ.

This is the long-neglected job of Christians. This is where the church has failed and where it must pick up the proverbial ball and begin again. We have failed to root, to build up, to establish and teach our own children. The churches have dropped the ball, as have Christian families. That ball needs to be picked up.

Of this verse Calvin said that "ingratitude is very frequently the reason why we are deprived of the light of the gospel, as well as of other divine favors." To be ungrateful is to be unsatisfied with what God has given. It is the refusal to be thankful to God, the refusal to live with a sense of gratitude or to be appreciative.

Appreciation requires discrimination. It requires the ability to discriminate, to recognize and draw careful distinctions. The differences between a thing of high quality and a thing of low quality are often small matters of detail that reflect large differences of substance.

The difference between living faithfully and not living faithfully is a matter of quality, of character, of caliber, and timbre. A high quality life, or excellence of character, is characterized by elegance, refinement, and accomplishment. While these things are often thought to come from wealth, they don't. Not really. They are learned skills, but not everyone who studies them learns them. Why not? Because their mastery involves more grace than effort, more gift than purchase. They are character qualities, not things that can be bought and sold.

Discrimination

Elegance reveals a sense of beauty that is ingeniously simple, both efficient and direct. Elegance is not derivative. Elegance must always be authentic or it is not elegant. Whatever it is, it cannot be bought. It's a grace, a gift. And yet, to a degree, it can be taught—learned and improved. It can be rooted, built up, and established.

Refinement involves a process of removing impurities in order to make a thing pure. Think of gold. In terms of Christian character, we are talking about the abandonment of impure thoughts and habits. Christians are called to personal refinement—not snootiness or uppity presumption, nor pomposity, but the real thing, the authentic thing. Refinement is an art, and art can be learned and improved. It's a matter of practice. It can be rooted, built up, and established.

Accomplishment, applied to character, reveals a commitment to discipline. For instance, an accomplished musician has mastered his instrument by way of personal commitment and discipline—practice. The accomplished person has gained skills and abilities through hard work and training.

And yet, the truly accomplished have exceeded their training by discovering their gift. The truly accomplished are often described as being gifted. All Christians are gifted by God with various graces for the world, for use in the world. And yet discovering our gifts of grace always involves the hard work of discipline, training, and commitment. The gift is given, but making something of it is hard work. It too can be rooted, built up and established.

Interestingly, those who are genuinely elegant, refined, and accomplished are thankful and grace-full. Over the centuries people have turned these things into the crass privileges of the rich, as if they can be bought and sold. People have made them more a function of vanity than humility. And so we tend to associate them with wealth and privilege.

But this is backwards. It is not the way it actually works—arsy varsy. It is not that the wealthy have access to elegance, refinement, and accomplishment, but that elegance, refinement, and accomplishment usually produce wealth. While wealth cannot buy superior character qualities, superior character qualities usually produce wealth. These qualities are the same qualities that make for a good worker—honesty, integrity, industry, consistency, etc. And good work habits increase income. People may not get rich personally, but as a general rule, people with good work habits do better than people without good work habits.

There are two primary reasons for ingratitude. Some people are ungrateful to God because they think they deserve more than what they have been given. They feel cheated because they covet what others have, and justify their coveting by insisting that justice means equal results rather than equal opportunity. Others are ungrateful because they deny God and refuse His grace. The ungrateful are unaware of the fruits of God's grace. In either case ungratefulness is an expression of disregard and disobedience to God.

In contrast, obedience to God—faithfulness to Jesus Christ—is both fulfilling and joyful. To trust the Lord for salvation is satisfying beyond description. Jesus Christ died on the cross in order that we can live our lives in Him. His death paid the price for our redemption. In Christ we are free of the burden of the law—not free from the law itself, but from its burden and punishment.

In Christ we enjoy the gift of grace, the satisfaction of obedience and the assurance of salvation. This joy is not an empty promise nor a thoughtless, emotional effervescence, but is a Rock-solid commitment to God's truth that is nothing more than the assumption that God's Word is true—because it is!

Tribe Mentality

In a recent article, it was suggested that a loyal network of friends and family can be the most powerful tool available for overcoming depression. According to the book, *Creating Optimism* (Bob Murray, Mc-Graw-Hill, 2005), "Depression is about a disconnect in relationships somewhere along the line." Depression and anxiety problems are associated with childhood experiences and environment—parental failures.

The authors advise reconnecting with our "hunter-gatherer" sense of morality and social practices. But how can enlightened people think that going back to a caveman mindset can help alleviate one of the most tenacious problems of contemporary society—depression? Isn't the suggestion to return to pre-Modern social structures a lot like the fundamentalist desire to return to the 16th Century or the Islamic desire to return to the 7th? History does not and cannot run backwards.

Nonetheless, *Creating Optimism* provides the three Rs of tribal bonding: Rules, Roles, and Rituals. The article then offered this idea:

> "While many of our social and cultural taboos have been erased
> because they are not feasible in a multicultural society, we still
> need boundaries in relationships to maintain safety and emotional
> security."

Dismissed without consideration is the fact that in large measure those "erased" taboos are part of the foundational morality of Christianity. Does this mean that Christian morality is not feasible in a multicultural society? If so, why not? Is every understanding of morality in a multicultural society feasible except that of Christianity?

It was suggested that those old taboos—Christian rules, roles, and rituals—have been erased from the minds of contemporary people—*erased*, not forgotten. Forgetting happens accidentally, but erasing is intentional. Words have meaning and ideas have consequences.

Apparently, people need to set the ground rules, not only for various categories of relationships, but for each relationship. The kinds of relationships cited were partners (not marriage), friends, colleagues, and family. And on what basis can individuals establish or define these ground rules? We are told to tell others what we need or want from them to make us happy. The satisfaction of our own desires are to be the criteria for our new relationship rules.

So, I tell other people what I need from them to make me happy, and, they tell me what they need to make them happy. The stated goal of these new relationship rules is self-satisfaction and self-esteem. Everyone is to demand from others what they want or need. Rules are not optional, but mandatory.

This idea couldn't be more opposed to biblical Christianity. Christians are not to demand from others what they want for themselves, but are to live according to God's rules and in self-sacrificial service to Jesus Christ and the needs of others. In Christianity, living by our own rules is called sin. Christianity teaches that people are selfish and self-centered because they have a fallen nature. So, Christians live by Christ's rules, and His rules are aimed at the glory of God and the establishment of human justice. Justice is required because human desires overlap and conflict. And Christ's rules minimize that conflict by focusing people on service to others rather than demanding self-centered satisfaction.

Apparently, new social roles are also needed. And these new roles are not to be determined by age and gender. Traditional roles such as mother, father, son, daughter, husband, and wife are identified as sources of depression. These are all gender and age based roles.

The new roles are to be determined by "ability and inclination," both of which are actually functions of desire. How so? Desire leads to practice and practice leads to ability. People are to define and establish their own social roles. Doesn't this make life self-centered? In contrast, Christian roles are determined by one's calling and God-given gifts in the service of God and the greater good of society.

Do breadwinners or employees fit into this new role scenario? A lot of people don't seem to have an inclination to work, nor to be responsible members of society. This allows for people who want to be criminals and bullies, if they have the ability and need it for their self-esteem. Again, this is the complete opposite of the Christian perspective.

Rituals also play a key role in overcoming depression. But it's odd that Christian rituals are not even mentioned. After all, Christianity is one of the most potent forces of ritual establishment on the planet.

The authors recommend returning to a tribal society because tribes, carefully defined and maintained, provide many benefits. However, each person needs to define his or her own tribe, and mandate to them how they want to be treated. This is supposed to maximize each person's ultimate satisfaction. I'm supposed to sit my friends and family down and demand (rules are mandatory!) that they make me happy.

Go back to the supposed hunter-gatherer tribal social structures? I don't think so. Though Christianity has had limited success in America to date, it would be utter foolishness to abandon the world's greatest and most effective social system because it hasn't yet been perfected. Rather than abandon it, we need to engage it more seriously. Did I mention that the authors suggest that spirituality is central to the treatment of depression? Well, they did. So, did they mention Christianity, the most common "spirituality" in America? No.

The failure of this article and book to recommend Christianity as being the most effective and readily available cure for depression, can only be a symptom of ideological blindness. The idea that people create their own tribes, whose purpose is to serve their own needs, implies that each person would be the chief of his or her own tribe, and that the highest goal of each individual would be the satisfaction of their own self-centered desires. I can't imagine anything that would result in more conflict. Such an idea depresses me.

OBSESSION

In response to an Internet post by me about my reaction to the movie, Obsession—Radical Islam's War Against the West, I wrote a letter, which follows.

> Obsession is a Clarion Project film about the threat of radical Islam to Western civilization. Using unique footage from Arab television and expert interviews, it reveals an "insider view" of the hatred the Islamists are teaching, their incitement of global jihad, and their goal of world domination. The film also traces the parallels between the Nazi movement of World War II and the Islamic radicals of today and the Western world's response to both threats.

December 9, 2008

Bruce R. Barbour
Nashville, TN 37204

Dear Bruce,

I wasn't suggesting that I had a book length response proposal to Obsession (the movie). But when I told my son of your interest he got interested in the idea—he is an aspiring novelist and theologian. I was hoping to involve him but his college schedule precludes his involvement at this time.

I said that Obsession required a Christian response because I did not see a Christian response in the movie presentation. And you asked what such a response would look like. Let me poke at it.

First, I'm no expert on Islam, and some expertise would be required to make the case that the Koran does in fact teach and promote terrorism as Obsession suggests. And if it does—and it does, then how can we explain Muslims who are not extremists? Such an explanation is key to a Christian response.

Simple. Moderate Muslims are similar to moderate Christians or moderate Jews because the forces of Postmodernism (Moderatism, if I may coin a word) tend to rip the heart out of religion by its emphasis on relativity. Postmodernism does not believe in absolutes or objectivity. So, the absolutes and objectivity that are essential to religious revelation are discounted as merely myths and stories, and not God's actual, trustworthy Word. Postmodernism (Moderatism) is the fruit of liberalism, and liberalism is the dominant worldview of the West. Liberalism is the celebration of moderation and the repudiation of extremism. Our culture is saturated in Postmodernism.

This means that moderate Muslims don't really believe the Koran, just as moderate Christians and Jews don't really believe the Bible. Moderates just go to religious services out of habit or for the fellowship, networking, or whatever. Oh, they might talk the walk, but moderates don't walk it. That's why the liberals love moderate religionists. While all liberals are not moderate religious believers, all moderate religious believers are liberal.

And again, Postmodernism is an instance or fruit of liberalism. It is the success of Postmodern liberalism that is the source of the growth of sin in the West. Liberalism encourages people to not take their religious beliefs seriously, where serious belief is extreme belief. To love the Lord with all one's heart and with all one's soul and with all one's mind (Matthew 22:37) is defined by Postmodernists as extremism. Moderates define such extreme commitment to God as evil simply because it is extreme. The more extreme it is, the more evil they would dub it.

But human beings have been designed to love in an extreme way. Love itself is an extreme or ultimate commitment, and true love is even more extreme. From the perspective of the Bible, the correct object of our love should be God first. But because of sin we misapply our love to many other things and neglect God. We love too many other things more than we love God. And that misapplication of our love (which is sin) has made a wreck of our society. Add to this that our sin is also the source of the Islamic hatred of the West and the extent of the problem begins to take shape.

Muslim terrorists are hell-bent on destroying the Great Satan—America (and all of the Judeo-Christian liberal West)—because what the West calls freedom they call sin. From a biblical perspective America and the West are awash in sin—just follow the news! But, in fact, Christians and Jews—real Christians and Jews, not the liberal moderates who don't really believe—are actually in agreement with the Islamic extremists about the sin problem in the West. And that scares liberal moderates spitless because they mistakenly think that Christians promote the same cure for sin that Islam does (or that the God of Christianity is the same as the god of Islam). Not being believers, liberals mistakenly think that all conservative or fundamental religionists have the same treatment program for the problem—death and destruction.

The liberals, of course, want to paint all religious extremists (those who actually believe and love God extremely) with the same brush. And that is somewhat understandable because there is much agreement among Christians and Muslims about the sin problem. We do agree that the liberal abuse of freedom is the source of much of the West's sin. But painting Christians and Muslims with the same brush is, a serious error because Christians have a different understanding of God, and an extremely different treatment plan for sin—forgiveness vs. imposed submission.

An interesting aside is that the more the West sins (or tries to expand its freedom throughout the world), the harder Islam fights to destroy it. Less sin in the West would provide less of a foil against which militant Islamics could rail—and that would provide a serious benefit for the current War Against Terror because it would hamper their recruitment efforts. Thus, the promotion of serious Christianity, genuine revival and reformation, in the West may actually provide a real end to the Islamic conflict by eliminating that which they are fighting against. This assumes that revival and reformation would reduce sin in the West, and it is a reasonable assumption. By "serious Christianity" I mean mostly Reformed Christianity (or any other branch that can stand the heat of faithful scholarship and evangelical conflict. Most of the liberal world would describe such serious Christianity as extreme Christianity and mistakenly put it in the same camp as Islamic extremists.) Why would this kind of a focus help the War Against Terror? Because where Christianity is strong Islam is not—and Christianity is not hell-bent on destroying its enemies.

The problem is that to attack Islam directly will simply create more Islamic martyrs, and Islam loves martyrs. Islamic jihad feeds on martyrs. So, on the one hand the current strategy to not name Islam as the overt target of our war is a good idea. But to lionize religious moderation (Moderatism) as the solution to religious extremism is madness. Moderation cannot defeat extremism because extremism will always have the advantage of superior personal commitment. The only weapon against "true believers" is right belief. Moderation does not inspire committed disciples. An extreme commitment to moderation is self-defeating because the more extremely such a commitment is held, the less of a commitment it becomes.

We must acknowledge that the current War Against Terror is a spiritual war. It is a religious war, like it or not. Islam knows this because it is the aggressor and has defined it as a religious war. They know that they are fighting a jihad. They've been fighting the same war (to them) for 1400 years. To deny this fact will result in the loss of the war. To win a war you have to know who you are fighting. This war cannot be won militarily because it is not a military war (though military forces are involved). It cannot be won politically because it is not a political war (though politics play a part). It cannot be won financially because it is not a financial war (though both sides must be financed). We must know what it actually is in order to engage the appropriate assets to defeat it. And the only asset we have access to which can defeat it is Jesus Christ. As Luther said, "He (Christ) must win the battle." Liberals will hate this answer and fight against it from within America, thus aiding and abetting the enemy without realizing it.

Again, to fight or even to name Islam directly as the enemy will be counter productive. It will generate more martyrs. So, the best offense is to support the forces of serious Christianity in order to provide sufficient Christian cultural momentum to reduce sin in the West and eventually to convert Muslims to Christ. The Christian argument for God is much superior to the Islamic argument, as is Christian culture. Surely, liberals can agree with this.

This means engaging the Reformed doctrines of faith as the central engines of our own cultural development by the leaders of America, all of her leaders—political, cultural, social, religious, academic, artistic, etc. It doesn't mean jumping to a Right Wing position or imposing Christian views or beliefs on anyone. But it does mean the serious cultural discussion of the doctrines of grace. Ben Stein understands the need for open dialog of ideas and how the current cultural milieu tends to shut dialog down. That's all I'm lobbying for. It all begins with dialog or it doesn't begin at all. Of course, I believe that Christianity provides superior arguments and will ultimately win the whole world to Christ. Great advances in Christianity have been made in the last forty years, but they have yet to manifest in other than small communities.

The Muslims want to destroy the West, but the Christians want (or should want because the Bible teaches us) to offer Christ as the solution to the sin problem. Christ came to save the world, not to destroy it. Where Islam wants to destroy Christians, Christianity does not want to destroy Muslims. We want to convert them, but not against their own will. Because we believe that only Christ can change hearts, we believe that Christianity needs the freedom to publicly call upon Christ to do that. And because we understand that revival and renewal begin with the church, we need to pray publicly that Christ will change the people in our own pews first! Revival and reformation are for the church.

Obsession (the movie) has Jewish roots, which is only to say that it is more Jewish than Christian. And that was my initial problem. The Jews don't have a solution, other than treating Islam as Islam treats them. Both Jews and Arabs seem to be committed to the destruction of the other. It's been going on for a very long time. Just as Islam had demonized the West, the Jews are demonizing Islam. And round and round she goes! Thus, it is only Christianity—real Christianity—that has the solution.

Obsession offers other solutions to the problem that can only fail in one way or another. For instance, one person in the movie said that it is the duty of all moderate Muslims to stand up and speak against the hate of the extremists. But if the Koran actually teaches terrorism, and it does, moderates cannot do that with integrity. They might call for a reformation of Islam that would write out of the Koran the extremist elements. (Fat chance!) But when have moderates ever inspired anyone to do anything so radical?

The moderate Christian response is no better. Moderate Christians want to love bomb-toting terrorists into accepting a moderate view of God. It will never happen! Moderate Christians also want to engage in dialog. But dialog cannot solve the problem because the terrorists are interested in dialog only long enough to garner sufficient strength to move their jihad forward. Moderation is simply not able to the task. It's the wrong tool, the wrong asset, the wrong weapon.

Therefore, extremist (faithful) Islam must be met with extremist (faithful) Christianity, but not directly—at least not now. We must fight fire with fire—by that I do not mean fighting terror and violence with terror and violence, but religious commitment with religious commitment. Terror and violence are not the problem, they are symptoms of the problem. We need to reduce American sin and its export.

The problem we face with jihad is religious commitment, and the answer is not no religious commitment (secularism) or less religious commitment (moderation), but right religious commitment, commitment to Christ, the Prince of Peace. No other religious or cultural option can meet the challenge presented by extremist Islam. Extremist Islam cannot be defeated militarily. They love the fight! It gives meaning and purpose to their otherwise insignificant lives. The more we fight the more they fight. The more we sin the more they fight. The more we dialog, the more they prepare to fight another day.

Extremist religion must be met with extremist religion in order to capture and control the commitment. But before you jump to any conclusions about this radical statement, please realize that extreme Christianity will neither conquer nor kill Muslims. Bible believing Christianity is "extreme" where "extreme" means "extremely faithful." Even the Muslim extremists believe themselves to simply be faithful to their beliefs. Real Christianity will convert everyone to Christianity, to the superior wisdom and culture of Christ. This is what Christians believe. Islam's only defense against such an effort is to kill Christians and ban the practice of Christianity. It knows that anything less will lead to its own demise. That's why they have such a radical view of Christianity.

Part of the problem is that Muslims understand all of Christianity to be liberal Christianity, which is not much different than the sinful worldliness that Muslims hate. They hate Christianity because they don't really understand it. They don't see biblical Christianity practiced anywhere (neither do I). They hate liberal Christianity because it is only warmed over humanism. They don't understand or hear Christ's radical call to self-sacrificial love and service, nor His call to self-death through baptism and regeneration (a la Romans 6). They don't hear it because they don't see it.

The more liberal Christians and moderate Muslims call for religious tolerance and moderation, the more radical Islam will fight. But if sin can be reduced by revival and reformation of the church, Christians may be able to call more widely for radical commitment to Christ in our own society. And hearing such an extremely radical call to Christ, the passion of the extremist Muslims might be rechanneled into Christian extremism, understood as radical commitment to Christ (not in a pseudo-Christian, militant, Right wing, gun-toting, red-neck, narrow-minded way, but in a genuine Christian, worship-centered, peace-loving, self-sacrificial concern for the well-being of others, servant-minded way). Think of it as spiritual judo where the attacker's momentum is used against him.

Human beings have been created for extreme and radical commitment—to God through Christ. People everywhere are actually pining for deep-seated, radical religious commitment. Liberals often misunderstand this as the call of Romantic love, and movies and media provide a siren song for the freedom of passionate authenticity (misguided, of course, but very real nonetheless).

I have argued in my books that genuine freedom is the freedom to become a slave (servant) to Jesus Christ. God didn't give Old Testament Israel freedom from Pharaoh to go out into the desert to do whatever they wanted to do. He gave them freedom from Pharaoh to go worship God because it is the worship of God that provides maximum human freedom.

Again, the best candidate for the job of reaching Muslims is Reformed Christianity because it shares some of the broader theological concerns and language with Islam. For instance, the Reformed teaching of God's sovereignty and election provides a correction to Islam's doctrine of fate and submission. Reformed Christians are likely the most extreme (faithful) Christians, and are therefore more likely to reach other extreme religionists because they are comfortable using extreme (ultimate) language.

Another line of argument might be that, in the same way that "all things work together for good, for those who are called according to his purpose" (Romans 8:28), the converse can be argued—that all things work together for evil, for those who are are called according to the purpose of evil. What this means is that just as all good comes from and leads to God, conversely, all evil comes from and leads to Satan.

This is why Islam, which is a tool of Satan in that it teaches lying, cheating, and killing (evil) as legitimate means to an end (its own propagation), has made much progress in the world. All sin and corruption everywhere are exploitable by Islam, the master of sin and corruption. Islam has mastered the dark arts. So, as sin and corruption have increased in the West, Islam has been able to make inroads. Islam can make inroads wherever sin and corruption exist because Islamic extremists, being counter cultural to whatever society in which they live easily make alliances with other counter culturalists and with criminals and blatant sinners who also live in the counter culture. The language of Islamic extremists is similar to the language of criminality.

Conclusion: to defeat Islam requires defeating our own sin.

Sincerely,

Phillip A. Ross

The Demise of and Hope for American Capital

(October 12, 2008) The pundits are searching feverishly for the causes and cures of the current market meltdown. At this writing the most likely culprits have been identified as the housing bubble (inflated housing prices), loose lending practices (inflated credit ratings) and complex packaging of investment vehicles (inflated creativity and marketing). These are certainly among the culprits, and more will come to light as the crisis unfolds. I'm not an economist, nor an economist's son, so I can't provide any help in that regard—other than the application of common sense (reason) to these various arguments. I'll leave the economic arguments to the experts because there is another, deeper, more important concern.

Correct diagnosis is essential for proper treatment. The culprits listed above are more symptoms than causes. They are indeed causes of the financial meltdown, but they are symptoms of something else, something deeper, something more important. And if we can get to the root from which these symptoms have irrupted, we may have a better opportunity to provide a real cure.

Moral Capital

That deeper, more important concern is a moral concern, a concern regarding the demise of American moral capital. The demise of American moral capital is the deeper issue. What is moral capital? There are many theories, but I will appeal to the most commonly believed theory based on the biblical concept of righteousness, which broadly means conformity with biblical moral principles, where moral means concerned with principles of right and wrong or conforming to standards of behavior and character based on those principles. The root of the word righteous is right, which is understood as correct or justifiable, and is related to justice. To be moral is to do the right thing, the correct thing, the just thing—according to some standard of rightness, correctness, and justice.

There are many proposed standards, but the Bible, which promotes the most common standard in America today, states that God is the source of all righteousness, and that is the foundation for what follows. I am arguing that the Bible has been given to us for times such as these, that the Bible has lots to say about the kind of financial crisis we are currently in. You may disagree with this, and are certainly free to do so. I am also free to believe it, to argue it publicly and to build upon this

foundation as an expression of Christian faithfulness and American political freedom.

Most financial analysts tell us that our market meltdown developed
because credit dried up, and without credit lending cannot happen,
which means that businesses cannot get the capital they need to function. That is essentially correct. The problem is that credit is drying up.
But credit is not money, nor is it currency. Credit is the problem because we have a credit-based financial system.

But money is not the root problem. Money problems are a symptom of the credit problem. Money is simply a measure of value. It measures worth. When a thing costs a lot, it means that it is worth a lot. The
more people want something, the more they are willing to pay for it. It
is not scarcity alone that drives prices up. Something scarce that nobody
wants is still cheap. Money is simply an indicator of value. It's like a gas
gage of value on the ship of state. It's a measure of wealth, of prosperity
and the values and policies that create wealth and prosperity. Money is
an indicator of what people value. So, a money crisis suggests a values
problem, a credit or credibility problem.

Values

Values are tricky, hard to understand. What people value the most
are the things that they believe most strongly. Values are the expressions
of our beliefs. Or to say it another way, our most fundamental beliefs
create our values—and this is not only related to our current credit crisis,
but is at the very heart of it.

The word credit means to have trust in something, or to trust in the
truth or veracity of something. It's root (source) is the Latin credite or
credo, which means believe. Lenders give credit to those who they believe will pay them back with interest. Financial pundits tell us that we
need to have trust in the fundamental soundness of the market, that our
trust in the market is what makes the market sound. But there is a fundamental error in this thought, an error that marks the difference between a dupe and a cautious skeptic.

Trust in the market is fine, unless the market is itself untrustworthy.
And when a market is untrustworthy it is foolish to trust it. So, rather
than emphasize our trust in the market, it makes more sense to emphasize the market's trustworthiness. In the former case the burden is on the
people to exercise trust in the market, in the latter case the burden is on
the market to exercise it's own trustworthiness. The two things are re-

lated, but the trustworthiness of the market must precede the trust of the people. To trust something untrustworthy is foolish.

What makes the market untrustworthy? Toxic credit is credit that has been issued by unscrupulous lenders to untrustworthy borrowers in order to create notes (agreements, paper) to sell for a quick profit before the debt drives the person into bankruptcy or foreclosure. Toxic credit is a form of greed and corruption, and it has infected the markets. Toxic credit is actually a form of false belief, and unfortunately false beliefs tend to cluster together. A false belief about one thing tends to lead to false beliefs about other things. Toxic credit produced bad debts and creative financiers creatively repackaged those bad debts by mixing them with good debts, dividing them into various investment packages and reselling them. We can think of those bad debts as a kind of poison that was sprinkled throughout the markets through broad-based investment instruments.

Morals

My concern is the fundamental cause of the loss of American moral capital, which set up the inflationary aspects of the market by lacing it with toxic credit/debt in order to inflate the value of various investment vehicles. The value of the market inflated as a result of the over valuing of bad credit, which was hidden from investors by the complexity of the investment instruments. This in turn led to the meltdown of market trust or confidence when the ruse was discovered and made public.

Market trust and confidence are not based upon finances, but upon morality, upon righteousness—honor, honesty, truth, trust, trustworthiness, etc. Being wealthy does not make a person moral, and it often takes a certain amount of immorality to garner wealth in a debt-based economy. It is not the trust or confidence that people have for the market that is critical, but the trustworthiness and honesty of the market that calls forth the trust of the people. Consequently, market confidence cannot be recovered by the infusion of financial capital. Rather, what is required is an infusion of moral capital into the market.

So, the question is how to recover moral capital that has been lost. This is the same issue as building moral capital in the first place, for it is recovered in the same way(s) that it is first acquired.

The Christian tradition affirms that moral capital is acquired by the grace of God alone. It is not something that people can conjure up for themselves, but rather it comes as a gift from God through faith (trust) in Jesus Christ. Moral capital is increased by adherence to the Bible and its teachings. Consequently, the demise of moral capital comes at the neglect of God's grace and the teachings of the Bible. Apart from Christ as the center of trustworthiness, as the foundation upon which social values are built, trust diminishes—particularly when no adequate substitute is provided as a foundation of faith and trust (fiduciary trustworthiness). To denigrate, deny, or eliminate Christ is to denigrate, deny, and eliminate the foundation of fiduciary trustworthiness for most Americans.

The root source of the market meltdown is the worldview of the people who are currently at the helm of leadership all across America. It is the worldview of pride and greed that lifted the financial regulations that in previous times had protected the market from the kinds of abuses that led to our current crisis. It is the worldview of moral self-centeredness that led Wall Street to hire physicists and mathematicians to develop arcane and convoluted financial instruments in which to hide toxic debt in order to make a buck in the short run. And it is the worldview of moral irresponsibility that led various mathematicians and physicists to work with those who perpetrate such criminal activities upon the American people.

Education & Worldview

But where did all of these people acquire this worldview that has been so harmful to American society? They all have at least one thing in common. They are all products of the sweeping changes that have come to American education over the past 40, 50, 60 years. The root of the worldview that has produced this crisis is American education. It is the cream of the crop of students that find their way into success, the success that bred the crop of financial and political leaders who are responsible for the collapse of the financial market.

And because these people have the worldview that they have (an un-Christian worldview) they will not be able to lead us out of this current crisis. More than the collapse of the financial market, our current crisis is really the collapse of the worldview or philosophy that has caused it. It has shown the bankruptcy of that worldview. Why is this true? Because there is no substitute for Christ as the source of all human righteousness.

And how can that un-Christian worldview be described? It is godless, liberated, multicultural, relativist, secular, evolutionist, indulgent, prideful, selfish, greedy, etc. In a word it is not the traditional worldview of the people who founded America, nor those who brought it to world power. It is the exact opposite of a biblical or Christian worldview. Whatever Christianity values, this other worldview devalues and despises. It is a foreign worldview, foreign to American hearts and minds. And yet it is the dominant worldview in every aspect of American education today.

This does not mean that all teachers are un-Christian. It only means that the philosophical content of the curriculum that is taught at American schools—Kindergarten through College—is decidedly and intentionally not Christian. Most educators so believe in the worldview they hold that they think that it is a function of Christian values to teach un-Christian values. They believe that multicultural fairness requires the denigration of the role of Christ in society. Their substitute for the role of Christ regarding social righteousness is self-righteousness (human righteousness), which has always proven to be a disaster.

Righteousness

The long term fix for the financial crisis is more likely to be an infusion of righteousness into American society and education than an infusion of capital into failing institutions. And those who are currently in charge will not be able to provide such a fix because they neither believe in the value of righteousness—and certainly not Christ's righteousness, nor will they have the integrity to accept responsibility for the problem, nor the vision or values to see beyond the worldview that has shaped them.

The kinds of change that are needed are not in the purview of those currently in positions of power. All we will get from those currently in power is more of the same worldview that brought us to this financial crisis. What is needed are new hearts and minds, not just for Wall Street and Washington, but for Main Street and City Street, not just for Obamaites, but for McCainites.

Nor can we simply start with our children in the hope that the future belongs to them. Rather, we must start with the teachers of the children, and the parents of the children, and the grandparents of the children, for if the teachers, parents, and grandparents of the children don't have new hearts and minds that give them new eyes for a new vision of renewed righteousness, the children will continue to learn the same old things from the same old people and continue in the same old rut that we are currently in. This crisis didn't happen in a day or a week or a month, or a year, nor will it be resolved in a day, week, month, or year.

American has had a leadership role in world development since its inception, but we all agree that we have taken a wrong turn somewhere. The wrong turn that has been taken, that has led to our current financial crisis, is a product of both Democrats and Republicans, Independents and Libertarians. The wrong turn has been the turn away from Jesus Christ.

Our collective rejection of traditional Christianity over the past decades has been so sever as to embed that rejection into the legal policies of our social institutions, which will make recovery more difficult than most people imagine. So, what can the average person do at this point? How will you and I find an infusion of righteousness? Good question. I suggest that we think about it, and pray about it—but do not pray to the god of your own choosing, nor rely upon faith in anything but Christ alone. There actually is no other hope, no other way.

> Amos 3:6 "If a calamity occurs in a city, has not the Lord done it?"
>
> Isaiah 45:7 "I form the light and create darkness, I bring prosperity and create disaster; I, the Lord, do all these things."
>
> Ecclesiastes 7:14 "When times are good, be happy; but when times are bad, consider: God has made the one as well as the other."
>
> Lamentations 3:37-38 "Who can speak and have it happen if the Lord has not decreed it? Is it not from the mouth of the Most High that both calamities and good things come?"

Find a Bible and read Luke 16:1-13. Lord, have mercy.

FED CRED

Ad fontes—to the source!

"Holy Cow, Batman! What about the credit crisis?"

"Well, Robin, it's not really about money."

"Not about money?! Then what is the problem?"

"Some say it is a credit crisis. Some say its a lack of market confidence, that people need to trust the market. But I say, *ad fontes*."

Ad fontes was a motto of the Protestant Reformation that suggests that in order to correctly understand the issues we need to return to the primary sources. They meant the Greek and Hebrew texts of the Bible, but that's not what I mean. I mean that we need to return to the primary definitions of the English words that describe our current financial crisis.

Most financial analysts tell us that the problem is that credit is drying up and without credit lending cannot happen, which means that businesses cannot get the capital they need to function. That is essentially correct. But what is really behind the money problems. The problem is that credit is drying up. But credit is not money.

Money is not the problem. Money problems are a symptom of the problem. Money is a measure of value. It measures worth. When a thing costs a lot, it means that it is worth a lot. The more people want something, the more they are willing to pay for it. It is not scarcity alone that drives price. Something scarce that nobody wants is still cheap. Money is simply an indicator of value. It indicates what people value. So, a money crisis suggests a values problem, a credit or credibility problem.

Those who cannot manage their money actually have a values problem that manifests itself through the wrong or inappropriate things they spend money on. People in America aren't actually poor, they have a values problem. They don't correctly value education, learning, discipline, hard work, etc. Giving poor people more money is seldom the solution to their problems. If their problem is poor personal management, they will simply manage more money just as poorly, and they will remain unable to accumulate capital, to get out of the hole they're in. Everyone who lives beyond their means, regardless of how much money they make, is in this category.

In addition, money won't solve drinking problems, gambling problems, marital problems, etc. In fact, money doesn't solve any of our most serious problems. It can't, it's only a measure of value. I understand that this doesn't make common sense to most people. But then again the fact that certain values are common doesn't make them sensible either.

Values are tricky, hard to understand. What people value the most are the things that they believe most strongly. Values are the expressions of our beliefs. Or to say it another way, our most fundamental beliefs create our values—and this is not only related to our current credit crisis, but is at the very heart of it.

The Fed wants to provide sufficient market liquidity to keep the market from crashing in the hope that the problem can be fixed by regulation. The bail out is a short-term fix that will continue a broken system. Maybe it will buy enough time to fix the problem, and maybe not. Nonetheless, once the wolf of depression is chased off the doorstep, the question remains as to whether market credibility can be legislated.

Of course, legislation—the right legislation—will help. But credibility like morality cannot be legislated. Legislation helps by making certain practices illegal. So, in the same way that other kinds of laws help retard some expressions of criminality, legislation will help. But legislation won't help unscrupulous people curb their greed, selfishness, and pride.

What we really need is an infusion of righteousness (integrity), where righteousness (integrity) means adhering to moral principles, doing things right—not just for personal gain, but because doing things right is the right thing to do. This crisis we face is actually more of a righteousness or integrity crisis than a credit crisis. It's more about our cumulative social morality, our cumulative social integrity or righteousness than our money. How can I say this? Well, if unscrupulous financiers hadn't hidden toxic notes in the bundling of investment vehicles, and if the credit industry and investors weren't so infected with greed by shoving credit (cards) down the throats of every man, woman and dog in America, we wouldn't be here.

But we are. And the fact that we are here means that our money, which is a measure of the things we value, is tainted. Tainted with what? Tainted with immorality, unrighteousness and a lack of integrity —sin.

We know that righteousness fixes sin. But we (the corporate we, the social we, the market we) don't seem to have any righteousness—or certainly not enough. So the most helpful question to ask is, Where will we find it?

Ad fontes!

FINANCIAL CRISIS OR RELIGIOUS CRISIS?

If the doctor fails to correctly diagnose the illness, her treatment plan is both risky and dangerous. The wrong medicine may kill the patient. On the other hand, a correct diagnosis of cancer may require chemotherapy, which will make you feel horrible and you'll lose all your hair, but you will live. Diagnosis is everything.

The financial "experts" tell us that we need to recapitalize the market or it will fail. It is, after all, a capitalist market. It feeds on capital. Or does it?

By the magic of fractionalized banking, the bank is able to lend out many times as much money as is deposited. When you deposit $100, the bank can loan out, say, $900. It needs to hold back a fraction of your deposit in order to have cash on hand in case you or some other depositor wants to withdraw some cash. I'm working with 10% because it makes the math easier.

So, we put money in the bank and the bank lends it out at, say 5% interest. So the bank makes 5% of $900 on your $100 deposit each year. When the bank needs cash, it sells some of its loans at a discount. Say that all of your payments over the life of the loan amount to $1000, over say 5 years. The bank can sell your loan to another institution for say $800 and receive that cash tomorrow. Your bank is happy because it has needed cash now, and the buying institution is happy because it will make money on your loan.

The stock market performs similar feats of magic. Wherever and whenever capital accumulates, the market moves to put it to use. When your business begins to accumulate cash, someone will find out and make an offer to buy it. They can buy it for more than its current value because they can take that accumulated cash and invest it elsewhere and because of the magic of fractionalized banking, it grows. Now this is a grossly oversimplified example, but it gives you the idea of how the system works.

But what is actually being bought and sold in these kinds of lending/borrowing transactions? It's called paper. It's the document you signed that got you the loan. It is actually your promise to pay back the loan. And the paper is only as good as your promise. Bankers and Wall Street are actually buying and selling promises, yours and mine.

Buying and selling such promises might be okay and it might not be. But before you jump to a conclusion about that, let's try to determine exactly what a promise is. In this case it is your commitment to pay back your loan. If you honor that commitment, everyone wins—you get your loan and pay the interest, the bank gets to make its loans and gets its interest, and the final holder of the paper gets his money back with interest. Everyone is happy. This capitalist system has worked longer and better than any financial system in the history of the modern world.

The financial experts are telling us that trust is the leading commodity of market stability, that we just need to trust in the system and it will all work out fine. So, they want to restore trust to the markets. However, it is not actually our trust that makes it work. Many a trusting buyer has been taken to the so-called cleaners, and that is not how the system is supposed to work. Everyone is supposed to benefit, not just the crooks.

So, if it isn't our trust that makes the market work, what is it? It is the market's trustworthiness. The responsibility is not on us to trust the market, but is on the market to actually be trustworthy. And, of course, the market is not an occult, other worldly entity. It's just people, buyers and sellers—which means that the people who are involved in the market need to be trustworthy in order for the market to work correctly. And that's the rub.

The market can absorb a certain amount of untrustworthiness because the margins of profit are large enough that small amounts of untrustworthiness—understood as failure to make good on your promise—won't adversely effect the system. But at a certain point the volume of untrustworthiness reaches a tipping point and threatens to have an adverse effect upon the whole system. Those untrustworthy promises act like a poison. A little can be tolerated, too much will kill you.

The current market crisis (2008) is the result of too many untrustworthy promises in the system. What that means is that the people invested in the system—anyone who uses a bank, credit card or has financed a home—are more untrustworthy than the system can handle. Of course, the reality is more complex because Wall Streeters have leveraged their investments by hiding the untrustworthiness of the paper they are selling. Why would they do that? Because it has been very profitable.

But at some point the proverbial hen comes home to roost. In this case, it means that the shady practices of bundling in order to hide the untrustworthy paper, in order to sell it for more than it is worth has come to light. Market players discovered that they were holding bogus paper that they paid too high a premium for, and no one else wants to buy it at the price they need to sell it at to keep from going broke themselves.

The 700 billion dollar bail out provides a way to keep the system functioning as it is, but it will not and cannot fix the problem. It only bails out those who are currently holding the bad paper. The culprits are those who created the bad paper. It may be difficult to charge the particular individuals or companies responsible, but the industries that are responsible are the credit regulators and/or the entire credit industry, which has been offering its poison to families and children (college students) for a long time.

The heart of the problem is that my debt is someone else's profit. There is a place for this kind of thing, but it has gotten out of hand. The problem is that the more I'm in debt (or you), regardless of my ability to repay the debt, the greater someone else can profit—if they conceal my low credit rating (and yours) by cleverly and complexly burying that information by mixing and matching various notes, they can then sell the packaged notes and make their profit before anyone notices. But someone will be left holding the bad paper.

Should it be the taxpayers?

The root problem is untrustworthy promises that manifest as toxic loans. Those who make good promises make good promises about everything they make promises about. When they say they'll do something, they'll do it. There's more to it than money and marriage. There are a thousand little promises that their friends know about. A person is either good at promise making and keeping, or they are not.

Promise making is the core of Christianity. God has made certain promises, and Christians make other promises in return. Promise making involves more than money. It's about honesty, integrity, industry, character, and honor.

FEMINIZATION

I grew up and was educated during the blossom of the feminine spirit. My years in seminary witnessed a vicious attack on everything masculine—including pronouns! Ordinary sentence structure was convoluted beyond common sense and the basic rules of English grammar collapsed in the wake. The gender of one's pronouns trumped the value of the content of one's thoughts and ideas. Women were angry and society was on "pins and needles." A "new" social movement was afoot. Everything was being retooled, rethought, and repackaged.

We learned about the historical subjugation of women by a patriarchy that had dominated Christianity since Moses brought down the proverbial Ten Commandments. Renewed efforts to throw off the shackles of masculine imperialism that reached back into the late 1800s and early 1900s was in full swing. In seminary we were taught that existentialism, feminism, and Marxism were a matter of social justice and political freedom (usually called Liberation Theology) that was "informed" by Scripture. Riding on the coattails of both the Women's Movement and the Civil Rights Movement was the homosexualization of Christianity in the name of a "loving" Jesus.

I later discovered that all I had learned was, in fact, not true. Biblical theology had been hijacked by just about everyone under the sun, except faithful Christians who were afraid to speak "Thus says the Lord." The church had indeed been "fishers of men" and had gutted every one it caught.

Further study has revealed a completely different landscape. For instance, Leon Podles book, *The Church Impotent: The Feminization of Christianity* (Spence Publishing, Dallas, 1999) provides an astonishing contrast to popular opinion regarding women and Christianity. Podles observed that the growing weakness and ineffectiveness of American churches coincided with the decrease of male participation and wondered why.

The established churches have long made a parade of their concern for civil rights and for the plight of minorities. But there is one minority whose cause they quietly ignore: black men. The problem of criminality and drug abuse among inner-city black men is a problem of a distortion of masculinity. But the liberal churches have little to say about masculinity except to condemn it as an obstacle to women's liberation. Churches that spend their energy hunting out and obliterating the last vestiges of patriarchy are in no position to help black men attain the status they so desperately need for their own good and the good of black women and children: that of patriarchs, responsible fathers who rule their families in justice and love (p. xvi).

Podles' book is a must read for Christians of every stripe because he has put the issue in its real historical context by uncovering its pre-modern roots in the Scholasticism of the Middle Ages and the consistent unfolding of that particular flower over succeeding centuries. He clearly demonstrates that feminized Christianity is not new to the modern or postmodern world, nor is it a result of the Enlightenment, though the Enlightenment gave it a boost, as it gave a boost to every idea that was not biblical. Podles shows that the roots of Christianized femininity are found in a particular strain of apostasy and mysticism that has dogged the Christian church from its inception.

The fundamental error of the church in this regard, says Podles, supplanted the biblical definitions by smuggling in and Christening Aristotle's definitions of masculinity and femininity. From these Greek rather than Hebrew definitions the feminine flower has blossomed.

Aristotle was especially interested in the contraries of form and matter, and he placed the male on the side of form, the female on the side of matter: "The Female always provided the material, the male that which fashions it." As the giver of form, man rules; as the matter that is given form, the woman obeys.

> In the order of nature, the woman is therefore inferior to the man. Nevertheless, in the order of grace, Christian Aristotelians taught, the woman is above the man, precisely because of her natural inferiority: "Mary...herself became a kind of material for the formative power of God. Her perfect identity as nonresistant material for the working of the Holy Spirit led to her complete absorption of the wisdom of God. Therefore (for St. Albert the Great) it followed that Mary knew everything that God knew.... Precisely because they (women) are more like the raw material on which form is imposed, they are more open to the formation of the Holy Spirit. Men have a form already — a form which gets in the way of the shape of Christ that the Holy Spirit wishes to imprint on the human person. Women, relatively lacking in form, are more open to receiving another form. This analysis eventually permeated all medieval discussion of gender. As Ann Astell says, "In the metaphysics of sexuality, every person, male and female, is more feminine than masculine in relation to God — because receptive, dependent, and small."

The philosophical and theological explanation for women's greater devotion to Christianity was in place (p. 111–112).

Podles argues that this line of thinking is wrong because it is not based upon biblical precepts, yet it continues to fuel the feminization of Christianity. Podles' work is interesting, engaging, well-written and academic in that it is highly footnoted and contains an extensive bibliography of sources.

Get it. Read it. Digest it.

Values Voting

Tom Krattenmaker writes in USA Today, November 12, 2006, *Confessions of a Values Voter,* as a political and religious "progressive" (which means Liberal) that conservatives and/or Republicans do not have a corner on the values market. And, of course, he is absolutely correct.

Writers often use words and terms without defining them, assuming that the readers will know what they mean. Unfortunately, such assumptions always lead to confusion and misunderstanding.

Values are nothing more (or less) than the beliefs of a person or social group in which they have an emotional investment either for or against something. Note that values are beliefs. And beliefs are almost always religious. When people speak about beliefs they usually intend to reference ultimate concerns such as the origins and/or the purpose of the world or of humanity, etc. And the concern is not merely to delve into the past, but to chart a course for the present. This is only to say that people are guided by their beliefs.

Beliefs are understood to be religious when they pertain to God. Most of the time we think of beliefs as positing some true statement(s) about God. Such beliefs are considered to be religious in a positive way. But there are also negative beliefs that operate in the same manner.

For instance, atheists believe that it is true that God does not exist. They hold a belief or set of beliefs about God that they believe to be true —that God does not exist. Thus, the atheist is every bit much a religious believer as is the most ardent or conservative Christian, Muslim, Jew, Hindu, etc. They believe something about God to be true—that He doesn't exist. Nonetheless, it is a belief about God, and therefore a religious belief.

Why have I gone through the exercise of demonstrating that atheism is a religious belief? Because I want to agree with Mr. Krattenmaker's argument that no one has a corner on values, and that everyone who votes always votes their values. And I want to argue that values voting (and there is no other kind of voting) is always religious, even when one is not a member of any particular church or religious group. Whether or not he realizes it, Krattemaker is arguing that voting is an exercise of religious expression.

The point that I want to make with this is that the effort of the civil government to regulate speech by religious organizations through its 501(c)(3) regulations regarding the endorsement of particular candidates

is, in fact, a violation of the separation of church and state. But it is not
the kind of violation that most people expect. Most people think that the
separation of church and state is supposed to keep the church (or religious concerns) from influencing the civil government. But what has
happened is that the concerns of the civil government have encroached
upon the freedom of religious expression by attempting to control such
expression by legitimizing and certain kinds of religious expression, and
illegitimizing other kinds of religious expression through 501(c)(3) regulations.

In support of his argument Krattemaker invokes the leading Liberal
(progressive) religion in the U.S.

> "William Sinkford, president of the Unitarian Universalist Asso-
> ciation, invokes values in describing the approach to sexuality ed-
> ucation adopted by the theologically liberal Unitarians—an ap-
> proach that directly acknowledges that people will have sex out-
> side of the opposite-sex, husband-and-wife contexts. 'Sexuality
> education is about much more than just biology and rules,' Sink-
> ford wrote recently. 'It is about values, including self-worth, sex-
> ual health, responsibility, justice and inclusivity and communica-
> tion.'"

In short, it is about politics.

Note the role that sexuality plays in this discussion of politics. Notice that the values that govern (or fail to govern) one's sexual practices
issue from the same values that people vote with. How is it that bedroom behavior and voting behavior are related?

Because of the fundamental unity of human experience, a unity, not
of religious organizations or even of diverse people, but the unity of individual personal experience. It is this unity that is the basis for referring
to us (human beings) as "individuals." Our experience in life is not only
individual and unique, but it is both of those things precisely because of
the unity that defines it as one life.

I am here arguing against the fragmentation of humanity and of human experience that is the defining characteristic of Modernism, and
which has become the foundation of Postmodernism. This fragmented
and schizophrenic understanding of life attempts to isolate various kinds
of experience from one another. In politics we find it as the belief that
one's private life and one's public life are categorically different, as if the
values of one do not bleed into the values of the other. The effort to separate these different areas of human experience amounts to the fragmen-

tation of human character into isolated compartments, and is the antithesis of personal integrity. It is an expression of moral schizophrenia.

Integrity is not merely moral soundness, but is the undivided or unbroken completeness or totality of human and/or individual experience. To have integrity is to be whole, complete. It is to acknowledge that there is one set of values that rule all of life, public and private, the bedroom and the boardroom.

Thus, the issue regarding values and values voting is not that some people have values and some don't. Such an idea is absolutely absurd. Rather, the issue is that some people define good values differently than others. The chief concern of the Christian is that the values that he or she holds are biblical, that the Bible defines good and evil, not man—not you or me, and not society, but God.

Why can't we human beings identify good and evil? Because we are the most adaptable creatures ever created, and our natural tendency is to adapt to our own desires. That is to say that people are naturally selfish and self-centered. We justify all of our behavior as moral or "good enough."

The Bible is categorically opposed to our defining good and evil on our own, and identifies such an effort as sin, even as Original Sin. This kind of sin is the chief protagonist in Scripture. All of the biblical values mitigate against such a self-centered society or world. In contrast, biblical values are about service and sacrifice, not self-fulfillment, selfishness or self-expression. The values of self-centeredness (self-fulfillment) are precisely the problem because they are at odds with the traditional, biblical values of self-sacrifice.

Yes, all voters always vote their values, but all values are not equal in anyone's sight. And that is the issue. The central dispute of our time is not values per se, but traditional, biblical Christian values.

Culture As The Platform For Economic Development
(May 2006)

Introduction

My friend Hyppolite Pierre has written an interesting article ("Culture, Development, and Changing Politics in Democratic Haiti") on his (now defunct) website about Haiti's need for culture as a prerequisite for economic development. This essay is a response to Pierre's article.

The concern is close to my heart for several reasons. First, it is a family matter. My brother (Scott) has adopted two Haitian girls, which makes them my nieces. Second, I live in Appalachia, a broad section in the American heartland known for its persistent poverty. We, too, need economic development, and there are many, many organizations and institutions in our area working toward that end. They have been doing so for generations. However, what they are doing is not working. Consequently, I believe that Haiti and Appalachia have some common concerns.

I understand that there is a world of difference between the poverty in Haiti and the poverty in Appalachia. If we could transpose a section of Appalachia into Haiti, we Appalachians would suddenly be rich by comparison. The point here is not to vie for poverty bragging rights. Rather, it is to examine Pierre's article for broader application. If he is right that culture is the foundation upon which economic development is built—and I believe he is, then we both may benefit from intellectual cross pollination.

At the outset, however, I have a problem that I must confess if I am to approach this subject with any degree of honesty. My problem is that I have a particular perspective that effects my entire process of thinking and evaluation. Everything that I think, say, and do is colored by my particular perspective. All incoming information is filtered through my particular perspective and all outgoing information I produce is correspondingly shaped by it.

There are three aspects or poles that contribute to my particular perspective. The first is my own personal history. I am who I am in great part because of the experiences I have had in my life. This aspect of my particular perspective has been shaped by my family background, my upbringing, my education, and my work experience. This pole could be called the personal pole of my particular perspective. I am a white

(Scots/Irish to be specific), middle class, college educated, American baby boomer. Let us note that these things will effect my perspective.

The second pole that needs to be taken into consideration was mentioned previously. I am a Twenty-First Century American. I mention this because my national culture has a tremendous effect upon my particular perspective, as does everyone's. I am a product of American culture, and everything that I think, say, or do will reflect that fact. While the previous pole can be considered to be individual and personal, this pole is decidedly social and public, and could be called the social pole. Every human being is both personal and social. These two poles are necessary constituents of every human personality and of every human perspective.

The reason that I mention these things at the outset is that I believe that no human being can ever escape the influence that these factors have in terms of shaping human character, understanding, and perspective. Every human being has a particular perspective that is different from every other perspective. People are unique. No two people share the same history. At the same time, people who live in the same culture have many common experiences. While their histories are not identical, they are in fact similar in many regards. But they are not similar in every regard. And that insight brings us to the third pole that I need to confess so that you will understand my bias.

Preamble

I am a Christian, which means that God Himself through the power and presence of His Holy Spirit has called and empowered me to be more than I am in and of myself able to be. I have been a Christian pastor for many years. As I say this I am aware that a wall of misunderstanding has been erected by this simple confession. What I intend for the purpose of clarity all too easily becomes a source of confusion. Yet, the failure to disclose this bias would be dishonest on my part. So, there it is.

Yes, I have a bias, but so do you. So does everyone. There is no such thing as a person without a bias. For the sake of clarity let's define bias as "a preference or an inclination, especially one that inhibits impartial judgment." That's the dictionary definition, and we'll accept it. But it begs a question: Is it possible for any human being to make impartial judgments? Aren't all human judgments made from particular, personal perspectives that are effected by various aspects of a person's own particular history and culture? I ask this question because Christians have a particular perspective that necessarily effects the answer to this question. Christians and non-Christians have historically differed radically about the answer to this question, and the nature and extent of those differing answers suggests that being a Christian is a watershed issue.

I know what being a Christian means to me, and I know what it means historically, but I don't know what it means to you. The first difficulty that we have is that everyone already has an idea of what it means for a person to be a Christian, but closer examination reveals that those ideas are not the same. In fact, they differ widely, radically. There are a million different ideas about what it means to be a Christian from a Christian perspective, and another million from a non-Christian perspective. You see the difficulty? I have an idea about what it means to be a Christian, and you have an idea about what it means to be a Christian, but the two ideas may have little in common.

Communication requires that people have the same definitions of words. To communicate we must share a common lexicon, a common understanding of the meanings of words. Conversely, communication is impossible if words have different meanings to different people. If I use the word "blue" and you understand it to mean "gray," then the idea of the color in question has not been correctly communicated. When one or both of us is color blind we talk past one another about the color blue. Those who are not color blind share a common experience of the color blue. Apart from that common experience there is no way to accurately describe the color blue. Communication appeals to a common experience or common understanding and without it communication fails.

Are Christians the only group of people who have a bias? Not at all. Buddhists, Moslems, Hindus, indeed every religious person has a bias. What about people who aren't religious? There aren't any. How so? Everyone is religious. To be religious is to have a belief about God, and even not believing in God is still a belief about God. It is the belief that God is not real, or that God does not exist, or that God does not matter.

This is much more than a linguistic or logical game of playing with words. It is a true statement about the reality of being human. To believe in God is to have a bias in one direction, but to not believe in God is to have a bias in a different direction. Neither belief is objective because belief about God is about the standard for objectivity itself. If God is real, then objectivity requires belief and to deny Him is to be blinded to reality. And if God is not real, then objectivity requires unbelief and to believe in Him is to be similarly blinded to reality.

It will not do to say that my belief is okay for me, and the belief of an atheist or a Buddhist, etc., is okay for someone else. Nor will it do to say that God exists for me but not for an atheist. God either exists or He doesn't, and human belief does not call God into existence. More to the point, it is specifically the God of the Bible that makes the problem the most difficult because the God of the Bible claims the entire human race and the entire world as His own creation and property. To accept the God of the Bible is to accept a particular belief that necessarily effects every human being in every nation in every time of history. That most certainly qualifies as a bias.

But the denial of the God of the Bible also qualifies as a bias that has the same scope of historical application. The only reason to think that objectivity requires not believing in God is that such a person denies a priori the existence of God as the fundamental presupposition that establishes the criteria for the definition of the meaning of objectivity.

Indeed, belief in God is not about some bearded ancient in the sky, but is about the criteria that establishes what we accept as truth or reality itself. When you say something is true, how do you know it is true? When you say something is false, how do you know it is false? This area of inquiry is the primary ground of religion. Religion is about presuppositions—faith, and all human existence and communication require the making of presuppositions of one sort or another. It is inescapable.

What does this have to do with my being a Christian? Everything. By confessing that I am a Christian I confess that everything I think, say, and do is effected by the fact that I am a Christian. And at this point, I have another serious communication difficulty to deal with.

Many people say that they are Christians, but there is no discernible difference between what they think, say, or do and those who say they are not Christians. George Barna, a popular Christian sociologist, has established that there is no significant sociological difference between contemporary Americans who go to church and those who don't. Both groups share similar statistics with regard to the practice of premarital sex, abortion, smoking, drinking, divorce, etc. In other words, there is no significant moral (behavioral) difference between those who say they are Christian and those who don't. So, how can I say that being a Christian effects everything I think, say and do?

I must further qualify my Christianity by noting that there may be a real difference between those who claim to be Christian and those who actually are. This means that not everyone who is self-identified as a Christian actually is. This fact is verifiable in the Bible itself. Jesus said,

> "Not everyone who says to me, 'Lord, Lord,' will enter the king-
> dom of heaven, but the one who does the will of my Father who
> is in heaven" (Matthew 2:21).

Self-identification is necessary but not sufficient to establish one's iden-tity as a follower of Jesus Christ. There is another element that is re-quired.

While self-identification corresponds to the personal pole of human character or personality, group-identification or community member-ship corresponds to the social pole. There is no such thing as a com-pletely isolated human being. Human beings are necessarily communal beings. And every individual human being necessarily belongs to vari-ous groups and is excluded from other groups. For instance, I am white not black. I am American not Haitian. I am male not female, etc. The point is that being a Christian requires acceptance by other Christians. But this begs the question, how do Christians know if someone else is a real Christian or not?

The answer is that Christianity is communicated from one person to another via the Holy Spirit. However, in order for communication to be successful a common experience or understanding is required. There are two elements of that commonality, and as you might expect one pole is personal and one pole is social. The personal pole or aspect of Christian commonality is the experience of being born again.

Jesus said that regeneration is a necessary part of being a Christian. One night a man named named Nicodemus, a ruler of the Jews came to Jesus by night and said to him,

> "Rabbi, we know that you are a teacher come from God, for no
> one can do these signs that you do unless God is with him."

Jesus answered him,

> "Truly, truly, I say to you, unless one is born again he cannot see
> the kingdom of God" (John 3:1-5).

I pray that you will hear what Jesus has said here. Apart from being "born again" people cannot even see the kingdom of God. Apart from being born again, the reality of the God of the Bible does not even show up on someone's radar. In other words, like the color blue, it cannot be known apart from a direct experience of it. The implications of this are very important.

Such an experience is essential for a person to be a Christian, but it is not sufficient. To illustrate this Jesus said,

> "Not everyone who says to me, 'Lord, Lord,' will enter the kingdom of heaven, but the one who does the will of my Father who is in heaven. On that day many will say to me, 'Lord, Lord, did we not prophesy in your name, and cast out demons in your name, and do many mighty works in your name?' And then will I declare to them, 'I never knew you; depart from me, you workers of lawlessness'" (Matthew 7:21-23).

Jesus rejects these people who thought that they knew Him, but were mistaken.

The people who came to Jesus in Matthew 7:21 claimed to know Jesus. They even claimed to have worked miracles in His name. Yet, Jesus rejected them as being true disciples. This means that there is more to being a Christian than simply having an experience and claiming Christ.

The other element corresponds to what I have called the social pole of human personality or character. Just as no one is human in and of him- or herself because we necessarily exist in community with others, no one is a Christian in and of him- or herself because Christians exist in Christ. Rather, being a Christian necessarily requires recognition by the historic community of faithful Christians. In other words, Christians share an experience of being born again personally, but they also share a common Christian lexicon, a common vocabulary that is both social and historical. It is social because it belongs to a group of people, and it is historical because that group of people has existed in continuity over many generations.

At this point, yet another communication difficulty arises. I apologize for what might seem like a mass of difficulties, but life is complex. There are many trees in the forest and they are not all alike.

The next difficulty that I must point out is the fact that there are many Christian communities, all of which claim to be faithful to "true Christianity." Please understand that the fact that there are many pretenders who claim the thrown does not invalidate the fact that the throne is real. But neither does the reality of the throne justify the veracity of all who claim it. Again, we are faced with the epistemological problem of discerning the criteria by which to evaluate the definition of truth and faithfulness. How can we know what we think we know to be true? On what basis is something true or false? By what standard do we evaluate truth and falsehood?

The question deserves an answer, but it is a very complex and difficult question. However, it is not that truth is complex or difficult to understand in and of itself. Rather, it is complex and difficult because many very smart people have denied and denigrated the truth for eons and have poisoned the well of conversation about it. Many people find the truth to be threatening. Many people find that truth stifles the imagination. Why? Because if you know the truth, you don't have to imagine what the truth might be. In fact, whatever we *imagine* it to be is necessarily false.

Allow me, for the sake of time, to provide a simple answer to the complex question of how to know what is true and what is not. My underlying presupposition is that truth is necessarily objective and eternal. What is true is true regardless of what you or I might say or believe about it. We might misunderstand the truth, but our misunderstanding does not change the truth. Think of math. Two times two is four regardless of whether I think it is five or six. Human error does not change the nature of truth. If I witness an automobile accident, my perception of it does not change the truth of what happened. I cannot see everything that happened from my limited perspective, and I may misperceive something for a number of reasons. But none of that changes the truth about whatever happened during or preceding the accident.

Sociologically, then, allow me to categorically state that the truest things in the world are the things that have lasted the longest. This is based on the fact that truth is objective and eternal. This is an historical argument for truth. Because truth doesn't change, that which persists in stable continuity for the longest period of time is the most true. The Bible and the community of people who believe in the reality of the Biblical God and who are associated with the preservation and proclamation of the truths of the Bible constitute the longest lasting continuous human community in the history of the world. I know that is a big statement and that defending or establishing it will take a lifetime of study, but it is important to get it on the table for consideration so that you will understand my bias. I've been working on it for many years.

Part of the difficulty of making such a statement is that many historians do not recognize the element of continuity that runs through the various groups and communities that have defended and proclaimed biblical truth. For instance, distinctions between the Old Testament and the New Testament are often understood as discontinuity rather than continuity. There are subgroups of both Jews and Christians who argue for the discontinuity of the Old and New Testaments. Nonetheless, faithful Christians believe that the same God is behind both the Old and New Testaments and has been working over a very long period of time, but always teaching and utilizing the same method of salvation—by grace through faith in Christ alone through Scripture alone. Again, the fact that some people don't see something doesn't mean that it isn't there. But when a group of people do see something significant, and that group has continued to proclaim the same truth of that fact throughout history, and that community has been responsible for the most significant developments of history, it suggests that something significant is there. And the prudent person will investigate it.

Calvin

This brings me to my final confession. I am a Calvinistic Christian. I am convinced after many years of wide-ranging religious studies that John Calvin was essentially correct in his assessment of God and Scripture. That does not mean that he was right in everything that he said. But it does mean that he was more right than he was wrong, and that he was more right than most other Christian scholars. What made him right was not his keen intellect or any other human ability he may have had. Rather, what made him right was his simple faith that the Bible is true in all that it says, and his unwavering consistent application of that belief to his study of it. As such, should you be interested in understanding the truth of Christianity, you will find no better exposition of it than his book, *Institutes of the Christian Religion*. You will find no better or more faithful and comprehensive treatment of Christianity or the Bible in print. To engage the *Institutes* as an introduction to Christianity will save countless hours of wasted time trying to sort through the mass of material that is currently available.

Now that I have confessed my own bias in an attempt to put my so-called cards on the table for the sake of honesty and clarity, allow me to interact with Pierre's article in order to demonstrate how all of this applies to what he has said. In what follows I will be arguing in agreement with the fundamental insight of his essay, that culture is indeed the true foundation for economic development. But I will disagree with several of his definitions and use of various words and ideas—and in particular his total disregard (and probable ignorance) of genuine Christianity in general and its role as a viable cultural engine for economic development. It is my intention to provide a wider and deeper understanding of culture in order to apply Pierre's fundamental insight more broadly in the hope of establishing a stronger, broader, and clearer foundation to support his fundamental insight that culture is the essential foundation of economic development.

By any measure the Bible—and in particular Reformed Christianity (another term for Calvinism)—is the single most historically effective cultural and economic engine in history. Yet no mention of either is found in Pierre's essay, not even an intellectual nod in passing.

It must be noted that the history of Haiti is an extension of the culture of modern France, a nation that has attempted to completely disengage itself from all expressions of Christianity because of abuses, both real and perceived, prior to and during the French Revolution. Indeed, one of the primary consequences of the French revolution was the national repudiation of Christianity.

John Calvin, a Frenchman by birth, found it necessary to leave France because of the cultural forces arrayed against genuine Christianity in France two centuries prior to the historic French revolution. It may not be too strong a statement to suggest that France as a nation has never known genuine Christianity, by which I mean Protestant Calvinism, to effect its national life. And if this is true for France, it is most certainly true for Haiti.

Haitian patriots, identified here as the indigenous Haitian ruling class, many of whom according to Pierre have interbred with the French, have been educated by the French during the Modern and Postmodern periods. I mention this because it is very unlikely that any correct, orthodox understanding of Calvinism would be taught in such a milieu. The combination of slavery, no doubt associated with the name of a faulty expression of Christianity, and the modern education of Haitian nationals into the culture of France appear to have eclipsed any expression of biblical Protestant Christianity in Haiti among the ruling class enough to effect Haitian culture. Christianity appears to have played no significant role in Haitian history, which, I believe and will try to establish, is the primary reason for the fact that Haiti is the most impoverished nation in the Western hemisphere.

It may be argued that there are many Christians in Haiti. Census reports suggest that as many as 80 percent of Haitians are Roman
Catholic. Others suggest that a similar percentage of the people practice
Voodoo. Contrary to what may be popular opinion, genuine Christians
will not practice Voodoo or any religion other than Christianity. No
doubt there are Christians in Haiti, but I am suggesting that very few of
them in terms of the overall population will be true Christians, by which
I mean orthodox in their beliefs and practices. In any case, my point is
not simply about Christians in Haiti, but about the influence of Calvinism in Haiti. Christianity was present in Western Europe for a thousand
years, but only when the Reformation recovered orthodox (or true)
Christianity did Europe begin to flower culturally and economically.

Pierre, in another essay, "Building a Democratically Structured
State: Challenges for the Next Administration" (his newsletter, April 25,
2006), makes exactly this point. He writes in the conclusion,

> "Any chart that one looks at and which displays results of studies
> on kleptocratic governments (institutionalized theft in the name
> of government), shows the nasty correlation between corruption,
> poverty, and underdevelopment index. Nations that are other-
> wise rich in human and natural resources are behind and stay be-
> hind because of the effect of corruption" (p. 22).

He acknowledges that corruption is the culprit, but again fails to
define the term. We turn to the dictionary to define corruption:
"marked by immorality and perversion; depraved; v. tr. to destroy or
subvert honesty or integrity." Clearly, corruption is an expression of
rampant immorality, perversion, depravity, and deceit.

The question that Pierre needs to look into is whether the institution of government is able to remedy personal and social corruption
without the enforcement of strict totalitarianism. Can government correct personal corruption? Pierre argues persuasively for a broad-based
development of democratic freedom in Haiti. He is not arguing for totalitarianism in any sense and does not want to see such a development. I
have introduced the idea of totalitarianism into the discussion because I
believe that a governmentally based solution to the problem of personal
and social corruption will require oppressive governmental enforcement
of moral behavior as the only cure for corruption. The problem is that
civil government can only impose legislation upon its people. Corruption is a personal problem and government is a social institution. All
government can do is impose and enforce its recommendations upon

people and institutions. Neither legislation or education can change human character.

The difficulty is that the enforcement that is needed to control corrupt people stands in stark conflict with the personal freedom that is requisite for the flowering of a successful democracy. In other words, the democratic government of a corrupt people will insure corruption, not remedy it. Why? Because corrupt people love corruption. They know nothing else, and believe that corruption is the nature of reality itself. Please understand that love of corruption is not unique to Haiti, but is common to all humanity. Those who benefit from corruption love (or prefer) it, and will not voluntarily abandon it apart from a change of personal character, a change of values, a change of heart.

I will argue that there is a better solution that does not require totalitarianism, that does not further the causes or practices of corruption, and is built upon the foundation of a representative government like that of the United States. It should be noted that the United States is not now, nor has ever been a form of pure democracy but is, rather, a democratic republic. The difference is important with regard to the improvement of a corrupt people.

Let me also note that any effort to merely educate morally corrupt people results in only in smarter people who are morally corrupt. This has been documented in American prisons, where there have been significant efforts to redeem criminals through education, but have only produced a lot of smart criminals. I am not saying that moral redemption doesn't happen in prisons. It does, but it is not a function of governmental education. Neither am I discounting the importance of education, only the fact that education doesn't change character, it only helps people to become more effective. Thus, criminals become more effective criminals through education. What is needed to change morally corrupt people is a radical change of heart, a change of mind, a change of character, a change of values, a change of perspective. And this is precisely the purpose and specialty of Christianity. The impact of genuine Christianity on both individual aspects of character and the social aspects of culture is very significant.

Culture

Pierre begins by quoting a 1992 Patrick Buchanan comment about the cultural war raging in America. Unfortunately, this paragraph is filled with confusion and contradictions. We read that liberals and conservatives alike agreed that Buchanan's observation that America is caught in a cultural war is "heretical." However, such an idea is impossible apart from some agreed upon doctrine(s) deemed to be orthodox by both groups. No such body of doctrine exists. Heresy is a meaningless term apart from Christian doctrine. Therefore, the term heretical cannot apply. Usually, when non-Christians apply the label heretical to something it just means that they don't like it.

In addition, the charge of Buchanan's so-called heresy is followed by the admission that Buchanan was in fact right according to both Time Magazine and the success of George W. Bush's presidential 2004 win. Pierre said that Bush "won on cultural issues, exactly those that Patrick Buchanan related to in his 1992 speech: religious convictions with Christian values as corollary."

The problem with Pierre's essay from the outset and as found in this example is that he has failed to define or adequately understand the idea of culture. To work toward a remedy for this problem we again turn to the dictionary, where we find the following: Culture:

1. The totality of socially transmitted behavior patterns, arts, beliefs, institutions, and all other products of human work and thought.

2. These patterns, traits, and products considered as the expression of a particular period, class, community, or population: Edwardian culture; Japanese culture; the culture of poverty.

3. These patterns, traits, and products considered with respect to a particular category, such as a field, subject, or mode of expression: religious culture in the Middle Ages; musical culture; oral culture.

4. The predominating attitudes and behavior that characterize the functioning of a group or organization.

Properly defining exactly what culture is will help to put Pierre's idea on a better foundation and clarify the confusion. And, by the way, the confusion regarding the nature and meaning of culture is not entirely Pierre's fault. It is a very difficult idea to understand and there is much widespread contemporary confusion about it.

For instance, in 1828 Webster defined culture as "any labor or means employed for improvement, correction or growth." I mention Webster's definition because he defined it as verb while the contemporary definition treats it as a noun. So, is it a verb or a noun? Is culture a thing or an action, an object or a process?

One of the differences between these two definitions is that the contemporary one is more abstract. It describes what is essentially an idea, while Webster's definition is more concrete. It describes an activity. In general, abstraction contributes to complexity, and in this case I think unnecessary complexity. If we can think of reality in terms of a spectrum, without regard to the nature of the spectrum we can say that what is increasingly abstract is increasing unreal. And conversely, what is more concrete is by definition more real. This lobbies for Webster's 1828 definition over the contemporary one found on the Internet Free Dictionary. Culture cannot be disassociated from the activity of cultivation—growth. It is an activity, a process engaged for improvement, correction or growth. This is an excellent working definition of culture.

A corresponding confusion exists with regard to determining the extent of culture. How can it be identified and measured? The contemporary definition begins by suggesting that culture is the totality of all human work and thought. The problem with this definition is that to say that something is everything is to say nothing distinguishable about it. In other words, this definition is too big to be of any practical use, except obfuscation. In light of the amazing diversity and complexity of human societies any definition of culture that encompasses everything the entire human race does will be so broad that it will essentially mean nothing. Any meaningful definition of culture must recognize that human society is a complex of cultures, many of which exist in stark contrast and conflict with others. The history of human warfare stands as a testimony to this fact.

Everything hinges on the correct definition of culture because to fail to define it will result in a failure to understand it. Wikipedia (an Internet encyclopedia) provides a cogent definition:

> "The word culture, from the Latin colo, -ere, with its root meaning 'to cultivate,' generally refers to patterns of human activity and the symbolic structures that give such activity significance. Different definitions of 'culture' reflect different theoretical bases for understanding, or criteria for evaluating, human activity. Anthropologists most commonly use the term 'culture' to refer to the universal human capacity to classify, codify and communicate their experiences symbolically."

Theologians, on the other hand, find that the job of classification, codification, and communication of what is found on the earth has been given to humanity by none other than God Himself (Genesis 1:28, 2:19-20). It is a religious activity.

Wikipedia goes on to say, "This capacity is taken as a defining feature of the genus Homo." This is quite true. However, it is significant to note that this defining feature of humanity is not a natural proclivity, but has been given by God. In other words, God Himself has provided the defining feature of the genus Homo. This fact of biblical history is very significant, though it is generally ignored by most anthropologists. The point is that the different theoretical bases for understanding and the differing criteria for evaluating human activity not only produce different definitions and understandings of culture, but they actually produce different cultures.

By definition, then, belief—another word for the theoretical basis for evaluation—is the engine of culture. In other words, the definition of culture is a product of one's theoretical basis for understanding human activity. A theoretical basis for understanding is always a product of assumptions and speculation—or belief. And different beliefs produces different cultures.

Thus, to speak meaningfully we must speak of cultures in the plural, not of culture in the singular. Even the contemporary Free Dictionary is confused about the definition of culture, though Wikipedia returns to the definition of culture as a verb. But this confusion should not surprise us if we understand Buchanan's insight that there is a culture war currently in process as being the simple realization that such a conflict is not unique to our time in history, but that such conflict has always been an essential ingredient of human history—and our time is no different. Again, the evidence is the history of warfare.

Buchanan was not so much calling for a culture war as he was simply acknowledging that cultural conflicts do exist in America. Given the current state of the world and the so-called "War On Terror," it will be better to describe the situation on American soil as a cultural conflict rather than a cultural war. Of course, this is only a difference of degree. Nonetheless, I pray that this conflict will find a peaceful resolution and not escalate any further. This essay is an attempt to bring clarity to this confused topic in the hope that clarity will facilitate understanding and understanding will facilitate peace.

Webster's definition of culture is concrete, simple, and elegant. Consequently, it is also superior in that it is more discernible, practical, and useful. Culture is, then, best defined as any labor or means employed for improvement, correction, or growth. But while this definition is sufficient it is not complete or comprehensive.

There is more.

Van Til

Henry R. Van Til said that culture is religion externalized (*The Calvinistic Concept of Culture*, Henry R. Van Til, Baker Academic Books, Grand Rapids, MI, 1959.). In other words, culture is a product of religion, of beliefs and values. A correct understanding of Henry Van Til requires familiarity with the writings of his cousin, Cornelius Van Til (www.vantil.info), a modern Christian scholar who stood on the shoulders of John Calvin. It should be noted that the basic idea conveyed in Henry's insight is readily available to the most uneducated person apart from all the background reading. However, anyone who is serious about understanding the nature of human culture will find the reading to be most helpful. I recommend reading Calvin's *Institutes* first, unless you are unfamiliar with the Bible. In that case, start with the Bible.

The reading of the Bible is not a minor recommendation, but a major concern. Familiarity with the Bible is a requisite for understanding this essay and/or the role of culture as the foundation for socioeconomic development. Apart from biblical familiarity it is impossible to make an intelligent comment, much less enter into critical evaluation of the present thesis.

In addition, understanding Henry's insight requires a definition of religion. Again, The Free Dictionary tells us that religion is

> "belief in and reverence for a supernatural power or powers regarded as creator and governor of the universe, and/or a personal or institutionalized system grounded in such belief and worship."

It needs to be emphasized that religion is an activity that issues from a belief, or an activity that issues from a presupposition (Presuppose: To believe or suppose in advance; from the Free Dictionary). Like culture, religion is not an abstract thing but a concrete activity or process.

The Free Dictionary calls religion "a personal or institutional system." A system of what? A system of human organization. In other words, religion is the organizational engine for human activity—culture. It provides the subjective motivation for cultural activity—moral and cultural improvement. It provides the context in which individual activity makes comprehensive sense. It allows individuals to understand their lives and their purpose in a context that is greater than themselves, which in turn provides the glue of human community. Community adhesion can also be defined as love, and is often described as the impetus for social interaction. It also provides the teleological purpose or end for which both individual effort and social structures exist in a comprehensively meaningful way. Through cultural expression (or the expression of belief or faith) human activity is integrated into a meaningful, purposeful goal of cultivating what is best for all humanity and for each individual member of society. In precisely these ways we see that religion serves human improvement and growth, which is the definition of culture as a verb.

One of the problems found in any attempt to define culture is that people with different belief structures use different criteria for organization and evaluation. As a result, discussion moves into the philosophical area known as epistemology.

> "Historically, epistemology has been one of the most investigated and debated of all philosophical subjects. Much of the debate in this field has focused on analyzing the nature of knowledge and how it relates to similar notions such as truth, and belief. Much of this discussion concerns justification. Epistemologists analyze the standards of justification for knowledge claims, that is, the grounds on which one can claim to know a particular fact. In a nutshell, epistemology addresses the question, 'How do you know what you know?'" (from Wikipedia).

The most significant division in epistemology results from whether or not a person accepts the Bible as a valid and reliable source of genuine knowledge. There are two important concerns here: 1) the grounds upon which the Bible is either accepted or rejected as a valid and reliable source of knowledge, and 2) the consequences of that belief? This is why being a Christian is watershed issue.

American Culture

According to Pierre, Bush won the presidency in 2004 on the basis of cultural issues—"religious convictions with Christian values as corollary." Exit polls during the same election attributed the win to the large number of people who cited moral values as the key election issue. They voted Republicans across the board on the basis of moral values. But I suspect that they voted more in opposition to Democratic moral values than they were actively embracing Republican moral values. These insights are related because while not all moral values are religious, all religious people espouse moral values of one sort or another. The clear implication is, as Pierre acknowledges, that not merely religious values but Christian values in particular determined the outcome of the vote. Bottom line—American Christianity is a major political player because it is still a major cultural influence.

The larger question that is still vehemently debated in this regard is whether the United States of America was or is a Christian nation. Unfortunately, the question is more difficult to answer than we would prefer. Evidence on both sides is voluminous.

Without regurgitating the various arguments pro and con, allow me to acknowledge that it was the intent of the Puritans and Pilgrims who first settled in America prior to the establishment of the Constitution to create a Christian society. That desire was not unanimous among all of the inhabitants of the land, however. And the result was that the Founding Fathers implied a foundation of Christian beliefs and values in the founding documents, but did not explicitly reference Christianity or the Bible. Nonetheless, the fact that the laws of this nation were built upon the model and incorporated the values of the Bible as understood by the Early American settlers, who were overwhelmingly Calvinistic Christians, is indisputable.

Dr. Gary North suggests that there was an intentional effort by the Founding Fathers of the United States, several generations removed from the Early American Puritan settlers, to eliminate the references to and reduce dependence upon biblical Christianity—and in particular Calvinism—in the development of the U.S. Constitution in order to provide for a greater union, to get more people to support their effort to found a nation. It was an effort to develop a form civil government that was more universally appealing than Calvinism was thought to be. In other words, the Founding Fathers were more interested in growing a nation than in biblical fidelity.

Thus, while the Founders had the opportunity to write the name of Jesus Christ into the Constitution, they did not. Yet, they preserved many biblical phrases and words that would suggest the incorporation of Christian principles and values without the actual commitment related to naming Jesus Christ. Theirs was an effort toward the unification of the people residing here, and they were very aware that there were a plurality of views about Christianity and about the Bible. So, they sought a compromise, a middle way that would satisfy those who wanted explicit Christian references in the Constitution and those who explicitly did not. Their achievement dominates the world today in as much as America is the only remaining so-called superpower, and is the model for all current economic development. The American Empire and economy are unparalleled in world history, and are to some extent the fruit of biblical culture. I contend that the socioeconomic success of America is the direct result of the values and practices of Protestant Christianity.

The point to notice is that Christianity was the civilizing force that settled America and gave rise to its Constitution, both in content and structure—and that early American Christianity was Reformed in its theology across several denominations (Congregational, Baptist, Presbyterian, Lutheran, and Episcopalian). But for the sake of nation building, Christianity was not specifically referenced in the Constitution, which allowed for the more diverse forces—values, policies, and procedures—of nation building to take the lead while the forces of Reformed Christianity took an increasingly smaller role in civil government over the centuries.

Today, American civil government—indeed, the bulk of American culture—is infected with a virulent strain of anti-Christian secularism that is bound and determined, not merely separate church and state, but to virtually eliminate all vestiges of Christianity in public life, and Calvinism in particular. I single out Calvinistic Christianity because, while all forms of Christianity are hated by secularists, none is more hated than Calvinism—and for good reason. None pose more of a threat to the secularist agenda than the Calvinistic strain of Christianity. Why? Because of its uncompromising and consistent commitment to the values, policies, and procedures of the Bible for all of life. No theological position is more consistent or comprehensive, which means that no theological position is less tolerant of civil corruption than historic Calvinism. And that is the issue.

At the same time, there is no theological, philosophical, or political position that is more suited to seriously address the concerns of individual and social corruption than historic Calvinism. I understand that this is a very serious statement. And I invite you to seriously consider it—not to shout it down in public discourse, nor to demonize it with a program of populist sloganeering, but to carefully and genuinely provide substantive intellectual and moral evaluation and criticism of this historic social movement. This cannot be done apart from serious study of Calvinism, and I believe that serious study—in conjunction with a genuine desire to solve the problems of moral corruption—will confirm its veracity.

Liberalism

Contemporary Christianity in America is decidedly pluralistic, so much so that it would barely be recognizable as Christianity at all to Christians of former generations. In fact, those who actually believe and practice Calvinistic Christianity in the contemporary world compose a very small minority within the Christian camp, and much smaller in the wider society. The dominant theological perspective in contemporary American Christianity is that of Liberalism. Virtually every church body has grown and is growing increasingly liberal over time, without regard for denominational or theological distinctives.

According to The Free Dictionary, Liberalism is

> "a political theory founded on the natural goodness of humans
> and the autonomy of the individual and favoring civil and politi-
> cal liberties, government by law with the consent of the gov-
> erned, and protection from arbitrary authority."

It must be understood, however, that Liberalism did not just suddenly appear in full flower without any prior history. Liberalism is the theology of American Civil Religion. It may be impossible for non Americans to understand American Civil Religion because of its sheer vastness and its ability to absorb both competing and complementary ideas and forces into itself.

What follows is a brief introduction to American Civil Religion by www.facsnet.org:

> Civil religion is an often unstudied and unacknowledged topic.
> Like many things that are ignored, omitted or hidden, it has a
> way of being found; and once it is discovered, the floodgates
> open. Apparently, this has been the case for the many readers
> who are drawn to this topic.
>
> The United States, which began as a few small colonies in Massa-
> chusetts and Virginia almost four hundred years ago, is now the
> most powerful country on earth. Accordingly, "the eyes of all
> people are upon us." These are the words of John Winthrop,
> leader (ordained Christian minister) of the Massachusetts Bay
> Colony, who delivered his oft-quoted "city on a hill" (Matthew
> 5:14) sermon in 1630 en route to the New World.

> Winthrop's sermon turned out to be prophetic: The eyes of the
> world are on the United States; and from foreign shores, those
> eyes are often mystified, puzzled, or sometimes maddened by this
> creature known as the American. Americans themselves are often
> unaware of their own motivations, values and beliefs. It is impos-
> sible to look in a mirror and see oneself as others see you. Besides,
> as some might say, "What's there not to like?"

> This study attempts to explain the American ethos, in terms of
> civil religion, for both Americans and non-Americans alike—
> journalists in particular.

As well as being the most powerful country, the United States is the
most diverse country in the world—religiously, ethnically and otherwise.
Americans are not defined by race, tribe, or religion. The vast majority
of Americans are not descendants of John Winthrop's colonists. Yet
those first Puritan settlers began a notion—a notion greatly expounded
upon by the nation's founders in 1776 and 1787—that lives on one way
or another in every person who claims "American" as his or her nationality. Echoes of this notion travel across time from Abraham Lincoln,
Martin Luther King, to Bob Dylan and George W. Bush. Some call it
civil religion; some explain it in the terms of a "social contract;" some
call it a "creed;" others say there's no such thing as any of it.

This piece attempts to show American civil religion for what it is,
regardless of what it's called, in its many contours. Civil religion is more
easily understood through its direct expression than a dictionary-type
definition. Throughout this piece, we attempt to reveal the meaning of
civil religion primarily through the words of Americans as they speak—
on issues ranging from war, culture, diversity to church and state.

You may want to spend some time reading the articles on the
www.facsnet.org website to better understand the nature and extent of
American Civil Religion. But don't let it distract you from our prior
concerns here. It plays a key role in the current American cultural ethos.
It is religion without God. It could be called an atheistic religion or an
agnostic religion. But regardless of what it is called, its defining theology is Liberalism. And the defining characteristic of Liberalism is syn-
cretism, which is a violation of the First Commandment (Exodus 20:3).

Is the theology of Liberalism Christian? Not according to J. Gresham Machen, a theologian of note who wrote *Christianity and Liberalism* in 1923, which is now in public domain and available on the web.
Machen's conclusion was that Liberalism is not Christianity by any defi-

nition, but is a different religion altogether. Why is this important? Because contemporary Christianity is dominated by a theology that is not Christian. Most churches have not completely succumbed to Liberalism at this time. But the vast majority have accepted its fundamental presuppositions and are in the process of making accommodations to it. The implications of this insight are many and significant. In fact, this insight constitutes a very serious accusation in the life of contemporary Christianity.

Liberation

Pierre speaks of the role of Vodou (his spelling) in the liberation of Haiti from it's French colonizers as the organizing cultural force of resistance (http://www.irsp.org/culture/faith1.htm, now defunct). The spirit of historic Haitian liberation was, according to Pierre, full of violence and atrocity and was led by Vodouists Makandal, Boukman, Duvalier and others.

Christians are not strangers to oppression, but have a long history of struggle against the forces of oppression in many different cultures all over the world. The fact that French (and many other) colonizers abused and enslaved people in the name of Christianity (but not in the true Spirit of Christianity) does not negate the reality that no cultural force in history as done more to free oppressed peoples all over the world than genuine Christianity. I wish that I did not have to distinguish between genuine Christianity and fake Christianity, but history is replete with abuses of power by those who claim to be Christian but do not actually believe in or practice the most basic Christian values. As such it is an error to blame Christianity for abuses by people who do not practice genuine Christian values and are liars who falsely claim to be Christian.

A simple comparison of the methods of Christian resistance to oppression with the methods of Vodou resistance to oppression reveals a world of differences. Where Vodou leaders have taught people to respond with hatred, violence, and rebellion, Jesus taught people to respond with patience, perseverance, humility, and submission to God. Vodou culture continues to be dominated by ignorance, poverty, and repression, where Christian culture has lead to education, widely shared economic development, and political freedom. The fruits of Christian liberation stand in stark contrast to the fruits of Vodou liberation. The two religions and their respective cultures—Christianity and Vodou—couldn't be more different. Christianity has produced education, science, technology, and economic development, where Vodou has left people in ignorance, superstition, and poverty. According to Pierre, the values of Vodou encourage its practitioners to take selfish advantage of others for their own gain as a matter of principle—because Vodou actually teaches that might (or power) makes right, that power is itself an expression of righteousness. Christianity, on the other hand, could not be more different.

For example, in the modern era Duvalier

> "came to realize that in no way could a leader in Port-au-Prince effectively control the murky politics of Haiti until and unless such leader not only recognized, but also accepted the validity of Vodou. Years later after he had become president of Haiti and had begun his reign of terror (1957-1971), everyone would realize as he had made it known, that he was himself a practitioner of that faith" (Pierre, www.irsp.org/culture/faith2.htm).

Pierre himself notes that the practice of Vodou has repeatedly produced political deceit and repression in Haiti.

> "All in all, the ultimate goal in Vodou is power, not the improvement of the self for some higher moral reason."

Compare this with the John Acton quote,

> "Power corrupts, and absolute power corrupts absolutely."

If Acton is right, and his understanding of power is generally held to be true by most people and more so by Christians, who understand the power of sin, then Haiti's quest for Vodou is a quest for corruption through deceit, greed, and political repression. And to no one's surprise corruption is a primary characteristic of Haiti, as identified by Pierre.

Later Pierre opines,

> "For too long, Haiti's traditional community leaders have been wrongly used by individualistic and power-hungry individuals who only cared about themselves rather than the country."

Yet, that is precisely the fruit of the teaching and ideals of Vodou. How can he identify the central teaching of Vodou as self-centered power grabbing and then complain that those who practice it aren't doing good for the country? He appears to be suffering from cognitive dissonance in this matter.

He acknowledges that the

> "difficulty is in processing the faith (Vodou) so that its positive
> figures can be acknowledged and used, while the negative ones
> are socially, morally, and intellectually discarded,"

but fails to understand that the dualistic character of the Vodou philosophy absolutely requires such opposites. The bad elements of Vodou cannot be cleansed from the religious and cultural practices because they are
inherent to Vodou. Eliminate the duality and Vodou is no longer
Vodou.

Rather, what is required is an entirely different philosophical and religious system. Contrary to Pierre's thesis that Vodou has benefited the
enslaved people of Africa who were brought to Haiti against their will
because it was the organizing force that led to the independence of
Haiti, Vodou appears to be the force that has bound Haiti in continuing
ignorance, superstition, and poverty.

According to Pierre, the Catholicism of Haiti blended with the
African culture of the slaves very early in its history. He acknowledges,
as do others, that beliefs and practices of the imported African slaves and
the religion of Vodou were incorporated into popular Haitian Catholicism. Pierre admits that "most people who practice Vodou will also tell
you that they are Catholics." This practice is called religious syncretism,
and is forbidden in biblical Christianity by the First Commandment
("You shall have no other gods before me" (Exodus 20:3).

Unfortunately, Catholicism has a long history of religious and cultural assimilation (or syncretistic) practices as a means of expansion.
Throughout history the Roman Catholic Church has incorporated various aspects of indigenous religions and cultural practices into itself as it
has gone into new areas. As such, Catholicism has a long practice of
"Christianizing" various beliefs and practices that are anathema to biblical Christianity. But because this practice is old and its history long,
many people have come to think that these "Christianized" beliefs and
practices are actually Christian. They are not. They undermine and corrupt biblical Christianity and have contributed greatly what I have called
fake Christianity.

The intent of the Reformation in the 1500s (led by Martin Luther
and John Calvin) was to reclaim the original beliefs and practices of biblical Christianity, which had been corrupted by the Roman Catholic
Church and its program of assimilation. The Reformation recovered the
historic gospel of Christianity, not perfectly, but enough to bring about
a significant shift in Western culture. It is the Christianity of the Refor-

mation that is defined here as genuine Christianity, and the engine of economic development. Yet, care must be taken because the contemporary world is awash again in same kinds of corruption that now taint the historic Reformed Christian denominations. However, it should be noted that such corruption—contemporary or historic—does not disprove the validity of the biblical teachings, but in fact provides significant evidence for their veracity.

Cultural Imperative

This has been a long diversion regarding my analysis of Pierre's article, and yet it is essential for an understanding of the role that religion and culture play in the social and economic development of a nation—any nation. In order to say anything significant about culture we must first understand what culture is and the role it plays in society. Because culture is the outgrowth of beliefs, presuppositions and values—in a word, religion—all cultural conflict is understood as the result of religious differences. And because Christianity stands opposed to all other religions, based upon the First Commandment and the Great Commission (Matthew 28:18-20), the resolution of religious conflict cannot be syncretistic. Christianity cannot be blended with or melded into any other religion, philosophy, or belief system. Christianity is unique in the religious history of the world.

But Christianity has in fact been blended with other religious and philosophical beliefs, beliefs apart from those described as biblical faithfulness, from very early in its history. The work of Cornelius Van Til has established this fact, and it is common knowledge that the Early Catholic Church worked toward the accommodation of pagan beliefs and practices as a mode of evangelism. Its method was to absorb non-Christian cultural practices and to Christianize them over time. Van Til documents that the Roman Catholic church has accommodated pagan Greek philosophy into the theology of the church through the work of Aquinas and others. The celebrations of Christmas and Easter are examples of such accommodation. However, the result of this effort has only succeeded in spreading a version of Christianity that is itself syncretistic, and therefore not faithful to the God of the Bible.

The Reformation of the 1500s was an attempt to cure the Christian church of this syncretistic tendency, and was only partially successful. But it was successful enough to demonstrate the power of genuine biblical faithfulness and culture as Holland, England, and later, the USA manifested sufficient biblical culture to ignite the scientific and techno-logical development that gave birth to the Industrial Revolution and free market economies. Contrary to popular opinion, science, technology, and free markets all have their origins in the Bible and the practice of biblical beliefs and values. Those not familiar with Scripture may doubt this, but only because of their lack of biblical knowledge.

In addition to these difficulties, over the past hundred or so years there has been a systematic effort to dismantle Christianity and the bibli-cal culture it has developed. This effort has no doubt been driven by genuine fear of the power unleashed by science, technology, and free markets. The various ecological and "Green Movements" are examples of this reactionary mindset. Without a doubt much damage has actually resulted from these forces, which have been dominated by the syncretis-tic corruptions of lust, power, and greed that sometimes operate in the name of but not in the true Spirit of Christianity. Of this there can be no doubt. But what is yet to be discovered is that the abuses done in the name of Christianity have been done by those people and institutions that are the least Christian. In fact, we can say that they are not Christian at all, except that they have infiltrated and corrupted historic Christian institutions and operate from within those institutions. Read Jude.

Thus, those unfamiliar with the gist of this essay may believe that the contemporary corrupt and diluted expressions of Christianity are ac-tually Christian. They are not! Any serious study of the historic Re-formed branch of Christianity will bear this out. Whether or not you agree with the historic Reformed position, it will be undeniable that the contemporary version of Christianity is not the Reformed version.

It is the thesis of this author that all genuine socioeconomic devel-opment—sustainable development—must be built upon the foundation of genuine biblical culture, and that the most consistent and compre-hensive expression of that culture is found to be in harmony with his-toric Calvinism. It must be noted, however, that Calvinism has been un-der attack from within and from without for centuries, and that great care must be taken to avoid the natural human urge toward sin and syn-cretism. Indeed, modern education itself teaches and applauds the ability to synchronize various views, values, philosophies and religions, and has abandoned its historical Christian roots. As a result, this practice syn-cretism is widespread. In fact, syncretism is exactly the philosophical po-sition of Liberalism and American Civil Religion—but it is not Chris-tian!

Indeed, the only protection available from the acids of unbelief comes in the name of Jesus Christ and from the regenerating power of the Holy Spirit. The extent of human sinfulness is so great that it can only be overcome by God Himself, through what Jesus called being "born again." And that is exactly what has happened and will continue to happen as God continues to unfold His story of the salvation of the world through His Son, Jesus Christ.

I pray that this essay may be used by the Lord for His own purposes in the hope that it may facilitate greater understanding of the concerns I have raised.

Born Or Made

Ellen Goodman lambastes the Pope in a recent article in the Boston Globe, "Nature or nurture?"[12] accusing the Roman Catholic Church of backsliding on the homosexual issue. She complains that the dividing line over gay issues has moved since the Pope Benedict XVI has banned sodomites[13] from Catholic seminaries. There are many good reasons to come down on the Roman Catholic Church, but this is not one of them.

Of course there is a sense in which she's right. The line did move. For over 3,500 years of recorded history every culture has considered sodomy to be taboo, which includes all of the history of Christianity—until about thirty years or so ago. Some cultures (like the Greeks) have more or less tolerated homosexuality, but none have embraced it as a social norm.

Two months before the Stonewall uprising in New York (1969)—generally recognized as the beginning of the modern gay and lesbian rights movement—the United Church of Christ's Council for Christian Social Action declared opposition to all laws criminalizing private homosexual relations between adults. The council also opposed the exclusion of homosexual citizens from the armed forces. This action constituted a complete reversal of all historic Christian and United States belief and practice.

In 1972 William Johnson became the first openly homosexual person ordained to the ministry by a Christian church. He was ordained by the Golden Gate Association, a group of United Church of Christ congregations in Northern California. Johnson has had one of the most effective ministries in modern times. A virtual revolution of views and values has occurred worldwide since that time. The line, as Goodman has referred to it, has rotated 180 degrees in most mainline churches. This revolution, more than any other single factor, has resulted in the gutting of mainline Christianity.

But the so-called line didn't actually move in the Roman Catholic Church. Pope John Paul ordered the issue to be studied, but didn't issue any official teaching regarding homosexuality. Goodman quotes from some Catholic study materials, but fails to mention that the study documents did not and do not reflect official Catholic doctrine. Of course,

---

12 http://www.boston.com/news/globe/editorial_opinion/oped/articles/2005/12/02/nature_or_nurture/

13 Using the term "sodomites" helps to frame the issue in the traditional biblical perspective.

many Catholic priests have argued vociferously in favor of sodomy within and without the church, but the arguments of priests do not constitute official Roman Catholic doctrine. Benedict has merely brought the study to a close by issuing an official proclamation. That's his job.

Goodman doesn't have a proverbial leg to stand on regarding the Catholic Church. The Pope decided not to move the Catholic line after years of institutional study. It is his job to make such decisions. There is, however, a point to be made regarding the mainline Protestant churches because they did move the line. But Goodman won't appreciate the point.

History aside, the nub of Goodman's concern appears to be whether sodomites are born or made. She errantly claims that the research favors the idea that homosexuality is a born trait. The National Association for Research & Therapy of Homosexuality (NARTH) provides extensive research to the contrary.

Friedman and Downey, psychiatric researchers at Columbia University, offered a strongly worded conclusion opposing the essentialist (or genetic) argument:

> "At clinical conferences one often hears...that homosexual orientation is fixed and unmodifiable. Neither assertion is true...The assertion that homosexuality is genetic is so reductionistic that it must be dismissed out of hand as a general principle of psychology" (2002, p 39).

Yet many national organizations continue to offer the essentialist argument as a guide for law and public policy. No reputable scientist on either side of the political spectrum would disagree with the conclusion of Friedman and Downey. Even the gay-activist researchers themselves, whose studies have been used by the media to trumpet the message that homosexuality is biologically determined, do not support the "born that way"[14] myth.

Matt Foreman's comment that it "doesn't matter what you do or believe or practice. If you are gay there is no making that better in the eyes of the church" reflects a complete misunderstanding of Christianity. Paul noted that among the Corinthian Christians were former homosexuals.

> "Do you not know that the unrighteous will not inherit the
> kingdom of God? Do not be deceived: neither the sexually im-

---

14 https://wiki2.org/en/A._Dean_Byrd

> moral, nor idolaters, nor adulterers, nor men who practice homo-
> sexuality, nor thieves, nor the greedy, nor drunkards, nor revilers,
> nor swindlers will inherit the kingdom of God. And such were
> some of you. But you were washed, you were sanctified, you
> were justified in the name of the Lord Jesus Christ and by the
> Spirit of our God" (1 Corinthians 6:9-11).

No sin (except the unforgivable sin—Matthew 12:31) is so great that it cannot be forgiven. But the forgiveness must be personally received, which necessarily involves repentance.

The critical issue regarding homosexuality in the church has little to do with homosexuality per se, but everything to do with repentance. First, understand that Christianity is for Christians, and Christians are necessarily forgiven and repentant sinners. It is not sin that keeps people from Christ, it's a lack of repentance that God cannot countenance. This should be clearly understood by all Christians, but is too often misunderstood by Christians and is widely misunderstood in contemporary society. Again, the issue is not the nature of any particular sin, but the change in the heart of the sinner that leads to revulsion of sin—all sin.

From a Christian perspective it doesn't matter whether homosexual orientation is genetic or learned. Because of the Fall (or what is called "original sin") sin is the natural condition (orientation, proclivity and/or tendency) of all human beings from birth. Critical to this issue is the biblical teaching that sin is the natural condition, but not the original condition of humanity. The purpose of Jesus Christ is to restore the original condition. The issue is not about the nature of homosexuality, but the power of sin and the greater power of Jesus Christ to conquer sin.

The destruction of Jerusalem established the fact that Christianity is not about the nation or the race of Israel. Christianity is not about genetics, but faithfulness. The birth, life, and death of Jesus Christ established that the power of God is greater than the power of the flesh (genetics). In Christ regeneration produces power over the flesh, over natural orientations, proclivities, and tendencies for all sinners, not just homosexuals. God trumps genetics. In Christ, Christians rise above their natural tendencies to sin and live in their original tendencies to faithfulness and holiness—not all at once, of course, but over time.

There are only two considerations pertinent to the issue of sin—any sin: 1) Can it be forgiven? And 2) is the sinner repentant (growing in grace and godliness, living according to the desires of Jesus Christ rather than the desires of self)? Being a Christian requires that each question be answered with an unqualified *yes.*

All sin involves natural tendencies, proclivities, and orientations. But the power of Christ through forgiveness and regeneration overcomes our natural tendencies, proclivities, and orientations and provides Christians with godly tendencies, proclivities, and orientations. This is what makes the gospel of Jesus Christ "good news."

MORAL VALUES AGAIN

Moral values are in the news again, thanks in large part to former President Jimmy Carter. Carter is promoting his new book and has taken careful aim at the morality of the current Bush administration and Republican leadership. Carter's concern has been picked up by the Islamic Republic News Agency. The list of moral issues is growing: the war in Iraq, the Abu Ghraib prison scandal, the CIA's secret prisons, the Libby and Delay indictments. There will be more.

One of the more accurate accusations comes from Kevin Leahy, who writes in the Northern Star Perspective,

> "The Republican party is particularly adept at wrapping itself in the kind of symbols and values-laden language that appeal to voters: God, family, community. They are consummate salesmen. After half a decade of unfettered Republican rule, however, it has become apparent the GOP's product doesn't match its sales pitch."

Ouch!

Implicit in Leahy's language is the suggestion that the Republican Party uses God, family, and community values as political weapons, and that their use of them betrays at best a shallow faith. My concern has long been that too many Republicans are more Republican than they are Christian. This is only slightly better than the Democrats who for the most part are openly anti-Christian—except for their support of Liberal Christianity. (If you are thinking that Liberal Christianity is another form of Christianity, see *Christianity and Liberalism*, by J. Gresham Machen.)

The biblical position on moral values is clear, consistent, and comprehensive. There is no morality apart from the Christ of Scripture. God invented morality and defined it in Scripture, any other definition lacks integrity. Of course, the word *moral* doesn't appear in the Bible. Rather, Scripture knows morality by its biblical name—righteousness.

The traditional doctrine of total depravity teaches that sin has effected the totality of the person. Because of sin and the Fall (Adam's fall from grace in the Garden of Eden) no aspect of being human is free from the effects of sin, those effects being the inability to be or become righteous, good, or moral apart from regeneration by the Holy Spirit. Apart from regeneration, nothing a human being thinks, says, or does is good, righteous, or moral in and of itself. In the shadow of the Fall, righteousness is not a human possibility.

Note that none of this so-called religious talk has anything to do with going to church or being a member of a political party. Rather, it is about thinking, perceiving, and making decisions—any and all thinking, perceiving, and decision-making. The issue pertains to the character or essence of righteousness. Is it our righteousness because we have become more Christ-like as we have grown in faithfulness? Or is it Christ's righteousness because growth in Christian faithfulness requires the death of the old self. It is the latter because the new self is not ours at all, but is entirely Christ's. The truth is that righteousness is so remote from being human that any degree of righteousness is entirely impossible for all human beings, apart from divine intervention.

Jesus Christ is that divine intervention, given freely to all who believe. The downside of all of this is that apart from belief in Jesus Christ even the idea of real righteousness (or morality) cannot even be conceived. In other words, no human idea of righteousness can compare to biblical righteousness. Biblical righteousness is infinitely more perfect than human righteousness because it comes from the mind of God.

The Republican Party would do well to harmonize their moral vision with their moral performance. Public repentance would be appropriate because the only way to harmonize moral vision with practice is to claim and profess the righteousness of Jesus Christ. Only in Christ can people fall short of moral perfection without losing moral credibility. Only the grace of God's forgiveness is able to neutralize the effects of sin and provide for moral improvement over time. Perfection belongs to eternity, but improvement belongs to history.

Of course, harmonizing ideals and actions requires more than lip service. The Republican Party is very unlikely to bring Jesus Christ into the Big Tent by name, but a few Republicans may yet repent.

Of Looting and Looters

Looters in the aftermath of hurricane Katrina and her annihilation of New Orleans and neighboring coastal areas has sparked questions about how and why looters loot. What is going on the minds of people who break into stores and carry out TVs and other nonessentials during a catastrophic disaster? What is wrong with these people!?

The question reflects a concern about the law. How can otherwise law abiding citizens so blatantly break the law in such circumstances? This question assumes too much. First, what makes us think that those who loot are otherwise law abiding citizens? There is a huge criminal underground in America—and everywhere else for that matter. Is it possible that the worst of the looters are not otherwise law abiding citizens? Absolutely. In fact, it is probable.

People who have no respect for the law during normal times will take advantage of the lack of law enforcement during difficult times. And that is most likely what we are seeing.

But to say that all looters are criminals prior to the onset of their looting during a catastrophe says too much. Some are, for sure, but not all. Many people will be encouraged to loot simply by witnessing others who are looting. It's a kind of copycat crime. Some do it because they don't want to look like wimps to the looters. Some do it to fit into what they perceive as a social order (though that order is criminal in nature). Others do it because they are afraid that the looters will come out with an unfair advantage by their looting, so to make things "even" they join to looting as a way of protecting themselves from falling behind is some perceived advantage.

However, I must condemn those television hosts and celebrities who justify looting during a catastrophe on the basis of "survival," saying or suggesting that its okay for people to loot to obtain food, water, diapers, or baby formula. Looting, which is never more than theft, is always destructive of society. It undermines the trust that is necessary for all social order, and apart from social order society quickly devolves into chaos and destruction. Katrina brought chaos to the social order of New Orleans, and the first order of recovery is the reestablishment of social order. All rescue and recovery efforts will succeed only through the deployment of order. And all looting undermines and destroys social order.

Another word for social order is *law*.

Behind the looting phenomena lies the issue of law. What is the proper role of law in society? And how is law best inculcated—taught

and assimilated? This issue comes to the fore during a catastrophe because disaster strips away the veneer of social custom to expose the core
values that people actually hold. How people respond to catastrophic
disaster is a function of their most deeply held values. Many articles have
been written to demonstrate that stress reveals character. The way that
people handle stress is a function of character, and character is a reflection of core values. And catastrophes are stressful.

But to say that looters lack moral character and respect for the law is
platitudinous drivel. Everyone knows that (except the looters, of course
—and those who justify their behavior). Looters are not expressing a
change of character during a catastrophic event that has stripped them of
their inner morality. Rather, looters reveal the character of their core
values that are otherwise obscured by the distractions of ordinary life.

The deeper issue is about how people view law in general. And the
issue is necessarily religious because all religion is about understanding
one's place in the order of the universe and of society. Everyone has a
place and everyone has an understanding of that place regardless of what
they think about God. Being religious is not an option for human beings. To define one's self as a human being is necessarily a religious expression because human beings always have a particular place in the universe and individuals have particular places in society. The issue not
whether or not to be religious, but only how to be religious. Even atheists define themselves in the context of God.

God provides order. Religion provides an orderly way of life, a way
of living or lifestyle that contributes to social order. According to the
Bible, God is the original law giver. That's important because it means
that God provided all original human or social order. People may deny
the reality of God, but no sane person can deny the historical role that
religion has played in the historical development of social order. Like it
or not, God is a key concept in the historical development of humanity,
and religion plays a key role therein.

With this brief background let me suggest that looters have a particular understanding of law. Looters view law in terms of enforcement.
The power of the law is the power of enforcement. And that means that
when the law cannot be enforced it is not in force. If it cannot be enforced, then people believe that it is no law at all. They believe that enforcement is the only consequence of breaking the law. If you don't get
caught, then you're not guilty. Religious antinomians might even mis-

takenly say that the failure to get caught is an expression of God's grace. But this is a perverted understanding of grace.

This begs the question of how people view or understand the general concept of law. Is law necessarily tied to enforcement so that obedience is always tied to the fear of temporal punishment? Or can the general conception of law be viewed or understood apart from immediate, temporal enforcement and punishment? Can people want to obey the law without regard for enforcement?

According to traditional Christianity, there are people who obey the law simply because they don't want to get caught. Such people view the law in terms of enforcement. But there are also people who view the law in terms of the maintenance of social order. These people are not concerned with getting caught—not simply because they don't break the law (and they do make every effort not to), but because they understand that social order is dependent upon conformity to the law by all people. Conformity to the law provides social order, which helps to preserve and protect their assets and interests. Such people are in essential agreement with Christianity, whether or not they recognize that fact. Christians are, of necessity, law abiding people.

Those who view the law in terms of enforcement are quick to take personal advantage of the lack of enforcement. And those who view the law in terms of the maintenance of social order are quick to take personal advantage of the benefits of social order. Each works out of his or her own personal advantage—people are designed to do that, as Adam Smith observed in his book, *The Wealth of Nations*. But regardless of which view is believed and acted upon, both views are essentially social and religious. And both have certain religious consequences.

Honesty Is Not A Management Strategy

On June 23, 2005, MSNBC reported about "a handbook of aphorisms that has become an underground hit among corporate chieftains." That hit is called *Swanson's Unwritten Rules of Management* and sets forth maxims developed by William Swanson, the chief executive of No. 4 U.S. defense contractor Raytheon Co.

His aphorisms are reportedly too basic to be ignored: to have fun; to make the hard decisions even if that results in criticism; and to learn to say "I don't know" when appropriate, and then to go find the right answer. Another is that "you can't polish a sneaker," meaning that it is a waste of time trying to improve something high on style but short on substance.

Deborah Kolb, the Deloitte Ellen Gabriel Professor for Women and Leadership at Simmons School of Management in Boston, acknowledged that another of Swanson's aphorisms, "looking for what is missing," is a great piece of advice. But she questioned the one about saying "I don't know" too often. "There may be situations where it opens up inquiry," she said. "But people may lose confidence if they look to you for guidance. If you're a woman in a leadership position and say 'I don't know,' people may ask why you're in that role."

Honestly acknowledging what you know and what you don't know is a critical life skill that is too often blatantly disregarded across the social spectrum. Leaders are particularly afraid to admit that they don't know something for exactly the reasons stated above by Dr. Kolb.

So, they make something up. Leaders have mastered the art of looking confident and sounding knowledgeable. That's what leadership is about, right? So, it's just a matter of projection, image, and inflection. This is not the stuff that gets reported in the news. It's more a matter of daily interfacing at work: Look good, stand tall, project confidence, and most of the time your ignorance won't matter.

But Swanson's advice is on the right track. When you don't know something, admit it. The alternative is to lie. Dr. Kolb apparently thinks that admitting ignorance is okay as long as it isn't overused. If you are in a situation where you should know but don't, your admission of ignorance could get you some negative attention. You don't want people to lose confidence in you, so you…what?! Make it up? Change the subject? It probably won't matter as long as you look good, stand tall, and project confidence.

Here's the rub—Dr. Kolb seems to be suggesting that honesty (admitting the truth that you don't know something) should be used as a leadership strategy to insure that you are rightly positioned as the leader you believe you are. When honesty supports your leadership position, by all means use it. But when it puts you in a negative light, you might want to pull something else out of your leadership hat—especially if you are a woman in a leadership role. I wonder if she'd argue that way for a man?

Regardless of your gender, when honesty submits to politics (where politics is a matter of making and sustaining power alliances) it ceases to be honest. When honesty as a character quality is buffered or disengaged for any reason it dies. Honesty is not a management strategy to be engaged here or there as the situation determines. Rather, it is a consistent way of life or it is nothing.

Self Evident Political Correctness

This article is in response to a family discussion on Facebook about the value and merits of Jordan Peterson, in particular to Caitlin Flanagan's article, "Why the Left Is So Afraid of Jordan Peterson." Peterson speaks much about Political Correctness.

Political Correctness is a slippery term that defies definition. It is generally thought to exclude or diminish particular categories or groups of people. And interestingly, there is both a conservative version of Political Correctness and a mutually exclusive liberal version. In addition, there is an ideological version that focuses on ideas, and a demographic version that focuses on people groups. The primary problem with the use of Political Correctness is that different groups use the same term to refer to different things. The Left argues that the Right uses it to suppress or limit Left leaning ideas and people, and the Right argues that the Left uses it to suppress or limit Right leaning ideas and people. Both usages are correct to a point.

In addition both the Left and the Right have different people and methods of political enforcement. Each group has intellectuals who argue logically and carefully to articulate their respective views as being the best representations of truth and reality. Each argues that their view or worldview, their perspective, is objective and the other is not. But each side also has people who use intimidation, bullying, protesting, and violence to enforce their particular view of Political Correctness by creating public news events designed to frame Political Correctness in their own favor. Each side then complains about the actions of the other's activist group, but never acknowledges the unsavory actions of their own activist group.

The Left argues that their view originates in the cradle of Western civilization—the traditions of Greek philosophers who were in pursuit of the truth and objectivity of human reality. And there is much to commend this line of argument which has amassed a great deal of great literature in support of it. Secular philosophy departments have claimed the high ground of objectivity in the effort to establish secular objectivity in contemporary universities, colleges, and the various endeavors they support.

The Right also argues that their view originates in the cradle of Western civilization—the traditions of Christianity which also pursue the truth and objectivity of human reality mitigated by the Bible (Protestants) and the traditions that claim biblical foundations

(Catholics). And much earlier departments of Theology claimed the high ground of objectivity, provided by the Bible and Christian traditions, in the service of God who Himself works to establish Christian and/or biblical objectivity in all of society.

The history of political correctness is found in the idea and practices of social moral enforcement or social norms—traditional sex roles, marriage and sexual expression, manners and norms of behavior, etc. For the most part these things have been inherited through the institutions of traditional Christianity—including universities which were invented by Christians, and were conservative in nature because people generally believed the cautions against idolatry and faithlessness found in the Bible. People believed that the Bible provided accurate information about various personal and social tragedies that had historically resulted from ignoring such cautions (God's judgments in history recorded in the Bible). Political Correctness of every stripe works to standardize morals and mores in the interest of both truth and peace.

The liberal versions of Political Correctness have long worked to undermine and/or change the existing morals and mores in the interest of a greater version or vision of truth and objectivity, a vision that promised to set people free of the shackles of ancient, outdated ideas that limited self-expression and human potential (Genesis 3). And because of sin and corruption, Christian institutions too often do harden into self-serving bastions of small-minded sinners who used Political Correctness to bolster their own power. In fact, over time every individual and institution falls into the snare of particularity, when individuals or institutions claim and/or attempt to speak for all people. Thus, this problem or reality of Political Correctness is very old. It did not originate in the 1980s. Yet the 80s did conceive a new term for it: Political Correctness.

In addition, in the 1980s some avaunt guard universities introduced a new department of study: Queer Theory, the objective of which was to "study" social norms and to free society of various limitations that held back human "progress." The result of this effort has been the very successful queering (https://wiki2.org/en/Queering) of traditional American norms. There has been vast and broad-based support for this effort. Indeed, everyone who has a beef with traditional America, Christianity, or God find themselves in support of this effort to dislodge what has come to be called "white privilege," the term that vilifies the value of social norms and mores by suggesting that existing norms and mores are, if not evil, then less than desirable. White privilege is synonymous with the traditional norms and mores of Western civilization, and particularly of the part of Western civilization that purports to be Christian.

Moira Weigel in her article, "Political correctness: how the right invented a phantom enemy." acknowledges the creation of the new term (Political Correctness), but frames it as an invention of the Right that intends to vilify a "phantom enemy." Her use of this term means that she either is not aware of the history of American liberalism and its capture of the levers of society and government (https://www.washingtonpost.-com/opinions/us-policy-has-gone-liberals-way-for-70-years/ 2014/04/08/8dffa2b2-b906-11e3-9a05-c739f29ccb08_story.html) or is in active denial of it. Political Correctness is nothing more than a new term that describes the establishment, enforcement, or change of social morals and mores. She apparently has no awareness or experience of what came before, so she calls it a "phantom enemy," which supports the presupposition of her own self-evident "objectivity."

Amanda Taub's article, "The truth about 'political correctness' is that it doesn't actually exist," suggesting that Political Correctness doesn't exist could be better argued by saying that the term in meaningless for reasons stated above. A term that means whatever you want it to mean means nothing in particular. But this fact does not stop people from using accusations of Political Correctness to divert or shut down those with whom one disagrees. Both Liberals and Conservatives use it thusly!

Zack Beauchamp's article, "Data shows a surprising campus free speech problem: left-wingers being fired for their opinions," provides a case study of not seeing the forest for the trees. The examination of official cases where free speech rights were challenged fails to grasp the subtle realities of social moral and moeurs enforcement techniques. As Jerry Z. Muller argued in 1990:

"Institutions in which characteristics of restraint, altruism, and moral autonomy are cultivated are in need of public defense, not (as some conservatives imagine) primarily in the political realm, where the stakes are the use of governmental force, but in the public sphere of cultural and educational institutions. The proper role of cultural conservatism so conceived is to proclaim—or better yet, to explain—that some institutions really are better than others. Some will proclaim on the basis of faith, maintaining that conservative morals conform to divine will; others may argue on the philosophical grounds of natural law. Or, like many of the masters of social science, they may attempt to weigh the costs and benefits of historical institutions, to discover not only why some institutions may be in need of reform or replacement, but also why certain traditional institutions are irreplaceable. What we should learn from the Jeremiahs of anti-capitalist doom and gloom is not to repent of economic liberalism, but to mind our manners and morals." (https://www.firstthings.com/article/1990/04/minding-our-manners-and-morals)

Beauchamp's treatment of counting up the official cases where free speech was challenged falls far short of serious treatment of the cultural aspects of Political Correctness. It is simply a short-sighted effort to bolster his own self-evident "objectivity."

Why Trump?

I don't know what to make of the article, "American political con-
sultant admits foreign money was funneled to Trump inaugural." It
sounds bad, but I have no idea how much is true or what it means generally or for Trump. I don't think that anyone can become a billionaire
without some financial shenanigans (involvement in corruption). And
I'm sure that politics is seriously corrupt, and that such corruption is not
new with Trump. From the beginning it has been clear to me that
Trump has never been part of the ruling elite, that they (the American
upper crust and the media who work for them) have despised Trump for
a long time. They very much did not want him to be President. Why
not? Likely because they knew that they could not control him, as they
have controlled the past several Presidents.

I voted for Trump because he would be a disrupter, and because Hi-
lary was much more dangerous. She would have continued the American Liberal political trajectory that had been in play for 40 years and was
greatly accelerated by Obama. I have stood against that trajectory almost
all of my adult life. History will show that Trump is God's man, but
don't confuse "God's man" with a "godly man." He's not a godly man.
He's a man who is being used by God. (I'd say a "flawed man," but who
isn't?) Nonetheless, God has put Trump in office for His (God's) own
reasons. God always uses flawed people; He has no other choice.

Trump is an instrument of God's judgment. How so? God is expos-
ing our hypocrisy through Trump. Yes, I mean Trump's hypocrisy, of
course, but also that of those who oppose him, the American upper crust
—Liberal and Conservative, Democrat, Republican, and Libertarian.
Lord, have mercy! Had Hillary won, the exposure of corruption in
American politics would have been much less. Trump has ripped off the
cover and we are in free fall (to mix metaphors). I'm not saying that
there would be less corruption had Hillary won, but that the existing
corruption would have gotten less public exposure. If Hillary had won,
what would we have made of Russian collusion? Not much!

It seems to me that the Democrats are much more likely to have
colluded with the Russians. The Dems have been flirting with socialism
for many decades. And if the Russian objective is to sow doubt and confusion into the American system, I'd say that they have succeeded
grandly, and that all parties are playing right into their hands. But it is
the Left that is driving the doubt and confusion. The Left wants to
blame Trump for the confusion, and he has his share of the blame. But

most of the serious doubt about America has come from the Left over the past 40 years. Mostly through colleges and universities, which have been hotbeds of Marxism and Socialism for decades.

The media is a department of the entertainment industry, not the truth industry. The media is not about truth, never has been. It's about entertainment, and that's why it can play so loose and fast with truth, and why politicians have no fear of lying to the media. Essentially, the media is a means of promoting gossip. Their business is two-fold: to sell stories that people want to buy, and advertising (to sell stuff). With regard to advertising, the media avoids liability through "puffery." From Wikipedia:

> "Puffery: In everyday language, puffery refers to exaggerated or false praise. In law, puffery is a promotional statement or claim that expresses subjective rather than objective views, which no 'reasonable person' would take literally. Puffery serves to 'puff up' an exaggerated image of what is being described and is especially featured in testimonials."

> "Puff piece is an idiom for a journalistic form of puffery: an article or story of exaggerating praise that often ignores or downplays opposing viewpoints or evidence to the contrary."

Indeed, puffery is standard operating procedure for the media. Trump uses puffery all the time, but the Left-leaning media ignore this and try to take him literally, proving that they fail to register as reasonable people.

> "The United States Federal Trade Commission (FTC) defined puffery as a 'term frequently used to denote the exaggerations reasonably to be expected of a seller as to the degree of quality of his product, the truth or falsity of which cannot be precisely determined.'"

> "The FTC stated in 1984 that puffery does not warrant enforcement action by the Commission. In its FTC Policy Statement on Deception, the Commission stated: 'The Commission generally will not pursue cases involving obviously exaggerated or puffing representations, i.e., those that the ordinary consumers do not take seriously.' e.g., 'The Finest Fried Chicken in the World.'"

The media are presenting us with two rival puff pieces of political corruption: 1) Trump and Russian collusion (the narrative of CNN, MSNBC, WAPO, etc.), and 2) the corruption of the FBI, DOJ, the Media, and Deep State (career politicians and government workers, represented by Mueller; the narrative of Fox, Hannity, Linbaugh, etc.). Both of these stories (narratives) make sense, and both are media puff pieces. Political reporting falls under the puffery category. To make things worse, it seems like the Media are asking us to choose one or the other. The dueling narratives divide us.

But because the Media are a major part of the corruption, doing what the Media wants us to do plays into their hands. How so? If we choose to believe the Trump narrative, then Mueller's Deep State becomes the fall guy and Trump ends up colluding with the American upper crust because he remains in office without official opposition. And if we choose the Mueller narrative, then Trump is the fall guy, and Mueller ends up colluding with the American upper crust, again because official opposition would be defeated with Trump's downfall. Having a "fall guy" is a handy way to adjudicate the case because we can blame the fall guy, and life goes on without really dealing with the underlying issues—our own corruption as a nation, a people, and individually. So I reject the option of believing one or the other of the competing narratives.

The other choices are: both stories (narratives) are true, or both are false. The problem with discounting the second alternative is that both narratives supply fairly compelling evidence of the guilt of the opposing party, so it is difficult simply discount them.

Both narratives could also be true, which means that there is horrendous corruption throughout the American (world's) political system(s), top to bottom, stem to stern. And the primary mode of that corruption is hypocrisy, "the practice of claiming to have moral standards or beliefs to which one's own behavior does not conform; pretense."

And that brings us to Jesus Christ, who provides a cure for hypocrisy—faith in the God of the Bible. But lest our faith also be hypocritical, it must be real, genuinely integrated into our own lives.

The transition from political corruption to Jesus hinges on hypocrisy, the underlying mode of the corruption. Jesus demands real honesty, and real honesty is the only cure that will reduce puffery and clarify the facts. Some people argue that people can be honest without Jesus, but the only way to avoid the claims of Jesus is to deny them, but that denial undermines the history of Western civilization.

The Liberal American upper crust has demonstrated its disgust with Christ's cure over the last 40+ years. Obama was a member of the United Church of Christ (my former denomination) when he entered office. That denomination is thoroughly apostate (corrupt in both theology and practice—full of hypocrisy), but is a favorite among the upper crust.

Trump, who is theologically ignorant, and barely Christian (if at all) has sided with and is supportive of Evangelicals, many of whom are a bit wild and crazy. Nonetheless, like the last national election, we must choose between bad options. Consequently, I throw my lot in with the Evangelicals, in spite of their faults—of which they have many—because they generally believe the God of the Bible more (or better) than the Liberals do.

It all really comes down to a matter of faith, not in Trump, but in Jesus. Trump is systematically undoing the Liberal state, which represents the fulfillment of the Godless, secular, corrupt American system that the Left has been building for 40+ years. This is why I support Trump. What is at play are two vying historic visions of America, Christian vs. secular.

www.ingramcontent.com/pod-product-compliance
Lightning Source LLC
Chambersburg PA
CBHW060239100426
42742CB00011B/1580